The Interpreting Spirit

The Interpreting Spirit

Spirit, Scripture, and Interpretation in the Renewal Tradition

HANNAH R. K. MATHER

PICKWICK *Publications* • Eugene, Oregon

THE INTERPRETING SPIRIT
Spirit, Scripture, and Interpretation in the Renewal Tradition

Pickwick Publications
An Imprint of Wipf and Stock Publishers
199 W. 8th Ave., Suite 3
Eugene, OR 97401

www.wipfandstock.com

PAPERBACK ISBN: 978-1-7252-7318-4
HARDCOVER ISBN: 978-1-7252-7319-1
EBOOK ISBN: 978-1-7252-7320-7

Cataloguing-in-Publication data:

Names: Mather, Hannah R. K., author.

Title: The interpreting Spirit : Spirit, scripture, and interpretation in the renewal tradition / Hannah R. K. Mather.

Description: Eugene, OR: Pickwick Publications, 2020 | Includes bibliographical references and index.

Identifiers: ISBN 978-1-7252-7318-4 (paperback) | ISBN 978-1-7252-7319-1 (hardcover) | ISBN 978-1-7252-7320-7 (ebook)

Subjects: LCSH: Holy Spirit | Bible—Hermeneutics | Pentecostalism

Classification: BS476 M38 2020 (print) | BS476 (ebook)

Manufactured in the U.S.A. SEPTEMBER 28, 2020

For those whose names are in these pages

Contents

Preface

The Interpreting Spirit is the revised version of my doctoral dissertation, which I researched for and wrote whilst a student at London School of Theology. I defended my dissertation in March 2019 and was delighted to pass without corrections. Amongst other things, this book appreciates that context is important. It seems fitting, therefore, to use this preface to provide some personal context from which it has been written.

My parents were involved with the beginnings of the charismatic movement in Britain in the 1960s and 1970s, and I grew up in charismatic Anglican churches where my father was the vicar and my mother also was later ordained. In adulthood, I worked for roughly a decade in business development in London's busy advertising sector, where my lifestyle was fast-paced and ultimately lonely. I finally came to my own faith in 2008 through a powerful but tender experience of the Holy Spirit that proved to me that God was real and wanted a close, personal relationship. After attending a mission school in Mozambique run by Heidi and Rolland Baker of Iris Global, I (reluctantly) decided that the charismatic ministry I felt God calling me to was best served by studying theology academically and I started at London School of Theology in 2011. I do not consider myself Pentecostal, but I have deep affection for, and long-standing friendship with, my Pentecostal comrades, which I cherish.

This book has emerged out of a combined love of scripture and for the self-effacing Spirit. Over the course of my research, I have had the pleasure of meeting and becoming friends with some of those whose thoughts are considered in these pages. As my research unfolded, I realized that I wanted to present an understanding of the Spirit's role in the interpretation of scripture in a way that enabled me to celebrate, but also draw from, develop, and unite those original voices. It is also around fifty years since this topic of pneumatic interpretation re-emerged on the scholarly arena, steered particularly by Pentecostal and charismatic scholars, and so this work seems timely.

The book has also grown out of encountering situations throughout my teenage years and adult life where there have been seeming impasses in perspective and understanding between two or more Christians. I have been personally involved in some of these situations, and a relative bystander with others. Reasons for impasses such as these—which usually involve conflict and misunderstanding to varying extents—are, of course, complex and multifaceted; yet they have all collectively led me to the same questions: how is it that a person discerns truth by the Spirit? And, perhaps more importantly, what is the Spirit's role in the interpretive process?

The Interpreting Spirit is a book that celebrates others, so I take this opportunity to celebrate two people amongst the many who have supported and surrounded me as I thought, researched, and wrote about this subject of pneumatic interpretation. These two are Reverend Doctor William Atkinson and Professor Graham Twelftree. As my doctoral supervisor, I am grateful to William for the time and belief he invested and his formational role in my scholarly development. William consistently believed in me more than I believed in myself, he called out the scholar in me, and—crucial for someone like me who tends to "feel" deeply—he (almost) always had a box of tissues in his office! Graham arrived at London School of Theology in 2016 from Regent University School of Divinity in Virginia Beach, USA. His continuing friendship, care, and support are much valued, especially our conversations gloriously intertwining things personal and academic. I am further appreciative of Graham for his commitment to guiding me on the transition from student-to-scholar and dissertation-to-book.

Finally, a note of explanation about the practical side of the book. The chapters are structured diachronically to reflect the way understanding often unfolds over time. Therefore, inclusion of someone's written thought (when it pertains to pneumatic interpretation and is not supporting material) is integrated according to the date it was first published. Although a full bibliography with dates is given at the back of the book, there are points when this date is helpful to see on the page. Hence, the date is given where that person's thought is discussed in detail, or where it is relevant. It is also often given when referring to a scholar's work outside the era of consideration (for example, referencing Moltmann, *Spirit of Life* [f.pub. 1991] in chapter 5). "Pub." (published) refers to works (articles, chapters, books, etc.) that have either been published once or where the first edition was used. There are four instances where I used a second or further edition and these cases are marked clearly in the footnotes. "F.pub" (first published) refers to reprinted or translated works. For example, Land, *Pentecostal Spirituality*, was first published in 1993 but I have used the 2010 reprint. Land's contribution is therefore included in chapter 3 in accordance with the 1993 date. Balthasar, *Theo-Logic III*, was first published in German in 1987 but not published in English until 2005; his thought is incorporated into chapter 2 according with the 1987 date. To the best of my knowledge these details are correct.

Hannah R. K. Mather
Scotland, March 2020

Abbreviations

AF	*The Apostolic Faith*
AJPS	*Asian Journal of Pentecostal Studies*
ANVIL	*ANVIL: Journal of Theology and Mission*
BA	*The Biblical Archaeologist*
BCE	before common era
BSac	*Bibliothecra Sacra*
CE	common era
cf.	compare
CTJ	*Calvin Theological Journal*
diss.	dissertation
Dei Verbum	*Dogmatic Constitution on Divine Revelation Dei Verbum*
DTh	Doctor of Theology
ed.	edition
e.g.	for example
EPTA	The European Pentecostal Theological Association
et al.	*et alii*, and others
etc.	*et cetera*, and so forth
Evangel	*Evangel Journal*
ExAud	*Ex Auditu*
f.pub.	first published
fn., fns.	footnote, footnotes
HeyJ	*The Heythrop Journal*
i.e.	that is to say
IJPT	*International Journal of Practical Theology*

Interpretation	*Interpretation: A Journal of Bible and Theology*
JBPR	*Journal of Biblical and Pneumatological Research*
JEPTA	*Journal of the European Pentecostal Theological Association*
JETS	*Journal of the Evangelical Theological Society*
JPT	*Journal of Pentecostal Theology*
JPTSup.	*Journal of Pentecostal Theology Supplement Series*
JSPSup.	*Journal for the Study of the Pseudepigrapha Supplement Series*
JSOTSup.	*Journal for the Study of the Old Testament Supplement Series*
MTh	Master of Theology
NICNT	*New International Commentary on the New Testament*
no.	*number*
nos.	*numbers*
n.p.	*no page*
NTS	*New Testament Studies*
OTE	*Old Testament Essays*
PhD	Doctor of Philosophy
Pneuma	*Pneuma: The Journal for the Society of Pentecostal Studies*
The Pneuma Review	*The Pneuma Review: Journal of Ministry Resources and Theology for Pentecostal and Charismatic Ministries and Leaders*
PSCF	*Perspectives on Science and Christian Faith*
pub.	*published*
SC	*The Spirit & Church*
sic	denoting an error in quoted text
SPS	The Society for Pentecostal Studies
St.	Saint
SVTQ	*St. Vladimir's Theological Quarterly*
TIS	theological interpretation of scripture
TrinJ	*Trinity Journal*
TS	*Theological Studies*

TynBul	*Tyndale Bulletin*
WARC	World Alliance of Reformed Churches

1

Laying the Foundations

1.1 INTRODUCING A HISTORICAL AND PNEUMATOLOGICAL ANALYSIS

How does the Holy Spirit work to communicate with us[1] as we engage with scripture?[2] This original work is an attempt to answer this question. It is the first comprehensive analysis of a conversation concerning this topic[3] that has been taking place amongst renewal scholars[4] since 1970. It highlights key voices, recognizing their individual importance, and yet arranges them in a collectively coherent way.

Accordingly, *The Interpreting Spirit* is an analysis[5] of the Spirit's role in the interpretation of scripture (pneumatic interpretation, outlined in 1.3). It

1. Use of "our," "we," and "us" in this work refers only to myself as the author and to the Christian reader.

2. Scripture: sacred writings of Judaism and Christianity in the Christian Bible considered inspired and authoritative for Christian faith and practice. This definition is sufficient for this work's purposes and follows definitions of "Bible," "canon," and "Scripture(s)," in Gorman, *Scripture and Its Interpretation*, 403, 421. Gorman defined scripture as "sacred writings, especially those of Judaism and Christianity" (421).

3. Discussed further in 1.5.

4. In this work's terms, a renewal scholar, voice, or conversationalist is someone who emphasizes the Spirit and accentuates the Spirit's role in their hermeneutical considerations. The term encompasses those who might not describe themselves as charismatic or Pentecostal but whose perspective contains a degree of reference to the Spirit that identifies with the renewal tradition and renewal thought. E.g., Kevin Vanhoozer. Explained further in 1.2.

5. Analyze: "to examine in detail in order to discover meaning, essential features, etc." *Collins English Dictionary*, 69.

is approached by engaging with a conversation surrounding this topic that has been taking place between renewal scholars since 1970 when renewed emphasis on and experience of the Spirit began to impact hermeneutical conversations. The work charts historical progress of the conversation[6] and concentrates on identifying common, uniting features of scholarly thought amidst hermeneutical diversity. The purpose is twofold: 1) to build understanding of pneumatic interpretation by drawing on and developing—and in this process celebrating—such scholarly thought; and 2) to foster appreciation and understanding between scholars.

As stressed throughout, central to pneumatic interpretation is personal experience *of* and intimate relationship *with* the triune God through pneumatic encounter. Affect, ethics, and cognition are three dynamically interrelating[7] aspects of this intimate relationship and therefore integral to consideration of pneumatic interpretation. Within this lies a paradox that whilst the Holy Spirit of God is all-powerful, receptivity to the Spirit's communication through scripture is either helped or hindered by ethical action and choice. It also highlights that seeking understanding of the Spirit's role in the interpretation of scripture requires consideration of the relational nature of the triune God from a pneumatic starting point. Consequently, the Spirit's relationship with the Father is reflected on as well as the Spirit's relationship with the Son. The work's core emphasis is that pneumatic interpretation is *holistic* and cannot be restricted to interpretation of the scriptural text. The Spirit always works *through* and *beyond* the written words, interpreting and appropriating scriptural truth in our lives in ways that align with scripture and transform and draw us holistically into knowledge of God as Father, Son, and Spirit, to whom the scriptural narrative, and therefore the Spirit through scripture, ultimately points.

The Interpreting Spirit purposefully asks something about God and seeks to reflect aspects of the Spirit's interpretive nature in its method and style.[8] As such, it is both a historical and pneumatological analysis, charting

6. The conversation: the conversation about the Spirit's role in the interpretation of scripture from scholars across or identifying with the renewal tradition. This incorporates Pentecostal hermeneutics, pneumatic hermeneutics, Spirit hermeneutics, charismatic exegesis, pneumatic exegesis, and renewal hermeneutics, specified accordingly.

7. Dynamic: "concerned with energy or forces that produce motion." A dynamic process is characterized by constant change, activity, and progression. Interrelate: "To place in, or come into a mutual or reciprocal relationship." *Collins English Dictionary*, 614, 1013. Use of these terms in this work adheres to these definitions.

8. Thank you to Amos Yong for alerting me to the significance of aligning one's method and style of writing with the argument itself. Amos Yong, *Spirit–Word–Community*, 24. Also discussed in fn. 359.

historical progression of the conversation,[9] and through this progression building a diachronic understanding of the Spirit's role in the interpretation of scripture. This approach allows allusion to certain inherent aspects of the Spirit's interpretive nature, and therefore of pneumatic interpretation: firstly, and most significantly for this work, that the Spirit never communicates directly but always through another object or movement;[10] secondly, illustrated by the diachronic style of the analysis and the deliberately open-ended nature of the conclusions, that the Spirit unfolds truth over time; thirdly and fourthly, that the Spirit communicates in ways that unify and that celebrate the other.

I approach this analysis as a charismatic scholar working within the context and perspective of the renewal tradition. Insights from scholars outside the renewal tradition are considered as they identify with and/or assist renewal thought.[11] Underlying my approach is the belief that discussions of pneumatic interpretation in the academy must ultimately be translatable to Christians (and non-Christians) outside the academy for this is a conversation relevant to all desiring personal relationship with God. *The Interpreting Spirit* is addressed to those within the academy, but those outside the academy were on the edge of my thinking throughout my writing and research.[12] This is the necessary preface to that work of translation.

Considering the Spirit's role in the interpretation of scripture by engaging with the historical conversation that renewal scholars have been having surrounding this topic, has enabled me to highlight the many varied and unique, yet also collectively coherent renewal voices. The work provides an answer to the question, "What does the Spirit *do* in the process

9. See fn. 6 (the conversation).

10. Object: "a person or thing seen as a focus or target for feelings, thought, etc: *an object of affection* [and] that towards which cognition is directed." Movement: "The act, process, or result of moving." Understanding affect, ethics, and cognition as movements for this discussion's purposes. *Collins English Dictionary*, 1365, 1282 respectively (emphasis original).

11. Consideration of the Spirit's role in the interpretation of scripture has chiefly been brought by those in or identifying with the renewal tradition (see 1.2), but smaller contributions have come from scholars who would not identify with the renewal tradition (in this work's terms), e.g., arguably some evangelical scholars considered in chapter 2, and reformed scholars in chapter 4. These contributions are included to assist understanding of pneumatic interpretation as discussed by renewal conversationalists. *Comprehensive* engagement with such thought lies outside the scope of this analysis because focus is within the renewal tradition and over-consideration external to this remit distracts attention; and time constraints and study length requires this.

12. *The Interpreting Spirit* is a revised version of my 2019 PhD dissertation undertaken at London School of Theology under Reverend Doctor William P. Atkinson, and examined by Doctor Andrew Davies and Professor Tony Lane.

of scriptural interpretation?" recognized as a notoriously difficult question to address.[13] However, it is a hope that *The Interpreting Spirit* will also be seen as a celebration of renewal scholarship in the years since 1970, serving to foster appreciation and understanding amongst those considering pneumatic interpretation. An aim steering my thought has always been to encourage the collective development of understanding concerning the Spirit's role in the interpretation of scripture. This conversation, and the individual discussions within it, is strengthened when scholars work together, where appropriate, across specialisms and research areas, with sensitivity, generosity, honor, and respect. I offer *The Interpreting Spirit* heuristically to those involved in the pneumatic interpretation conversation, and to those who will be in the future, with the hope that recognizing and celebrating each other, and giving generously of our own research, when we recognize it will be developed better by or with another, will increase as time goes on and serve to enrich this precious conversation about the Spirit's role in the interpretation of scripture.

1.2 THE RENEWAL TRADITION

In this work, "the renewal tradition" describes global charismatic movements and scholars in these groups who emphasize the Spirit and accentuate the Spirit's role in their hermeneutical considerations. What characterizes renewal Christians, or those who identify with this term, is a degree of reference to the Spirit that is missing in other streams of Christianity.[14] Hence, scholars identifying with but not as renewal Christians might not describe themselves as charismatic or Pentecostal, but their perspective (written and/or expressed in daily faith-life) contains a degree of reference to the Spirit that identifies with the renewal tradition and renewal thought.

The renewal tradition is often known as the Pentecostal and charismatic movement(s), within which three interrelated, global waves of the Spirit are traditionally described. Classical Pentecostalism (the first wave) refers to denominations that began in the 1900s, often traced to Charles Parham and Bethel Bible School, and William Seymour and the Azusa Street Revival. The charismatic movement refers to the second wave of the

13. Discussed further in 1.5.

14. This follows the definition given by Kevin Spawn and Archie Wright: "This expression [the renewal tradition] refers to global charismatic movements and scholars in these groups who maintain that pneumatological commitments and experiences have implications for the hermeneutical project." Spawn and Wright, *Spirit and Scripture*, xvii.

Spirit beginning in the 1960s in historic mainline churches (for example, Anglicans, Roman Catholics), and the third wave beginning in the 1980s in new independent churches. The second wave is often traced to Dennis Bennett, who was relieved of his position as pastor of Saint Mark's Episcopal Church, California, in 1960 after announcing to his congregation that he had received the gift of tongues.[15] The third wave is often associated with John Wimber and the Vineyard movement.[16]

In the work, "the renewal tradition" is used primarily to stress inclusivity of scholars across or identifying with all three waves, emphasizing contributions from scholars associated with classical Pentecostalism alongside those associated with the charismatic movement, and secondarily to reduce confusion over application of Pentecostal and charismatic terminology. Craig Keener's decision to use "Spirit hermeneutics" terminology in *Spirit Hermeneutics* was partly based around confusion over this terminology. Keener explained that scholars use "Pentecostal" in two ways; referring to Pentecostalism, and to all who share pentecostal spiritual experience as shown through Acts 2. The former is often with a capital "P" and the latter

15. In Britain, the second wave is traceable to a prayer meeting in February 1963 at St. Mark's Gillingham where John Collins was vicar. Collins is often overlooked for his role in the beginnings of the British charismatic movement for well-known figures like David MacInnes, David Watson, and Michael Harper. However, MacInnes and Watson were Collins's curates until 1961 and 1962 respectively, and Harper was a friend and invited speaker at the prayer meeting. Bennett visited St. Mark's in 1963 as the church was experiencing renewal. Hocken, *Streams of Renewal*, 99–103; Harrison, "C of E's Spirit Level," n.p.

16. For explication of classical Pentecostalism and the charismatic movement, including inception, history and differences, see Lederle, *Theology with Spirit* (chapters 3 to 5 discussing the three waves). For summary, see Cartledge, "Charismatic Movement," 9–11. Also, Burgess and van der Maas, *New International Dictionary of Pentecostal and Charismatic Movements*, xvii–xxiii. For perspective presenting all three waves as phases of Pentecostalism, see Anderson, *Introduction to Pentecostalism*. For summary, see Anderson, "Pentecostalism," 641–44. For summary of the charismatic movement, inception and history, see Robeck, "Charismatic Movements," 145–54. For the early charismatic movement in Britain (until 1965), see Hocken, *Streams of Renewal*. For (early) explication of the charismatic movement from British, charismatic-evangelical perspective, see Buchanan et al., *Charismatic Movement in the Church of England*; Smail, Walker, and Wright, *Charismatic Renewal*. For (early) explication of the charismatic movement from Roman Catholic perspective, including discussion of Pentecostal and charismatic theology, see Congar, "Renewal in the Spirit," 145–212. For summary of the Roman Catholic charismatic movement, see Robeck. "Charismatic Movements," 145–54. For global assessment of the charismatic movement, see Hocken, "Charismatic Movement," 477–519. For explication of classical Pentecostalism, including inception and history, see Anderson, *Introduction to Pentecostalism*; Synan, *Holiness-Pentecostal Tradition*. For summary, see Robeck, "Classical Pentecostalism," 553–55. My synopsis broadly follows Lederle's explication and Cartledge's summary.

with a small "p" (application is inconsistent).[17] Researching and writing for this book, I found that Pentecostal scholars discussing a Pentecostal approach to interpretation (Pentecostal hermeneutics) generally, but not always, use "Pentecostal" in the ecclesial sense with a capital "P" within which there is usually an implicit, if not explicit, addressing of the Spirit's involvement. "Pentecostal," in this analysis, is therefore used in this ecclesial sense but noted where terminological use differs. The work therefore understands that Pentecostal hermeneutics is mainly concerned with defining an interpretive identity for the Pentecostal tradition within the academy, within which implicit or explicit consideration to the Spirit is usually given. Pentecostal hermeneutics is therefore wider than scriptural interpretation and includes a range of related topics including pneumatic interpretation.

As Keener also noted, a similar terminological problem occurs with "charismatic," used both in reference to the charismatic movement and to Paul's depiction of spiritual gifts (Rom 12:6–8; 1 Cor 12:4–11).[18] The former is often with a capital "C" and the latter with a small "c" (again, application is inconsistent). Keener emphasized that the pentecostal or charismatic experience of the Spirit is open to all believers (Rom 12:4–6; 1 Cor 12:12–30).[19] Whilst concurring, pneumatic experience is prioritized by, and therefore characteristic of, those in or identifying with the renewal tradition. Accordingly, "charismatic" is here used with a small "c" simultaneously in respect of both aspects. "Charismatic" (with small "c") is adopted as the encompassing term over "pentecostal" but to reduce potential confusion, "renewal" is used where appropriate.

Amidst ecclesial and theological diversity, common features unite those in the renewal tradition. As Mark Cartledge explained, "Essential to these features is the emphasis on an *encounter with the Holy Spirit*. This encounter is free, spontaneous, dynamic, transformative, and should be an ongoing experiential reality with the purposes of God."[20] Whilst agreeing with Cartledge, the purpose of pneumatic encounter is not simply encounter for encounter's sake but a *relational encounter* with the triune God by which the Spirit works to bring transformation in personal relationship with God, in our own self-understanding, and in relationships with those around us. Cartledge gave four helpful features characterizing renewal spirituality, and

17. Keener, *Spirit Hermeneutics*, 7–8.

18. Keener, *Spirit Hermeneutics*, 8.

19. Keener, *Spirit Hermeneutics*, 8.

20. Cartledge, "Charismatic Spirituality," 215 (emphasis original), noting that Cartledge used "Charismatic" terminology. For alternative perspective oriented around classical Pentecostalism giving less attention to spirituality in the second and third waves, cf. Kärkkäinen, "Pentecostal Identity," 14–31.

which can work to serve the purpose of this relational pneumatic encounter: 1) worship and praise, including prayer ministry; 2) inspired words, that is tongues, prophecy, words of wisdom and knowledge, discernment of spirits, and personal testimony; 3) living a sanctified life, emphasizing gradual "growing in Christ"[21] through life in the Spirit; and 4) witnessing, stressing that this action, empowered by the Spirit, breaks barriers between cognitive and affective aspects of life, holistically uniting people and communities.[22]

As the analysis will show, whilst there has been much research concerning Pentecostal hermeneutics, within which consideration to pneumatic interpretation has been given, *Spirit and Scripture: Exploring a Pneumatic Hermeneutic* by editors Kevin Spawn and Archie Wright, was the first published account[23] to intentionally recognize and explore pneumatic interpretation in a wider renewal context. (They referred to this as a pneumatic hermeneutic.) With Spawn and Wright,[24] my purpose is not to give a detailed history of the renewal tradition and the three interrelated waves, or to explicate a renewal spirituality, but to initially recognize these contexts in order to incorporate thought from scholars across or identifying with the renewal tradition and foster understanding of pneumatic interpretation.

Finally, as stated, in order to consider the Spirit's role in the interpretation of scripture, the work draws upon and develops thought from those in or identifying with the renewal tradition since 1970 who have emphasized the Spirit and accentuated the Spirit's role in their hermeneutical considerations. The analysis is therefore characteristic of, and also a celebration of renewal thought. However, at the outset it is imperative to stress that pneumatic interpretation cannot be limited to the renewal tradition, for to one extent or another, the Spirit through scripture communicates knowingly or unknowingly (on our part) to, with, and through all Christians.[25]

21. As noted, this analysis emphasizes intimate relationship with the *triune* God through pneumatic encounter and therefore also incorporates and emphasizes consideration of the Father.

22. Cartledge, "Charismatic Spirituality," 216–23 (221).

23. Spawn and Wright, *Spirit and Scripture* (f.pub. 2011). For earlier attempt, see May, "Role of the Holy Spirit in Biblical Hermeneutics" (MTh diss., 1999).

24. Spawn and Wright, *Spirit and Scripture*, xvii.

25. Cf. similar discussion from Spawn and Wright, "Cultivating a Pneumatic Hermeneutic," 196–98. The question of the Spirit's communication through scripture to non-Christians lies beyond the remits of this analysis. However, I would argue that if intimate relationship with God is central to pneumatic interpretation, then the Spirit, at some level, is always seeking to draw a person closer into that relationship. Acknowledging that this verges into questions about predestination and election, also beyond the remits of this work.

1.3 WORKING TERMINOLOGY AND UNDERSTANDING

The following working terminology and understanding is explicated throughout the analysis.

1.3.1 Pneumatic terminology

"Pneumatic interpretation" refers to the conscious or subconscious perception, discernment, or reception of truth brought by the Spirit through the interpretation of scripture.[26] "Pneumatic discernment" refers to conscious or subconscious judgment, perception, and assessment of truth brought by the Spirit in situations wider than interpretation of scripture.[27] "Pneumatic appropriation" is an act of communication brought by the Spirit through our engagement with scripture. This communication is to personal and contemporary contexts, and coheres with the original passage and its surrounding context in some way.[28] "Pneumatic hindrance" describes hindrances upon ability to perceive, discern, or receive truth brought by the Spirit in situations including, but not limited to, the interpretation of scripture.

26. This definition supports that given by Spawn and Wright but emphasizes more *the Spirit's* communicative activity over *our* interpretive methodology. Spawn and Wright explained, "A pneumatic hermeneutic is defined as a scholarly approach attempting to account for the role of the Holy Spirit in biblical interpretation. This general approach may consist of either the development of principles and practices of classical scholarship or an emphasis placed on the Holy Spirit in the interpretation of biblical and related literatures." Spawn and Wright, *Spirit and Scripture*, xvii.

27. "[Discernment] is concerned with the ability to decide, to see into the reality of the situation, to avoid being deceived by external appearances and misleading information." Kay, "Spiritual Discernment," 130.

28. Appropriate: "Right or suitable; fitting." From fifteenth-century Latin, *appropriāre*: to make one's own. *Collins English Dictionary*, 98. Appropriation: "1) generally, the utilization of Scripture for contemporary belief and practice; 2) sometimes . . . understood as the final step in the interpretive process, following distantiation and contextualization, with the goal of deriving meaning and life transformation." Gorman, *Scripture and Its Interpretation*, 402 (emphasis removed). Goldingay argued for an "essential link between historical, exegetical study and the response of appropriation, which involves experiencing the realities of which the text speaks." Goldingay, *Models for Interpretation of Scripture*, 252. For consideration of appropriation incorporating postmodernist thought (notably Ricoeur and Gadamer), and biblical criticism, see Schneiders, *Revelatory Text*, 169–78. Neither Goldingay or Schneiders directly referenced the Spirit.

1.3.2 Affect, ethics, and cognition

As stated, the work's core stress is that pneumatic interpretation (and associated terminology) is *holistic*. Following Steven Land, the heart is recognized as "the integrative center" of the emotions, will, and mind,[29] and therefore the locus of discernment, from which affect, ethics, and cognition stem. Themes similar to affect, ethics, and cognition were also present in *Pentecostal Spirituality*, where Land explicated orthopathy (right affection), orthopraxy (right practice), and orthodoxy (right belief), as three interrelating components of Pentecostal (and wider Christian) spirituality.[30] Land's contribution and influence is discussed in 3.1.

"Affect" is understood as an overarching descriptor of emotion and desire.[31] Thus, particular affections are wide-ranging, including love, joy, desire, sorrow, gratitude and compassion.[32] "Ethics," broadly understood as moral principles or values held by an individual or group which influence behavior,[33] is here specific to action and conduct and therefore aligns with orthopraxy, understood as "action in harmony with God's purposes in which we can discover God and his truth."[34] "Cognition" is understood as "the mental act or process by which knowledge is acquired, including

29. Land, *Pentecostal Spirituality*, 128, cf. 31. Land's definition of heart is sufficient for this work's purposes and will be followed.

30. Land, *Pentecostal Spirituality*, 30–31, 182–83. Dale Coulter highlighted that Theodore Runyon, aiming "to capture John Wesley's focus on experience . . . coin[ed] the term *orthopathy* to describe how right affections fuse right beliefs (orthodoxy) and right practices (orthopraxis) within Wesley's thought." This influenced scholars like Land discussing divine encounter and spiritual development. Coulter, "Introduction: Language of Affectivity," 5, 25 note 2 (5). Runyon explained that he first discussed orthopathy in an address in 1984, developing the term in Runyon, "A New Look at Experience," *Drew Gateway* (Fall 1987) 44–55. See Runyon, *New Creation*, 251, note 2, and 146–49 discussing orthopathy, orthopraxy, and orthodoxy. Land credited Runyon for helping develop his thought. Land, *Pentecostal Spirituality*, 32–33. Also concerning orthopathy, orthopraxy, and orthodoxy, Jackie Johns, "Yielding to the Spirit," 70–84; and, concerning orthopathy, Cartledge, "Affective Theological Praxis," 34–52.

31. Following Coulter, "Introduction: Language of Affectivity," 8. Coulter and Yong's colloquy, *Spirit, the Affections, and the Christian Tradition* contains a range of essays considering affect throughout Christian tradition from a renewal perspective. For overview of terminological and conceptual shifts concerning affect, see Coulter, "Introduction: Language of Affectivity," 8–14, shown further through the essays.

32. See Coulter, "Whole Gospel," 158.

33. *Collins English Dictionary*, 675. For further, see O'Donovan, discussing the process of coming to moral conclusions including the foundational incorporation and use of scripture. O'Donovan, "Christian Moral Reasoning" 122–27.

34. Stevens, "Living Theologically," 6.

perception, intuition, and reasoning."[35] Affect always relates to an object, and is therefore interrelated with cognition,[36] and the same can be understood for ethical action. All understanding, regardless of whether it is Spirit-given, involves the interrelation of affect, ethics, and cognition. Aligning with Land's use of orthodoxy, cognition is understood both as an aspect of intimate relationship with God *and* as a framework facilitating understanding (discussed further in chapter 3).

A consistent emphasis throughout is that central to pneumatic interpretation is intimate loving relationship with God through pneumatic encounter, focusing on affect, ethics, and cognition as dynamically interrelating aspects of this relationship. The Spirit draws us into relationship with God as Father, Son, *and Spirit*—for to be drawn by the Spirit into relationship with God is also to be drawn into relationship with the Spirit through the Father and the Son—and in this process our human affections become aligned with God's affections. Affectivity aligns, ethical action follows, and both correspond with cognition.[37] This, affective-ethical with cognition, alignment or transformation is a continual process as we grow in intimate relationship with God and are drawn holistically by the Spirit into knowledge of God as Father, Son, and Spirit.[38] Because this process *is* continual, and, in our fallen human nature, is a work in progress, this transformation evolves but never completely aligns.

Highlighting the importance of recognizing and exploring the Spirit's role within discussions concerning affect, Dale Coulter explained that the Spirit "draws forth a delight in the law of God . . . serv[ing] as the intersection between divine affectivity (Spirit as bond of love) and human affectivity." Coulter insightfully stressed, "This places pneumatology front and center

35. *Collins English Dictionary*, 398.

36. Coulter, "Whole Gospel," 158. See fn. 10 for definition of object (undefined by Coulter).

37. Gordon Fee wrote of the *purpose, pattern, principle, and power* of Christian ethics. The purpose is the glory of God, the pattern is Christ, the principle is love, and the power is the Spirit. The Spirit "empowers the believer for ethical behavior," and "reproduces the pattern and the principle of that behavior." Spirit people are therefore *expected* to exhibit changed behavior. Fee, "Spirit and Ethical Life," 879. See text for scriptural references.

38. Villafañe described a vertical and horizontal process of being transformed into the image of Christ with "ever-increasing glory" (2 Cor 3:18) and following the example set by Christ "in similar obedience of the Father's missional calling (Luke 4:18–19)." He stressed, "both of these foci and goals can only be carried out in the power of the Spirit, and undergirded by God's love." Villafañe, *Liberating Spirit*, 167–68 (168) (for pneumatic interpretation, see 205–11). For critique of *Liberating Spirit*, see Cartledge, *Mediation of the Spirit*, 16–18.

in the discussion of affectivity."[39] Complementing Coulter, Eldin Villafañe described how the love of the Father in the Son, experienced, initiated, and mediated by the Spirit, transforms a person. Villafañe stated, "Love becomes the dominant relationship of the believer to God and to other persons. Love becomes the source, motive and power of the living in the Spirit, even our ethical walk."[40] However, as Villafañe also emphasized, relationship with God is *hindered* by sinful "actions and attitudes of the believer that 'cut' the relationship of love and thus grieve the Holy Spirit."[41]

These preliminary thoughts show affect, ethics, and cognition to be dynamically interrelated, especially concerning the affective-ethical aspect. The Spirit shapes our affections and actions and this influences cognition; yet paradoxically, our ethical actions can also hinder this shaping process. This is analyzed throughout chapters 2 to 6 in relation to pneumatic interpretation and associated terminology, pneumatic discernment, pneumatic appropriation, and pneumatic hindrance.

1.4 NOTE ON INTERPRETIVE METHOD

Within the conversation there has been much debate about interpretive method, which has included discussion over contexts and frameworks[42] surrounding and supporting pneumatic interpretation. Some reading this may feel that there are points where a vast swathe of literature is glossed over within which is much diversity of opinion concerning interpretive method (see, for example, 3.4.3). This could be a valid critique, but my reasoning for this approach is twofold and interrelated.

Firstly, this analysis is focused on *the Spirit's role* in the interpretation of scripture; it is not an analysis of (our) interpretive method. Put alternatively, *my concern is with the Spirit's interpretive method over our own.* As emphasized throughout, conversations about (our) interpretive methods, if overly attended to, can and has drawn focus away from the Spirit and into a medley of interpretive techniques and concepts. This applies to those prioritizing community approaches, involving understanding the community framework surrounding ourselves as we approach scripture, *and* those

39. Coulter, "Introduction: Language of Affectivity," 7.

40. Villafañe, *Liberating Spirit*, 167. Villafañe did not use affective terminology.

41. Villafañe, *Liberating Spirit*, 170, referencing Romans 15:30, Ephesians 4 and 5 in discussion. He broadly described these sinful attitudes and actions as disobedience to God, injustice and alienation, and unbelief and idolatry. Land also acknowledged this (discussed in 3.1), but Villafañe's emphasis was more overt.

42. This work largely uses "framework" instead of "context," aiming to bring freshness of understanding to this much debated issue of context.

prioritizing historico-grammatical approaches, involving understanding the framework surrounding the scriptural text in its original[43] historical location. Both these frameworks are important, but for those seeking understanding concerning the Spirit's role in interpretation,[44] they must assist and not overwhelm consideration of the Spirit's role. Therefore, recognizing this problem with over-attention, all discussion concerning (our) interpretive methodologies is aimed at supporting and not distracting from consideration of the Spirit's role. Hence, discussion concerning (our) interpretive methods are incorporated but simplified.[45]

Secondly, when analyzing these discussions about interpretive method, the focus is intentionally on commonalities over differences. This is part of the stated purpose to chart overall progress of the conversation but concentrate on identifying common, uniting features of scholarly thought amidst hermeneutical diversity, and in this process, build a diachronic understanding of the Spirit's role in the interpretation of scripture. Another, by no means less important aim is that this work would foster collective appreciation and understanding amongst those presently in the conversation and who might be in the future. Taking this approach allows allusion to the third aspect of the Spirit's nature discussed in 1.1, and therefore a hallmark of pneumatic interpretation, that the Spirit, through scripture, *unifies*. This focus on identifying common, uniting features of thought amidst scholarly diversity is evident throughout the analysis and articulated in most detail in chapter 5.

43. Original context and original meaning: Throughout *Spirit Hermeneutics*, especially part III, Keener emphasized the original context in which scripture was written as a foundational, grounding principle for pneumatic interpretation. He reasoned that "observing the designed sense, or what we might call the sense projected by the ideal author or at least the ancient cultural sense, is a vital and foundational objective for interpreting Scripture." Keener, *Spirit Heremeneutics*, 99. Keener also spoke of the range of senses original meaning can have, including authorial intention, stages of the text's production, what the first audiences heard, and who they were. To retain focus, Keener spoke "simply of this range of senses" (339–40, note 1) as do I.

44. Noting that amongst conversationalists, the Spirit's role in interpretation has not always been the central focus. E.g., Kenneth Archer (chapter 4), Jacqueline Grey (chapter 5), Lee Roy Martin (chapters 4 and 5).

45. For full-length studies concerned with interpretive method, see Grey, *Three's a Crowd*; Keener, *Spirit Hermeneutics*.

1.5 WHY THIS APPROACH? A BRIEF HERMENEUTICAL THEOLOGY OF THE SPIRIT

During the early stages of research I came across two short works: a historical analysis of pneumatic interpretation discussions from Kevin Spawn and Archie Wright,[46] and a brief critique of the conversation from Kevin Vanhoozer.[47] The genesis of thought for *The Interpreting Spirit* came from these two offerings and it is with gratitude that I acknowledge these scholars. From Spawn and Wright's chapter came the idea to offer an analysis. Hence, this is the first comprehensive analysis of the conversation surrounding pneumatic interpretation that has been taking place amongst renewal scholars since 1970.[48] An observation from Vanhoozer would lead to recognizing that successfully addressing the Spirit's role in the interpretation of scripture, required an approach *through* something else, whilst taking care to both celebrate but not overly attend to this aspect.

In his chapter, Vanhoozer observed that renewal scholars discussing hermeneutics had ironically not adequately addressed *how* the Spirit is involved in interpretation. He stated, "When it comes to giving a nitty-gritty account of the Spirit's role in hermeneutics, there is less a mighty rushing wind than a whispering shrug of the shoulders." Vanhoozer suggested that part of the problem was renewal scholars' "zeal for community."[49] In other

46. Spawn and Wright, "Emergence of a Pneumatic Hermeneutic in the Renewal Tradition" (f.pub. 2011), 3–22.

47. Vanhoozer, "Reforming Pneumatic Hermeneutics" (pub. 2014), 18–24.

48. The first comprehensive analysis of literature pertaining to the development of Pentecostal hermeneutics from scholars in the classical Pentecostal tradition came from Oliverio, *Theological Hermeneutics* (f.pub 2012). William Oliverio drew his understanding of theological hermeneutics from Yong, *Spirit–Word–Community*. He emphasized that for Pentecostal theology, hermeneutics must be broader than scriptural interpretation and that "a hermeneutics of the divine that fails to properly account for the interpretation of the extra-Scriptural world will ultimately sabotage the theological task." Oliverio, *Theological Hermeneutics*, 4–5 (5), quoting Yong, *Spirit–Word–Community*, 5. *The Interpreting Spirit* aligns with this perspective, but places scripture centrally whereas for Oliverio (and Yong, discussed in chapters 4 and 5), it was an aspect of consideration. Hence, Oliverio's scope aligned with the Pentecostal hermeneutics' conversation he considered in that it was wider than pneumatic interpretation but largely restricted to classical Pentecostalism.

49. Vanhoozer, "Reforming Pneumatic Hermeneutics," 21. Vanhoozer continued, suggesting that renewal scholars' focus on community and integration of renewal concerns with postmodernism had caused some renewal scholars to "have inadvertently sold their spiritual birthright for a mess of postmodern pottage" (21). Here, Vanhoozer referenced Archer, *Pentecostal Hermeneutic*; Oliverio, *Theological Hermeneutics*; contributor essays in Spawn and Wright, *Spirit and Scripture*; Vondey, *Beyond Pentecostalism*, 66–78; and Yong, *Spirit–Word–Community*. All included in this work. I disagree

words and in this work's terms, Vanhoozer suggested that renewal scholars were focusing on the contemporary community framework surrounding a person as they approach scripture at the expense of considering the Spirit's role.

Progressing through my research, I continued pondering over Vanhoozer's insight, and realized that this issue was not limited to those focusing on the contemporary community. Those concerned with historico-grammatical approaches, involving understanding the framework surrounding the scriptural text in its original historical location,[50] tended to have the same problem.[51] *It appeared that where focus on these two important interpretive frameworks increased, attention to the Spirit actually decreased.*

Insight into this problematic issue can be gleaned by considering the Spirit's self-effacing nature. Consider these thoughts from Hans Urs von Balthasar:

> The Spirit is breath, not a full outline, and therefore he wishes only to breathe through us, not to present himself to us as an object; he does not wish to be seen but to be the seeing eye of grace in us. . . . He is the light that cannot be seen except upon the object that is lit up: and he is the love between Father and Son that has appeared in Jesus. He does not wish to be glorified but "to glorify me," by "taking what is mine and revealing it to you" (Jn 16:14), in the same way that the Son neither wishes nor is able to glorify himself but glorifies only the Father (Jn 5:41; 7:18).[52]

Balthasar's beautifully articulated words present an understanding that the Spirit is seen and experienced indirectly through another object or movement.[53] Elsewhere he also emphasized this, writing that "every grasp or 'experience' of the Spirit is indirect."[54] Implications of such a perspective are

---

with Vanhoozer's inclusion of *Spirit and Scripture*, for the editors and contributors mostly (John Christopher Thomas aside) did not overly employ postmodernist thought. However, a valid critique raised by Walter Moberly (discussed in fn. 508) was that the *Spirit and Scripture* essayists had also not adequately tackled the Spirit's role.

50. See fn. 43 (original context and meaning).

51. Arguably, this is why the *Spirit and Scripture* essayists also did not adequately tackle the Spirit's role (see fn. 49), for their focus was largely oriented around historico-grammatical related concerns.

52. Balthasar, "Unknown Lying Beyond the Word," 111. Balthasar's theology and relevance for understanding pneumatic interpretation is considered in 2.3.

53. See fn. 10 for definitions of object and movement.

54. Balthasar, *Theo-Logic III*, 31. For complementary perspectives, see Atkinson, *Trinity After Pentecost*, 58–59, 61; Cartledge, "Locating the Spirit," 258–60; Moltmann, *Spirit of Life*, 205.

that if the Spirit, and therefore the Spirit's communication, is discerned and experienced indirectly through another object or movement, then analyzing and articulating the Spirit's role in interpretation also requires attending to whatever it is the Spirit is communicating through—and also glorifying (in the case of the Father and the Son), and illuminating and celebrating (in the case of everything and everyone else). For example, as the analysis will show, considering the Spirit's role in the interpretation of scripture involves a dynamically interrelated consideration of the Father, the Son, and the Spirit; the written words of scripture and their surrounding historical framework; the community framework surrounding a person as they approach scripture; and affect, ethics, and cognition. Broadly speaking, these are all objects or movements that the Spirit works, communicates, and interprets through. The issue is that whilst it is natural and necessary to consider these objects and movements, *overly* concentrating on them actually steers attention *away* from the Spirit.

Vanhoozer's observation, therefore, was important, for it helped identify that a reason scholars had ironically not adequately addressed the Spirit's role in the interpretation of scripture was because the Spirit, by nature, always looks beyond the Spirit toward the other; and therefore, scholars' interpretive work generally focuses accordingly.[55] Moreover, Vanhoozer's insight, together with Spawn and Wright's analysis, steered my own approach, recognizing that in order to consider pneumatic interpretation, it needed to be done through something else. The outcome was bringing analysis of the Spirit's role in the interpretation of scripture through the historical conversation that renewal scholars have been having surrounding this topic since roughly 1970. This approach allows me to draw together and present an understanding of pneumatic interpretation *and* highlight the individual contributions through whom my own contribution has been built. Hence, alluding to the fourth aspect of the Spirit's interpretive nature detailed in 1.1—that the Spirit communicates in ways that celebrate the other—this work is also *a celebration* of these renewal voices.[56]

At points in chapters 2 to 6, scholars are particularly critiqued for over-focusing on interpretive[57] frameworks and inadvertently steering emphasis away from the Spirit (see, for example, within 3.4 and 4.1). However, at the outset, I stress that because of the Spirit's self-effacing nature, studies concerning the Spirit's communication are *challenging*, for the task requires attention to whatever it is the Spirit is communicating through—and also

55. For a complementary perspective, see Yong, *Spirit–Word–Community*, 216.

56. See fn. 4 (renewal scholar/voice).

57. Also understood as cognitive frameworks (see 1.3.2).

glorifying and/or celebrating—together with awareness that over-attention can and does divert focus away from the Spirit and/or the task at hand.[58] This is highlighted, not as a personal disclaimer, but so as to foster understanding and appreciation amongst scholars.

1.6 LIMITATIONS AND OUTLINE

1.6.1 Limitations and overlapping conversations

There are many interrelating conversations surrounding scriptural interpretation.[59] The following overlap with this work but are not explored in detail. Hence, this section also notes potential areas of further exploration, touched upon at various points in chapters 2 to 5.

Early Jewish interpretation is discussed in 3.4.5 in reference to pneumatic interpretation but this is also a much wider discussion area. Related with early Jewish interpretation are conversations concerning the use of the Old Testament by New Testament writers,[60] and prophetic interpretation, also discussed in 3.4.5.

Ecumenical dialogue and interpretation is another overlapping area. After Vatican II, Roman Catholics and Pentecostals engaged in formal international dialogue. Reports from these discussions are noted in chapter 2 but not considered in detail.[61] Likewise, similar Reformed-Pentecostal dialogue is also noted in chapter 4.[62] The years post-2010 have seen increasing

58. Of course, some "diversions" lead to significant discussions in their own right, as has been the case with Pentecostal hermeneutics (see 3.4.1).

59. For non-exhaustive introduction to the wide-ranging hermeneutical approaches to scripture, see Joel Green, *Hearing the New Testament*; Porter, *Dictionary of Biblical Criticism and Interpretation*; Vanhoozer et al., *Dictionary for Theological Interpretation of the Bible.*

60. For general introduction, Beale, *New Testament Use of the Old Testament*; Hays and Joel Green, "Use of the Old Testament," 222–38. For collection addressing ancient contexts (e.g., Judaism and Hellenism) surrounding and influencing the New Testament, see Joel Green and McDonald, *World of the New Testament*. Also, Hays, *Echoes of Scripture*; Chilton, "Rabbinic Literature and the New Testament," 413–23. For further, see 3.4.5.

61. "Final Report 1972–1976," 85–95; "Final Report 1977–1982," 97–115; "Perspectives on Koinonia," 117–42. The title is different but "Perspectives on Koinonia" is the third report from dialogue held between 1985 and 1989.

62. From 1996 to 2000, representatives of the World Alliance of Reformed Churches (WARC) and classical Pentecostals engaged in the first formal international dialogue. The report from these discussions, "Final Report 1996–2000," 9–43, is discussed in chapter 4. Further perspectives on ecumenical interpretation include Kärkkäinen and Yong, *Pneumatological Theology*, 1–80; Wainwright, "Ecumenical Hermeneutic," 639–62.

numbers of scholars focusing on theological interpretation of scripture (TIS),[63] a broad, overlapping conversation, which is engaged with as TIS identifying scholars like Kevin Vanhoozer or Stephen Fowl have discussed pneumatic interpretation.[64]

Postmodernism's influence on the conversation is discussed throughout (for example, see 3.4.2), but active incorporation of postmodernist or philosophical approaches to interpretation is beyond the remits of this work.[65] Although pneumatic discernment is discussed, it is always in relation to pneumatic interpretation. Discernment[66] is therefore another overlapping research area, and relatedly, so too is revelation.[67]

Cultural interpretation[68] is a natural offspring from any discussions recognizing that the context surrounding a person as they read scripture (in relationship with the triune God by the Spirit) is important. Correspondingly, feminist hermeneutics,[69] along with liberation hermeneutics and

63. E.g., Bartholomew and Thomas, *Manifesto for Theological Interpretation*; Billings, *Word of God*; Treier, *Introducing Theological Interpretation of Scripture*; Fowl, *Theological Interpretation of Scripture: Classic and Contemporary Readings*; Fowl, *Theological Interpretation of Scripture: A Short Introduction*.

64. For active engagement, see Philemon, "Pneumatic Hermeneutics."

65. For overview, see Bartholomew, "Postmodernity and Biblical Interpretation," 600–607. Key thinkers include Martin Heidegger, Hans-Georg Gadamer, and Paul Ricoeur. E.g., Heidegger, *Logic*; Heidegger, *Being and Time*; Gadamer, *Truth and Method*; Dostal, *Cambridge Companion to Gadamer*; Ricoeur, *Essays on Biblical Interpretation*; Ricoeur, *Interpretation Theory*; Ricoeur, *Conflict of Interpretations*. Additionally, Schneiders, *Revelatory Text*; Wolterstorff, *Divine Discourse*. Also, the New Hermeneutic: for overview and key voices, see Thiselton, "New Hermeneutic," 78–107; Robinson and Cobb, *New Hermeneutic*, with contributions from Gerhard Ebling, Ernst Fuchs, John Dillenberger, Robert Funk, and Amos Wilder.

66. E.g., David Johnson, *Pneumatic Discernment in the Apocalypse*; Kay, "Spiritual Discernment," 130–33; Moberly, *Prophecy and Discernment*; Parker, *Led by The Spirit*. Also, McQueen, *Pentecostal Eschatology*.

67. E.g., Schneiders, *Revelatory Text*; Wolterstorff, *Divine Discourse*. Also, Francis Martin, "Revelation and Understanding Scripture," 253–72.

68. E.g., Castelo, "*Diakrisis* Always *En Conjunto*," 177–95; Levison and Pope-Levison, "Global Perspectives on New Testament Interpretation," 329–48; Yong, "Science, Sighs, and Signs of Interpretation," 27–42; Yong, "Science, Sighs, and Signs of Interpretation," 177–95; Yong, "Jubilee, Pentecost, and Liberation," 162–78.

69. E.g., Fiorenza "Feminist Biblical Hermeneutics," 366, cf. Power, "Holy Spirit: Scripture, Tradition, and Interpretation," 160–61; Cheryl Bridges Johns, "Grieving, Brooding and Transforming," 141–53; Moltmann, "Trinitarian Hermeneutics of 'Holy Scripture,' 138; Powers, "'Your Daughters Shall Prophesy,'" 313–37; Schneiders, *Revelatory Text*. Schneiders wrote from a self-confessed context as a Roman Catholic, "white, middle class, First World woman," and feminist (4). She explained her primary motivation to explore the New Testament's function as "a locus and mediation of revelatory encounter with God" (4) briefly recounting her journey of integrating her spirituality

social justice,[70] religious pluralism,[71] and postcolonial interpretation[72] are also all touched upon to one extent or another within the analysis.

Topics such as liturgical interpretation[73] and pneumatic preaching[74] are also beyond this work's remits, but they are natural conversation partners and there is opportunity for much dialogue. Equally, semiotics and pragmatics,[75] and metaphor[76] are briefly discussed in 5.1. Both research areas have potential for furthering understanding of ways the Spirit communicates through scripture but require more discussion space than is available here. Whilst remembering that pneumatic interpretation is concerned with the Spirit's role in scriptural interpretation over our interpretive methodologies (see 1.3), literary criticism,[77] narrative approaches,[78] and

with her scholarship and describing how this informed her writing (2–4). Schneiders largely did not actively discuss the Spirit's role in interpretation (see 72–75 for her consideration), and completed her study with a feminist interpretation of John 4:1–42 (*Revelatory Text*, 180–99).

70. E.g., Davies, "Spirit of Freedom," 53–64; Villafañe, *Liberating Spirit*; Archer and Waldrop, "Liberating Hermeneutics," 162–78.

71. E.g., Kärkkäinen, *Trinity and Revelation*, 27–29, 36–37, 45, 92–94, 269–70, 291–93, 358–62, referencing pneumatic interpretation, mainly regarding Moltmann; Yong, "Light Shines in the Darkness," 197–221.

72. E.g., Keener, *Spirit Hermeneutics*, 293–5; Sugirtharajah, "Postcolonial Biblical Interpretation," 535–52. Also, Grey, "Through the looking glass," 28–39.

73. E.g., Fletcher and Cocksworth, *Spirit and Liturgy*; Chris Green, *Pentecostal Theology of the Lord's Supper*; Chris Green, "Then Their Eyes Were Opened," 220–34. Also, Vondey and Chris Green, "Between This and That," 211–32; Porter, "Liturgical Interpretation," 206–10; Shin, "Radical Orthodoxy," 121–42.

74. E.g., Heisler, *Spirit-Led Preaching*; Heisler, "Spirit and Our Preaching," 197–202; Lim, "Pneumatic Preaching," 203–7. Also, Cheryl Bridges Johns, "Meeting God in the Margins," 20–25.

75. The following definitions from Chandler, and Mey are sufficient for this work's purposes: "Semiotics involves the study not only of what we refer to as 'signs' in everyday speech, but of anything that 'stands for' something else." Chandler, *Semiotics*, 2; "Pragmatics studies the use of language in human communication as determined by the conditions of society." Mey, *Pragmatics*, 6 (emphasis removed).

76. The following understanding of metaphor from Lakoff and Johnson is sufficient for this work's purposes: "The essence of metaphor is understanding and experiencing one kind of thing in terms of another," also explaining that how we perceive, think, experience, and relate is "fundamentally metaphorical in nature." Lakoff and Johnson, *Metaphors*, 5 (emphasis removed), 3. For further, see Archer, "Biblical Imagery," n.p.; McFague, *Metaphorical Theology*. Also, Rabens, *Holy Spirit and Ethics*, 37, 43–52; Ricoeur, "Metaphor and Symbol," 45–69.

77. E.g., Ryken, "Literary Criticism," 457–60.

78. N. T. Wright, "How Can the Bible be Authoritative?" 7–32. This was Wright's presentation of scripture as a five-act play, the first four acts comprising creation, fall, Israel, and Jesus. The first scene of the fifth act is the rest of the New Testament and the

reader response[79] are three further interpretive methods compatible with the study of pneumatic interpretation, noting reader response especially.

Practical theology and the social sciences is another natural, and overlapping conversation partner,[80] and also theology and the biological and physical sciences.[81] The work stresses that the Spirit works personally in the life of the person engaging in relationship with God via scripture, but this is also not a "how to" work, instead purposefully asking about the Spirit's interpretive nature and reflecting some of these aspects in approach and style. A natural outflow from an offering such as this would be exploring in greater depth how some of the concepts drawn out over these pages practically manifest and serve purpose in a person's life. This is where the expertise of practical theologians can be so valuable.

Theological considerations of Old and New Testament books are included as they relate to pneumatic interpretation. Due to the increasingly enlarging material related to interpretation, exegetical commentaries[82] are only included to strengthen positions already identified through the hermeneutical literature. Pneumatology and trinitarian theology is included as it has relevance for understanding the Spirit's role in the interpretation of scripture.[83] I also acknowledge wider consideration of pneumatic ethics,[84]

---

rest of the fifth act is the church and the people of God living under the authority of the biblical story. Later detailed in, N. T. Wright, *New Testament and the People of God*, 121–44; Tom Wright, *Scripture and the Authority of God*, 115–42. For analysis and application of Wright's five-act play to empirical theology and pneumatic interpretation, see Cartledge, "Empirical Theology," 119–21.

79. E.g., Fish, *Is There a Text in This Class?*; Parry, "Reader Response Criticism," 658–61; Joel Green, "Practice of Reading," 411–27; Vanhoozer, "Reader in New Testament Interpretation," 301–28. On the value of reader-response approaches for pneumatic interpretation, see Davies, "What Does It Mean to Read the Bible as a Pentecostal?" 225.

80. E.g., Cartledge, *Practical Theology*; Cartledge, *Mediation of the Spirit*; Parker, *Led by The Spirit*. Additionally, Cartledge, "Locating the Spirit," 258–60; Kay, "Philosophy and Developmental Psychology," 267–78.

81. Mitchell, "Let There Be Life!" 297–314; Tenneson et al., "Surprising Bedfellows" 279–96; Yong, "Social Psychology of Sin," 141–61; Yong, "Reading Scripture and Nature," 237–56.

82. For commentaries from Pentecostal perspective, see, for example, Fee, *Galatians*; Thomas, *1 John, 2 John, 3 John*; Thomas and Macchia, *Revelation*.

83. E.g., see incorporated thought from Hans Urs von Balthasar, Stanley Grenz, Steven Land, Jack Levison, Frank Macchia, Jürgen Moltmann, Clark Pinnock, and Amos Yong through the analysis. Also, William Atkinson, Veli Matti Kärkkäinen, Steven Studebaker, and Wolfgang Vondey.

84. E.g., Barth, *Holy Spirit and the Christian Life*; Castelo, "Tarrying on the Lord," 31–56; Fee, "Spirit and the Ethical Life," 867–81; Rabens, *Holy Spirit and Ethics*; Villafañe, *Liberating Spirit*, 163–222; Wenk, *Community-Forming Power*, 120–48.

affect,[85] and ethical interpretation,[86] but focus here is restricted to those in or identifying with the renewal tradition discussing pneumatic interpretation. Finally, engagement with Pentecostal hermeneutics is not exhaustive but is where scholars involved in these discussions have discussed pneumatic interpretation. Where Pentecostalism is discussed, this relates to those who trace their origins to Charles Parham, William Seymour, and the Wesleyan-Holiness tradition.[87] Because a focus of this work relates to the triune nature of God, work from Oneness Pentecostal scholars is not included.[88]

1.6.2 Outline

Broadly, consideration of the Spirit's role in the interpretation of scripture is approached with two overriding and interrelated foci: 1) intimate relationship with God as Father, Son, and Spirit through pneumatic encounter, with affect, ethics, and cognition as three dynamically interrelating aspects of this intimate relationship; and 2) the Spirit's relationship with scripture, discussed by considering the relational nature of the triune God from the starting point of the Spirit. Chapters 2 to 5 also emphasize personal responsibility to cultivate intimacy with the triune God through whom pneumatic interpretation comes. This involves recognizing aspects, including ethics, that may hinder receptivity to pneumatic truth.

The structure is chronological, commencing with the period 1970 to 1989 in chapter 2, and continuing through the 1990s and 2000s in the third and fourth chapters, up until the most recent era, 2010 to 2018 in chapter 5. Each chapter identifies themes pertaining to the development

85. E.g., Castelo, "Tarrying on the Lord," 31–56; work by James Smith including, Smith, *Thinking in Tongues*; and Smith, *You Are What You Love*. Also, Yong, *Spirit of Love*. Additionally, see fns. 30–31 (affect).

86. E.g., Hauerwas and Wells, *Blackwell Companion to Christian Ethics*, is a collection of essays introduced by Hauerwas and Wells, "Studying Ethics Through Worship," 1–50, and focusing on the relationship between Christian worship and ethics. Essays discussing scriptural interpretation include Scott Bader-Saye, "Listening: Authority and Obedience," 156–68; and Jim Fodor, "Reading the Scriptures" 142–55. Also, Brueggemann, *Interpretation and Obedience*; Hauerwas, *Sanctify Them in the Truth*, 21–23; Hauerwas, *Unleashing the Scripture*; Jackie Johns, "Yielding to the Spirit," 70–84; Volf, *Exclusion and Embrace*, 51–52. See also fn. 37 (Fee).

87. For historical origins and theological overview of second work, finished work, and oneness Pentecostalism, see Anderson, *Introduction to Pentecostalism*, 46–51; Oliverio, *Theological Hermeneutics*, 20–21.

88. For consideration of pneumatic interpretation from oneness Pentecostal scholar, David Bernard, see Bernard, *Understanding God's Word*. For critique, see Archer, "David K. Bernard," 131–32; Oliverio, *Theological Hermeneutics*, 141, 165–67.

of understanding of pneumatic interpretation and associated terminology. They are presented in such a way so as to also recognize and celebrate those scholars through whom thought is drawn and developed. Chapters 3 to 5 build on hallmarks identified in the previous chapter(s), thus enabling a diachronic and thematic unfolding understanding of the Spirit's role in the interpretation of scripture. Chapter 6 reflects back, drawing together key themes and offering a closing perspective.

2

Pneumatic Interpretation is Holistic

1970 to 1989

THE CONTEMPORARY CONVERSATION[89] ABOUT the Spirit's role in the interpretation of scripture began in earnest in the 1970s as the renewed emphasis on and experience of the Spirit brought by the charismatic movement began to impact hermeneutical conversations.[90] This seems to have stimulated the academy in the following ways: conversations about the Spirit's role in the interpretation of scripture surfaced amongst evangelical scholars;[91] others

89. There have been discussions about pneumatic interpretation throughout the history of the people of God. Within the context of *this work*, some of these discussions are noted, e.g., "pneumatic" interpretation practiced in early Judaism (see 3.4.5). For historical survey of pneumatic interpretation, from the early church to the twentieth century, highlighting key periods and figures, see Wyckoff, *Pneuma and Logos*, 12–51. "People of God": Hebrews, Israelites, and early Jews in Old Testament times, and early Jews, followers of Jesus, and early Christians in New Testament times, and Christians throughout church history until present day. For further terminological discussion, see fn. 324 (Wenell and Gorman)

90. Spawn and Wright suggested that scholars in the charismatic movement joined Pentecostal thinkers, but this chapter shows that those associated with the charismatic movement surfaced alongside, if not slightly before, Pentecostal scholars. Of course, the charismatic movement was the *second* wave of the Spirit amongst the global movement now known as the renewal tradition (see 1.2) with the first wave being Pentecostalism. Therefore, it seems reasonable to suggest that the second wave of the Spirit *galvanized* those in or identifying with both waves. Spawn and Wright, "Emergence of a Pneumatic Hermeneutic in the Renewal Tradition," 3 (for further, see 1.5). For historical roots of Pentecostal theology and hermeneutics, see William Oliverio, *Theological Hermeneutics* (see fn. 48).

91. Comprehensive engagement with evangelical thought concerning the Spirit's

began actively discussing this topic in light of the charismatic movement; engagement was seen from Roman Catholic scholars;[92] and Pentecostal scholars began developing a Pentecostal approach to scripture in what would develop into a wider pursuit for theological and ecclesial identity.[93] Pentecostal scholars started using and defining "Pentecostal hermeneutics"[94] almost immediately, but it would not be until 2011 that pneumatic interpretation as a method characteristic of the renewal tradition and those scholars identifying with it, was given adequate recognition and definition by Kevin Spawn and Archie Wright.[95]

As explained in chapter 1, this work is both a historical and pneumatological analysis. It charts the conversation about the Spirit's role in the interpretation of scripture from scholars in or identifying with the renewal tradition. In this process, common and uniting features are identified, thus working to build an understanding of pneumatic interpretation and associated terminology, pneumatic appropriation and pneumatic hindrance. The

---

role in interpretation lies outside this work's scope (see 1.1 and fn. 11 [those considering pneumatic interpretation], and 1.2). Evangelicalism is understood in accordance with Yong's statement, "Whereas 'Pentecostal' refers first and foremost to an event—the Day of Pentecost—'evangelical' refers to the good news itself, the Christian *evangelion*. Whatever else evangelicalism considers itself, it is at its heart a movement that proclaims, shares, and calls attention to the good news that human beings can be reconciled to God through Jesus Christ." Yong, "Word and the Spirit," 239 (emphasis original). I broadly appreciate evangelicalism from a British context and in accordance with the Evangelical Alliance basis of faith but many discussed in this work approach evangelicalism from a North American context. Evangelical Alliance, "Basis of faith," n.p.; Evangelical Alliance, "What Is an Evangelical?" n.p. For history and relationship between evangelicalism and Pentecostalism from North American context, see Yong, "Word and the Spirit," 235–52.

92. Comprehensive engagement with Roman Catholic scholarship concerning pneumatic interpretation lies outside this work's scope (see 1.1 and fn. 11, and 1.2). I interact primarily with Hans Urs von Balthasar (see 2.3), because his work contains a degree of reference to the Spirit that identifies with renewal thought (see 1.2), and aspects of his thought are directly relevant to this analysis.

93. This period also saw the forming of the Society for Pentecostal Studies (SPS) in 1970, and *Pneuma: The Journal of the Society for Pentecostal Studies* began in 1979. The European Pentecostal Theological Association (EPTA) also formed in 1979. *EPTA Bulletin* began in 1981 and re-launched as the *Journal of the European Pentecostal Association* in 1996. For further, see SPS, "Who We Are"; SPS, "About Pneuma"; EPTA, "History of EPTA"; EPTA, "JEPTA." All n.p.

94. For definition of Pentecostal hermeneutics, see 1.2.

95. Spawn and Wright, *Spirit and Scripture* (see 1.2; 1.3; 1.5; and chapter 5). For this work's definition of pneumatic interpretation, which supports Spawn and Wright's definition, see 1.3. The term pneumatic appears to have been introduced by Howard Ervin (see 2.4.3). All applications of pneumatic in this chapter, beyond references to Ervin, are mine.

period 1970 to 1989 marks these conversational and considerational beginnings and this chapter analyzes evangelical, charismatic, Roman Catholic, and Pentecostal thought accordingly. It shows that although various terminologies were used,[96] the identified components of pneumatic interpretation, affect, ethics, and cognition (see 1.3), were themes from the start. Chapter 2 also begins to present a holistic understanding of pneumatic interpretation centered around the relational nature of the triune God.

2.1 EVANGELICAL THOUGHT

Slightly predating charismatic and Pentecostal scholars were evangelicals not actively writing from a renewal perspective.[97] J. I. Packer stated that historically, evangelical scholars had not taken the Spirit's role in interpretation seriously, identifying Arthur Pink as the only evangelical he knew after John Owen who had integrated the Spirit with interpretation.[98] Unbeknown to Packer, evangelical scholars *had* more recently been seeking to do this,[99] but Packer was correct to highlight the significance of Pink's contribution.

2.1.1 Honesty of soul and spirituality of heart (Arthur Pink)

In *Interpretation of the Scriptures*, Pink wrote, "The first and most essential qualification for understanding and interpreting the Scriptures [is] *a mind illumined by the Holy Spirit*."[100] Like other evangelical conversationalists of

96. See fn. 6 (different terms).

97. See fn. 11 (contributions outside the renewal tradition).

98. Packer, "Infallible Scripture and the Role of Hermeneutics," 418 fn. 75, referring to Owen, *Causes, Ways and Means* (1678).

99. Two contributions pre-dating 1970 were Ramm, *Contemporary Relevance of the Internal Witness of the Holy Spirit*, especially chapters III, IV; Cullmann, "Tradition," 59–99. Evangelical contributions post-1970 included: Anderson, *Living Word*, 34–35; Berkouwer, *Holy Scripture*, 105–15; Bloesch, "Sword of the Spirit," 14–19; Bromiley, "Church Fathers and Holy Scripture," 214; Bruce, *Canon of Scripture*, 281–83; Dunnett, *Interpretation of Holy Scripture*, 80, 142, 178; Frame, "Spirit and the Scriptures," 217–35; Fuller, "Holy Spirit's Role in Biblical Interpretation," 189–98; Henry, *God, Revelation and Authority*, 256–95; Keegan, *Interpreting The Bible*, 151–63; Klooster, "Role of the Holy Spirit in the Hermeneutic Process," 451–72; Marshall, "Holy Spirit and the Interpretation of Scripture," 66–74; Nash, *Word of God*, 121–32; Packer, *Keep in Step with the Spirit*, 238–41; Ramm, *Protestant Biblical Interpretation*, 7–18; Thiselton, "Word of God and the Holy Spirit," 85–92; Torrance, "Epistemological Relevance of the Holy Spirit," 185–86; Winn, "Holy Spirit and the Christian Life," 51–52; Zuck, "Role of the Holy Spirit in Hermeneutics," 120–29.

100. Pink, *Interpretation of the Scriptures* (f.pub. 1977), 15 (emphasis original). Pink

his day, Pink identified the Spirit's illumination with regeneration, speaking of a veil of ignorance and prejudice lying over the mind and the affections, preventing a person from recognizing truth.[101] Other evangelicals had identified a relationship between sin and pneumatic interpretation but they concentrated mainly on the context of regeneration. Although they detailed the ongoing relationship a believer has with God and the corresponding influence upon perception, this does not seem to have been their emphasis, or if it was, if was not clearly defined.[102] Pink's emphasis, by contrast, was clear. He wrote that the veil was not completely removed at regeneration,[103] and identified the heart[104] as the locus of discernment, not the mind.[105] Pink also spoke of the transforming knowledge the Spirit brings, but emphasized the corresponding responsibility to work with the Spirit in bringing this knowledge about.[106] Four relating qualifications facilitating ability to pneumatically interpret were identified: "an impartial spirit," "a humble mind," "a praying heart," and "a holy design" involving seeking, not to acquire scriptural knowledge, but to grow closer in relationship with God, be transformed by God's holy teaching, and understand God's will for our[107] lives.[108] For Pink, careful and diligent study of scripture was important,[109] but it was not enough; scripture must be approached prayerfully and holistically. He wrote:

> Something more than intellectual training is required: the heart must be right as well as the head. Only where there is honesty of soul and spirituality of heart will there be clearness of vision to perceive the Truth.[110]

(1886–1952) published little in his lifetime. *Interpretation of the Scriptures* was amongst the first of his works to be published posthumously.

101. Pink, *Interpretation of the Scriptures*, 16.

102. E.g., Henry, *God, Revelation and Authority*, 278; Klooster, "Role of the Holy Spirit in the Hermeneutic Process," 461–63; Ramm, *Protestant Biblical Interpretation*, 12.

103. Pink, *Interpretation of the Scriptures*, 16.

104. For definition of heart, see 1.3.

105. Pink, *Interpretation of the Scriptures*, 16. Also Klooster, "Role of the Holy Spirit in the Hermeneutic Process," 461–3; Fuller, "Holy Spirit's Role in Biblical Interpretation," 192; Berkouwer, *Holy Scripture*, 110–11.

106. Pink, *Interpretation of the Scriptures*, 17.

107. See fn. 1 (use of "our," "we," and "us")

108. Pink, *Interpretation of the Scriptures*, 17–19 (emphasis removed).

109. Pink, *Interpretation of the Scriptures*, 23. Similarly, Zuck, "Role of the Holy Spirit in Hermeneutics," 126.

110. Pink, *Interpretation of the Scriptures*, 13. Comparably, I. Howard Marshall

Pink emphasized the hindrance upon discernment that acting in the opposite spirit brought. He wrote, "There is a veil of *prejudice* over the affections. 'Our hearts are overcast with strong affections of the world, and so cannot clearly judge practical truth.'"[111] He explained that opposing impartiality was prejudice, which clouded discernment, and opposing humility was pride (self-conceit) resulting in spiritual ignorance. He also cautioned that those who did not approach scripture prayerfully, recognizing their dependence upon the Spirit to reveal truth, would be hindered in their interpretive pursuit.[112]

Pneumatic hindrance[113] was also highlighted by Roy Zuck and G. C. Berkouwer. Zuck wrote that "a Christian who is in sin is susceptible to making inaccurate interpretations of the Bible because his mind and heart are not in harmony with the Spirit."[114] Berkouwer used the Pharisees as an example, writing that they knew scripture but had not discerned its deep intent. He linked humility and the state of the heart with ability to interpret, asserting that meaning is missed when we do not listen sincerely, with willingness to be instructed and guided, stating, "We need insight (Eph. 3:18) as opposed to futile minds, darkened understanding, and ignorance due to hardness of heart (Eph. 4:17ff.)."[115]

2.1.2 Appropriating scripture to new situations

It is important to understand what these evangelical conversationalists were *not* talking about when they considered the Spirit's role in interpretation. Although they explored the Spirit's conveying of insight, received in a person's heart (and mind), most did not recognize the Spirit's appropriation of scripture for personal and contemporary contexts outside of

explored various issues concerning pneumatic interpretation, centering on the importance of the interpreter's relationship with God. Illustrating his own humility, Marshall started by acknowledging his ignorance of this research area. Marshall, "Holy Spirit and the Interpretation of Scripture," 66–74.

111. Pink, *Interpretation of the Scriptures*, 16 (emphasis original), quoting Manton (no further reference given).

112. Pink, *Interpretation of the Scriptures*, 17–18. On prayer and spiritual devotion, see Zuck, "Role of the Holy Spirit in Hermeneutics," 125; Marshall, "Holy Spirit and the Interpretation of Scripture," 73. For similar Roman Catholic charismatic perspective, cf. Dulles, "Bible in the Church," 5–27 (discussed in 2.2.2 and fn. 143).

113. For definition of pneumatic hindrance, see 1.3.

114. Zuck, "Role of the Holy Spirit in Hermeneutics," 125.

115. Berkouwer, *Holy Scripture*, 109–11 (110–11).

those presented in scripture.[116] Fuller's statement illustrates this: "The Holy Spirit's role [in interpretation] is to *change the heart* of the interpreter so that he loves the message that is conveyed by *nothing more than* the historical-grammatical data."[117] These conversationalists tended to see this appropriation within the context of exegetical preaching or reading. Pink, for example, understood prophecy within these boundaries, describing "prophet" as "interpreter," someone who declares and explains the mind and will of God to others,[118] whilst I. Howard Marshall described Paul's epistles as Paul's sermons, intended by Paul to reach the hearers of his messages in their situations, but intended by the Spirit to reach subsequent hearers in their situations.[119] These were cautious or even non-charismatic approaches to pneumatic interpretation, but it should also be appreciated that because the charismatic movement had only just started to influence scholars, these were early conversations, which would develop as understanding of the charismata increased. This also illustrates the importance of identifying, where possible, faith perspectives underlying a person's writing, for without this appreciation, interpretation of their material risks distortion.

Those beginning to articulate that the Spirit uses scripture to speak personally in situations outside that presented in scripture included Clark Pinnock, James D. G. Dunn, and Richard Hays.[120] Pinnock wrote of a system of truth deposited by the Spirit in the words, through which new insights and changes of perspective will come,[121] whilst Dunn and Hays both considered Paul's use of scripture.

In *Jesus and the Spirit*, Dunn discussed the interpretive work of the Spirit in the Pauline epistles and John's gospel.[122] Referring to Pauline lit-

116. For definition of pneumatic appropriation, see 1.3.

117. Fuller, "Holy Spirit's Role in Biblical Interpretation," 192 (emphasis added). Also Berkouwer, *Holy Scripture*, 57. Similarly, Bloesch, "Sword of the Spirit," 18; Klooster, "Role of the Holy Spirit in the Hermeneutic Process," 451; Pink, *Interpretation of the Scriptures*, 38; Ramm, *Protestant Biblical Interpretation*, 18.

118. Pink, *Interpretation of the Scriptures*, 31, referencing Charles Hodge (no further reference given).

119. Marshall, "Holy Spirit and the Interpretation of Scripture," 69–70. Marshall's accompanying example was John Wesley's conversion when Wesley came to understanding justification by faith in his *heart* through his *hearing* of Luther's preface to the epistle to the Romans. Similarly, Bloesch, "Sword of the Spirit," 17–18; Pink, *Interpretation of the Scriptures*, 25, 91–97. For John Wesley, see 3.1.

120. Also Lee, "Taking Ourselves More Seriously," 149–59.

121. Pinnock, "How I Use the Bible" (pub. 1985), 27.

122. Dunn, *Jesus and the Spirit* (pub. 1975), 236–38, and 351–54 respectively. Dunn highlighted that in John, the relationship with God through the Spirit is an individual affair, whereas in Paul it is more community focused (354).

erature, Dunn used the term charismatic exegesis, which he described as teaching denoting "*a new insight into an old word from God*."[123] He suggested that Paul's use of Israel's past scriptures illustrated this charismatic interpretation "to the ever changing needs and situations of the believing communities,"[124] further proposing that whilst not all of the passages identified as charismatic exegesis illustrate a spontaneous insight (for example, Rom 4:3–22; 1 Cor 10:1–4), "Paul probably regarded the initial insight as a charisma."[125] Dunn also emphasized that the Paraclete passages in John (specifically 14:26; 15:15; 16:12–15) show the interconnection between the new revelation and the old revelation. He wrote, "The new revelation has the continual check of the old revelation," identifying that it is through the old revelation that the new one is drawn out.[126]

A decade later, and with similar thinking, Dunn proposed developing an evangelical hermeneutic, which, to the best of my knowledge, he did not pursue further beyond some initial thoughts. These were to develop an interpretive approach that prioritized historico-grammatical approaches to scripture whilst appreciating that God speaks by the Spirit through scripture into a person's life. The method would be steered by looking to the New

123. Dunn, *Jesus and the Spirit*, 237 (emphasis original). As is discussed in 3.4.5, Aune used "charismatic exegesis" similarly, stating, "'charismatic exegesis' is an extremely complex phenomenon which (at least for early Judaism and early Christianity) appears to be rooted in the belief that the Torah can only be properly understood if God himself grants divine insight to his people. Charismatic exegesis does not consist of a particular type of interpretation identifiable on the basis of its distinctive form, content, or function. Rather, charismatic exegesis is essentially a *hermeneutical ideology* that provides divine legitimation for a particular understanding of a sacred text which is shared with others who understand the text differently." Aune, "Charismatic Exegesis" (pub. 1993), 148–49 (emphasis original). Dunn and Aune's understanding of charismatic exegesis aligns with *sensus plenior*, which Moo explained as "the idea that there is in many scriptural texts a 'fuller sense' than that consciously intended by the human author—a sense intended by God, the ultimate author of Scripture. It is this meaning, an integral part of the text, that is discerned and used by later interpreters who appear to find 'new' meaning in Old Testament texts. This 'new' meaning is, then, part of the author's intention—the divine author and not necessarily the human author." Moo, "Problem of *Sensus Plenior*" (pub. 1986), 201 (see 201–4 for discussion, including treatment of Raymond E. Brown. *"Sensus Plenior" of Sacred Scripture*. Baltimore, MD: St. Mary's University Press, 1955). Dunn, Aune, and Moo, then, all understood that God brought new insight as a person engaged with "old" texts. For value of *sensus plenior* to pneumatic interpretation, see Grey, *Three's a Crowd* (pub. 2011), 99–102. Grey is discussed in 5.3.4.

124. Dunn, *Jesus and the Spirit*, 237–38 (238).

125. Dunn, *Jesus and the Spirit*, 237. Dunn also suggested that it was possible that the "teaching" Paul envisaged in 1 Corinthians 16:6, 26, was an elaboration of a charismatic insight received by an individual before the delivery of the message.

126. Dunn, *Jesus and the Spirit*, 351–52 (352).

Testament authors when they interpreted scripture for their contemporary contexts. Dunn described this hermeneutic as "historical exegesis with a prophetic openness to the Spirit now."[127]

This work focuses on the Spirit's interpretive activity over our interpretive methodology. Differentiation can be subtle between the two emphases, but Dunn's proposition, certainly by its name, suggested more of an emphasis on our interpretive methodology. Nevertheless, his idea corresponds with this work's understanding of pneumatic appropriation (see 1.3) as an act of communication brought by the Spirit through scripture to personal situations and surrounding contexts and which coheres with the original passage and its surrounding context in some way.

Hays also considered Paul's use of Israel's scriptures for new contexts,[128] assessing whether Paul used a particular hermeneutical approach,[129] and if this could be applied today.[130] He identified Paul's discussion of letter and Spirit in 2 Corinthians 3:1—4:6 as central, thereby identifying a Pauline hermeneutic as pneumatic at its core.[131] Like Dunn, Hays identified historico-grammatical methods of interpretation as important tools with limitations. Using Paul to illustrate this, he explained that "the 'original' meaning of the scriptural text . . . by no means dictates Paul's interpretation, but it hovers in the background to provide a *cantus firmus*[132] against which a *cantus figuratus* can be sung."[133]

127. Dunn, *Living Word* (pub. 1987), 126–36 (132). Cf. 3.4.4 re the prophetic aspect. Cf. Fee (see 2.4.2), writing that historico-grammatical study should not be a freestanding structure on its own but provide a framework for the Spirit: "The letter and the Spirit are not opposed to one another. It is only when one has the letter alone that it kills or only when one has the Spirit alone that the structure is sure to collapse." Fee, "Genre of New Testament Literature," 126.

128. Hays, *Echoes of Scripture* (pub. 1989), chapter 1.

129. Hays, *Echoes of Scripture*, chapter 4.

130. Hays, *Echoes of Scripture*, 154–92 (180). For arguments in favor of using 2 Corinthians 3 hermeneutically, see Käsemann, *Perspectives on Paul*, 138–66; Hooker, "Beyond the Things that are Written?" 295–309. For opposing views, see Plummer, *Commentary*, 87; Westerholm, "Letter and Spirit," 229–48.

131. Hays, *Echoes of Scripture*, 156.

132. "An existing melody that becomes the basis of a polyphonic composition." Apel, *Harvard Dictionary of Music*, 130.

133. Hays, *Echoes of Scripture*, 178. Correspondingly, Donald Bloesh and William LaSor both considered the appropriation of past scripture for a new context (Christ) by the New Testament authors. Bloesh called this a christological hermeneutic and stated that the Spirit was within this process. LaSor was clearer on the method's prophetic attributes but did not apply this to contemporary contexts or attribute a role to the Spirit. Bloesch, "Christological Hermeneutic," 78–102; LaSor, "Prophecy, Inspiration, and *Sensus Plenior*," 49–60. Also, and without mentioning the Spirit, Sheppard, "Canonization,"

2.1.3 Evaluation

The value of these early evangelical scholars' insights at this work's outset are twofold: firstly, their recognition of a relationship between ethical conduct and pneumatic interpretation; and secondly, their emerging investigations concerning how the Spirit communicates personally to a person through scripture in ways cohering with the historico-grammatical data.

These scholars, and Pink especially, identified the heart as the locus of discernment, and cautioned that when our hearts (and minds) are not in harmony with the Spirit, discernment will be hindered (Pink, Zuck, Berkouwer). Pink's four qualifications for ability to pneumatically interpret—impartiality, humility, prayerfulness, and seeking to grow closer in personal relationship with God—are worthy of further exploration. His identification that partiality and pride can hinder ability to pneumatically interpret and discern is important for developing understanding of pneumatic hindrance. These thoughts provide a base understanding for pneumatic hindrance, building from the definition offered in 1.3, which will be developed throughout chapters 2 to 6. Pink is a key figure at the start of the conversation, juxtaposing worldly affections with affections from the Spirit. He thereby effectively identified affective and ethical components of the Spirit's role in interpretation and linked the two together.

When incorporating thought from evangelical scholars it should be recognized that at this time, most saw the Spirit providing no new revelation outside of the historico-grammatical data. They believed that the Spirit could speak personally through scripture but only within these constraints, tending to see this correspondence within exegetical preaching or reading. Dunn, Pinnock, and Hays were exceptions to this, beginning to consider ways the Spirit speaks through scripture in personal situations outside those presented in scripture, identifying aspects that correspond with and support the understanding of pneumatic appropriation offered in chapter 1.

2.2 CHARISMATIC THOUGHT

Some scholars actively sought understanding concerning the Spirit's role in the interpretation of scripture in light of their involvement with the charismatic movement.[134] Discussions centered on developing interpretive

21–33; Goldingay, "Interpreting Scripture," 273. Cf. fn. 123 (*sensus plenior*).

134. For evangelical perspective on the charismatic movement, particularly regarding use and application of scripture, see Carson, *Showing the Spirit*, 170–83. For Roman Catholic charismatic perspective, see Congar, "Renewal in the Spirit," 145–212 (166–67,

methods that took the experience of the Spirit into consideration, thereby emphasizing the holistic nature of pneumatic interpretation.

2.2.1 A balanced dialectic of scripture and Spirit

James Jones credited the Pentecostal movement with "rediscovering the Spirit" but cautioned that the charismatic movement was prioritizing experience at the expense of reflection.[135] He emphasized that "the New Testament and the writings of the church fathers reveal that the early church not only experienced but thought about the Spirit"; in other words, they put their writings, reflections, and training at the service of their spiritual experience.[136] Jones recommended this approach should be prioritized, incorporating a healthy understanding of encounter and reflection upon the Spirit throughout church tradition.[137] He proposed that recovering "a dialectic of Word and Spirit as a balance where both receive equal weight"[138] alongside a parallel understanding of objectivity and subjectivity would result in greater theological sensitivity to the Spirit. Jones further emphasized that scripture is not an authority, only confirmed as such by the testimony of the Spirit.[139] Hermeneutical implications of his proposition become clearer through his statement:

> Refusing to subsume the Spirit under the Word frees the Spirit to do more than simply confirm the text and then shut up. . . . The Spirit is as much a guide to the Christian as the Bible. The Spirit does not contradict the Scriptures but his job is more than just repeating what one can find by reading there.[140]

Jones therefore *explicitly* gave the Spirit and scripture equal weighting, but by emphasizing that the Spirit confirms scripture as an authority, *implicitly* gave the Spirit greater weighting. He recognized coherence between Spirit and scripture and hermeneutically prioritized the Spirit over scripture.

210–11 for pneumatic interpretation, noting that for Congar, "Word" is Christ [211]).

135. Jones, *Spirit and the World* (pub. 1975), 1–2 (1). Also, Congar, "Renewal in the Spirit," 166–67.

136. Jones, *Spirit and the World*, 2–3 (2).

137. Jones, *Spirit and the World*, 3.

138. Jones, *Spirit and the World*, 98.

139. Jones, *Spirit and the World*, 97–99.

140. Jones, *Spirit and the World*, 99.

2.2.2 The charism of scholarship & corrosion by historico-criticism

Scripture and the Charismatic Renewal is the proceedings of a Roman Catholic conference, held in 1978 "to examine the theological and pastoral issues concerning the use of scripture in the charismatic renewal."[141] Like Jones, the delegates considered how charismatic application of scripture could progress healthily. They recommended continuing dialogue between theologians and people in the churches experiencing the charismatic renewal. This would help prevent scholars from being disconnected from the experience of God in the churches, and protect people from misuse and misunderstanding of charismatic forms of biblical interpretation.[142] Scholarship was affirmed as a charism but they warned that if it was not "dynamically related to the other gifts of the Spirit and . . . firmly rooted in Christian community," it would actually corrode faith.[143] The delegates applied this directly to historical criticism, stating, "Historical criticism when used alone corrodes faith, [for] not every form of scripture teaching builds faith."[144]

The proceedings of the Lutheran conference, *Welcome Holy Spirit*, held in 1981,[145] took a similar position, asserting that the charismatic movement's perspective of experiencing and practically applying scripture presented a significant intellectual challenge to the academy, challenging the naturalism and rationalism dominating it.[146] The delegates asserted that

141. George Martin, *Scripture and the Charismatic Renewal* (pub. 1979); Martin, "Introduction," 2.

142. O'Brien, "Summary and Conclusion," 99–100.

143. O'Brien, "Summary and Conclusion," 117. Cf. Pink on hindrance (2.1.1). Similarly to Pink, but from a Roman Catholic charismatic perspective, Avery Dulles suggested that the Bible is an expression of faith and devotion to God, and must be read with similar faith and devotion, along with prayer, for this facilitates communion with God. Dulles referenced Vatican II's *Constitution on Divine Revelation Dei Verbum* (hereafter *Dei Verbum*) no.12, "Holy Scripture must be read and interpreted in the sacred spirit in which it was written," and 25, "prayer should accompany the reading of sacred Scripture so that God and man may talk together." Dulles, "Bible in the Church" (pub. 1979) 14–16 (16); Vatican, "*Dei Verbum*," n.p. After Vatican II, Roman Catholics and Pentecostals engaged in formal dialogue. For perspective on these discussions as they related to issues of pneumatology and interpretation, see Kärkkäinen, *Spiritus ubi vult spirat* (pub. 1998) 86–149, 426–27; Lee, *Pneumatological Ecclesiology* (pub. 1994), 51–96. See fn. 203 (Kärkkäinen, Lee) fn. 187 (Ervin).

144. O'Brien, "Summary and Conclusion," 117.

145. Christenson, *Welcome Holy Spirit* (pub. 1987). The conference was attended by Lutherans with pastoral and theological experience and training, and who had experienced the charismatic renewal. Christenson, "Introduction: A View from Within," 11.

146. Christenson, "Biblical Interpretation in the Charismatic Renewal," 43–44. Similarly, Power, "Holy Spirit: Scripture, Tradition, and Interpretation," 154.

"what charismatics most strongly take issue with in historical-critical studies, however, is not its methodology as such, but precisely an *un*critical use of this method, whereby one imposes on the text a presupposition, such as an antisupernatural bias, that is basically alien to the biblical world."[147]

2.2.3 Inner healing as an interpretation of Romans 6:5–7 (Francis Martin)

In *Theological Reflections on the Charismatic Renewal*,[148] Roman Catholic priest and scholar Francis Martin considered how to bridge the hermeneutical gap from author to interpreter. He argued that "an interpretation is not the same as the description of an object; it is the re-presentation of an act of communication" in a different time, space, or experience.[149] Martin emphasized that new experiences bring new confrontations with scripture. He advised structuring a hermeneutical process beginning with faith experience (of the charismatic movement)[150] writing that the charismatic movement's most essential characteristic was that it was "an experience [or] style of consciousness" of the realities of the good news in Christ and it was in this that our anthropology was challenged.[151] Martin brought this proposition into conversation with aspects of Paul's teaching on *soma*, concluding that Paul's teaching showed the charismatic movement "the true meaning of the move toward community." He emphasized, "A true community is a place of 'mystical union' in which the totality of our personality and spiritual, emotional, and physical life is taken up in union with these same dimensions of the risen Lord."[152]

Martin suggested viewing the practice of inner healing advocated by the charismatic movement as an interpretation (or *re-presentation*) of Romans 6:5–7 ("the body ruled by sin" and the new life brought by dying to

147. Christenson, "Biblical Interpretation in the Charismatic Renewal," 45 (emphasis original). Another charismatic Lutheran seeking to integrate his faith with interpretation of scripture was Serenius, *That They May Be One*. For criticism of the Lutheran charismatic position, see Bird, "Experience Over Scripture in Charismatic Exegesis," 5–11.

148. Haughey, *Theological Reflections on the Charismatic Renewal* (pub. 1978). These proceedings of a conference held in Chicago in 1976, particularly referred to Roman Catholic charismatic spirituality. Ranaghan, "Preface," viii.

149. Francis Martin, "Charismatic Renewal and Biblical Hermeneutics," 4, cf. 31, fn. 13.

150. Francis Martin, "Charismatic Renewal and Biblical Hermeneutics," 4–8.

151. Francis Martin, "Charismatic Renewal and Biblical Hermeneutics," 13 (emphasis removed).

152. Francis Martin, "Charismatic Renewal and Biblical Hermeneutics," 27.

this sin).[153] He explained inner healing as a "healing of memories" brought about through "word[154] and prayer," yielding a person to the action of God within them and releasing them from the bondage of past associations. Martin argued that this yielding and releasing was a process, not a one-off event, and that these bondages were "most apparent in the fear and anger that they carry, and in the *living knowledge of God the Father* that they prevent."[155]

Thus, Martin recognized the holistic nature of the Spirit's role in interpretation, showing this through the physical and emotional spiritual experiences that were hallmarking the charismatic movement. He also implicitly recognized that past experiences, which have caused emotional hurt, can hinder pneumatic discernment and interpretation, but that inner healing—*healing of the heart* through the work of the Spirit—can help correct this. Once again (see 2.1.1; 2.1.2), this places the heart as the locus of discernment and argues that pneumatic interpretation should be understood holistically.

2.2.4 Evaluation

These early charismatic conversationalists were much more cautious of historico-grammaticism than evangelical scholars, advising incorporation only as part of wider, more holistic understandings of charismatic forms of interpretation. This probably illustrates the differing faith perspectives underlying their work. These scholars emphasized the importance of continuing conversations whilst engaging with church tradition (Jones), and with people in the churches experiencing the renewal first hand. The delegates of *Scripture and the Charismatic Renewal* identifying the scholarly calling as a charisma is a beautiful affirmation to all scholars, but the accompanying warning should be heeded: scholars must be actively engaged with Christian community and incorporate other gifts of the Spirit with their scholarly gift. The fruits of the Spirit could also be included here. Drawing from and building upon Jones's contribution, a person's scholarly writing, reflection,

153. Francis Martin, "Charismatic Renewal and Biblical Hermeneutics," 19–20 (emphasis added).

154. I interpret this to mean words spoken to a person, either directly by the Spirit, as scripture is read, or by the words of another person, often using scripture, which work to correct false perceptions and bring healing.

155. Francis Martin, "Charismatic Renewal and Biblical Hermeneutics," 19–20 (emphasis added). Similarly, Power, "Holy Spirit: Scripture, Tradition, and Interpretation," 159. Cf. Pink's juxtaposing of the affections of the world with the affections from the Spirit (2.1).

and training are in mutual relationship with, and at the service of, Spiritual experience, not prior to it.

Martin appreciated that interpretation was a physical, emotional, and mental spiritual experience. His *re-presentation* of inner healing as a contemporary, charismatic interpretation of being set free from the body ruled by sin (Rom 6) is a tangible example of the more holistic, charismatic approaches to interpretation being explored by these scholars. Incorporating Romans 8 (the new life through the Spirit) could develop the biblical basis for this further. Martin's insights align with Pink's in 2.1.1, with both contributions (Pink's explicitly) placing the heart as the locus of discernment. Pink and Martin's thought-commonality garners insight as to how perception, discernment, or reception of truth brought by the Spirit can be hindered. Understanding inner healing as being set free by the Spirit through word and prayer from past bondages is significant, for it helps to again recognize the affective and ethical components of the Spirit's role in interpretation. This time, the emphasis is not so much on our ethical conduct but the actions of others, which can cause emotional harm, damage the heart, and hinder ability to discern truth. Distorted discernment and interpretation can, of course, lead to distorted conduct, increasing potential to cause emotional harm to others. Only through and with the Spirit can these distorted affections, actions, and perceptions be corrected.

2.3 ROMAN CATHOLIC THOUGHT (HANS URS VON BALTHASAR)

As identified, contributions to "Charismatic Thought" came from Roman Catholic scholars.[156] Additionally, the following aspects of Hans Urs von Balthasar's pneumatology directly pertain to the affective, ethical, and cognitive components of pneumatic interpretation.

156. Further contributions from Roman Catholic scholars included: Congar, "Renewal in the Spirit," 166–67, 210–11; Dalton, "Composition," 144; Power, "Holy Spirit: Scripture, Tradition, and Interpretation," 152–78; Rahner, "Experience of the Spirit," 189–211. Also Dulles, "Bible in the Church," 5–27; "Scripture," 7–26; Francis Martin, "Charismatic Renewal and Biblical Hermeneutics," 1–37 (discussed in 2.2). Whilst I interact primarily with Balthasar (see fn. 92), Yves Congar is noted.

2.3.1 The Spirit (self)-interprets God as Father, Son, and Spirit

For Balthasar, "the Spirit's entire role is to guide us into the truth and to declare it."[157] The Spirit "is the love between Father and Son by being simultaneously their fruit and hence their witness," and the Spirit is therefore "the interpreting Spirit." The Spirit is also identifiable with the truth and so "the space between Father and Son, into which the Spirit introduces us, is in a certain respect the Spirit himself."[158] Guidance into truth is "transmutation into the realm of the divine" and this happens by the Spirit's operation of insight and virtue.[159] This is "trinitarian truth," declared by the Spirit, appearing in Christ and illuminating the Father. Reception of the Spirit's truth inspires lived faith, imparts unity, and enables discernment between spirits of truth and error.[160]

Furthermore, because all wisdom and knowledge is held in Christ (Col 2:3), the truth the Spirit communicates is infinite, and new vistas of perception open up as it is translated and declared through the ages. "Sometimes," Balthasar stated, "if the Spirit wills, we can suddenly become aware of entirely new aspects of the infinite truth as they come under the spotlight, aspects that had always had their place within faith's spiritual horizon but were somehow neglected."[161]

2.3.2 Pneumatic interpretation: reachable yet also beyond grasp

Applying these aforementioned aspects of Balthasar's pneumatology to pneumatic interpretation, and a view emerges that as we read scripture, the Spirit (self)-interprets God as Father, Son, and Spirit to us.[162] Moreover,

157. Balthasar, *Theo-Logic III* (f.pub. 1987), 17. Balthasar's *Theo-Logic* series focuses on what God speaks about God. *Theo-Logic III* concluded the series and was published a year before Balthasar's death in 1988. Balthasar's abiding principle in *Theo-Logic III* was that the Spirit declares the works of the Father and Son personally to us (13).

158. Balthasar, *Theo-Logic III*, 18.

159. Balthasar, *Theo-Logic III*, 19.

160. Balthasar, *Theo-Logic III*, 21, 23–24 (24), cf. 65 concerning the discernment of spirits, Qumran, and prophecy.

161. Balthasar, *Theo-Logic III*, 21

162. Balthasar, *Theo-Logic III*, 28, also 30. Balthasar developed this further in "Interpreter," 61–104 (part of *Theo-Logic III*), explicating the Spirit's interpretation (self-disclosure) of God through the Old and New Testament, reaching a "final simplification" and simultaneous "highest fullness" in John, around which discussion is centered. He started with the Spirit's disclosure of truth in the Old Testament and wider Jewish literature (63–67 [66, 67]), and then considered the Spirit's interpretive activity in John (69–84), Paul, Luke, Matthew and Mark, and the Old Testament (85–100) and the church fathers (101–4).

this pneumatic (self)-interpretation does not just cognitively inform; it is a *holistic interpretation*, which transmutes us into the image of God and into the realm of the divine. In Balthasar's words, "the illuminating Spirit . . . takes complete possession of the theologizing human subject. . . . Through his own mystery, the Spirit grants insight in to the mystery of the Son who interprets the Father."[163] Here, there is a point of differentiation, for as this quote indicates, together with the holistic nature of the Spirit's interpretation, Balthasar emphasized the Spirit who reveals the Son who interprets the Father.[164] Whilst not necessarily disputing this, the emphasis brought through this analysis, which will becomes clearer as it unfolds (for example, see 3.2 and 4.2), is that the Spirit, through scripture, also interprets the Father to us.

Furthermore, and as Balthasar highlighted, God as Father, Son, and Spirit, is both invisible, and yet at the same time, incarnate. It follows, therefore, that if God's triune nature is invisible, and yet at the same time, incarnate, the Spirit's communication, being communication *from* God and which also interprets God *to* us, will carry the triune God's invisible and incarnate nature. Emphasizing this aspect of the triune's God's nature *and* communication, Balthasar explained that whilst the Spirit's act of interpreting comes to light in Christ, the incarnate Son, truth given by the Spirit is "both interpretable and beyond interpretation."[165] Elsewhere Balthasar related this to experience, stating that we can never have a direct experience of God (compare 1.5) and *must live in the space between knowing and not knowing*. He wrote, "If you think you have grasped it, it is certainly not God."[166]

163. Balthasar, *Theo-Logic III*, 30.

164. Balthasar's works are vast and I do not speak for his theology in all of them, merely the portion mentioned here.

165. Balthasar, *Theo-Logic III*, 28–29 (29).

166. Balthasar, "Preliminary Remarks" (f.pub. 1974), 338. Rahner also addressed this tension, asking whether there was an experience of the Spirit that could help us to understand and authenticate scripture. Rahner, "Experience of the Spirit" (f.pub. 1983), 191. Rahner's proposition was to understand scripture's testimony that all can experience the Spirit, and which would help prevent overlooking, not admitting to, or suppressing daily experiences of the Spirit. Rahner explained this as mysticism open to all, integration of the transcendental experience of the Spirit with concrete experiences of life. He stated, "Concrete experience of life . . . whether we are explicitly aware of it or not, are experiences of the Spirit, assuming only that we cope with them in the right way." Rahner, "Experience of the Spirit," 195–200 (200). For further, see Rahner, "Man as the Event," 116–37; Caponi, "Aspects," 7–17, discussing Rahner and Balthasar's pneumatologies. For complementary perspective to Rahner, cf. Moltmann, "Theology of Mystical Experience," 55–83 (not discussing scripture).

These thoughts of the invisible, and in contrast, incarnate nature of God *and* God's communication illuminate that truth brought by the Spirit through scripture is always trinitarian truth, holistically (self)-interpreting the Father and the Spirit to us as well as the incarnate Son. *All* truth brought by the Spirit, whether through scripture or another medium, necessarily carries the invisible, yet at the same time, incarnate nature of the triune God. Consequently, the truth the Spirit communicates through scripture—because this truth self-interprets God as Father, Son, and Spirit to us—is always *both interpretable and beyond interpretation; reachable, yet nevertheless also beyond grasp.*

2.3.3 The paradox of affective receptivity and ethical willingness

> "Imagination" and "obedience" are so little opposed to each other that in fact they much more demand and require each other. Wherever one comes up too short, the other will certainly suffer.[167]

In "Preliminary Remarks on the Discernment of Spirits,"[168] Balthasar explicated the affective and ethical components of pneumatic discernment. Here he emphasized that the Spirit can be "blocked" through immoral behavior, therefore hindering pneumatic discernment. As he explained, the Spirit, as "the personified love of God, the highest, freest power," is at the same time vulnerable to obstruction through human rebellion because of God-given freedom of individual choice.[169]

In order to perceive God, we have to make room for God, and to make room for God is to be (self)-interpreted by the Spirit, the personified love, fruit and witness of the Father and Son.[170] This is done through acknowledging the paradox of receptivity and spontaneity, a concept Balthasar developed in detail.[171] This paradox concerned the active and passive nature of God as Father, Son, and Spirit, and the active and passive nature of divine love leading us into truth. Drawing on and building from Balthasar's

167. Balthasar, "Preliminary Remarks" (f.pub. 1974), 346.

168. Balthasar's reflections on the discernment of spirits were partly in response to having observed "astonishing phenomena of spiritual renewal, zeal in prayer and apostolic commitment" in Pentecostal and charismatic churches, therefore showing critical awareness of the renewal tradition. Balthasar, "Preliminary Remarks," 348.

169. Balthasar, "Preliminary Remarks," 340.

170. Balthasar, "Preliminary Remarks," 340–43; cf. Balthasar, *Theo-Logic III*, 18.

171. Balthasar, "Preliminary Remarks," 341–46.

insights, I posit that as we engage with scripture, the Spirit (self)-interprets us through our receptivity, bringing affectivity, and consequently ethical conduct, into alignment with the Father and the Son. However, within this pneumatic interpretation there is also an active, ethical requirement. As Balthasar wrote:

> We are baptized into his *death*. And because we have died and been buried, we must lead a life free from sin (Rom. 6:1–2). The rising with the Lord is here spoken of only in the future, even if the power to live a sinless life already belongs to us from Christ's Resurrection. . . . The Spirit given to us is the Spirit breathed out to us from the dying breath of the Lord: eternal life from death. And this is what makes the discernment of spirits concrete.[172]

The paradox is that when we are most affectively receptive to God we are also most ethically willing to actively make room for the Spirit by modifying behavior, and to be in a state of passive reception, active behavior is also required. This interaction between affect and ethics—and the passive and active aspects within both components—impacts cognition, facilitating pneumatic interpretation.[173]

2.3.4 Evaluation

The overriding recognition engaging with Balthasar's pneumatology brings is that to understand the Spirit's role in the interpretation of scripture, we must seek to understand the nature of the triune God. All incorporation of Balthasar's thought should be understood in respect of this. His assertions that pneumatic truth is infinite and translatable to different contexts, and that it is reachable, yet also beyond grasp, are particularly relevant here, respectively recognizing that all wisdom and knowledge is hidden in Christ; and that the triune God, and the communication the Spirit brings through scripture which (self)-interprets the triune God to us, is both interpretable, yet paradoxically at the same time also beyond interpretation.

This pneumatic (self)-interpretation does not just cognitively inform; it changes and simultaneously transmutes us into the image of God and into the realm of the divine. Therefore, pneumatic interpretation with Balthasar presents the Spirit not only drawing us into knowledge of God but also possessing us holistically, affectively, ethically, and cognitively drawing us into the love, fruit, and witness of Father, Son, and Spirit. Immoral behavior

172. Balthasar, "Preliminary Remarks," 345–46 (emphasis original).

173. Cf. Balthasar, "Preliminary Remarks," 342, 346.

obstructs the Spirit, preventing this process and hindering pneumatic interpretation and discernment. Room is made for the Spirit by being affectively receptive to God and ethically willing to actively modify behavior.

2.4 PENTECOSTAL THOUGHT

Around the same time as charismatic conversationalists, Pentecostal scholars began developing an approach to interpretation, which quickly became known as a Pentecostal hermeneutic.[174] Roger Stronstad identified work from three scholars in the development of a Pentecostal hermeneutic: Gordon Fee, "Hermeneutics and Historical Precedent"; William Menzies, "The Methodology of Pentecostal Theology"; and Howard Ervin, "Hermeneutics: A Pentecostal Option."[175] Stronstad argued that they were "seminal strategists" who had "drawn attention to important components in an overall Pentecostal hermeneutic," but that each had a partial focus.[176]

2.4.1 Embodying the message of scripture (Rickie Moore)

Retrospectively, Stronstad could have identified Rickie Moore and "A Pentecostal Approach to Scripture" as a fourth seminal strategist and work, for here Moore addressed components of an approach to scripture that have remained integral throughout the conversation.[177] Moore recognized the uniqueness of Pentecostalism as "a particular historical community," and proposed an interpretive approach to scripture that protected Pentecostals from sabotage "by the powerful and pervasive teaching impact of non-Pentecostal methods."[178] He also described how a central component of a

174. Fee appears to have first used the term but William Menzies used it more explicitly. Fee, "Hermeneutics and Historical Precedent" (pub. 1976), 119–31; William Menzies, "Synoptic Theology" (pub. 1979), 14–21.

175. Stronstad, "Trends in Pentecostal Hermeneutics" (pub. 1988), 1–12, referencing Fee, "Hermeneutics and Historical Precedent" 119–31; William Menzies, "Methodology of Pentecostal Theology (pub. 1985), 1–14; Ervin, "Hermeneutics: A Pentecostal Option" (pub. 1985), 23–35. Stronstad's article was revised and reprinted in Stronstad, *Spirit, Scripture, and Theology* (pub. 1995), 11–30. See also, William Menzies, "Synoptic Theology." 14–21.

176. The genre of Luke-Acts (Fee), the integration of theology and hermeneutics (Menzies), and the pneumatic continuum between the experience of the contemporary Pentecostal and the ancient biblical world (Ervin). Stronstad, "Trends in Pentecostal Hermeneutics." n.p.

177. Moore, "Pentecostal Approach to Scripture (f.pub. 1987), 11–13.

178. Moore, "Pentecostal Approach to Scripture," 13.

Pentecostal approach to scripture is recognizing that "the Holy Spirit addresses us in ways which transcend human reason."[179] Moore wrote:

> There is a vital place for emotion as well as reason, for imagination as well as logic, for mystery as well as certainty, and for that which is narrative and dramatic as well as that which is propositional and systematic. Consequently, we appreciate Scripture not just as an object which we interpret but as a living Word which interprets us and through which the Spirit flows in ways that we cannot dictate, calculate, or program. This means that our Bible study must be open to surprises and even times of waiting or tarrying before the Lord.[180]

Moore recognized the Spirit's role in interpretation similarly to Pink, and Martin, also aligning with Balthasar's discussed pneumatology and application to pneumatic interpretation. The common, uniting feature amongst all four scholars and the varied ecclesial situations from which they wrote, is that each identified and emphasized the *holistic* nature of the Spirit's interpretive activity. Moore understood that we *embody* the message of scripture. These early written thoughts of Moore's, reinforced by interaction with Pink, Martin, and Balthasar, help bring a perspective that we do not just interpret scripture. Rather, as we engage with scripture, the Spirit reaches through it and *interprets us* in ways that affect, surprise, inform, and extend into our lives.

Moore's hermeneutical approach was Pentecostal in the ecclesial sense, reflecting ways in which Pentecostals engage with the Spirit and scripture. However, whilst he may not have realized this, because he centralized the Spirit, Moore's approach was *also* a renewal approach and therefore necessarily inclusive for anyone regardless of ecclesial tradition interested in and focusing on the Spirit's role in hermeneutical considerations (see 1.2).

2.4.2 Evangelical and Pentecostal methods (Gordon Fee and William Menzies)

Fee argued for retaining and integrating evangelical, historico-grammatical methods of interpretation, which scholars like Moore were distancing themselves from.[181] In "Hermeneutics and Historical Precedent," Fee cautioned

179. Moore, "Pentecostal Approach to Scripture," 11.

180. Moore, "Pentecostal Approach to Scripture," 11.

181. Similarly to Fee, see Johnston, "Pentecostalism and Theological Hermeneutics," 51–52. Similarly to Moore, see McLean, "Pentecostal Hermeneutic," 48–49.

Pentecostals against disregarding these principles (also including literary genre) over experience.[182] William Menzies took a different position, arguing for the importance of identifying a distinct Pentecostal theology. He saw methodology as the central issue and suggested developing a unique Pentecostal method, with inductive (careful exegesis) deductive (consideration of biblical theology) and verification (application to contemporary experience) stages of interpretation, calling this a "Pentecostal hermeneutic." Menzies incorporated historico-grammatical methods, but only as the first stage of a larger interpretive process.[183] He argued against Fee, describing his hermeneutical principles—Fee had been critical of using Luke-Acts as a hermeneutical model[184]—as "overly restrictive and somewhat subjectively derived."[185] Menzies placed Luke-Acts centrally within his method.[186]

182. Fee, "Hermeneutics and Historical Precedent (pub. 1976)," 119–31. Similarly, Fee, "Genre of New Testament Literature," 105–27.

183. William Menzies, "Methodology of Pentecostal Theology," 1–14; Menzies, "Synoptic Theology," 14–21. Russell Spittler similarly saw historico-critical methods as "both legitimate and necessary, but inadequate." Spittler, "Scripture and the Theological Enterprise," 76. Correspondingly, see Karl Barth's three stages of scriptural interpretation—observation, reflection, and appropriation. Barth, *Church Dogmatics I/2* 722–39. For complementary approach to historical criticism, see Barth, *Epistle to the Romans*, 1–15 ("Preface to the First Edition" and "Preface to the Second Edition"). Additionally, see Dulles, "Scripture: Recent Protestant and Catholic Views," 8–9 (regarding Barth).

184. Fee, "Hermeneutics and Historical Precedent," 124–26.

185. William Menzies, "Synoptic Theology," n.p. I am not surprised offense was taken as a result of Fee's article for his comments lacked sensitivity. E.g., "[Pentecostal] attitude toward Scripture regularly has included a general disregard for scientific exegesis and carefully thought-out hermeneutics. In fact, hermeneutics has simply not been a Pentecostal thing. . . . In place of scientific hermeneutics there developed a kind of pragmatic hermeneutics—obey what should be taken literally; spiritualize, allegorize, or devotionalize the rest." Fee, "Hermeneutics and Historical Precedent," 121. Fee restated this twice, with slight variations, in Fee, *Gospel and Spirit* (f.pub. 1991), 85–86; Fee, "Exegesis and Spirituality" (pub. 2000), 8, omitting specific reference to Pentecostals. He expanded and explained this perspective in Fee, "Why Pentecostals Read Their Bibles Poorly" (pub. 2004), 4–15, where he also discussed evangelical Christians' poor Bible reading practices. For similar perspective to mine, cf. Atkinson, "Worth a Second Look?" (2003), 49, 53 fn. 3.

186. William Menzies, "Methodology of Pentecostal Theology," 7. Scholars starting to apply a Pentecostal hermeneutic more widely than biblical interpretation included, McLean, "Pentecostal Hermeneutics," 35–56; Sheppard, "Pentecostals and the Hermeneutics of Dispensationalism," 5–33.

2.4.3 Personal, holistic communication (Howard Ervin)

Ervin's ecumenical positioning—a Baptist minister turned college professor and scholar, holding evangelical, Pentecostal, Roman Catholic, and Orthodox affiliations—provided a vantage point that is reflected in his hermeneutical approach.[187] He also appears to have been the first to use the term pneumatic. His consideration of Pentecostal hermeneutics was meant as a reflection upon the interpretation of scripture in light of the pentecostal or charismatic experiences of the Spirit across the renewal tradition and was not intended to be restricted within Pentecostalism.[188] Ervin is included here to respect his influence upon Pentecostal hermeneutics and theology[189] (he is often recognized as a Pentecostal scholar)[190] and also to show that confusion over application of Pentecostal hermeneutics' terminology existed from the start of the conversation (see 1.2).

Complementing Moore's approach, Ervin suggested that what was needed was not just a hermeneutic but a pneumatic epistemology. Ervin wrote:

> What is needed is an epistemology firmly rooted in the biblical faith with a phenomenology that meets the criteria of empirically verifiable sensory experience (healing, miracles etc.) and does not violate the coherence of rational categories. A pneumatic epistemology meets these criteria.[191]

187. Farah and Durasoff, "Biographical and Bibliographical Sketch," xi–xii. Ervin was influential in the Roman Catholic-Pentecostal dialogue. See also, Ervin, "Ties that Divide," 255–56. Briefly mentioning pneumatic interpretation in the Roman Catholic-Pentecostal dialogue was Dalton, "Composition," 145. Cf. fns. 143, 203 (Kärkkäinen).

188. Ervin, "Hermeneutics: A Pentecostal Option" (pub. 1985), 34.

189. For recent biography, crediting Ervin's Pentecostal, charismatic, and ecumenical influence, see Isgrigg, *Pilgrimage into Pentecost*.

190. E.g., Pneuma Review, "Tribute to Professor Ervin," n.p. This also begs the question, what constitutes a Pentecostal scholar? Noting Ervin as an exception, this work considers Pentecostal scholars to be those who self-identify Pentecostalism as their ecclesial and theological home. However, a renewal scholar can also be an (ecclesial) Pentecostal scholar. See 1.2, and 5.2.

191. Ervin, "Hermeneutics: A Pentecostal Option," 23. Cf. Torrance, "Epistemological Relevance of the Holy Spirit" (f.pub. 1971), 185–86. Thomas Torrance wrote that "biblical statements" were merely "time-conditioned and space-conditioned limitations of their human authors, and when left to themselves can only be interpreted in that way." He continued, stating that "[through] the activity of the Holy Spirit . . . they become diacoustic and diaphanous media through which God discloses Himself to us in His own Word and Reality and makes us capable of knowing Him beyond ourselves." Torrance stressed, "Apart from this work of the Holy Spirit all the forms of revelation remain dark and opaque but in and through His presence they become translucent and transparent" (185 [emphasis removed]). Torrance also considered the relationship

Ervin believed that we can only reach the core of the message of scripture with the Spirit, and interpretive methods not considering this were therefore inadequate. He wrote, "It is the testimony of Scripture that it is not possible to penetrate to the heart of its message apart from the Holy Spirit."[192] In stating this, he did not suggest that scripture cannot be understood without the Spirit but that the *core* of scripture's message can only be reached with the Spirit.[193] He asserted that the grounds for a pneumatic hermeneutic lay in the incarnation of Christ, writing:

> The hearing and understanding of the word is qualitatively more than an exercise in semantics. It is theological (*theoslogos*) communication in its deepest ontological context i.e. the incarnational. The incarnation makes truth personal. . . . It is not simply grasping the kerygma cognitively. It is being apprehended by Jesus Christ, not simply in the letter-word but the divine-human word.[194]

Ervin therefore recognized that truth communicated by the Spirit through scripture and received by us has a cognitive component but is *also* communicated and received *personally* and *holistically*. He asserted that "precisely because of the incarnation," cognitive, historico-grammatical methods were indispensable, but only a first step in the interpretive process. He explained, "It is only as human rationality joined in ontological union with 'the mind of Christ' (1 Cor 2:16) is quickened by the Holy Spirit that the divine mystery is understood by man."[195]

---

between cognition and the Spirit (175–76); the Spirit's work of creating and revealing through "created realities and forms of thought and speech," e.g., scripture (184–86 [184]); and knowledge of God taking place within the structures of personal and communal life (188–92). Also McDonnell, "Determinative Doctrine of the Holy Spirit," 144–45.

192. Ervin, "Hermeneutics: A Pentecostal Option," 29.

193. Similarly, Arrington, "Hermeneutics," 382. For critique of Ervin, especially referring to his more controversial statement, "there is no hermeneutic unless and until the divine *hermēneutēs* (the Holy Spirit) mediates an understanding"—Ervin, "Hermeneutics: A Pentecostal Option," 27—see Atkinson, "Worth a Second Look," 52–53. For critique of Ervin and Arrington, see Kärkkäinen, *Spiritus ubi vult spirat*, 137–48; Lee, *Pneumatological Ecclesiology*, 68–71.

194. Ervin, "Hermeneutics: A Pentecostal Option," 28. Cf. Ervin, "Ties that Divide," 251–52.

195. Ervin, "Hermeneutics: A Pentecostal Option," 29 (emphasis removed). Similarly to Ervin, French Arrington suggested building on a Pentecostal hermeneutic by developing a pneumatic epistemology, which saw "knowledge not as a cognitive recognition of a set of precepts but as a relationship with the One who has established the precepts by which we live." He recommended developing this by considering the divine and human elements of scripture, arguing that historical criticism was an important

2.4.4 Evaluation

1970 to 1989 saw the birth of Pentecostal hermeneutics and this marked the beginnings of Pentecostal scholars' pursuit for a distinct theological and ecclesial identity within the academy. A tangential effect of this pursuit would be increased differentiation between Pentecostal and charismatic scholars. However, as engagement with Ervin has shown, not every scholar using Pentecostal hermeneutics' terminology meant this in reference to Pentecostalism itself but as an approach to scripture incorporating pentecostal or charismatic experience.

Like charismatic conversationalists, Pentecostal scholars began to move away from interpretive methods dominated by historico-grammaticism, exploring more holistic approaches to pneumatic interpretation. These approaches reflected a Pentecostal worldview, and recognized emotional and sensory experience as components alongside rational thought. However, where these hermeneutical approaches intentionally centralized the Spirit's role in the interpretation of scripture (for example, Ervin, and Moore),[196] they were also renewal approaches, and necessarily inclusive for anyone regardless of ecclesial experience interested in and focusing on the Spirit's role in hermeneutical considerations. Ervin's focus was ecumenical, whilst Moore's hermeneutical interests lay within the Pentecostal community.

Moore's identification that the Spirit can communicate in ways that transcend reason complemented similar emerging efforts by charismatic and Pentecostal scholars to rebalance evangelical approaches that had overemphasized reason. Moore and Ervin were key strategists, their approaches aligning with Arthur Pink's identification of the heart as the locus of discernment and interpretation (see 2.1.1) and Francis Martin's *re-presentation* of inner healing (see 2.2). Corresponding particularly with the engagement with Balthasar's pneumatology and application to pneumatic interpretation discussed in 2.3, but also with Pink and Martin, Moore recognized that we embody the message of scripture. His insights help bring a perspective that we do not just interpret scripture, but the Spirit through scripture interprets us, whilst Ervin suggested that the truth the Spirit communicates through scripture was personal and holistic knowledge including, but extending beyond the cognitive, bringing a person closer to the mind of Christ.

---

component. Arrington, "Hermeneutics" (f.pub. 1988), 382, 387 (382). Kärkkäinen has credited Ervin and Arrington for their attempts to establish a pneumatic epistemology. Kärkkäinen, *Spiritus ubi vult spirat* (pub. 1998), 138, 141. I am sorry not to have brought Arrington into the main section of 2.4 for his contribution was also seminal.

196. Also Arrington (see fns. 193, 195).

2.5 EVALUATION

The primary theme from evangelical, charismatic, Roman Catholic, and Pentecostal thought between 1970 and 1989 is that *pneumatic interpretation of scripture is holistic.* Affect, ethics, and cognition are three interrelating components of this. Understanding the heart as the locus of discernment, from which affectivity stems, helps to appreciate this holistic understanding, and gives further weight to the emphasis identified by engaging with Balthasar's pneumatology applied to pneumatic interpretation, further strengthened by engagement with Moore, that we do not just interpret scripture, but that the Spirit, through scripture, *interprets us*. Drawing from Balthasar, the illuminating Spirit takes complete, holistic possession of us as the Spirit (self)-interprets God to us. Chapter 2 therefore commences the emphasis, which will be developed in chapter 3, that pneumatic interpretation involves the Spirit not only drawing us into the knowledge of God through our engagement with scripture, but also possessing (or interpreting) us holistically; affectively, ethically, and cognitively drawing us into the love, fruit, and witness of God as Father, Son, and Spirit.

Engaging with Balthasar's pneumatology also helped to identify an important paradox that when we are most affectively receptive to God, we are also the most ethically willing to actively modify behavior, yet in order to be in a state of passive reception, active effort is also required. This interaction between affect and ethics impacts cognition, facilitating (or hindering) pneumatic interpretation.

Like Balthasar, evangelical scholars recognized a link between ethical conduct and ability to receive truth brought by the Spirit through scripture. Pink's identification of pneumatic hindrance, with his emphasis on partiality and pride, is especially relevant. Pink also juxtaposed worldly affections with affections from the Spirit, thereby illustrating further a relationship between the affective and ethical components of pneumatic interpretation. Pink's significance at the start of this conversation is noted. Francis Martin's interpretation of the inner healing experienced by people across the charismatic movement is an example of efforts by renewal and Pentecostal scholars to understand and recognize pneumatic interpretation in contemporary, more holistic constructs. This interpretation (or *re-presentation*) further highlights that past experiences that have caused emotional hurt can hinder the ability to discern and receive truth brought by the Spirit.[197] All

197. Conversing with John Christopher Thomas, he offered, "No doubt the healing of past pain does help us discern more properly, as there is less chance that our discernment is being unduly influenced by ego centric needs growing out of our pain and as we grow healthier we are stronger and have more energy and alertness for the task at

these thoughts concerning the interrelation between affect and ethics, with impact on cognition, and pneumatic hindrance, build on the preliminary discussion in 1.3 and will continue as the analysis develops.

Within these discussions was an emphasis that a major purpose of the Spirit's role in interpretation is to bring union with Christ. Martin described this as bringing all aspects of a person (personalities, spiritual, emotional and physical lives) into union with the same aspects in Christ, whilst Ervin described this as joining ontologically with the mind of Christ.[198] Aligning with Balthasar, this work stresses that this union is not just in relation to Christ and emphasizes the Father alongside the Son, with the Spirit. In this perspective, as we read scripture, the Spirit, through scripture, holistically (self)-interprets God as Father, Son, and Spirit to us. Moreover, because God as Father, Son, and Spirit is both invisible, yet at the same time, incarnate, the truth the Spirit communicates through scripture, because this truth self-interprets the triune God, is always simultaneously both interpretable and beyond interpretation, reachable, yet nevertheless also beyond grasp.

A secondary theme was the application of historico-grammatical methods. Generally, charismatic and Pentecostal conversationalists were much more cautious of incorporating these methods than evangelical scholars, advising doing so only as aspects of wider interpretive methods and seeking to rebalance their dominance. However, evangelical, charismatic, and Pentecostal scholars all acknowledged a relationship between the original content and context presented in scripture and the Spirit's appropriation of this to contemporary situations. Even though evangelical conversationalists only recognized pneumatic appropriation within the historico-grammatical data presented in scripture, they still perceived a relationship. Engaging with Balthasar provided a perspective of pneumatic appropriation based around the nature of Christ, as he asserted that because all wisdom and knowledge is hidden in Christ, pneumatic truth (understood as the Spirit's [self]-interpretation of the triune God to us) is infinite and translatable across different contexts through the ages.

---

hand." Personal email correspondence with John Christopher Thomas, March 17, 2018. Cf. Lewis, "Pentecostal Epistemology," 123.

198. Implicit within this is the role of the body, i.e., the physical component. Martin, Moore, and Ervin all alluded to a physical component but did not explicitly state as such. If we do *truly* embody the message of scripture *holistically* then it follows that the Spirit *can* bring interpretation in ways that bring physical transformation. Correspondingly, I suggest that pneumatic hindrance can also *sometimes* manifest physically (e.g., physical ailments). Consideration of physical aspects of pneumatic interpretation lie outside this work's remit.

3

Through and Beyond Scripture I

1990 to 1999

During the 1990s more Pentecostal scholars entered the conversation and pursuit for a distinct theological and ecclesial identity for Pentecostalism within the academy garnered strength.[199] The predominant terminology therefore became "Pentecostal hermeneutic." Evangelical[200] and charismatic[201] conversationalists did not continue conversing with the same collective vigor as Pentecostals, but Clark Pinnock and Kevin Vanhoozer made contributions.[202] Veli-Matti Kärkkäinen and Paul Lee brought Roman Catholic-Pentecostal perspectives.[203]

199. In this period, the *Journal of Pentecostal Theology* (*JPT*) and the *Asian Journal of Pentecostal Studies* (*AJPS*) began (1992 and 1998 respectively). BRILL, "Journal of Pentecostal Theology," n.p.; Asia Pacific Theological Seminary, "Asian Journal," n.p.

200. Those considering pneumatic interpretation from evangelical positioning included: Erickson, *Christian Theology*, 273–85; Fowl, "How the Spirit Reads," 97–127; Goldingay, *Models for Interpretation of Scripture*, 188–89; Grenz, *Theology for the Community of God*, 379–404; McCartney and Clayton, *Let the Reader Understand*, 75–80; Thiselton, *New Horizons in Hermeneutics* (minimal consideration largely concerning historical scholarship and Pauline literature); Waltke, "Exegesis and the Spiritual Life," 28–35; N. T. Wright, "How Can the Bible Be Authoritative?" 14–16, 26, 31.

201. Considering pneumatic interpretation from renewal perspectives were: Cartledge, "Empirical Theology," 115–26; Herholdt, "Pentecostal and Charismatic Hermeneutics," 417–31; May, "Role of the Holy Spirit in Biblical Hermeneutics," n.p.

202. Pinnock, "Work of the Holy Spirit," 3–23; Pinnock, "Role of the Spirit," 491–97; Vanhoozer, "Spirit of Understanding: Discerning and Doing the Word," 407–31. Also, Vanhoozer, "Spirit of Understanding: Special Revelation and General Hermeneutics," 131–65, with ensuing critique from Willard, "Hermeneutical Occasionalism," 167–72.

203. Kärkkäinen, and Lee considered divergences between Roman Catholics and

Grouping scholars by ecclesial tradition in chapter 2 helped identify that pneumatic interpretation was an emerging conversation across (and beyond) the renewal tradition in the 1970s and 1980s. This emphasis will continue throughout chapters 3 to 5, focusing on renewal thought (see 1.2). However, because the majority of 1990s conversationalists were Pentecostal, and in order to keep the primary focus on pneumatic interpretation, this chapter is not structured around these groups but around contributions that help to develop understanding of the affective, ethical, and cognitive components of pneumatic interpretation.

Themes similar to affect, ethics, and cognition were also seen in Steven Land, *Pentecostal Spirituality: A Passion for the Kingdom*, and Land's work is used as a framework for this 1990s chapter. Theological consideration to the Spirit's relationship with scripture is given, before discussing intimate relationship with God as affective, ethical, and cognitive, and considering various cognitive frameworks for interpretation. Following Land, cognition is identified as an aspect of intimate relationship with God and as a framework facilitating knowledge. These latter discussions particularly concern interpretive method, a major conversation during the 1990s as postmodernism influenced hermeneutics and as Pentecostals investigated methods befitting their tradition.

3.1 STEVEN LAND: ORTHOPATHY, ORTHOPRAXY, AND ORTHODOXY (AFFECT, ETHICS, AND COGNITION)

Steven Land noted the absence of Pentecostal thought that directly addressed the relationship between spirituality, theology, and method.[204] He sought to fill this gap by presenting Pentecostal spirituality as "the ongoing integration of beliefs, affections, and actions" (orthodoxy, orthopathy, and orthopraxy),[205] describing this as a spirituality with a pneumatic starting point, centered on Christ and directed toward the Father.[206] Land explained

Pentecostals regarding interpretation and the Spirit subsequent to dialogue post-Vatican II. Kärkkäinen, *Spiritus ubi vult spirat*, 86–149, 426–27 (pneumatic interpretation, 137–48); Kärkkäinen, "Authority, Revelation, and Interpretation," 89–114; Lee, *Pneumatological Ecclesiology*, 51–96 (pneumatic interpretation, 60–71). See fn. 143. For evangelical-Roman Catholic perspective, see Dorman, "Holy Spirit, History, Hermeneutics and Theology, 427–38; Power, "Holy Spirit: Scripture, Tradition, and Interpretation" (pub. 1989), 152–78.

204. Land, *Pentecostal Spirituality* (f.pub. 1993), 15–16.

205. Land, *Pentecostal Spirituality*, 30–31 (30).

206. Land, *Pentecostal Spirituality*, 182, cf. 163. For trinitarian emphasis, see 21, 31, 169, 200–201.

that in doing this he was seeking to overcome unhelpful dichotomization between spirituality and theology, which tended to "fragment into intellectualism, sentimentalism, and activism,"[207] (or, rephrasing in this work's terms, the cognitive, affective, and ethical). He explained:

> To state this claim in a more formal way: orthodoxy (right praise-confession), orthopathy (right affections), and orthopraxy (right praxis) are related in a way analogous to the interrelations of the Holy Trinity. God who is Spirit creates in humanity a spirituality which is at once cognitive, affective, and behavioral, thus driving toward a unified epistemology, metaphysics, and ethics.[208]

Land located the affections (orthopathy) as the integrating center of Pentecostal spirituality, shaped and expressed by behavior (orthopraxy) and belief (orthodoxy).[209] He wrote, "If the heart is understood to be the integrative center of the mind, will, and emotions, then it is clear that affections are more than mere feelings and Christian affections are meant to characterize a person's life."[210] Pausing here, Land almost dichotomized affect, appearing to present an affection as a God-given emotion but not something already present in a person. This may not have been intentional and it may simply be a phraseology issue. Nevertheless, here, affect is understood slightly differently, as an over-arching descriptor of emotion and desire, with the Spirit aligning our already present affect with that from the triune God (see 1.3.2).

Land argued that the core of Pentecostal spirituality lay with the first ten years of Pentecostalism,[211] stressing impact of the Wesleyan and Holiness movements with their emphasis on personal holiness[212] and noting influence of Jonathan Edwards and John Wesley, concentrating on Wesley.[213]

207. Land, *Pentecostal Spirituality*, 30.

208. Land, *Pentecostal Spirituality*, 31.

209. Land, *Pentecostal Spirituality*, 182

210. Land, *Pentecostal Spirituality*, 128. For discussion of the affections, see 117–80. Land described affect in relation to Christianity generally (127–33), but emphasized three *Pentecostal* affections: gratitude (thanks/praise), compassion (love/longing), and courage (confidence/hope). He explained that whilst all Christians have these affections, gratitude, compassion, and courage, together with overriding emphasis, carry distinct Pentecostal ethos (133–59).

211. Land, *Pentecostal Spirituality*, 49–116.

212. See Land, *Pentecostal Spirituality*, 37–43, 183, 201–5 for Wesleyan-Holiness inheritance, and 139–53 for holiness (framed within compassion).

213. "The Christian affections are the heart of the spirituality of Edwards and Wesley. They are likewise the heart of Pentecostal spirituality." Land, *Pentecostal Spirituality*, 33–34. For Edwards and Wesley, see 32, 128–31, 183, for Wesley, see 202. For further, see Edwards, *Religious Affections*; Edwards, "Careful and Strict Inquiry," 3–93; Edwards, "Dissertation on the Nature of True Virtue," 122–42. See fn. 220 for Wesley.

He therefore placed the early Pentecostal community as the cognitive framework for understanding Pentecostal spirituality, with holiness as a hallmark,[214] framing orthodoxy and orthopraxy (roughly cognition and ethics) alongside affect.

3.1.1 Relationship with this work

Four aspects of *Pentecostal Spirituality* are important for this analysis. Firstly, Land considered pneumatic interpretation, but within his emphasis that "the Spirit does not exist *only* to illumine Scripture" but to gift and guide in daily life and community.[215] Whilst affirming this, pneumatic interpretation of scripture is the central focus of this analysis.

Secondly, although Land presented a spirituality that integrated cognition, affect, and ethics, by placing affect as the integrating center, he did also prioritize affect over cognition and ethics. This priority was subtle,[216] but more noticeable when he discussed pneumatic interpretation or discernment, with Land tending to emphasize the way affect shapes and influences ethics and cognition over their influence upon affect.[217] Land's starting point, aligning with the pneumatic starting point of his method, was the Spirit's work in us conforming us into the image of Christ, transforming our affectivity and influencing our behaviors and beliefs. Within his wider scope—for example, when discussing Wesleyan and Holiness influence—Land emphasized behavioral issues such as ethical conduct, but his

214. Hallmarks of Pentecostal spirituality shown during the first ten years were an apocalyptic mindset, participation in the story of God, and worship and witness. Holiness, prayer, and Bible reading were subsets within this. Land, *Pentecostal Spirituality*, 159–63 (scripture and Spirit); 163–72 (prayer).

215. Land, *Pentecostal Spirituality*, 28 (emphasis added). For pneumatic interpretation, see 28–30, 43, 66–67, 92, 94–96, 163. Cf. Moltmann's similar emphasis in *Spirit of Life*, 2–3. Land did not use "pneumatic interpretation" or "pneumatic discernment." These are this work's terms (see 1.3), applied in understanding of Land's thought.

216. E.g., "The fruit of the Spirit is the character of God [orthopathy] and therefore it is depicted fully and narratively for believers in the life of Jesus. But the acts of Jesus [orthopraxy] must be taken together with the acts of the Spirit [orthopathy] and the story of God the Father throughout Scripture [orthodoxy], for all three of these are part of the one story which should evoke and shape the Christian life for the kingdom of God." Land, *Pentecostal Spirituality*, 163 (similarly, 128).

217. Land, *Pentecostal Spirituality*, 28–30, 66, 94, 163 concerning the affections and pneumatic interpretation. This aligned with Land's Spirit-scripture emphasis discussed in 3.2.1 and 3.2.2. For approach to pneumatic interpretation starting with orthodoxy, see 43 (women in ministry).

suggestion that ethical conduct influences pneumatic discernment was implicit, and even less apparent when considering pneumatic interpretation.[218]

Thirdly, although Land was developing a spirituality specific to Pentecostalism, his use of John Wesley, Anglican minister, founder of Methodism, and grandfather of Pentecostalism,[219] justifies application to a wider renewal context, especially when developing interpretive methods that incorporate affect and ethical responsibility, which Wesley's doctrine of perfection focused on.[220]

Fourthly, the emphasis on the role of community, the context of early Pentecostalism, and focus on affectivity that has emerged in Pentecostal hermeneutics' conversations since the 1990s can all be traced to Land's influence. John Christopher Thomas (see 3.4.4) and Kenneth Archer (see

218. For implicit links between pneumatic discernment and ethical responsibility, see Land, *Pentecostal Spirituality*, 142, 143, 161, 163, 167–69, 174, 202–3. If *witness* is understood in terms of *perception*, more explicit links are identified, e.g., sins against the Spirit hinder the witness and distort the affections (168, also 179). Remembering that Land was explicating a *spirituality*, not a scriptural hermeneutic, nor analyzing pneumatic discernment.

219. Allan Anderson and Vinson Synan both placed theological origins of Pentecostalism with John Wesley. Synan emphasized that Pentecostalism's origins lay in eighteenth-century Britain, traceable through Anglicanism, Roman Catholicism and Methodism. Anderson highlighted German Pietism's influence upon Wesley, outlining that Wesley's doctrine of entire sanctification and possibilities of spiritual experiences subsequent to conversion are the foundations of the Holiness movement, from which emerged Pentecostalism. On this basis, Wesley can be credited as grandfather of Pentecostalism. Anderson, *Introduction to Pentecostalism*, 26–27; Synan, *Holiness-Pentecostal Movement*, 217. Also, Lederle, *Theology with Spirit*, 50–56.

220. John Wesley (1703–91) wrote on experiencing the reality of perfection throughout his career and his theology of perfection (entire sanctification) was woven into many of his sermons. Wesley wrote two sermons summarizing his idea of perfection: "Sermon 40, On Christian Perfection" and "Sermon 76, On Perfection," written in 1741 and 1784 respectively. Additionally, "Sermon 17, On the Circumcision of the Heart" and "Sermon 127, On the Wedding Garment," written in 1733 and 1790 respectively, represent the beginning and end points of Wesley's theological development of holiness and perfection. Sermons forty and seventy six were written partly to clarify persistent confusion surrounding the doctrine, and the forty-three-year gap between them illustrates continuing confusion this doctrine evoked. Much of this confusion surrounded Wesley's theology concerning the ability to sin in this life and disputes over the word "perfect." "Sermon 13, On Sin in Believers," written in 1763, was produced to clarify this, and in a letter to his brother, Charles Wesley in 1767, John explained, "By perfection I mean the humble, gentle, patient love of God and man ruling all our tempers, words, and actions, the whole heart by the whole life. I do not include an impossibility of falling from it, either in part or in whole. Therefore, I retract several expressions in our hymns, which partly express, partly imply, such an impossibility." John Wesley, "Letter to Charles Wesley," similarly stated in John Wesley, *Plain Account of Christian Perfection*, 112.

4.1.2) are both major proponents of the roles of community (Thomas and Archer) and the context of early Pentecostalism (Archer) to interpretation. These two scholars are key influencers within Pentecostal hermeneutics. Land's published written thoughts, however, preceded both Thomas's and Archer's. The post-2010 conversation has particularly emphasized affect within pneumatic interpretation and this is discussed in chapter 5. Land's voice is still present in current research some quarter of a century after *Pentecostal Spirituality* was published.[221]

Although Land's scope was wider than pneumatic interpretation, he deserves particular mention because of the corresponding nature of orthopathy, orthopraxy, and orthodoxy with affect, ethics, and cognition. He merits further recognition because of the relevance of his method to a wider renewal context, and his influence on subsequent Pentecostal thought.

3.2 THE SPIRIT'S RELATIONSHIP WITH SCRIPTURE I

In this section, thought from scholars who factored a theological understanding of the Spirit as a major feature of their hermeneutical considerations is considered and developed, concentrating on contributions from Land, Jürgen Moltmann, Clark Pinnock, and Kevin Vanhoozer.

3.2.1 The Spirit forms a life for God (Steven Land)

Land made an analogy between the Spirit's forming of Christ in Mary, and the Spirit using scripture to form Christ in us.[222] He posited, "The relation of the Spirit to Scripture is based on that of the Spirit to Christ. Even as the Spirit formed Christ in Mary, so the Spirit uses Scripture to form Christ in believers and vice-versa."[223]

Through scripture, as Land asserted, the Spirit "illuminates, teaches, guides, convicts, and transforms,"[224] but scripture is only the medium, the *purpose* is the forming of a life for God. He explained, "The power of the Spirit forms a life for God as Christ was formed in Mary's womb."[225] Land

221. The 47th Annual SPS Conference 2018 included "A Panel Discussion of *A Passion for the Kingdom: Reflections after 25 Years*, by Steven Land," co-chaired by Rickie Moore and John Christopher Thomas, with panelists, and Steven Land responding.

222. Land also noted the trinitarian nature of pneumatic interpretation. Land, *Pentecostal Spirituality*, 163. See also fn. 206 (trinitarian emphasis).

223. Land, *Pentecostal Spirituality*, 94.

224. Land, *Pentecostal Spirituality*, 94.

225. Land, *Pentecostal Spirituality*, 202–3.

presented this as a continual journey requiring daily choice: scripture is the path and the Spirit is the light; cultivating the fruit of the Spirit increases sensitivity to the light.[226] Although the application to pneumatic interpretation was indirect (through analogy of the forming of Christ in Mary in both passages), Land incorporated Wesley's doctrine of perfection, understanding that at the center of Wesley's doctrine lay the pursuit for wholehearted love, facilitating affective-ethical transformation.[227] Within this, Land also stated that "sin is a betrayal, a willful resistance of that purpose for which we were called."[228] Whilst he did not explicitly link this with pneumatic discernment or interpretation (see 3.1.1, remembering that Land was explicating a spirituality, not a scriptural hermeneutic), Land's thoughts highlight that whilst the Spirit works in us, affectively forming our life for God and as a consequence transforming our ethics, active ethical action is also required. This ethical aspect is considered further in 3.3, discussing the centrality of intimate relationship with God to pneumatic interpretation.

3.2.2 The Spirit reaches through and beyond scripture (Steven Land, Clark Pinnock, and Jürgen Moltmann)

Land's statement that the Spirit uses scripture to form Christ in us places the Spirit's authority prior to scripture's authority, a position also held by Moltmann in *The Spirit of Life*. Their emphasis is helpful because it recognizes a mutual relationship between Spirit and scripture but also understands that because the Spirit is not bound to scripture, pneumatic interpretation therefore reaches through and beyond scripture, effecting and/or appropriating scriptural truth holistically in our lives. Moltmann described this as a "mutual relationship," whilst Land described this as a fusion, or marriage, warning that separation or divorce will come "at great peril and price to the church and believer."[229] Instead of "scripture," Land used "Word," seemingly implying a twofold understanding of "Word" as Christ and "Word" as

226. Land, *Pentecostal Spirituality*, 163, 203, cf. 161.

227. Land, *Pentecostal Spirituality*, 201–3 (also 128–32, discussing Wesley and Edwards).

228. Land, *Pentecostal Spirituality*, 202.

229. Moltmann, *Spirit of Life* (f.pub. 1991), 3; Land, *Pentecostal Spirituality*, 94, cf. 28. For assessment of Land's Spirit-scripture position as illustrative of Pentecostal scholars' distancing themselves from evangelicalism, see Ellington, "Pentecostalism and the Authority of Scripture," 23–24, cf. Moltmann, *Spirit of Life*, 1–2. For critique raising awareness of the dangers of subjectivity within the Spirit-scripture position, see Kärkkäinen, "Authority, Revelation, and Interpretation," 98; Kärkkäinen, *Spiritus ubi vult spirat*, 115.

scripture. This implied and/or assumed twofold understanding is considered as the analysis develops (see, for example, 4.2.1; 5.4.2; 6.2).

Pinnock differed slightly, asserting that the Spirit *was* bound to scripture but *chooses* to be bound to it, also describing this as subordination on the Spirit's part.[230] He argued that the principle of the Spirit "being tied" to scripture was established by the Nicene Creed's identification of apostolicity as the fourth mark of the church—"we believe in one holy catholic and apostolic church"—arguing that apostolicity in this context denoted that the church is founded on the testimonies of the original apostles, as evidenced in the Bible.[231] Like Land and Moltmann, Pinnock recognized the Spirit's appropriation of scriptural truth, describing this as the Spirit's "controlled liberty." In this controlled liberty, the original meaning[232] of the scriptural text is honored alongside appreciation of the text's ability to procreate, and via this process, God, by the Spirit, speaks personally today through the meaning of the biblical authors.[233]

Understanding the Spirit-scripture relationship as a marriage instead of viewing the Spirit as bound or subordinate to scripture (voluntarily or otherwise) is more valuable in establishing a theological basis for how the Spirit reaches through and beyond scripture, interpreting scriptural truth holistically in our lives, whilst also synonymously remaining in relationship with scripture's written words. Moltmann's emphasis on the creational, or life-bringing nature of the Spirit's work in relationship to scripture helps to establish this further. He wrote:

> The Spirit is the subject of determining the Word, not just the operation of that Word. The efficacies of the Spirit reach beyond the Word. Nor do the experiences of the Spirit find expression

230. Pinnock, "Work of the Holy Spirit" (pub. 1993), 12, 11.

231. Pinnock, "Work of the Holy Spirit," 11; Anglicans Online, "Nicene Creed," n.p. Pinnock wrote about pneumatic interpretation between 1985 and 2009, during which time his theological perspective transitioned. In 2009 he spoke of his journey from rational, evangelical forms of interpretation toward embracing the plurality of meaning the Spirit can bring through scripture. "Work of the Holy Spirit" (pub. 1993), and "Role of the Spirit" (pub. 1993), show him midway on this journey, engaging with evangelical hermeneutical thought as a major part of both papers but critiquing and moving away from it. Also Pinnock, "Biblical Texts: Past and Future Meanings" (pub. 2000), 71–81; Pinnock, "Work of the Spirit" (pub. 2009), 158–59 (discussing his growing interest in the Spirit's role in the interpretation of scripture). Pinnock freely acknowledged his transition, writing of his theological pilgrimage from Augustine (emphasizing the sovereignty of God) toward Arminius (emphasizing human freedom), also describing it as a pilgrimage from Luther toward Wesley. Pinnock, "Augustine to Arminius," 15–30.

232. See fn. 43 (original context and original meaning).

233. Pinnock, "Work of the Holy Spirit," 9. Similarly, Welker, *God the Spirit*, 275–76.

> in words alone. They are as multifarious and protean as sensory reality itself. The Spirit has its non-verbal expressions too. The indwelling of the Spirit "in our hearts" goes deeper than the conscious level in us. It rouses all our senses, permeates the unconscious too, and quickens the body, giving it new life (1 Cor. 6:19f.). A new energy for living proceeds from the Spirit. To bind the experience of the Spirit solely to the Word is one-sided, and represses these dimensions. The non-verbal dimensions for their part show that the Word is bound to the Spirit, but that the Spirit is not bound to the Word, and that Spirit and Word belong in a mutual relationship which must not be conceived exclusively, or in merely intellectual terms.[234]

By placing the Spirit as prior to scripture, Moltmann was able to highlight the Spirit's non-verbal expressions alongside the Spirit's verbal expressions (scripture's written words). This perspective facilitates our developing understanding of pneumatic interpretation: it recognizes the mutuality of the Spirit-scripture relationship and also helps highlight the holistic nature of pneumatic interpretation in reaching beyond or *through* scripture, bringing non-verbal expressions from verbal expressions. Thus, Moltmann's perspective, applied to pneumatic interpretation, strengthens a key insight gained in chapter 2, that whilst we may approach scripture seeking to interpret its written truth, in this act the Spirit may reach through scripture and interpret us.[235]

3.2.3 The Spirit interprets the Father (Jürgen Moltmann) and the Son (Kevin Vanhoozer)

Moltmann aligned with Balthasar (see 2.3), emphasizing the Spirit's relationship with the Father and asserting that the Spirit's communication was trinitarian in nature and not singularly related to Christ. When he spoke of the Spirit's non-verbal expressions (see above), Moltmann particularly

234. Moltmann, *Spirit of Life*, 3. Moltmann's surrounding context was that experiences of the Spirit precede and determine written, or verbal words. He explained that as the words in the Bible sprang from experiences of the Spirit, words of proclamation from Christians today also spring from pneumatic experience.

235. Also Vanhoozer, "The Word exposes—exegetes!—us, the interpreters." Vanhoozer, "Spirit of Understanding: Discerning and Doing the Word," 427. Vanhoozer described the Spirit as the efficacy of scripture, rendering scripture effective. He explained scripture as a communicative act, addressing a person in diverse ways, trying hearts and minds, and exposing and exegeting and restoring the senses (427–28). This was within incorporation of speech act theory using locutions, illocutions, and perlocutions (see fn. 242). Cf. Herholdt, "Pentecostal and Charismatic Hermeneutics," 423–24.

referred to the life-bringing function of the Spirit's communication. He attributed the "far-reaching decision in favour of the *filioque*" for an over-emphasis of the redemptive aspect of the Spirit's work at the expense of the creational aspect. He continued: "This has meant that the Holy Spirit has come to be understood solely as 'the Spirit of Christ,' and not at the same time as 'the Spirit of the Father.' As *the Spirit of Christ* it is *the redemptive Spirit*. But the work of creation too is ascribed to the Father, so *the Spirit of the Father* is also *the Spirit of creation*."[236] In *Experiences in Theology*, Moltmann presented a "Trinitarian hermeneutics of 'holy scripture.'"[237] Here, he explained that whilst "the Spirit of truth communicates . . . knowledge of Christ and of the God who raised him," the Spirit also communicates "something new and specific to the Spirit, over against what Christ and God the Father have done and do."[238] In Moltmann's view, as we engage with scripture pneumatically, the Spirit brings eschatological truth and sanctification.[239] Moltmann further wrote:

> The sending of the Spirit is at the same time *the sending of life* [and] from this we can conclude that a "spiritual interpretation of scripture" has to be a *biographical* interpretation. Through the ways in which we express our lives we interpret the scriptural texts we live with.[240]

236. Moltmann, *Spirit of Life*, 8 (emphasis original). Cf. 4.2.3 (Grenz).

237. Moltmann, "Trinitarian Hermeneutics of 'Holy Scripture,'" 134–50. This was published in 2000 as part of Moltmann, *Experiences in Theology*, but is included here to illustrate Moltmann's thought. Similarly, Stanley Grenz, chapter 4, Jack Levison, chapter 5.

238. Moltmann, "Trinitarian Hermeneutics of 'Holy Scripture,'" 145. Like Balthasar (see 2.3.1), Moltmann emphasized John's gospel, particularly the Paraclete passages, as the basis for a trinitarian hermeneutic with a pneumatic starting point. Further contributions emphasizing John's gospel and the paraclete passages as basis for pneumatic interpretation came from Mark Cartledge, Jackie Johns and Cheryl Bridges Johns, and Stephen Fowl. Cartledge's focus was illustrating the value of empirical theology to evangelical-charismatic hermeneutics, and Johns and Johns's was "formulat[ing] a hermeneutic that takes seriously the dynamics of the Pentecostal faith." Fowl used John's gospel to provide trinitarian grounding for pneumatic interpretation, and the book of Acts to incorporate pneumatic community experience. All recognized the reaching of the Spirit through and beyond scripture, effecting and appropriating scriptural truth personally. Cartledge, "Empirical Theology," 115–26; Johns and Johns, "Yielding to the Spirit," 110, 113–16 (110); Fowl, "How the Spirit Reads," 97–101, 126–27. Also, Cheryl Bridges Johns, *Pentecostal Formation*, 130–40.

239. Moltmann, "Trinitarian Hermeneutics of 'Holy Scripture,'" 145.

240. Moltmann, "Trinitarian Hermeneutics of 'Holy Scripture,'" 146 (emphasis original).

Drawing from, and developing these insights, a perspective emerges that the Spirit therefore (self)-interprets God as Father, Son, and Spirit to us as scripture is read. However, because the Spirit is the source of life through the Father creationally and the Son redemptively, the Spirit cannot just communicate but *must also create and redeem* through this communication. This life-bringing creational and redemptive work brought by the Spirit through scripture as we engage with it, necessarily extends biographically into our lives.

Vanhoozer also used the *filioque* to explicate his understanding of the Spirit's relationship to scripture but was more positive about the clause than Moltmann. For Vanhoozer, "the Holy Spirit is the Spirit of the Word—the Spirit of Christ—and ministers Christ, the matter of Scripture, to its readers."[241] Vanhoozer believed that the Spirit did not alter the meaning of scripture or add to the revelation given through the original author. He stated, "The Spirit is the 'Lord of the hearing' not because he makes the words of the Bible mean something other than they say but because he guides and directs the effects of Scripture's communicative action."[242] The Spirit's role

241. Vanhoozer, "Spirit of Understanding: Discerning and Doing the Word" (pub. 1998), 429. Vanhoozer acknowledged that not every theologian affirmed the *filioque* but argued that the same point could be made through Barth's discussion of revelation (448, note 188). However, quite possibly, the *filioque* influenced Barth in the development of *his* theology. Citing the table of contents in Barth, *Church Dogmatics I/2*, xiii, Vanhoozer noted Barth's division of his discussion into two parts: Jesus as the "objective reality of revelation" and the Spirit as the "subjective reality." Vanhoozer, "Spirit of Understanding: Discerning and Doing the Word," 409. Barth stated, "The Holy Spirit is the Spirit of the Father and of the Son, of the Father who reveals Himself in his Son and only in His Son. But that means that He is the Spirit of Jesus Christ . . . to speak about the Holy Spirit and his work we must expound the biblical testimony to the revelation in Jesus Christ." He further elucidated that the biblical testimony is "God's Word" brought to a person's hearing in revelation, clarifying, "God's Word, i.e., God's revealed, incarnate Word spoken to all other men in the man Jesus of Nazareth." Barth, "The Holy Spirit as the Subjective Possibility of Revelation," in *Church Dogmatics I/2*, 247. Barth's influence on Vanhoozer is particularly evident through Barth's statement, which arguably shows *filioque*-stemmed influence: 'The work of the Holy Spirit means that there is an adequate basis for our hearing of the Word, since it brings us nothing but the Word for our hearing. It means that there is an adequate basis for our faith in Christ and our communion with Him, because He is no other Spirit than the Spirit of Jesus Christ.' Barth, *Church Dogmatics* I/2, 248. For further perspective involving Barth's theology, see Molnar, "Role of the Holy Spirit," 16–20.

242. Vanhoozer, "Spirit of Understanding: Discerning and Doing the Word," 429, quoting Barth (unreferenced). Vanhoozer used speech-act theory (locutions, illocutions, and perlocutions) to explicate the relationship and communication from the Father (locutions), the Son (illocutions), and the Spirit (perlocutions) (427–29), explaining that the Spirit's role is to (perlocutionally) persuade and convince the reader of the Son's (illocutional) claims (410). He stated, "As the Spirit proceeds from the Father and the Son, so perlocutions proceed from locutions and illocutions" (429, cf. 488,

in interpretation for Vanhoozer is therefore to persuade the reader of what is already present in scripture, not to communicate anything extra to it. Although Vanhoozer acknowledged the Father, he did so only within the context of the *filioque*, placing greater emphasis on the Spirit's relationship with the Son.[243]

Vanhoozer's perspective illustrates Moltmann's point that the addition of the *filioque* has served to neglect the creational work of the Spirit as the Spirit of the Father. Factoring this creational, life-bringing aspect of the Spirit's work within pneumatic interpretation means acknowledging, in alignment with Moltmann and against Vanhoozer, that the Spirit *does* convey something new over against the content of scripture. Furthermore, this perspective also affirms that the "new" truth the Spirit conveys is always in relationship with scripture's content through which the Spirit (self)-interprets the Father, the Son, and the Spirit to us. This (self)-interpretation is holistic and biographical, creating and redeeming, sanctifying and eschatologically informing.

3.2.4 Evaluation

Seeking understanding of the Spirit's role in the interpretation of scripture requires us to consider the Spirit's relationship with scripture. Sequentially, this involves contemplation of the Spirit, the Spirit's nature, and the Spirit's relationship with *the Father* as well as the Spirit's relationship with the Son. These theological considerations should underpin conversations about pneumatic interpretation, providing a foundation upon which hermeneutical thought can build.

Consideration of pneumatic interpretation in the renewal tradition—which prioritizes personal experience of and communion[244] with God—should take seriously the Spirit's relationship with the Father. Moltmann's

note 188). This further illustrates Vanhoozer's alignment with the *filioque*. Similarly, Vanhoozer, "Speech Acts to Scripture Acts," 15; Vanhoozer, "Spirit of Understanding: Special Revelation and General Hermeneutics," 155–58. For key text engaging speech-act theory and divine discourse (but not directly considering the Spirit), see Wolterstorff, *Divine Discourse* (cf. 1.6.1 [postmodern and philosophical approaches, and revelation]). Largely those located outside the renewal tradition and influenced by philosophical thought have developed speech-act theory in relation to interpretation so it is not included as a major theme here.

243. Evident through Vanhoozer's explication of locutions, illocutions, and perlocutions (fn. 242). Pinnock also used the Nicene Creed as a basis for establishing the Spirit's relationship with scripture (see 3.2.2).

244. Commune: to engage in intimate conversation, share and exchange thoughts, emotions or feelings. Cf. *Collins English Dictionary*, 412.

theology, aligning with Balthasar's in chapter 2, is therefore integral, helping recognize the creational (Spirit–Father) aspect of pneumatic interpretation alongside the redemptive (Spirit–Son) aspect. This helps us to understand why we can argue that the Spirit does communicate new things over against scripture's content as it is read. Furthermore, continuing the perspective brought in 2.3.2, that as we engage with scripture, the Spirit (self)-interprets the Father, the Son, and the Spirit to us, strengthens understanding that these new things communicated by the Spirit will always remain in mutual relationship with scripture's written content. I therefore suggest adjusting Land's emphasis that the Spirit uses scripture to form Christ in us, recognizing that the Spirit's formation (or [self]-interpretation) is triune and not singularly related to Christ.[245] In this understanding, scripture, therefore, does not go beyond the Spirit, because scripture reveals the triune God and this is a work of the Spirit through, in mutual relationship with, but also beyond, written scriptural content.

Consequently, in this theological understanding, the Spirit—and therefore pneumatic interpretation—always reaches through and beyond scripture, effecting and/or appropriating scriptural truth holistically (creationally and redemptively) in our lives. In this way we interpret scripture pneumatically, but through this process the Spirit reaches through scripture and interprets us. So, as the Spirit (self)-interprets Father, Son, and Spirit to us, we are pneumatically transformed into that (self)-interpretation. Returning to, and drawing from Land's original insight (see 3.2.1), whilst scripture is the Spirit's medium, the Spirit's *purpose* is the forming of a life for God.

3.3 INTIMATE RELATIONSHIP WITH GOD: AFFECTIVE, ETHICAL, AND COGNITIVE I

Land placed the affections as the integrating center of his spirituality because he recognized their relational and transformational nature, identifying the heart as the locus of affectivity and God (as Spirit, Son, and Father) as object and source.[246] With this work, Land saw affect as central to spirituality which prioritizes intimate relationship with God.[247] Differing from

245. Understanding Christ as the incarnate image of the unseen God. Colossians 1:15. This also aligns with Land's own trinitarian emphasis. See 3.1, also fns. 206, 222 (trinitarian references).

246. Land, *Pentecostal Spirituality*, 130–1

247. Robert Baker applied affect directly to scriptural interpretation, emphasizing that interpretation of scripture involved affect *and* cognition. Baker concentrated on a

this work, however, whilst Land acknowledged the transformation of ethical conduct as a consequence of the Spirit's working in and through affect, he did not emphasize ethical conduct as an active, influencing component of pneumatic discernment and cognition (see 3.1.1 and 3.2.1).[248] Land's consideration of active ethical action was clearest when he incorporated John Wesley's doctrine of perfection, and this interaction with Wesley further emphasizes the paradox of affective receptivity and ethical willingness brought when engaging with Balthasar in 2.3.3 and 2.5. Essentially, the affective-ethical paradox recognizes that as the Spirit works in us, our affect and consequently ethics are transformed, yet at the same time active ethical action is also required.[249] Wesley's doctrine was, after all, a pursuit for wholehearted love, indicating our own involvement.[250]

Land's approach is still valuable in developing understanding of the relationship between affect and ethics, and this section recognizes and develops thought from scholars, which shows different aspects of this affective-ethical, or ethical-affective relationship. Scholars in this section emphasized intimate relationship with God, and their contributions highlight affective, ethical, and cognitive aspects of this relationship.

3.3.1 The struggle and the grace (Paul Lee and Kevin Vanhoozer)

Paul Lee spoke of God effecting gradual, holistic conformation and transformation within us, alongside the continual struggle to abandon immoral ways of living. This was part of a critique of Pentecostal approaches to pneumatic interpretation[251] in which Lee suggested that Pentecostals needed to clarify more precisely *how* the community or individual approached

---

Pentecostal-specific approach to interpretation over consideration of the Spirit's role. Whilst Baker explored affect, he did not consider relational aspects. Baker's strength lay in his recognition that traditional evangelical scholarship had over-emphasized rational approaches to interpretation at the expense of affect. However, his description that New Testament scholarship generally exhibited "symptoms of paranoid schizophrenia" in approaching interpretation, and that Pentecostal scholarship presented a healthier, more holistic approach, was not productive in fostering understanding between scholars of different ecumenical traditions. Baker, "Pentecostal Bible Reading" (pub. 1995), 34–48 (34).

248. Similarly Pinnock, "Role of the Spirit," 496.

249. Land, *Pentecostal Spirituality*, 202–3.

250. See 3.2.1 and fn. 220 (Wesley).

251. Lee, *Pneumatological Ecclesiology* (pub. 1994), 68–71 ("Critique of Pentecostal Pneumatic Exegesis"). Lee concentrated on Ervin and Arrington's attempts to build on a Pentecostal hermeneutic by developing a pneumatic epistemology. See 2.4.3.

pneumatic interpretation.[252] Possibly because his primary focus was pneumatic interpretation and not Pentecostal identity, Lee questioned whether a specific Pentecostal hermeneutic was necessary.[253] He suggested that the issue of pneumatic interpretation was best addressed by viewing ourselves as "Spirit-event[s]," explaining:

> The human person is an event of God's creative dialogue . . . drawn and converted to God as he reveals himself in a continuing dialogue. Conversion involves not only some dramatic events or experiences, but it is primarily process, a gradual conformity and transformation of the human subject into the full stature of Christ in the Spirit. Abandoning the "carnal way" of life (cf. 1 Cor. 2:10–3:1) and living in the Spirit is *a constant struggle yet a graced dialectic*. In a Spirit-led life, a wholesome interpretation is possible. A spiritual exegesis involves the whole person who lives an earthly pilgrimage, yet with his eyes gazing on heaven.[254]

Lee further highlighted that living a faith-filled life changes behavior and reorients vision, bringing interpretation of scripture into alignment with the Spirit, who brings forth this "transformed perceptivity."[255]

Similar explication came from Vanhoozer who wrote of the struggle "against ourselves, against our lust for power, against the tendency to totalize and to lord it over others," alongside the Spirit's work of sanctification in us. He wrote, "The Spirit's illumination of our minds is . . . dependent on his prior transformation of our hearts," explaining that the Spirit sanctifies by purging us of "hermeneutic sin" that does "interpretive violence" and "conforms our interests to those of the text."[256] Within this, Vanhoozer—and

252. Lee, *Pneumatological Ecclesiology*, 70. Lee referred to the Pentecostal position on pneumatic interpretation stated in the 1990 report from the 1985–1989 Roman Catholic-Pentecostal dialogue: "Each Christian can interpret Scripture under the guidance of the Spirit and with the help of the discerning Christian community." "Perspectives on Koinonia," no. 26. For pneumatic interpretation discussed in the Roman Catholic-Pentecostal dialogue, see "Final Report 1972–1976," nos. 29, 43; "Final Report 1977–1982," nos. 7, 26–27, 52, 54–55; "Perspectives on Koinonia," nos. 2, 20–21, 24–26, 28. See also 1.6.1 (ecumenical dialogue and interpretation).

253. Cf. discussion of Pentecostal hermeneutics in 3.4.1. Lee's critique came within his chapter, "Scripture and *Koinonia* in the Spirit," 51–96, where he elaborated on the pneumatological dimensions of "Perspectives on Koinonia."

254. Lee, *Pneumatological Ecclesiology*, 71 (emphasis removed and added).

255. Lee, *Pneumatological Ecclesiology*, 66. Similarly, Herholdt, "Pentecostal and Charismatic Hermeneutics," 423–24.

256. Vanhoozer, "Spirit of Understanding: Discerning and Doing the Word" (pub. 1998), 413, cf. 427–28 (see fn. 235). Also Pinnock, "Work of the Holy Spirit," 22–23;

similarly William Atkinson[257]—asserted that pneumatic interpretation did not just involve a struggle against our own ethics, emphasizing that it also involved a struggle against evil spirits[258] seeking to distort our understanding of scripture. These brief observations bring two important insights. Firstly, immoral behavior effects false thinking and can feed distortion of scriptural truth by evil spirits. Secondly, closely connected with the Spirit's role in the interpretation of scripture is the ever-present reality of a spiritual battle against powers and principalities that seek to distort our ability to recognize truth. Pneumatic hindrance caused by evil spirits is discussed further in chapter 5.

From their differing Roman Catholic and reformed[259] perspectives, Lee and Vanhoozer emphasized that ethical conduct both influences and is influenced by pneumatic interpretation, with Vanhoozer highlighting that immoral behavior can effect pneumatic hindrance. Their insights, together with those from Land, strengthen the paradox that when we are most affectively receptive to God we are also the most ethically willing to modify behavior, and in order to be in a state of open receptivity to God, active effort is required. Lee's insights highlight the holistic nature of the Spirit's

"Role of the Spirit," 496 (discussed in 3.3.3). Similarly, Goldingay stated that "the Spirit is perhaps most crucially involved in softening the hard heart of the individual interpreter and the community, enabling them to see things that they would prefer to miss because these things will demand a change in commitments." Goldingay, *Models for Interpretation of Scripture*, 189.

257. Atkinson, *Now Read This*, 63 (without reference to the Spirit).

258. Vanhoozer's definition of evil spirits as principalities and powers that would distort understanding (Eph 6:12) is satisfactory for this analysis and will be followed. With Graham Twelftree, an evil spirit can also be understood synonymously as a demon. Vanhoozer, "Spirit of Understanding: Discerning and Doing the Word," 413; Graham Twelftree, "Spiritual Powers," 798.

259. Further reformed approaches came from Bruce Waltke, emphasizing that unethical conduct is a pneumatic hindrance and scripture must be approached with a pure conscience. Waltke, "Exegesis and the Spiritual Life," 33. Also, Dan McCartney and Charles Clayton, who emphasized that interpretation is not ethically neutral. McCartney and Clayton explained that sin, "a hindrance in any communication, especially in interpretation," colors desire and distorts interpretation of scripture. They also warned that distorted interpretation (or misinterpretation) of scripture was itself a sin and can lead to further immoral behavior, inducing a cycle of sin and distorted interpretation. McCartney and Clayton, *Let the Reader Understand*, 32–37 (quotes 34, 33 respectively). I am not sure I agree that misinterpretation is a sin in and of itself but they are right to emphasize ethical ramifications that may result from misinterpretation. However, although they considered ethical interpretation *and* pneumatic interpretation, they only indirectly linked the two aspects. See McCartney and Clayton, *Let the Reader Understand*, 75–80 for pneumatic interpretation. Their position on pneumatic interpretation was similar to Vanhoozer's (see 3.2.3) in that the Spirit guides people to recognize, understand, and apply truth but that this truth comes *only* by the words in scripture (78).

interpretive work, drawing us into affective and cognitive relationship with God, reorienting ethics, and influencing ability to pneumatically interpret through this communion.

3.3.2 Knowing God by living in response to God (Jackie David Johns and Cheryl Bridges Johns)

Jackie David Johns and Cheryl Bridges Johns argued for an approach to knowledge based around personal relationship with God, comparing *yada*, the Hebrew verb for "know" with the Greek verb *ginoskein*.[260] Citing Thomas Groome, they argued that *yada* is an approach to knowledge that is not measured around objectivity (as denoted by *ginoskein*), but a knowing "more by the heart than by the mind, knowing that arises not by standing back in order to look at, but by active and intentional engagement in lived experience."[261] In a later publication, Cheryl Bridges Johns wrote:

> Within the understanding of *yada*, if a person knows God, she or he is encountered by the one who lives in the midst of history and who initiates covenant relationship. Knowledge of God, therefore, is measured not by the information one possesses but by how one is living in response to God. A person is ignorant of or foolish not because of lack of awareness of facts about God but rather because of a failure to do the will of God.[262]

Subsequently, Johns and Johns presented knowledge as growing and unfolding because it comes through personal relationship with God, which grows and develops over time, further emphasizing that knowledge is manifest through ethical obedience to God.[263] They brought this means of know-

260. Johns and Johns, "Yielding to the Spirit" (pub. 1992), 109–34. For comparison of *yada* and *ginoskein*, see Groome, *Christian Religious Education*, 141–45. For discussion of *ginoskein* incorporating *yada*, see Bultmann, "γινώσκω," 689–719.

261. Johns and Johns, "Yielding to the Spirit," 112, quoting Groome, *Christian Religious Education*, 141. See also Cheryl Bridges Johns, *Pentecostal Formation* (pub. 1993), 35–41, 130–38. As Johns noted, she developed these ideas with Jackie Johns, and material in *Pentecostal Formation* is largely taken from Johns and Johns, "Yielding to the Spirit." Additionally, Jackie Johns, "Pentecostalism and the Postmodern Worldview," 89, 91–93; Jackie Johns, "Yielding to the Spirit" (pub. 1999), 78–79. For critiques, see Ellington, "Pentecostalism and the Authority of Scripture," 24–25; Cartledge, *Practical Theology*, 45–47.

262. Cheryl Bridges Johns, *Pentecostal Formation*, 35; similarly Johns and Johns, "Yielding to the Spirit," 112–13. See fn. 261.

263. Johns and Johns, "Yielding to the Spirit," 112–13; Cheryl Bridges Johns, *Pentecostal Formation*, 36, referencing 1 John 4:3, 16, 20, and 1 John 2:3–5; 5:1–5 respectively.

ing into conversation with the *paraclete* passages in John's gospel[264] and proposed an approach to group Bible study that followed this understanding. This had four interrelating elements: sharing of testimony, searching scripture, yielding to the Spirit, and responding in loving obedience.[265]

Johns and Johns emphasized the centrality of scripture[266] and focused on affective transformation brought by the Spirit through scripture. Although they did not use these terms, they recognized that cognitive knowledge comes through intimate relationship with God, transforming affect, and facilitating ethical obedience.[267] This raises the question: "Does ethical obedience (to God) itself display knowledge of God because it signals affective and cognitive intimacy?" Within this process Johns and Johns also emphasized the believer's ethical responsibility to yield to the Spirit, explaining this as "attending to the Spirit's living presence in the world."[268] Through this yielding, the Spirit brings transformative, contextual understanding of scripture and of self.[269]

3.3.3 Unfolding understanding of scripture and self (Clark Pinnock, drawing on Karl Rahner)

Pinnock stressed that the Spirit's role in interpretation was not primarily intellectual but to open scripture up in a way that develops friendship with God, recommending striking a balance between using and submitting cognition to the Spirit.[270] He also applied Karl Rahner's analogy of falling

---

Cf. Bultmann: "Christian knowledge is not a fixed possession but develops in the life of the Christian as lasting obedience and reflection." Bultmann, γινώσκω," 707.

264. Johns and Johns, "Yielding to the Spirit," 114–16. Cf. fn. 238 (John's gospel and pneumatic interpretation).

265. Johns and Johns, "Yielding to the Spirit," 124–33; Cheryl Bridges Johns, *Pentecostal Formation*, 130–38. Also, Cheryl Bridges Johns, "Meeting God in the Margins," 23–25.

266. Johns and Johns, "Yielding to the Spirit," 117–18.

267. See their discussion of praxis, which they explain as the "linking of knowing and doing," and integration with *yada* knowledge. Johns and Johns, "Yielding to the Spirit," 119–24 (119).

268. Johns and Johns, "Yielding to the Spirit," 133.

269. Johns and Johns, "Yielding to the Spirit," 131, 133.

270. Pinnock, "Work of the Holy Spirit" (pub. 1993), 22–23; "Role of the Spirit" (pub. 1993), 496. Similarly, Atkinson, *Now Read This*, 66; and Vanhoozer, asserting that "what the interpreter needs in order to read the Bible correctly is not scholarly tools but saintly training." Vanhoozer, "Spirit of Understanding: Discerning and Doing the Word," 411. Here, Vanhoozer drew on Hauerwas, *Unleashing the Scripture* (pub. 1993). Hauerwas argued against the *priority* given to historico-grammatical principles

in love to describe the Spirit's unfolding of scripture over time.[271] Rahner had used this concept to explain the development of dogma. Rahner wrote that at the beginning stages of love we cannot grasp all that is happening in our hearts and minds. As time progresses, however, understanding of the love that has begun *and* understanding of ourselves in relation to that love unfolds in our hearts and minds.[272] Pinnock suggested that correspondingly, through engagement with scripture, the Spirit draws us deeper into relationship with God, unfolding scriptural truth over time and bringing recognition and understanding of what is already present in scripture.[273] However, what Rahner *had* delineated but Pinnock did not, was the interrelationship between the unfolding understanding of love *and* the unfolding understanding of self. Rahner wrote:

> The lover knows of his love: this knowledge of himself forms an essential element in the very love itself. . . . Reflexion upon oneself (when it is accurate) in propositions (i.e. in *pensées* which the lover produces about his love) is thus a part of the progressive realization of love itself; it is not just a parallel phenomenon, without importance for the thing itself. The progress of love is a living growth out of the original (the originally conscious) love *and* out of just what the love has itself become through a

---

of interpretation, contending that if practices are wrong, interpretation will follow. He emphasized, 1) academic study of scriptural interpretation should not be separated from the believing community; 2) when the believing community has accommodated itself to "presuppositions of liberal democracies," ability to faithfully hear scripture will be damaged (9). Hauerwas wrote, "Our failure to understand what Paul 'really meant' is not the problem. Our problem is that we live in churches that have no practice of nonviolence, of reconciliation, no sense of the significance of singleness; so we lack the resources to faithfully preach and hear God's Word. If such an approach means I risk being 'unscholarly,' it is a risk well worth taking in order to free theology from its academic captivity" (8). Hauerwas further argued that a divided church breeds misinterpretation of scripture, but a unified church breeds correct interpretation. He understood unity as an expression of the Spirit (23). Whilst not directly discussing the Spirit's role, Hauerwas's thoughts highlight that pneumatic interpretation cannot be divorced from the ethical practices of the surrounding community and that cultivating relationship with each other, seeking unity and repairing division, are vital aspects. Cf. 1.6.1 (ethical interpretation).

271. Pinnock, "Work of the Holy Spirit," 15.

272. Rahner, "Development of Dogma" (f.pub. 1954), 63–65.

273. Pinnock, "Work of the Holy Spirit," 15. Cf. Fletcher and Cocksworth: "The language of love is complex and multi-layered but it certainly embraces both the fixed and the free, the given and spontaneous, the received and the newly made. The Spirit who inspires all genuine gestures of love directs our worship through both time-tested texts and actions . . . and spontaneous words and actions." Fletcher and Cocksworth, "Language of Love," 6–7 (7).

> reflexive experience of itself. It lives at every moment from its original source *and* from that reflexive experience which has immediately preceded any given moment.[274]

Recognizing Rahner's original emphasis in alignment with Pinnock's application to pneumatic interpretation strengthens further the growing perspective drawn from and through thought in this chapter, and building from chapter 2, that pneumatic interpretation of scripture is dynamically interrelated to pneumatic interpretation of self. In other words, as we approach scripture, seeking the Spirit's guidance in interpretation, the Spirit also reaches *through* scripture and *interprets us.*

Corresponding with his understanding of the unfolding nature of pneumatic interpretation, Pinnock recommended scripture be approached as a sacrament that can facilitate relationship with God.[275] He emphasized importance of cultivating this relationship though prayerfulness, being willing to hear, and adopting godly habits, further warning that the effects of the Spirit's work in an individual may not always feel positive because God may be doing a refining work, removing pneumatic hindrances such as sin, foolishness, unbelief, and sloth.[276] Pinnock wrote, "Just as a judge needs a judicial temperament, the believer needs a godly temperament if she or he hopes to hear the voice of the shepherd. There needs to be reverence, humility, patience and obedience among other spiritual and moral qualities which foster the hearing of God's word."[277]

In summary, Pinnock identified that immoral behavior hinders *both* personal relationship with God *and* ability to receive truth brought by the Spirit through scripture, aligning with Vanhoozer in highlighting pneumatic hindrance (see 3.3.1). These aspects of their contributions illustrate the interconnection between relationship and discernment, placing cultivation of personal relationship with God, with its affective, ethical and cognitive components, as a vital aspect of pneumatic interpretation. Pinnock's thoughts, taking into consideration Rahner's original emphasis, also highlight the unfolding nature of pneumatic interpretation, in relation to understanding of both scripture and self, as we journey in relationship with God.

274. Rahner, "Development of Dogma," 64 (emphasis original).

275. Pinnock, "Work of the Holy Spirit," 22.

276. Pinnock, "Work of the Holy Spirit," 22–23.

277. Pinnock, "Work of the Holy Spirit," 23.

3.3.4 Critical-charismatic interpretation of scripture and self (Rickie Moore)

Continuing his quest to integrate his Pentecostal faith with his scholarship (see 2.4.1), Rickie Moore proposed an approach to interpretation that integrated scripture's written content with ongoing charismatic experience and relationship with God.[278] He called this "Canon and Charisma in the Book of Deuteronomy," and argued that Deuteronomy showed this "dynamic integration" of canon and charisma through Israel's relationship with God.[279] He asserted that in seeking the Spirit's role in interpretation, Pentecostals were trying to negotiate their way through this dynamic interrelation. Moore located Pentecostals in the crossfire between liberal-critical and conservative evangelical interpretive approaches that he felt either rendered interpretation as an "open and merely human process" or as a "closed divine deposit" respectively. Insightfully, he emphasized that both approaches restricted interpretation to the reader and the text, limiting or altogether ignoring the Spirit's role.[280]

Developing this further in "Deuteronomy and the Fire of God," Moore proposed that encounter with God at Horeb was the core of the book and Deuteronomy was itself an act of interpretation simultaneously critical and charismatic.[281] He wove his personal story in with his interpretation of Deuteronomy, describing his own ongoing (charismatic) experience as he interacted with the Deuteronomic text over some years. This journey transitioned him from separating his Pentecostal faith from his critical scholarship (as he had been taught as a student), to seeking to fully engage the two together (as a lecturer and scholar). He explained that he found this dynamic interrelation, instead of compromising his critical study as he had

278. Moore, "Canon and Charisma" (pub. 1992), 75–92. Similarly, Moore, "'And Also Much Cattle,'" 35–48, interacting with the book of Jonah (see 36 for influence of Land and integration of affect, ethics, and cognition).

279. Moore, "Canon and Charisma," 91.

280. Moore, "Canon and Charisma," 75, fn. 1, cf. 91–92. Cf. Pinnock, who emphasized that the strong influence of rationalism in Western culture had neglected attention to the Spirit's role in interpretation, and evangelical scholarship had not focused on the Spirit's role because of a fear of subjectivity. Pinnock, "Work of the Holy Spirit," 4–8. See also, Pinnock, "Role of the Spirit," 491–97. Cf. 3.4.2 and 3.4.3. For critique of Pinnock, see Ellington, "Pentecostalism and the Authority of Scripture," 24.

281. Moore, "Deuteronomy and the Fire of God" (pub. 1995), 11–12. The purpose of this analysis is not to critique these claims and engage with Deuteronomic scholarship, which Moore did in his paper, but to interact with Moore's presentation and implications for pneumatic interpretation. For collection of Moore's essays, see Moore, *Spirit of the Old Testament*.

been led to expect, was actually "the most *critical* step [he] had ever taken in studying biblical texts," because it pushed him into "another dimension of criticism" where he was forced to engage his personal relationship with God and his expression of that relationship with his critical scholarship.[282] This also led him to recognize aspects of his ethics that were hindering his "critical" scholarship. For Moore this was seeking social conformity and allowing himself to be intellectually intimidated. He admitted, "I was secretly embarrassed about the uncredentialed heritage and humble status of my uneducated Pentecostal elders. . . . I was afraid of scholars and smart people. I was constantly intimidated by them and in awe of them, never realizing at the time that this was the fear of which worship is made."[283]

Moore believed that integrating his personal relationship with God, expressed through his Pentecostal faith, with his critical scholarship brought him to a clearer, cognitive vantage point of the text *and* of himself,[284] thus giving a personal illustration of Rahner's analogy and adding further emphasis to this chapter's growing perspective of pneumatic interpretation.[285] The story of the book of Deuteronomy, namely its critical-charismatic interrelation of scripture and relational encounter, had informed and interpreted Moore's own story, which had informed and influenced his interpretation of Deuteronomy. Moore recognized that he had both interpreted and *been* interpreted.[286]

282. Moore, "Deuteronomy and the Fire of God," 15–16 (16), 20 respectively (emphasis original). Cf. Marius Herholdt, explaining that Pentecostals and charismatics view the Spirit speaking personally, holistically, and relationally through scripture: "Believers use the body to uplift the human spirit to God, daring to reach out to Him because we have examples in the Word of people who dared to reach out. To understand the texts does not mean to take an objective stand. We therefore do not interpret the texts as much as follow the text, to be interpreted by the text. We understand the texts as much as we touch on the reality of God on the invitation and demand of the text. It is not understanding alone that is important, but also orientation." Herholdt, "Pentecostal and Charismatic Hermeneutics" (pub. 1998), 424.

283. Moore, "Deuteronomy and the Fire of God," 20 (also 16, 21).

284. For complementary evangelical perspective, cf. Grenz detailing how, through scripture, the Spirit calls and directs us toward new identity, addressing us personally in ways that align with, and cause our identity to arise from, the biblical story. Grenz, *Created for Community*, 169–71.

285. Rahner, "Development of Dogma," 64. See 3.3.3.

286. Moore, "Deuteronomy and the Fire of God," 12.

3.3.5 Claimed and transformed (Larry McQueen)

Citing Moore, Larry McQueen concluded a study of the book of Joel by documenting his personal journey encountering the scriptural content he was studying. McQueen described being claimed and transformed by the Spirit through his writing, stating, "I began to realize that the biblical text of Joel was not simply an object of study but rather was calling me to re-evaluate my own relationship with God." McQueen explained that he had sought to interpret Joel but was led on a journey where he believed that the Spirit, through the book of Joel, had interpreted *him*, bringing him fresh understanding and articulation of the book of Joel.[287] He also described the affective pain of this journey as his affective and cognitive understanding was repaired and integrated.[288]

3.3.6 Evaluation

Land, Lee, Vanhoozer, Johns and Johns, Pinnock (with Rahner), Moore, and McQueen all incorporated intimate relationship God into their hermeneutical considerations. Their thought, presented and developed here, emphasizes the following aspects of pneumatic interpretation relating to affect, ethics, and influence on cognition.

Moore and McQueen described ongoing relational experiences with God through pneumatic encounter with scripture that brought affective, ethical and cognitive transformation in their understanding of scripture and self, and McQueen emphasized that his transformation of understanding directly related to his relationship with God. McQueen's detailing of his affective pain as his cognitive understanding was adjusted suggests the removal of pneumatic hindrances highlighted by Pinnock and Vanhoozer. Moore described how his progressive encounter with Deuteronomy over a number of years impacted his ethics as he began to recognize and adjust the ways he had been thinking and behaving that he felt were hindering his ability to discern truth. Furthermore, Moore and McQueen's accounts both convey a sense of affective receptivity to God alongside active willingness to modify their ethics, strengthening the emphasis developed by engaging with contributions from Lee and Vanhoozer (and Balthasar), that ethical conduct both influences and is influenced by pneumatic interpretation. Adopting Moore's terminology, I suggest a working understanding

287. McQueen, *Joel and the Spirit* (f.pub. 1995), 106–9 (106). Similarly, McKay, "When the Veil is Taken Away," 17–40.

288. McQueen, *Joel and the Spirit*, 107.

that ethics and affect dynamically interrelate with each other. Moore and McQueen's accounts also suggest that they both actively sought the Spirit's leading in interpretation and were consequently interpreted pneumatically in ways that transformed their affect, ethics, and cognition. In Johns and Johns's terms, Moore and McQueen actively sought to yield to the Spirit.

Whilst Moore did not make many explicit references to the Spirit's role in interpretation, preferring to emphasize the integration of his Pentecostal faith (as did Johns and Johns, and McQueen), his weaving of his personal journey throughout "Deuteronomy and the Fire of God" can be viewed as a personal illustration of the crux of the argument presented in this chapter so far and further strengthened through considering and developing thought from Johns and Johns, and Pinnock and Rahner; that as we approach scripture, seeking the Spirit's guidance in interpretation, the Spirit also reaches through scripture and interprets us. This is an interrelating, dynamic relationship. Pneumatic interpretation cannot be understood solely in relation to scripture because the Spirit always works *through* and *beyond* scripture, effecting scriptural truth affectively, ethical, and cognitively, in ways that create and redeem (compare 3.2.4), and draw us deeper in intimate relationship with God. As this section has shown, there is also an active requirement on us to pursue intimacy with God, through whom pneumatic interpretation comes.

3.4 COGNITIVE FRAMEWORKS OF INTERPRETATION

Land asserted that the beliefs of a community shape understanding alongside affect and behavior. He therefore recognized that interpretation requires a cognitive framework, a mental structure or process by which knowledge is acquired, and placed the early Pentecostal community as his framework.[289] However, as shown in chapter 2 (see 2.1.2 and compare 2.2.4 and 2.4.2, summarized in 2.5), 1970s and 1980s conversationalists had previously considered interpretive frameworks in respect of pneumatic interpretation, and this section continues to build on the themes discussed there. Therefore, as the conversation developed through the 1990s, scholars kept considering, alongside Land, various cognitive frameworks and contexts for interpretation that incorporated the Spirit and allowed for personal faith expression.

289. Further consideration of the framework and context of early Pentecostalism came from Archer, "Pentecostal Hermeneutics: Retrospect and Prospect," 63–81; Clark, "Investigation," 4–52; Kärkkäinen, "Pentecostal Hermeneutics in the Making," 77–83; Smith, "Closing of the Book," 49–71; Pluss, "Azusa and Other Myths," 189–201. Cf. 3.1.1 (Archer's influence).

This led into discussions concerning application of postmodernist thought and its emphasis on subjectivity, use of historical grammaticism—involving understanding the framework surrounding the scriptural text in its original historical location, and community—involving understanding the framework surrounding the scriptural text as it is interpreted. A fourth conversation point surrounded early Jewish approaches to pneumatic interpretation and the role of prophecy within contemporary pneumatic interpretation. This section will consider each of these frameworks.

3.4.1 Interpreting as a Pentecostal

It was through these discussions over frameworks and contexts for interpretation that emphasis shifted from the Spirit's role in interpretation to interpretation as a Pentecostal.[290] In early Pentecostal hermeneutics' discussions (see 2.4), consideration of the Spirit's role in the interpretation of scripture was a corresponding factor alongside theological and ecclesial identity.[291] However, a consequence of the increasing focus on Pentecostal hermeneutical identity was a lessening focus on the Spirit's role in interpretation. Pursuit of understanding concerning the Spirit's role in the interpretation of scripture was still present within these contextual discussions, but became subsumed within the framework of Pentecostal hermeneutics.[292] This was not the case with early Jewish discussions, discussed in 3.4.5, which were not a focus of those involved in Pentecostal hermeneutics. Essentially, those writing outside Pentecostal hermeneutics, for example, Lee, Pinnock, and Vanhoozer (see 3.2, and 3.3), tended to retain primary focus on the Spirit's role,[293] whilst those writing within Pentecostal hermeneutics largely did not.

290. A typical example of this emerging and increasingly dominant emphasis on Pentecostal identity came from Richard Israel, Daniel Albrecht, and Randal McNally, who argued that a Pentecostal hermeneutic was "the interpretive activity in which Pentecostals search for an understanding of themselves." Israel et al., "Pentecostals and Hermeneutics: Texts, Rituals and Community," 161. They approached this by engaging with postmodernist thought, specifically with Ricoeur and Gadamer.

291. I realize some may disagree with this assertion, e.g., Archer, "Pentecostal Hermeneutics: Retrospect and Prospect," 63.

292. E.g., Anderson, "Pentecostal Hermeneutics Part 1," 1–11; Anderson, "Pentecostal Hermeneutics Part 2," 13–22; Archer, "Pentecostal Hermeneutics: Retrospect and Prospect," 76–79; Arrington, "Use of the Bible by Pentecostals," 101–7; Cargal, "Beyond the Fundamentalist-Modernist Controversy," 173–78; Clark, "Investigation," 163–65; Harrington and Patten, "Pentecostal Hermeneutics and Postmodern Literary Theory," 113–14; Thomas, "Women, Pentecostals and the Bible," 42. Also, Ma, "Biblical Studies in the Pentecostal Tradition," 52–69 (Ma's attention to the Spirit was minimal).

293. Also, Fowl, "How the Spirit Reads," 97–127 (see fn. 238).

As explained in 1.5, understanding the self-effacing nature of the Spirit is crucial within discussions about pneumatic interpretation. The Spirit always points beyond the Spirit toward the other. So, considering the Spirit's role in the interpretation of scripture necessarily requires focusing on those objects and movements that the Spirit is communicating through, and also purposefully celebrating and illuminating. The challenge, however, is that overly focusing on some of these objects and movements that the Spirit is communicating through, and also intentionally highlighting—in this case the Pentecostal community framework—will actually steer away from attending to the Spirit's role. However, at the same time, some of these foci are, and will turn into important conversations in their own right. In both respects, it seems, such was the growing case for Pentecostal hermeneutics.

3.4.2 Influence of postmodernism

Postmodernism influenced the conversation[294] through increasing awareness of the dominance of rational approaches to scripture that had emphasized objectivity but suppressed the notion of subjectivity.[295] Postmodern thinking, with its focus on subjectivity, was viewed by a group of scholars writing in *Pneuma* in 1993 as a natural affiliation with Pentecostal hermeneutics.[296] Hannah Harrington and Rebecca Patten articulated the appeal, writing:

> The work of such postmodernists as Paul Ricoeur and Hans-Georg Gadamer has provided a new way of approaching texts by focusing on the world the reader brings to the text as well as the world of the text. . . . The subjectivity involved in the reader's appropriation of the text is considered not only legitimate by postmodernists but indeed inevitable in the reading of any text.[297]

294. Comprehensive analysis of postmodernism's relationship with Pentecostal hermeneutics and pneumatic interpretation is beyond this work's remits. See fn. 65 (postmodernist and philosophical approaches to interpretation).

295. For analysis of interpretive issues surrounding modernity, the Enlightenment, postmodernism, Pentecostal hermeneutics, historical criticism, subjectivity and objectivity, see Ellington, "Pentecostalism and the Authority of Scripture," 16–38. Also Thomas, "Pentecostal Theology," 11–12. See fn. 470 (Enlightenment).

296. Byrd, "Ricoeur's Hermeneutical Theory and Pentecostal Proclamation," 203–14; Cargal, "Beyond the Fundamentalist-Modernist Controversy," 163–87; Dempster, "Paradigm Shifts and Hermeneutics," 129–35; Israel et al., "Pentecostals and Hermeneutics: Texts, Rituals, and Community," 136–61. Additionally, Autry, "Dimensions of Hermeneutics in Pentecostal Focus," 29–50 (also pub. 1993 but in *JPT*).

297. Harrington and Patten, "Pentecostal Hermeneutics and Postmodern Literary Theory" (pub. 1994), 109.

Others, writing subsequent to the *Pneuma* articles, recommended caution.[298] Kärkkäinen, Jackie Johns, and Gerald Sheppard all emphasized foundational differences over the centrality of God. Kärkkäinen stated:

> True, there are many potential convergences—plurality of meaning of any text, the plural meaning of the text itself, the role of the affections in the reading, etc.—but the convergences might exist only on the "surface level." Between Postmodernism(s) and Pentecostalism there is such a wide gap in terms of presuppositions that one is wise not to exaggerate apparent similarities. For example, there is no "big story" for Postmodernists, but there is one for Pentecostals; there is no absolute truth of any kind for Postmodernists, but there is *the* truth for Pentecostals. It is these kind of foundational philosophical presuppositions that should be considered carefully before the wedlock is celebrated.[299]

Noting Land, Jackie Johns emphasized that Pentecostalism is built on a relationship based around communication from, and response to, God. He posited orthodoxy as cognitive response to God, a dynamic interrelationship of giving glory to God and correct belief,[300] and asserted that Pentecostals must maintain this commitment.[301] Johns advised scholars to "consider carefully the distinctiveness of their own worldview and its implications for the postmodern era" before they committed themselves to postmodernist thought.[302] Sheppard was positive about the influence of postmodernism upon Pentecostal hermeneutics but also asserted that postmodernist methodologies could not address divine encounter in the hearing of scripture and subsequent response.[303]

298. Clark, "Investigation," 291–93; Harrington and Patten, "Pentecostal Hermeneutics and Postmodern Literary Theory," 109–14; Jackie Johns, "Pentecostalism and the Postmodern Worldview," 73–96; Kärkkäinen, "Pentecostal Hermeneutics in the Making," 97; Robert Menzies, "Jumping Off the Postmodern Bandwagon," 115–20; Sheppard, "Biblical Interpretation After Gadamer," 121–41.

299. Kärkkäinen, "Pentecostal Hermeneutics in the Making" (pub. 1998), 97.

300. Johns explained, "Orthodoxy, in both the sense of giving glory to God and in the sense of correct belief, is the purpose of knowledge. It is that toward which the church must always be moving." Jackie Johns, "Pentecostalism and the Postmodern Worldview" (pub. 1995), 92–93. Cf. Land, *Pentecostal Spirituality*, 130–31 (God as the object of the affections). See 3.3.

301. Jackie Johns, "Pentecostalism and the Postmodern Worldview," 96.

302. Jackie Johns, "Pentecostalism and the Postmodern Worldview," 96. Johns defined a worldview as "a disposition toward a perception of reality" (75), and considered characteristics of the postmodern and Pentecostal worldview throughout his paper.

303. Sheppard, "Biblical Interpretation After Gadamer" (pub. 1994), 136. Sheppard particularly referred to Ricoeur who he identified as hermeneutical mentor to Byrd,

Collectively, therefore, Kärkkäinen, Johns, and Sheppard cautioned that postmodernist approaches to interpretation do not address personal relationship with God and encounter with scripture as a consequence of that relationship. This, and factoring in the preceding discussion of Pentecostal identity and the self-effacing nature of the Spirit in 3.4.1, raises awareness that engaging with postmodernist methodologies can hinder analysis of the Spirit's role in interpretation by drawing focus away from encounter with God and into a medley of interpretive techniques and concepts. Whilst the value of postmodernism's emphasis upon subjectivity has been noted, as this chapter has been showing, recognition and incorporation of personal aspects of the Spirit's communication was present within the conversation beyond postmodernist considerations.

3.4.3 Incorporation of historical grammaticism (Timothy Cargal and Robert Menzies)

Postmodernist thought influenced discussion surrounding use and application of historico-grammatical methods of interpretation. Timothy Cargal and Robert Menzies differed significantly on the application of postmodernist thought to Pentecostal hermeneutics, with Menzies heavily criticizing Cargal for his propagation of it.[304] However, these scholars also appeared to misunderstand each other, and they talked at cross-purposes, particularly regarding historico-grammatical methods. Both asserted the importance of historical-grammaticism but viewed it from different perspectives. Menzies's concern was for the original intention of the biblical authors to be taken seriously, stating, "If we loose the meaning of a text from its historical moorings, how shall we evaluate various and even contradictory interpretations? How shall we keep our own ideologies and prejudices from obliterating the text?"[305] Cargal did not disagree. He just saw historico-grammatical methods as an important part of a larger process of interpretation involving

Cargal, and Dempster, and Israel, Albrecht, and McNally. See fn. 290. Sheppard also highlighted the importance of pre-modern hermeneutics, citing Schleiermacher and Barth particularly. He emphasized that Pentecostal approaches to scriptural interpretation are part of the long history of Christians interpreting scripture (128–33).

304. Menzies described Cargal's assessment of postmodernism as it related to interpretation of scripture as "triumphalist," and his article as "lucid, insightful, and ultimately disturbing." Robert Menzies, "Jumping off the Postmodern Bandwagon" (pub. 1994), 115.

305. Robert Menzies, "Jumping off the Postmodern Bandwagon," 117.

the Spirit acting as a bridge between the original author and the contemporary interpreter:[306]

> The traditional Pentecostal emphases upon spiritual experience in general and pneumatic illumination in particular for understanding Scripture (the major foci of most Pentecostal interpreters within parish settings) have been joined with an emphasis upon a unitary meaning of Scripture identified with the "intent of the inspired authors" (the major focus of Pentecostal academics, in part as a result of Fundamentalist and Evangelical influence). The result of this union has been that ancient biblical texts have a tremendous immediacy for twentieth-century Pentecostals because "the Spirit serves as the common context in which reader and author can meet to bridge the historical and cultural gulf between them" and "establishes both the existential and presuppositional continuum between the word written in the past and that same word in the present."[307]

Cargal and Menzies's articles illustrate evolving positions (compare 2.2.2, also 2.4.2) concerning the role of historico-grammatical approaches that have continued throughout the conversation. Generally, some Pentecostal scholars saw Menzies's position as an example of rational, evangelical principles of interpretation they were trying to rebalance or move away from as part of their pursuit for Pentecostal hermeneutical identity and understanding of the Spirit's role in interpretation.[308] However, all scholars considering historico-grammatical approaches within pneumatic interpretation and Pentecostal hermeneutics were seeking to address the relationship between the original meaning of the scriptural text and contemporary

306. For critique aligning with my perspective, see Harrington and Patten, "Pentecostal Hermeneutics and Postmodern Literary Theory," 113.

307. Cargal, "Beyond the Fundamentalist-Modernist Controversy" (pub. 1993), 180–81, quoting Arrington, "Hermeneutics," 382, and Stronstad, "Trends in Pentecostal Hermeneutics," 9, respectively. For perspective aligning with Cargal, see Arrington, "Use of the Bible by Pentecostals," 101–7. Arrington offered three issues as central to the development of a Pentecostal hermeneutic: historical and literary criticism, recognition of the Spirit's role in interpretation, and acknowledgment of the experiential dimension.

308. E.g., Archer, critical of Robert Menzies's and other scholars' alignment with evangelicalism and negative influence on Pentecostal hermeneutical identity, and Moore, referring to the crumbling canons of historical criticism. Archer, "Pentecostal Hermeneutics: Retrospect and Prospect," 74–75; Moore, "Canon and Charisma," 92, Also Arrington's belief that "the adoption of the methodology of Evangelicals has led Pentecostal scholars to emphasize the historical-context of the biblical texts and to reduce their meaning to the intent of the authors." Arrington, "Use of the Bible by Pentecostals," 101.

interpretation in some way[309] and differences lay with particular emphases and starting points.

3.4.4 Conversations about community (John Christopher Thomas)

As well as considering the early Pentecostal community as the framework for interpretation,[310] some Pentecostal scholars focused on the contemporary community surrounding scripture as it is read as a framework or context for interpretation. John Christopher Thomas steered this approach through his article, "Women, Pentecostals and the Bible: An Experiment in Pentecostal Hermeneutics."[311]

Thomas outlined reasons for developing a distinct Pentecostal hermeneutic including disappointment with rationalism and its influence on interpretation, lack of serious consideration of the Spirit's role in interpretation, and recent recognition amongst Pentecostal scholars that the role of community was an important part of interpretation.[312] He used the de-

309. This included: Anderson, "Pentecostal Hermeneutics Part 1," 1–11; Anderson, "Pentecostal Hermeneutics Part 2," 13–33; Archer, "Pentecostal Hermeneutics: Retrospect and Prospect," 63–81; Arrington, "Use of the Bible by Pentecostals," 101–7; Autry, "Dimensions of Hermeneutics in Pentecostal Focus," 29–50; Bloesch, *Holy Scripture*, 17–29; Byrd, "Paul Ricoeur's Hermeneutical Theory and Pentecostal Proclamation," 203–14; Cargal, "Beyond the Fundamentalist-Modernist Controversy" 163–87; Dempster, "Paradigm Shifts and Hermeneutics," 129–35; Dorman, "Holy Spirit, History, Hermeneutics, and Theology" 427–38; Elbert, "Spirit, Scripture and Theology," 55–75; Ellington, "Pentecostalism and the Authority of Scripture," 16–38; Fee, "History as Context for Interpretation," 10–32; Fowl, "How the Spirit Reads," 97–127; Goldingay, *Models for Interpretation of Scripture*, 183–99, 251–65; Harrington and Patten, "Pentecostal Hermeneutics and Postmodern Literary Theory," 109–14; Herholdt, "Pentecostal and Charismatic Hermeneutics," 417–31; Israel et al., "Pentecostals and Hermeneutics: Texts, Rituals, and Community," 137–61; Luke Johnson, *Scripture and Discernment*, 61–108; Robert Menzies, "Jumping off the Postmodern Bandwagon," 115–20; Robert Menzies, "Coming to Terms with an Evangelical History," 18–28; Moore, "Canon and Charisma," 75–92; Moore, "Deuteronomy and the Fire of God," 11–33; McQueen, *Joel and the Spirit*, 1–10; Pinnock, "Role of the Spirit," 491–97; Pinnock, "Work of the Holy Spirit," 3–23; Powery, "Ulrich Luz's *Matthew in History*," 3–17; Sheppard, "Biblical Interpretation After Gadamer," 121–41; Stibbe, "This is That," 181–92; Stronstad, "Pentecostal Experience and Hermeneutics," 53–78; Stronstad, "Pentecostal Hermeneutics," 215–22; Williams, *Renewal Theology*, 241–42.

310. See fn. 289 (early Pentecostal community).

311. Thomas, "Women, Pentecostals and the Bible" (pub. 1994), 41–56. Later republished in Thomas, *Spirit of the New Testament*, 233–46, as part of a collection of Thomas's essays.

312. Thomas, "Women, Pentecostals and the Bible," 41–42.

liberations of the Jerusalem council (Acts 15) as a model for a Pentecostal hermeneutic,[313] highlighting that the passage showed three elements dynamically interrelating: the community, the Spirit, and scripture.[314] Based around this he argued for a dynamic, holistic approach to interpretation that does not always start with scripture as the basis for interpretation but also seeks to discern, as a community, how the Spirit is working and moving in contemporary contexts, and incorporate this pneumatic discernment within consideration of scripture.[315] Thomas applied this model to women in ministry, asserting that pneumatic discernment of this much-debated issue[316] requires consideration of all three elements dynamically interrelating with each other.[317]

Thomas, along with other Pentecostal scholars considering the role of community,[318] effectively and insightfully argued that interpretive approaches that rigidly start with scripture and seek to determine meaning principally through historico-grammatical methodology without seeking

313. Those using Luke-Acts as basis for a pneumatic/Pentecostal hermeneutical approach included: Arrington, "Use of the Bible by Pentecostals," 106; Elbert, "Spirit, Scripture, and Theology," 55–75; Fowl, "How the Spirit Reads," 101–23; Luke Johnson, *Scripture and Discernment*, 61–108; Robert Menzies, "Coming to Terms with an Evangelical History," 18–28; Robert Menzies, "Essence of Pentecostalism," 1–9; Stibbe, "This is That," 81–192; Stronstad, "Pentecostal Experience and Hermeneutics," 53–78; Stronstad, "Pentecostal Hermeneutics," 215–22.

314. Thomas, "Women, Pentecostals and the Bible," 49–50.

315. Thomas, "Women, Pentecostals and the Bible," 49–56.

316. See Beck, *Two Views on Women in Ministry*, for discussion of egalitarian and complementarian views on women in ministry between scholars holding both views (Belleville, Blomberg, Keener, and Schreiner).

317. Thomas, "Women, Pentecostals and the Bible," 52–54. Similarly, Land described (perceived) experiences of the Spirit leading the early Pentecostal community to look afresh at scripture concerning the silence of women in churches. Land, *Pentecostal Spirituality*, 43, 95. Also Cartledge, *Practical Theology*, 158–61; Cox, "'Your Daughters Shall Prophesy,'" 123–57; Pinnock, "Biblical Texts: Past and Future Meanings," 79–80. For consideration of Thomas's approach by Archer, see "Pentecostal Hermeneutics: Retrospect and Prospect," 78–79.

318. E.g., Archer, "Pentecostal Hermeneutics: Retrospect and Prospect," 70–81; Arrington, "Use of the Bible by Pentecostals," 101–7 and Cargal, "Beyond the Fundamentalist-Modernist Controversy," 163–87; Hanson, "Scripture, Community and Spirit," 3–12; Israel et al., "Pentecostals and Hermeneutics: Texts, Rituals and Community," 154–58, 160–61; Harrington and Patten, "Pentecostal Hermeneutics and Postmodern Literary Theory," 111; Thomas, "Pentecostal Theology," 8–11. See also, fn. 313 (consideration of community relating to Luke–Acts). Like Thomas, Arrington and Cargal both argued that three elements were central to the development of a Pentecostal hermeneutic: historical grammaticism and original intent, recognition of the Spirit's role in interpretation, and acknowledgment of the experiential dimension. See 3.4.3, and fn. 307 (Arrington).

to discern, in dynamic interrelationship,[319] what the Spirit is doing within personal and communal contemporary contexts risk complicating and even hindering pneumatic interpretation.

3.4.5 The role of prophecy, and "pneumatic" interpretation in early Judaism (David Aune)

A final issue to be addressed within this section is discussion surrounding the role of prophecy within pneumatic interpretation. These conversations hinged upon the relationship between subjectivity and objectivity (compare 3.4.2 and 3.4.3), and recognition of the Spirit's communication of scripture to personal and contemporary contexts outside of those presented in scripture. J. Rodman Williams, and Mark Stibbe both described this as standing in pneumatic continuity with the text,[320] whilst John Goldingay argued for an "essential link between historical, exegetical study and the response of appropriation, which involves experiencing the realities of which the text speaks." Goldingay only indirectly (at best) linked the Spirit with appropriation, but his thoughts align with the growing understanding explicated thus far, that the Spirit through scripture interprets us. Specifically, Goldingay emphasized that appropriation "implies a reversal of movement in the process of interpretation," whereby a person becomes the object of interpretation with the text scrutinizing them.[321]

Discussions about subjectivity and objectivity and the Spirit's communication of scripture to personal contexts also led scholars like McQueen and Stibbe to suggest that this appropriation was prophetic. McQueen (see 3.3.5) described his personal experience engaging with the book of Joel as a prophetic hermeneutic, explaining this as "an interpretive event in which pathos and reason, Word and Spirit are integrated as the human subject is made aware of the Spirit's reinterpretation of a life situation or worldview." Stibbe, concerned to develop an interpretive approach that "not only pays careful attention to the original *meaning* of a text [but] also pays prayerful attention to its contemporary prophetic *significance*," recommended

319. Cf. Moore's interpretive interaction with Deuteronomy (see 3.3.4).

320. Williams, *Renewal Theology* (pub. 1990), 241–2; Stibbe, "This is That" (pub. 1998), 187, referencing Williams.

321. Goldingay, *Models for Interpretation of Scripture* (pub. 1995), 252, 255 respectively. Goldingay located his discussion within consideration of scripture, prophecy, and interpretation (139–265, see 188–89 for pneumatic interpretation). Similarly, Hanson, "Scripture," 3–21.

developing an objective (historico-grammatical) and subjective (prophetic reader response) hermeneutic.[322]

David Aune also considered this aspect of "pneumatic" interpretation.[323] His context was not contemporary interpretation but a form of biblical interpretation practiced in early Judaism and early Christianity,[324] where the implicit or explicit claim was that the interpretation had been divinely revealed,[325] and he described prophecy as a feature of this appropriation. He used the term "charismatic exegesis"[326] which he described as "a *hermeneutical ideology* that provides divine legitimation for a particular understanding of a sacred text which is shared with others who understand the text differently."[327] Aune explained that charismatic exegesis exhibited the following characteristics: it was commentary (the interpreter's understanding of the scriptural text in written form), divinely inspired,

322. McQueen, *Joel and the Spirit*, 108–9; Stibbe, "This is That," 182 (emphasis original). McQueen acknowledged Moore's influence on his thought. Moore himself described this process as prophetic in "Canon and Charisma" but later omitted the description in "Deuteronomy and the Fire of God" (see 3.3.4). For similar approaches, see McKay, "When the Veil is Taken Away," 17–40; Willis, "Prophetic Hermeneutics," 193–207.

323. Aune, "Charismatic Exegesis" (pub. 1993), 126–50. Subsequently published in Aune, *Apocalypticism, Prophecy, and Magic*, as part of a collection of Aune's essays. For earlier version, see Aune, "Christian Prophecy and Charismatic Exegesis" (pub. 1991), 339–46.

324. Judaism in the Second Temple period, after the return from Babylonian exile, (*circa* 536 BCE to 70 CE) and Christianity in the first century C.E. For explanation of the historical and cultural context surrounding Old and New Testament scripture including period terminology and dates, see Wenell, "Setting," 23–44 in Gorman, *Scripture and Its Interpretation*. Wenell termed Hebrews as "the ancestors of the Israelite nation (Abraham and Sarah to Moses)," Israelites as "the people of God from Moses to the Babylonian Exile (586 BCE)," and Jews as "descendants of the Israelites after the exile." Wenell, "Setting," 24–25 (emphasis removed). Wenell's definitions corresponded to use throughout *Scripture and Its Interpretation*. This work follows this terminology, using "the people of God in the Old Testament" or "Israel" as an overarching descriptor as necessary (see fn. 89 [people of God]). Israel: "the nation/people descended from the ancestors Abraham, Isaac, and Jacob (renamed Israel)." Gorman, *Scripture and Its Interpretation*, 413.

325. Aune, "Charismatic Exegesis," 126.

326. Aune noted other synonymous terms used as "inspired eschatological exposition" and "spiritual exegesis." He attributed the term charismatic exegesis to H. L. Ginsberg who used it in conversation with William Brownlee to described interpretation practiced at Qumran. Brownlee, "Biblical Interpretation," 60–61, fn. 24. Brownlee described charismatic exegesis as prophetic. Cf. Dunn's use of charismatic exegesis. See 2.1.2, particularly fn. 123 (Dunn and Aune's use of charismatic exegesis, and Douglas Moo on *sensus plenior*).

327. Aune, "Charismatic Exegesis," 149 (emphasis original).

eschatologically orientated, and a type of prophecy prevalent during the Second Temple period.[328]

Three aspects of Aune's discussion of charismatic exegesis in early Judaism and early Christianity are especially relevant to this work's growing understanding of pneumatic interpretation. Firstly, Aune cautioned that unless divine influence in interpretation was present in the text, either implicitly or explicitly, one could not be certain that it was charismatic exegesis. He further stressed that whilst there was plenty of evidence that the Qumran community believed God revealed truth to them, there was "precious little evidence to suggest *how* they thought the Spirit revealed truth."[329] Secondly, Aune recognized coherence in interpretive behavior and approach between the early Jews and early Christians. He emphasized that the eschatological significance of the Jewish scriptures for the early Christians, manifest through interpretations of the Old Testament in the New Testament, were similar to the concerns of early Judaism, particularly Qumran, and manifest through the *pesharim*.[330] Noting here that charismatic exegesis is related to *pesher*, explained by Emil Schürer as "the most characteristic type of Qumran exegesis . . . exemplify[ing] the genre which may be designated as a fulfilment interpretation, i.e. an exposition in which the meaning of an oracle, or of a presumed prophecy, is determined by the historical event or personality which the biblical author is thought to have predicted."[331] Thirdly, Aune explained that prophecy in early Judaism could

328. Aune, "Charismatic Exegesis," 126–27. For a one-volume history of the Second Temple period (including a useful glossary of terms), focusing on biblical interpretation and surrounding contemporary cultural influences, see Schiffmann, *Text to Tradition*. Also helpful are Schürer, *History I*; and Schürer, *History III:i*. Rabbinic literature: "The result of scholastic activity of the scribes and rabbis, consist[ing] mainly . . . of an academic exegesis of the text of the Bible." The purpose of the literature was "to develop Jewish law . . . and to enlarge on biblical history and evolve religious and moral ideals through a systematic combination of separate scriptural passages." This included the *talmudic* literature (teaching and study of the law), the *midrashim*, and the *targums* (traditional interpretation of scripture in synagogues). Schürer, *History: I*, 69 (68–114 for discussion). Midrashim: commentaries on scripture, passage-by-passage. Schürer, *History I*, 90. Midrash: an "interpretive genre . . . in connection with exegesis of a combination of biblical passages." Schürer, *History: III:i*, 420–21 (421). For further, see Neusner, *Introduction to Rabbinic Literature*; Strack and Stemberger, *Introduction to the Talmud and Midrash*; Chilton, "Rabbinic Literature;" 413–23.

329. Aune, "Charismatic Exegesis," 128 (emphasis original).

330. Aune, "Charismatic Exegesis," 143–44, cf. 128.

331. Schürer, *History III:i*, 420–21. *Midrash* and *pesher* were the two main interpretive genres at Qumran. For introduction to *pesharim* texts and genre see Lim, *Pesharim*. Also Berrin, "Pesharim," 644–47. For overview of Qumran community and their writings (the Dead Sea Scrolls), see Schürer, *History I*, 118–22; Schürer, *History: III:1*, 380–469; Vermes, *Introduction to the Complete Dead Sea Scrolls*. Also, Dimat,

be understood in at least two ways: via the direct inspiration of the prophet, or via the prophet's inspiration as mediated through the text.[332]

From this brief overview, charismatic exegesis in early Judaism appears to bear noticeable similarities to contemporary conversations about pneumatic interpretation by those in or identifying with the renewal tradition. Archie Wright has discussed this particular subject and his insights are considered in 5.3.3. Understanding the approaches and frameworks of these ancient communities can steer and enrich contemporary understanding, and this is a focus of a group identified as "Regent school," which includes Wright and is discussed in chapter 5.[333]

An example of the value of looking to these ancient communities to inform contemporary understanding of pneumatic interpretation can be seen through Aune's, and similarly Christopher Forbes's, consideration of prophecy. They asserted that whilst it can be appreciated that prophecy was a feature of charismatic exegesis in early Judaism,[334] there was less evidence for arguing this in early Christianity, the main argument being a lack of direct evidence linking prophecy and pneumatic interpretation in the New Testament.[335] Aune stated:

> Paranesis was never the exclusive province of either prophecy or biblical interpretation in the early church, and . . . prophets are never explicitly linked to the task of biblical interpretation. There is little evidence to substantiate the view that one of the major occupations of Christian prophets was the inspired exegesis of the Old Testament.[336]

"Qumran," 739–46; Hempel, "Qumran Community," 746–51. For use of the Old Testament in the New Testament, see 1.6.1.

332. Aune, "Charismatic Exegesis," 128–29. For prophecy and interpretation at Qumran, see Aune, "Charismatic Exegesis;" Aune "Christian Prophecy and Charismatic Exegesis;" Horgan, "Bible Explained (Prophecies)," 247–53. For prophecy and interpretation in Hellenism, and wider Second Temple Judaism, see Forbes, *Prophecy and Inspired Speech*, 230–32; Hengel, *Zealots*, 234–35. For prophecy and interpretation in the Old Testament, New Testament and today, see Goldingay, *Models for Interpretation of Scripture*, 141–99.

333. This group includes Mark Boda, Craig Keener, Jack Levison, Kevin Spawn, and Archie Wright.

334. Aune, "Charismatic Exegesis," 128–29, 132, 134–40; "Christian Prophecy and Charismatic Exegesis," 339–42; Forbes, *Prophecy and Inspired Speech*, 230, 232.

335. Aune, "Charismatic Exegesis," 146–48; "Christian Prophecy and Charismatic Exegesis," 342–46; Forbes, *Prophecy and Inspired Speech*, 232–37.

336. Aune, "Charismatic Exegesis," 147. Max Turner also aligned, stating, "It need not be doubted that prophecies had didactic and prescriptive elements. . . . But it is quite another matter to assert that inspired preaching, exegesis or teachings are actually (wholly or in part) what the New Testament *means* by prophecy." Turner, "Does

Ascertaining whether, or in what ways—for example, through appropriation of the scriptural text—prophecy is a feature of pneumatic interpretation, and therefore identifiable with pneumatic appropriation, requires analysis of the relationship between prophecy and interpretation in early Judaism and across the Old Testament, early Christianity in the New Testament, and contemporary Christianity (I suggest, in dynamic interrelationship).[337] This would require a three-stage exploration, interrelating; firstly, interpretive methods like *pesher* in early Jewish communities like Qumran; secondly, use of prophecy and pneumatic interpretation by early Christians in the New Testament, including eschatological use of past scriptures; and thirdly, contemporary use of prophecy and pneumatic interpretation by those across or identifying with the renewal tradition. As considerable further research is required, it would be misleading to suggest that prophecy is always a feature of pneumatic interpretation and appropriation *or* actively consider prophecy within pneumatic interpretation further in this analysis. Whilst the Spirit's appropriation of scripture to personal and contemporary contexts cannot presently be described as prophetic, there is a relationship between the context or framework presented in scripture and the Spirit's appropriation to personal contexts and frameworks. This can be understood as cognitive (interrelated with affect and ethics) appropriation involving perception, intuition, and reason.[338]

Prophecy Denote Charismatic Exegesis, Preaching or Teaching?" 206–12 (206, emphasis original). Similarly, Grudem, *Gift of Prophecy*, 139–44; Carson, *Showing the Spirit*, 161. Those arguing for more positive association between prophecy and pneumatic interpretation in the New Testament included, Boring, "Prophet as Interpreter of Scripture," 95–103; Dunn, *Jesus and the Spirit*, 172, 186 (cf. Forbes, *Prophecy and Inspired Speech*, 233, fn. 36); Ellis, *Prophecy and Hermeneutic*, 127–43 (and more generally 147–253). Selwyn, *St. Peter*, 134. For critiques of these positions, see Aune "Charismatic Exegesis," 146–49; Forbes, *Prophecy and Inspired Speech*, 232–37; Turner, "Does Prophecy Denote Charismatic Exegesis, Preaching or Teaching?" 206–12.

337. For an approach, see Goldingay, "Scripture as Inspired Word," 141–99, noting Goldingay gave minimal attention to pneumatic interpretation (see 188–89 for consideration).

338. Post-2000 contributions including/considering prophecy as an aspect of pneumatic interpretation are incorporated in chapters 4 and 5 whilst noting this resting position. These include, Boda, "Word and Spirit, 25–45; Crinisor, "Paraclete and Prophecy," 276; Davies, "Reading in the Spirit," 304; Dunn, "Role of the Spirit," 154–59; Fee, "Why Pentecostals Read Their Bibles Poorly," 8, fn. 1; Grey, *Three's a Crowd*; Herms, "Invoking the Spirit," 99–114; Keener, "Refining *Spirit Hermeneutics*," 205–6 (also referencing discussion of various roles of prophecy in *Spirit Hermeneutics*); Lee Roy Martin, *Biblical Hermeneutics*, 47–48; Lee Roy Martin, *Unheard Voice of God*, 61–63; Mather, "Welcoming *Spirit Hermeneutics*," 160–61; Moore, "Prophetic Calling," 17–20 (the prophet as messenger); Pinnock, "Work of the Spirit," 163; Westphal, "Spirit and Prejudice," 18; Archie Wright, "Second Temple Period Jewish Biblical Interpretation,"

3.4.6 Evaluation

All scholars agreed that the context or cognitive framework for interpretation *mattered*. In this respect they were not as different from each other as they perhaps thought they were, and their frameworks though different in location, approach and focus, should therefore be regarded as complementary.

As this chapter has consistently shown, pneumatic interpretation of scripture is dynamically interrelated to pneumatic interpretation of self, and self-in-community (Thomas). This places personal relationship with God centrally within consideration of the Spirit's role in the interpretation of scripture. Therefore, drawing from but also building upon Johns, frameworks of interpretation that do not centralize intimate relationship with the triune God through pneumatic encounter can be a hindrance in developing understanding of pneumatic interpretation. This raises a caution against over-using *both* historico-grammatical methods *and* postmodernist thought. A framework of pneumatic interpretation should primarily draw us toward intimate relationship with the triune God, not into a medley of interpretive techniques and concepts. However, because the Spirit, by self-effacing nature, always communicates through and never direct, this task is challenging, for it necessarily requires considering the frameworks that the Spirit communicates through (and also illuminates), whilst at the same time taking care not to over-focus, if concentration is to be kept on pneumatic interpretation.

Pentecostal emphasis (steered by Thomas) on the contemporary community surrounding the scriptural text as a framework for interpretation began to provide a healthy balance to interpretive approaches starting with the text and the historico-grammatical data. Thomas's recommendation of an approach to interpretation incorporating the contemporary situation (and surrounding cognitive framework), the Spirit, and scripture (and surrounding cognitive framework) dynamically interrelating with each other was brave and pioneering. This approach recognized that dependence on the Spirit's leading, as per Acts 15, is crucial, therefore prioritizing personal relationship with God. Consequently, the Acts 15 community framework is preferable to the postmodernist approach because it centralizes intimate relationship with God and retains focus on the Spirit's role in interpretation (providing all three elements *are* held in balanced, dynamic relationship).

Complementing Thomas's emphasis was Aune (and previously Dunn, see 2.1.2), whose insights show that charismatic exegesis in early Jewish communities like Qumran bore noticeable similarities to contemporary

---

73–98; Vondey, *Beyond Pentecostalism*, 72–75.

renewal explorations of pneumatic interpretation and appropriation. Seeking understanding concerning these early approaches and frameworks of interpretation can enrich contemporary understanding and this was illustrated through Aune's consideration of prophecy as a feature of charismatic exegesis, which showed disparity between evidence from early Judaism and the New Testament. A way to negotiate this disparity and resolve understanding as to whether prophecy *can* be established as a feature of pneumatic interpretation, and therefore identifiable with pneumatic appropriation, would be to take Thomas's approach and seek to pneumatically discern, as an academic community, whether prophecy can be appreciated as a feature of contemporary forms of pneumatic interpretation, incorporating this contemporary understanding and (believed) pneumatic discernment in dynamic interrelationship with evidence from early Judaism and across the Old Testament, and early Christianity in the New Testament. This exploration would involve interaction between scholars of different disciplines and research areas, and result in a strength and wealth of insight that would not be achievable without the interaction.

3.5 EVALUATION

The dominant theme drawn and developed from 1990s conversationalists is that *as we approach scripture seeking the Spirit's guidance in interpretation, the Spirit also reaches through scripture and interprets us*. This is a dynamic interrelationship. Pneumatic interpretation cannot therefore be understood solely in relation to scripture because the Spirit always works through and beyond scripture, in ways that create and redeem, and effect scriptural truth affectively, ethically, and cognitively in our lives. This understanding builds on chapter 2 where the primary theme was that pneumatic interpretation is holistic.

Reflecting theologically upon the Spirit's relationship with scripture established this theme, with Land's thoughts highlighting that whilst scripture is the medium, the purpose is the forming of a life for God. Interacting with Moltmann's insights developed further the perspective initiated through engagement with Balthasar's pneumatology in chapter 2 that, as we engage with scripture, the Spirit (self)-interprets the Father, the Son, and the Spirit to us, creating and redeeming through this communication. Factoring the creational (Spirit–Father) aspect of pneumatic interpretation alongside the redemptive (Spirit–Son) aspect means acknowledging that the Spirit *does* convey something new over against the content of scripture but also emphasizes that this new truth is always in relationship with scripture through which the Spirit (self)-interprets God to us. These theological considerations are important as they underpin and provide a foundation upon which hermeneutical thought can build.

Drawing on and building upon thought from scholars who intentionally incorporated personal relationship with God within their hermeneutical considerations further strengthened this theme. Intimate relationship with God was recognized as affective, ethical, and cognitive, and there was collective recognition of the importance of *pursuing* intimate relationship with God, through whom pneumatic interpretation (of scripture and self) comes. Engaging with these scholars helped further understanding of the relationship between affect and ethical conduct, with Land, Lee, and Vanhoozer's contributions strengthening the paradox that when we are most affectively receptive to God we are also the most ethically willing to modify behavior, and in order to be in a state of receptivity to God, active effort is required. Moore and McQueen's personal accounts emphasized this further, giving a sense of their affective receptivity alongside active willingness to modify conduct, influencing their cognition. I suggest, therefore, a working perspective that affect and ethics dynamically interrelate, influencing cognitive reception of truth brought by the Spirit through scripture. Vanhoozer and Pinnock were distinctive in emphasizing that immoral conduct, and evil spirits can cause pneumatic hindrance. Vanhoozer, and Atkinson's[339] brief observations on evil spirits highlight an important point: closely connected with pneumatic interpretation is an ever-present reality of a spiritual battle against powers and principalities that seek to distort our ability to recognize truth.

Cognition was therefore identified as an aspect of intimate relationship with God through whom pneumatic interpretation comes, *and* as a framework of knowledge. Cognitive frameworks of interpretation that assist understanding of the Spirit's role in the interpretation of scripture must place personal relationship with God centrally. The Acts 15 framework as outlined by Thomas centralized dependence on the Spirit's leading (requiring communion with God *and* with each other) and sought to incorporate *two* frameworks of interpretation: the framework surrounding the contemporary community or situation, and the framework surrounding relevant passages of scripture. This is a valuable model for pneumatic interpretation and appropriation *provided* all three elements *are* held in balanced interrelationship. Those involved in Pentecostal hermeneutics emphasized the contemporary framework over the framework surrounding scripture, but Aune's approach provided balance to those focused on the contemporary

339. Atkinson without reference to the Spirit (see 3.3.1).

community, showing that forms of pneumatic interpretation also existed in ancient Jewish communities. However, as cautioned when discussing the increasing enthusiasm for looking at the role of the Pentecostal community, *overly focusing* on cognitive frameworks *will* steer attention away from pneumatic interpretation.

In closing, I return to Land with whom this chapter started. Land cautioned that when the integration of orthopathy, orthopraxy, and orthodoxy fragments, it brings "affective distortions," "practical dilemmas," and "intellectual struggles" that require addressing and interpreting as symptoms of greater need.[340] Taking imperfect human nature into consideration, we can appreciate that, to one extent of another, these dilemmas, distortions, and struggles will always be present in the pursuit of understanding concerning the Spirit's role in the interpretation of scripture. A perfect integrative balance of affect, ethics, and cognition will probably never be achieved. Consequently, understanding of the ways the Spirit brings truth through scripture, as well as discernment of pneumatic truth itself, will always be fragmentary and imbalanced. However, as Wesley advocated through his doctrine of perfection,[341] this should not, and has not, stopped the pursuit.

340. Land, *Pentecostal Spirituality*, 192. Land phrased this as "intellectual struggles, affective distortions, and practical dilemmas," but I have re-ordered his words to correspond with orthopathy (affect), orthopraxy (ethics), and orthodoxy (cognition).

341. See fn. 220 (Wesley).

4

Through and Beyond Scripture II

2000 to 2009

In the 2000s, Pentecostal scholars continued to explore interpretive methods that integrated personal faith expression with academic expression and incorporated the Spirit. As with the 1990s, they were a large part of the conversation and Pentecostal hermeneutics' terminology was prevalent. During this decade reflections were produced,[342] and full-length studies emerged. Following Larry McQueen, who brought the first published monograph to the conversation,[343] Lee Roy Martin and Robby Waddell presented full-length studies of the books of Judges and Revelation that actively incorporated their Pentecostal faith,[344] whilst Kenneth Archer brought the first published monograph of Pentecostal hermeneutics.[345] From evangelical positioning, a key contribution to pneumatic interpretation came from

342. On Pentecostal hermeneutics: Atkinson, "Worth a Second Look," 49–54; Becker, "Tenet Under Examination," 31–34; Macchia, "Pentecostal Theology," 1121–23; Macchia, "Spirit and the Text," 53–65; Thomas, "'Where the Spirit Leads,'" 289–302. On Pneumatic interpretation: Thomas, "Holy Spirit and Interpretation," 165–66.

343. McQueen, *Joel and the Spirit* (f.pub. 1995, see 3.3.5). Noting John Wyckoff's 1990 PhD dissertation published in 2010 (this has no new sources after 1990). Wyckoff, *Pneuma and Logos* (see fn. 89).

344. Martin, *Unheard Voice of God* (pub. 2008); Waddell, *Spirit of the Book of Revelation* (pub. 2006).

345. Archer, *Pentecostal Hermeneutic* (f.pub. 2005). The first unpublished monograph on Pentecostal hermeneutics was Clark, "Investigation" (DTh diss., 1997). Offering a full-length, reformed evangelical perspective on pneumatic interpretation was Brown, *Holy Spirit and the Bible*.

Stanley Grenz,[346] and Frank Macchia reflected on pneumatic interpretation following Reformed-Pentecostal dialogue. Clark Pinnock was amongst a few scholars to intentionally incorporate renewal perspectives in their approaches,[347] and Francis Martin and Andrew Minto contributed from Roman Catholic charismatic perspectives.[348]

Paradoxically, although it was still the main channel through which consideration of the Spirit's role in the interpretation of scripture was emerging, Pentecostal hermeneutics was increasingly hindering discussions by restricting attention within Pentecostalism and focusing on the Pentecostal community as the cognitive framework for interpretation. This chapter addresses these issues before following a similar outline to chapter 3, giving theological consideration to the Spirit's relationship with scripture, and considering affect, ethics, and cognition as aspects of intimate relationship with God.

4.1 THE VALUE OF AND THE PROBLEM WITH PENTECOSTAL HERMENEUTICS

As engagement with Howard Ervin's seminal contribution highlighted (see 2.4.3), not everyone used Pentecostal hermeneutics' terminology in the same way. For example, Paul Lewis used "Pentecostal hermeneutic" to refer

346. Grenz, "Spirit and the Word," 357–74. Further evangelical contributions came from Brown, *Holy Spirit and the Bible*; Grenz, *Renewing the Center*, 209–11; Pinnock, "Biblical Texts: Past and Future Meanings," 71–81; Pinnock with Callen, *Scripture Principle*; Sparks, *God's Word in Human Words*, 171–203; Ward, *Words of Life*; Trueman, "Illumination," 316–18; Vanhoozer, "Discourse on Matter," 3–31; Vanhoozer, "Spirit of Understanding: Special Revelation & General Hermeneutics," 207–35 (this was a revised version of his earlier offering with similar name, see fns 202, 242); and Vanhoozer, "Speech Acts to Scripture Acts," 27, 40–43 (see fn. 242); Webster, "Biblical Theology and the Clarity of Scripture," 352–84; Webster, *Holy Scripture*; Yocum, "Clarity of Scripture," 727–30.

347. Pinnock, "Work of the Spirit," 157–71. Also, Elbert, "Contextual Analysis and Interpretation," 1–14; Lewis, "Pentecostal Epistemology," 95–125; Minto (see fn. 348); Tennison, "Charismatic Biblical Interpretation," 106–9.

348. Minto summarized the early church fathers' understanding of pneumatic interpretation and related it to pneumatic interpretation discussions in the renewal tradition, emphasizing the Roman Catholic charismatic renewal. He wove discussion around statements in *Catechism of the Catholic Church* and *Dei Verbum*. Minto, "Charismatic Renewal and the Spiritual Sense of Scripture," 256–72 (260–61); *Catechism of the Catholic Church* nos. 101–41; *Dei Verbum*, no.12 (cf. fn. 143 [Dulles]). Also, Kärkkäinen, "Authority, Revelation and Interpretation," 23–38 (this was a revised version of his earlier article with similar name, see fn. 203). For further from Francis Martin, see *Sacred Scripture*, particularly chapter 5 (study of *lectio divina*) and chapter 11 (reflection upon *Dei Verbum*, no. 12).

to a hermeneutic from those across the renewal tradition, whilst Amos Yong used "pentecostal" and "Pentecostal" hermeneutics to refer to a pneumatic interpretive approach, and hermeneutic characteristic of Pentecostalism in ways not altogether consistent or clear.[349] Generally, however, use was largely concerned with defining an interpretive identity for the Pentecostal tradition within the academy, within which consideration was given to pneumatic interpretation. This work continues to acknowledge Pentecostal hermeneutics within this context.

4.1.1 Over-emphasis of cognitive frameworks

As Pentecostals investigated interpretive methods fitting their tradition, shift from consideration of the Spirit's role in interpretation to interpretation as a Pentecostal strengthened. In particular, as attention on the contemporary community as the cognitive framework for interpretation increased, focus on the Spirit's role in interpretation decreased.[350] This can be attributed to postmodernism's influence, which appealed to scholars[351] through focus on subjectivity, helping to consider the contemporary community framework surrounding the scriptural text, and the interpreter within this framework,

349. Lewis, "Pentecostal Epistemology," 95–96; Yong, *Spirit-Word-Community* ix, cf. Hermeneutical Trialectic," 24. For later example of this confusion, Yong, "Foreword," in Keener, *Spirit Hermeneutics*, xviii–xxi.

350. This is a broad analysis of Pentecostal hermeneutics from the decade overall, factoring contributions from the previous three decades (see 3.4). It is not a statement of every contribution. E.g., this critique could not be made of Robby Waddell, who employed postmodernist methods of intertextuality to construct a Pentecostal strategy for interpretation, keeping focus on pneumatic interpretation and considering the community's role in interpretation. Waddell, *Spirit of the Book of Revelation*, 192–93.

351. Evangelical scholars also incorporated postmodernist approaches. One could assume that The Scripture and Hermeneutics Series edited by Craig Bartholomew et al., namely *Renewing Biblical Interpretation*, *After Pentecost*, and *Out of Egypt*, engaged with scriptural interpretation from renewal perspective, but this was a series from evangelical scholars integrating postmodernist thinking with biblical interpretation. Excepting Vanhoozer, "Speech Acts to Scripture Acts," and Webster, "Biblical Theology and the Clarity of Scripture," only minor consideration was given to pneumatic interpretation. See Andrew Lincoln, "Hebrews and Biblical Theology," 331–32; Olhausen, "'Polite' Response to Anthony Thiselton," 127–29, critiquing Thiselton for only briefly mentioning the Spirit's role in interpretation (Thiselton. "'Behind' and 'in Front of' the Text," 108); Ingraffia and Pickett, "Reviving the Power of Biblical Language: The Bible, Literature and Literary Language," 245–48, critiquing Vanhoozer's speech-act theory. Further fleeting references in essays in *Renewing Biblical Interpretation* mostly regard Vanhoozer's speech-act theory (see fn. 242). For series focus on postmodernism, see Bartholomew, *Renewing Biblical Interpretation*, xxv; Bartholomew, *After Pentecost*, xxii; Bartholomew, *Out of Egypt*, 7.

but not directly addressing personal relationship with God and pneumatic encounter with scripture as consequence of that relationship (see 1.5; 3.4.1; and 3.4.2). Pentecostal scholars were now more cautious of postmodernist methods, recognizing their limitations,[352] but influence was especially present where consideration was given to the contemporary community as the framework for interpretation.[353] These considerations were valuable to understanding pneumatic interpretation, balancing approaches starting with scripture and the historico-grammatical data. However, as outlined in chapter 3 (see 3.4.1; 3.4.2; and 3.4.6), over-emphasis of either of these frameworks (or concentrated discussions over their integration)[354] steer emphasis away from the Spirit and into a medley of interpretive techniques and concepts. As explained in 1.5 and 3.4.1, understanding the Spirit's self-effacing nature provides insight into this "problem."

I hesitate in this aspect of the analysis because I do not want to devalue discussions of Pentecostal hermeneutics. One cannot work for years considering the literature, and meeting and becoming friends with scholars in the conversation, without receiving a deep impression of the significance of these discussions in defining academic interpretive identity for Pentecostals, for

352. John Poirier and Scott Lewis aligned with Robert Menzies's warnings of the postmodernist influence (see 3.4.3) and defined "postmodernist" as "any approach opposed to the use or privileging of the historical method." Poirier and Lewis, "Pentecostal and Postmodernist Hermeneutics," 3–21 (6). Scott Ellington was softer, yet still cautious of Pentecostal scholarship's eagerness to embrace postmodernism. Ellington, "History, Story and Testimony" (pub. 2001), 245–63. However, he was later more welcoming of integration: "Postmodernism capitalizes on the fundamental failure of modern historiography to bridge the gap between historical account in the form of a historical text and the referent to which such texts belong." Ellington, "Reciprocal Reshaping of History and Experience" (pub. 2007), 18–31 (19). Kenneth Archer proposed forging a middle ground between the "pluralistic relativism of postmodernism" and "the objectivism of modernism," a pathway he located in early Pentecostal approaches to biblical interpretation." Archer, *Pentecostal Hermeneutic*, 208 (discussed in 4.1.3). Frank Macchia suggested Pentecostals be "guided by Karl Barth's insight that critical methods prepare one for hearing the Word of God in the 'strange new world of the Bible' but that such methods cannot guarantee the act of hearing itself." Macchia, "Spirit and the Text," 53–59, 65 (56). Waddell advised cautious integration, stating that "the relationship between Pentecostalism and modernity is quite antithetical and yet the 'postmodern' label does not quite fit either." Waddell, *Spirit of the Book of Revelation*, 112. Also, Kärkkäinen, "Hermeneutics: From Fundamentalism to Modernism," 3–21 (this was a revised version of "Pentecostal Hermeneutics in the Making," see fn. 298). For active incorporation, see Cross, "Proposal to Break the Ice," 44–73.

353. E.g., Archer, *Pentecostal Hermeneutic*, chapters 5 and 6; Lee Roy Martin, *Unheard Voice of God*, chapter 3; Waddell, *Spirit of the Book of Revelation*, chapter 3 (see fn. 350).

354. E.g., Archer, *Pentecostal Hermeneutic*, chapter 5 ("Current Pentecostal Hermeneutical Concerns").

self-understanding and for appreciation within the academy. Reflections of the early and contemporary Pentecostal community, such as those brought by Land (see 3.1) and Archer, have been vital to these discussions. However, by emphasizing the Pentecostal community and restricting attention to Pentecostalism, those involved in Pentecostal hermeneutics were paradoxically also hindering focus on pneumatic interpretation, and inclusivity of those across or identifying with the renewal tradition. From this context this section engages with Archer, Lee Roy Martin, and Andrew Davies, using their contributions as examples of wider trends across Pentecostal hermeneutics.

4.1.2 Spirit, scripture, and community (Kenneth Archer)

Archer's thesis was that "there exists within early Pentecostalism an authentic Pentecostal approach to interpretation that is rooted in and guided by Pentecostal identity which can be retrieved and critically re-appropriated with the current postmodern context."[355] His concern was to articulate an academic interpretive identity for Pentecostalism, and stemming from this he presented a Pentecostal approach to interpretation of scripture which incorporated the Spirit.[356] Although Archer stated the incorporation of community, scripture, and Spirit in interdependent dialogue, emphasizing that no element was subordinate to the other two,[357] his focus was on the Pentecostal community as the cognitive framework for interpretation, and he considered the Spirit and scripture in relation to this. This is evident throughout, but accentuated in his hermeneutical method where twenty-four pages are given to community, eight to scripture, and six to pneumatic interpretation.[358] In this respect, it could be argued that the balanced interrelationship he asserted was not actually presented.[359] When consider-

355. Archer, *Pentecostal Hermeneutic* (f.pub. 2005), 3.

356. Archer, *Pentecostal Hermeneutic*, 1.

357. Archer, *Pentecostal Hermeneutic*, ix, 213, 214–15, 252, 260.

358. Archer, *Pentecostal Hermeneutic*, 215–52. With thanks to Vanhoozer, "Reforming Pneumatic Hermeneutics" (pub. 2014), 20–21 for the insight.

359. *A Pentecostal Hermeneutic: Spirit, Scripture and Community* is a revised version of Archer's PhD dissertation, "Forging a New Path: A Contemporary Pentecostal Hermeneutical Strategy for the 21st Century." See Archer, *Pentecostal Hermeneutic*, ix. Unlike his revised title, this title does not imply balanced consideration of Spirit, scripture, and community. Retaining this would have lessened the emphasis, making this particular critique harder. It may be interesting to compare Archer with Yong. Both presented hermeneutical models interplaying Spirit, scripture/Word, and community as three interrelating components. Yong explained that he had sought to align his method of writing with his actual argument, explaining, "This method proceeds from my overall conviction that while arguments are important, so are the media through

ing pneumatic interpretation, Archer acknowledged the Spirit speaking through the community and scripture,[360] advocating John Christopher Thomas's Acts 15 model (see 3.4.4).[361] He also used (and celebrated) insights from French Arrington to assert that a person's openness to the Spirit was an important part of pneumatic interpretation.[362] This latter aspect, of course, aligns with this work's emphasis of the centrality of intimate relationship with the triune God (through pneumatic encounter) to pneumatic interpretation. However, Archer did not explore much beyond this in the six pages given over to the Spirit's role.

Archer's focus therefore, whilst valuable to Pentecostal identity, increased a trend[363] that was emphasizing the contemporary framework surrounding scripture as it is read (and the interpreter within this framework), but steering away from detailed and explicit consideration of the Spirit.

4.1.3 The early and contemporary Pentecostal community (Kenneth Archer and Lee Roy Martin)

Archer's attention to the early and contemporary community as the cognitive framework for interpretation unearthed another issue; within these community considerations were aspects particular to Pentecostalism *and*

---

which they are made." Yong, *Spirit–Word–Community*, 24. Yong's conviction made for a complicated writing style and presentation, balancing his complex and sometimes abstract theology (see also fn. 391). However, the overall idea that the media through which arguments are made should align with the arguments themselves is valuable. It is also an approach that this work seeks to employ (see 1.1 and fn. 8). For Yong, see 4.2.2. Also comparable, Vondey, *Beyond Pentecostalism*, 66–77. For critique of Archer, *Pentecostal Hermeneutic*, see Elbert, "Toward a Pentecostal Hermeneutic," 320–28.

360. Archer, *Pentecostal Hermeneutic*, 247. For further, see 195–200.

361. Archer, *Pentecostal Hermeneutic*, 197. Further considerations of Luke/Acts and Acts 15 incorporating pneumatic interpretation included: Noel, "Gordon Fee and the Challenge to Pentecostal Hermeneutics," 60–80; Thomas, "Reading the Bible from within Our Traditions," 108–22.

362. Archer, *Pentecostal Hermeneutic*, 252, referencing Arrington, "Use of the Bible by Pentecostals" (pub. 1994), 105. For Arrington, see fns. 195, 307.

363. A further example of this trend can be seen from John Christopher Thomas and Kimberly Ervin Alexander, who suggested that Mark 16:9–20 had been overshadowed by the Acts narrative as the template for Pentecostal identity and practice. There is *no attention* to pneumatic interpretation in this article, further emphasizing the increasing focus on Pentecostal identity and decreasing attention to the Spirit. Responding, Wall critiqued that whilst appreciative, his concern was that their approach was "overly sectarian" and not inclusive enough of those outside the Pentecostal tradition. Thomas and Alexander, "'Signs are Following,'" 147–70; Wall, "Response to Thomas/Alexander," 180. Also, Landrus, "Hearing 3 John 2," 70–88.

aspects that deserved to be placed in the wider context of the renewal tradition and recognized accordingly. Archer advocated the early Pentecostal "Bible Reading Method,"[364] and this shows a particular Pentecostal approach, but even so it cannot be completely separated from the wider renewal tradition for—as he noted—the method was adapted from one used by the Wesleyan and Holiness movements and used within the Pentecostal framework.[365] As established in 3.1.1, any interpretive methodology that draws from John Wesley's thought, justifies, if not demands, application to a wider renewal context. Furthermore, Archer's identified aspects of how early Pentecostals approached scripture such as recognizing the importance of openness before God, and a desire to believe and obey,[366] align with the central tenets of this work, which is intentionally inclusive of all who are in, or who identify with, the renewal tradition regardless of ecclesial expression. As a reminder, here, "the renewal tradition" is defined around those charismatic movements and scholars in those groups who unite around a central emphasis on the Spirit (see 1.2). Where the Spirit is central, the hermeneutical focus has to be ecumenical, inclusive, and unifying.

Correspondingly, in *The Unheard Voice of God: A Pentecostal Hearing of the Book of Judges*, Lee Roy Martin contained his discussion within Pentecostalism and used the early and contemporary Pentecostal community as a framework. However, he also described an approach to scripture and relationship with God shared by those in or identifying with the renewal tradition. Martin's thesis was about *hearing* and not just reading Judges, approaching scripture from the perspective of God's word to be heard and received (discussed in 4.3.3.).[367] Martin explained that he was not speaking for everyone in the renewal tradition but "as a practicing Pentecostal who for many years has struggled to integrate the critical interpretation of Scripture with the ongoing life of the Church."[368] Similarly to Archer, Martin based his concept of hearing from the oral tradition of early Pentecostalism but noted oral communication of texts across and beyond Christian traditions.[369]

364. Archer, *Pentecostal Hermeneutic*, chapter 3 and 4, particularly 99–102, 125–27, 128. For earlier thought, along similar lines as chapters 3 and 4, see Archer, "Early Pentecostal Biblical Interpretation," 32–70; Archer, "Pentecostal Story," 36–59 respectively.

365. Archer, *Pentecostal Hermeneutic*, 128.

366. Archer, *Pentecostal Hermeneutic*, 127.

367. Lee Roy Martin, *Unheard Voice of God* (pub. 2008), 53.

368. Lee Roy Martin, *Unheard Voice of God*, 59.

369. Lee Roy Martin, *Unheard Voice of God*, 64–68. Likewise, in *Spirit of the Book of Revelation*, Waddell explained his restriction to Pentecostalism, giving a history of Pentecostalism and noting the charismatic movement, but his approach also identified with renewal thought generally. E.g., "Pentecostals . . . read the Bible theologically as

4.1.4 Reading from a Pentecostal perspective (Andrew Davies)

Addressing "everyday practice of reading Scripture," Davies considered what it meant to read scripture as a Pentecostal,[370] suggesting that Pentecostals read scripture "to meet God in the text, and to provide an opportunity for the Holy Spirit to speak to our spirits."[371] He explained that encounter with God is prioritized over cognitive understanding, meaning that Pentecostals accept a degree of uncertainty and do not need to understand all that is read for an encounter with God to take place.[372] Davies further argued that the priority placed on spiritual gifts such as healing and tongues, and worship gatherings within open structures giving space for the Spirit to intervene, mean that Pentecostals are practically confronted with the tension between knowing and not knowing (compare 2.3.2) in ways that "do not afflict our sisters and brothers in other groups in quite the same way."[373] Referring to weakness in Pentecostal hermeneutics' research concerning *how* the Spirit is involved in interpretation, and with a similar insight to the one from Vanhoozer that influenced this work's beginnings (see 1.5), Davies stated:

> Here it seems to me that we need help from the work of systematicians. Whilst Pentecostals almost universally assume the role of the Spirit in guiding our interpretation, there is a notable weakness in the literature in terms of how this process is understood and defined. How does the Spirit truly guide us in interpretation? How do we listen?[374]

Davies's insights are valuable, but nevertheless they are not just relevant to Pentecostals but to *all* across and identifying with the renewal tradition who accentuate the Spirit's role in hermeneutical considerations. As this analysis has been showing, central to discussions of pneumatic

---

divinely inspired scripture which can and will speak directly to their present situations and will affect every aspect of their lives." Waddell, *Spirit of the Book of Revelation*, 103–8 (100–101, and see fn. 12). Cf. (Cf. fns. 350, 417 [Waddell's interpretive approach]).

370. Davies, "What Does it Mean to Read the Bible as a Pentecostal?" (pub. 2009), 218. Davies wrote from a British perspective referring to classical Pentecostalism (217). Similarly, Davies, "Reading in the Spirit," 304–5.

371. Davies, "What Does it Mean to Read the Bible as a Pentecostal?" 219.

372. Davies, "What Does it Mean to Read the Bible as a Pentecostal?" 220.

373. E.g., healing promised (Mark 16:18) yet unanswered, and tongues spoken by one and interpreted by another. Davies stated that "the unknowable and unfathomable" was the core of Pentecostal spiritual experience, noting common heritage with "mystical traditions of Christianity." Davies, "What Does it Mean to Read the Bible as a Pentecostal?" 220–21.

374. Davies, "What Does it Mean to Read the Bible as a Pentecostal?" 228. This weakness was also noticed by Cross, "Proposal to Break the Ice," 65, 70–73.

interpretation in the renewal tradition is the priority placed on personal experience *of* and intimate relationship *with* God as Father, Son, and Spirit, through pneumatic encounter. Whilst this *is* characteristic of a Pentecostal approach to interpretation, it is *also* characteristic of a renewal approach.

4.1.5 Evaluation

Emphasis on the early and contemporary Pentecostal community as the cognitive framework for interpretation was valuable for developing Pentecostal hermeneutical identity but less productive in fostering understanding of pneumatic interpretation and promoting inclusivity of all scholars across or identifying with the renewal tradition. The contemporary framework surrounding scripture as it is read, and the interpreter within that framework, is a necessary part of the conversation (along with appreciating the framework surrounding scripture in its original historical location), but focus on these contemporary frameworks was inadvertently steering attention away from detailed and explicit attention to the Spirit's role in interpretation and toward explications of Pentecostal identity. A reason for this problem lies with understanding the Spirit's self-effacing nature. Because the Spirit is self-effacing, the Spirit's role can only be considered through whatever it is the Spirit is communicating through and also glorifying and illuminating. Whilst it is natural and necessary to focus on these objects and movements, doing so can also draw attention away from the Spirit.

Additionally, the emphasis on the Pentecostal community as the framework for interpretation raises questions concerning aspects considered particular to Pentecostalism (whilst appreciating that no community lives in an historical or contemporary vacuum), and common features shared by those across or identifying with the renewal tradition.

Tendency to recognize approaches to scripture and spirituality such as those illustrated by Davies, Archer, and Martin as particular to Pentecostalism was now widespread across those involved in Pentecostal hermeneutics,[375] but this did not adequately recognize or include non-Pentecostals within or identifying with the renewal tradition who approached scripture and relationship with God similarly and who were *also* part of the

375. Additional to those already discussed, Allen, "'Forgotten Spirit.'" 51–66; Coulter, "What Meaneth This?" 38–64; Cross, "Rich Feast," 27–47; Davies, "Reading in the Spirit," 303–11; Ellington, "History, Story, and Testimony," 255–57; Ellington, "Reciprocal Reshaping of History and Experience," 27–31; Pinnock, "Divine Relationality," 3–26, even though he self-identified as "'third wave' evangelical" (5); Smith, "Thinking in Tongues," 27–31; Thomas, "Bible," 108–22.

conversation.[376] The conversation was reaching a stage where Pentecostal scholars writing in Pentecostal hermeneutics were the dominant voices, and those in or identifying with the charismatic movement were the minority voices struggling to be heard.

4.2 THE SPIRIT'S RELATIONSHIP WITH SCRIPTURE II

In this analysis, it has so far been asserted that seeking understanding of the Spirit's role in the interpretation of scripture requires consideration of the relational nature of the triune God, from the starting point of the Spirit. As has been argued, this requires reflection on the Spirit's relationship with the Father as well as the Spirit's relationship with the Son. The Spirit effects and/or appropriates scriptural truth holistically in ways that create and redeem and draw us affectively, ethically, and cognitively into knowledge of God as Father, Son, and Spirit, and of self. This communication is always in relationship with scripture's written content but also reaches beyond it. In this way we interpret scripture pneumatically but through this process the Spirit reaches through scripture and interprets us (see discussion in 2.3; 3.2; and 3.5). It has also been maintained that because God as Father, Son, and Spirit is invisible and, at the same time, incarnate—with the Spirit's act of interpreting coming to light in Christ, the incarnate one—the Spirit's communication will carry God's invisible yet also incarnate nature (see 2.3.2). Therefore, characteristic of those considering pneumatic interpretation will be conscious or subliminal recognition that the Spirit's communication is both interpretable and beyond interpretation; reachable, yet nevertheless also beyond grasp. This section continues and builds upon these themes, considering thought from scholars who sought theological understanding of the Spirit's relationship with scripture, also incorporating ongoing discussion (noted in 4.2.4) of the Spirit's appropriation of scripture to personal and contemporary situations and use of the historico-grammatical data.

376. Archie Wright addressed this in 2011, stating, "It is true that the majority of scholars working in the area of a pneumatic hermeneutic previously have been from Pentecostal circles, but to categorize the renewal tradition and a pneumatic hermeneutic as a Pentecostal endeavour is an unfair generalization." Wright, "We Are Not All Pentecostals," 177. Similarly, Herms, "Review of Robby Waddell," 15.

4.2.1 The Spirit and the Son (Frank Macchia and the Reformed–Pentecostal dialogue)

Between 1996 and 2000, representatives from the World Alliance of Reformed Churches (WARC), and leaders from classical Pentecostal churches engaged in formal dialogue, within which pneumatic interpretation was discussed.[377] In the official report, the participants affirmed Christ as "God's Son, . . . the eternal Word of God who became flesh," the decisive revelation of God and "the One in whom the fullness of the Godhead dwells." They additionally agreed, "God has revealed God's Self through the Scriptures and Scripture, as the Word of God, is not to be isolated from the agency of the Holy Spirit."[378] The participants further stated:

> Together, we stress the mutual bond of the Word and the Spirit. Through the Holy Spirit, the Bible speaks the Word of God. The indispensable action of the Spirit makes the text into a living and life-giving testimony to Jesus Christ, transforming the lives of people, for the Scripture is not a dead text.[379]

Like Land's seeming twofold understanding of "Word" as scripture and Christ (see 3.2.2), these Reformed and Pentecostal participants similarly appeared to combine Word as scripture and Christ as *Logos*. Whilst noting that this topic forays into areas beyond this work's remit and is too large to treat well here, the apparent twofold use of Word as scripture and Christ as *Logos* adopted by some conversationalists[380] carries pneumatological, patrological, and trinitarian implications that are important to this work's developing understanding of pneumatic interpretation. Some of these implications become more apparent by recognizing that the agreed Reformed–Pentecostal position presented the Spirit revealing the Son through scripture but did not address the Father or the triune relationship.[381] Effectively, the Reformed-

377. "Final Report 1996–2000," 9–43. For pneumatic interpretation in the Final Report, see nos. 19, 20, 22, 26, 28, 29, 33, 35 (within discussion "I. Spirit and Word," nos. 15–35). See also 1.6.1 (ecumenical dialogue and interpretation).

378. "Final Report 1996–2000," no. 19, referencing John 1:14, Hebrews 1:1–2, Colossians 2:3, 9.

379. "Final Report 1996–2000," no. 22, also cited by Macchia, "Spirit, Word, and Kingdom" (pub. 2002), 80–81.

380. E.g., Macchia "Reply to Rickie Moore," 18 (Macchia was responding to Moore, "Letter to Frank Macchia," 12–14, who was questioning on *sola scriptura* versus *solo spiritu*); Waddell, "Spirit of Reviews and Response," 25; also fn. 241 (Barth and Vanhoozer).

381. E.g., the Reformed/Pentecostal participants concluded the "Spirit and Word" section stating, "Pentecostal and Reformed Christians conclude that the Bible is the

Pentecostal position centralized Christ but restricted a wider pneumatological, patrological, and trinitarian perspective.

Frank Macchia reflected on these discussions and although he discussed trinitarian pneumatology, noting, "Pentecostals are Trinitarian with a christological focus," this reflection was external to the Spirit and scripture.[382] Following the Reformed–Pentecostal perspective, when discussing the Spirit's role in the interpretation of scripture, Macchia focused on the Spirit–Son relationship and did not discuss the Father or the triune relationship.[383] Macchia's theology has been influenced by Karl Barth, and Barth's christocentric emphasis is evident across Macchia's consideration of pneumatic interpretation. For example:

> Karl Barth's passion for encountering the living Christ as the living subject matter of the text and the related desire to place scientific and other interpretive methods in the service of the act of hearing by the Spirit of God might provide Pentecostals with a way beyond the limitation of a nonacademic reading of the biblical text.[384]

Whilst dialogue with reformed scholars is valuable,[385] reformed theology accentuates the Son more than the Spirit and the Father in hermeneutical

Word of God in its witness to Jesus Christ through the work of the Holy Spirit." "Final Report 1996–2000," no. 35. They also acknowledged that Pentecostals do not detach the Spirit's work from a trinitarian understanding. However, this was external to pneumatic interpretation, and presented the trinitarian relationship as "the Father through the Son in the power of the Spirit." "Final Report 1996–2000," no. 17.

382. Macchia, "Spirit, Word, and Kingdom" (pub. 2002), 78–80 (79) referencing "Final Report 1996–2000," no. 17. For Macchia's trinitarian theology, see Macchia, *Trinity, Practically Speaking*, Also, Macchia, *Justified in the Spirit*, 293–312. For assessment of Macchia's trinitarian theology, see Studebaker, *Pentecost to the Triune God*, 196–98.

383. Macchia, "Spirit, Word, and Kingdom," 80–85. Similarly, Macchia, "Reply to Rickie Moore," 16–19.

384. Macchia, "Spirit and the Text" (pub. 2000), 62. Also quoted in Macchia, "Pentecostal Theology," 1123. Similarly, Macchia, "Reply to Rickie Moore," 18–19; Macchia, "Spirit, Word, and Kingdom" 79. For Barth's position, see fn. 241 (Barth and Vanhoozer). Also incorporating Barth within pneumatic interpretation, Brown, *Holy Spirit and the Bible*, 10; Grenz, "Spirit and the Word," 365; Sparks, *God's Word in Human Words*, 171–78, 192; Vanhoozer (noted elsewhere); Yong, *Spirit–Word–Community*, 261.

385. Notably, John Webster. Rather than discussing how to interpret scripture, in *Holy Scripture* (pub. 2003), Webster went back one stage to establish the nature of scripture itself. He wrote, "The proper location for a Christian theological account of the nature of Holy Scripture is the Christian doctrine of God. In particular, theological assertions about Scripture are a function of Christian convictions about God's making himself present as saviour and his establishing of covenant fellowship" (39). Webster argued that scripture is holy—he always described scripture as "Holy Scripture"—and in order to describe scripture, "language of the triune God's saving and revelatory

conversations, and reformed thought is therefore largely external to the renewal tradition as understood in this work's terms.[386] Consequently, engagement with reformed scholars and their theology by conversationalists considering pneumatic interpretation should be approached with awareness of this christocentric emphasis.[387]

4.2.2 The Spirit, the Father, and the Son (Amos Yong, William Atkinson, and Mark Cartledge)

In *Spirit-Word-Community*, Amos Yong concentrated on developing a "trinitarian theological hermeneutic and method from a pneumatological starting point."[388] Yong's scope was broader than interpretation of scripture,

action" must be used (1). He described *Holy Scripture* as "a dogmatic ontology of Holy Scripture: an account of what Holy Scripture *is* in the saving economy of God's loving and regenerative self-communication" (2 [emphasis original]). Webster's *Holy Scripture* strengthens understanding that interpretation of scripture should be rooted in knowledge of the nature and communicative activity of the triune God. See his sketch of a doctrine of scripture within three primary concepts of revelation, sanctification, and inspiration in chapter 1 (the quote from page 39 is a summary of chapter 1), and consideration of the nature of reading in an economy of grace in chapter 3. In chapter 3 Webster incorporated thought from John Calvin, Dietrich Bonhoeffer, and Huldrych Zwingli, arguing that "grasping the nature of Scripture involves both rational assent and a pious disposition of *mind, will and affections*." Webster, *Holy Scripture*, 69 (emphasis added to stress complementarity with affect, ethics, and cognition). See also, Webster, "Biblical Theology and the Clarity of Scripture," 352–84.

386. Vanhoozer has been incorporated within this analysis because he engaged directly with the conversation and his work sometimes contains a degree of reference to the Spirit that identifies with the renewal tradition. *However*, his contributions are included with awareness and presentation of his reformed perspective. See 3.2.3 and fns. 241–42 (Barth's influence and Vanhoozer's alignment with the *filioque*). For direct engagement, see Vanhoozer, "Reforming Pneumatic Hermeneutics" (pub. 2014), 18–24; Vanhoozer, "Spirit of Light" (pub. 2015), 149–67.

387. E.g., having reflected on some of his earlier work, Vanhoozer brought "descriptive treatment of what actually happens in understanding." Vanhoozer, "Discourse on Matter: Hermeneutics and the 'Miracle' of Understanding' (pub. 2006), 4. Following Gadamer and Ricoeur, and centering on Barth's *Epistle to the Romans*, Vanhoozer posited that there is an active agent in the event of understanding that he called the *Sache*. Vanhoozer presented the *Sache* as the *matter* of the text and the key to understanding, arguing that it is through the relationship of the *Sache* to the interpreter that "the 'miracle' of understanding" takes place. Vanhoozer concluded with Barth that the *Sache* is Christ resplendent "the living *logos*, the 'true light that enlightens every man' (Jn 1:9)" (28). Vanhoozer was unclear regarding the Spirit's hermeneutical role, hinting that the miracle of understanding was an act of revelation given through the Spirit (10, 25–26, 28). There was no mention of the Father or the triune relationship.

388. Yong, *Spirit-Word-Community* (pub. 2002), 1.

and aimed at "interpreting and understanding from the perspective of faith not only the biblical text but also life and reality."[389] Here Yong's approach differs from this work, which has been centralizing scripture by considering the Spirit's role in its interpretation, and subsequently recognizing that *the Spirit reaches through scripture and interprets us* as we engage with scripture. Yong identified "the process of interpretation as including three distinct but interrelated moments captured by the metaphors, Spirit, Word,[390] and Community," explaining that his hermeneutic was based on "the perichoretic indwelling of the inter-Trinitarian relationships."[391]

Yong argued that approaching interpretation starting with the Spirit delivers a stronger trinitarianism than interpretive approaches beginning with the Son, especially prevalent in Western theology and which had too often relegated the Spirit as an afterthought behind the Father and the Son.[392] He stated:

> A pneumatological starting point, however, is both christological and patrological—the Spirit being the Spirit of Christ and the Spirit of the Father simultaneously—but in different respects. This difference stems from the fact that while the Spirit is related to the Son and to the Father, it is a dual relationship with different theological implications. Pneumatology therefore insists on a vigorous trinitarianism in a way that christology which draws attention to the Father–Son relationship does not.[393]

Yong's approach stemmed from desire to redress the subordination of Spirit resulting from Western Christianity's "inclination to accept the

389. Yong, *Spirit–Word–Community*, 7.

390. Yong's use of Word was wider than scripture or Christ as *Logos* but he also interchanged Word in both respects. E.g., Yong, *Spirit–Word–Community*, 17–18, 253–65; "Hermeneutical Trialectic" (pub. 2004), 27. For assessment of Yong's understanding of "Word," see Oliverio, *Theological Hermeneutics* (f.pub. 2012), 240–43.

391. Yong, "Hermeneutical Trialectic," 22, 23 respectively. As Yong explained, "Hermeneutical Trialectic" summarizes *Spirit–Word–Community*. See Yong, "Hermeneutical Trialectic," 22. William Oliverio highlighted Yong's brilliance at weaving together hermeneutics, ontology, epistemology, and metaphysics. Without disputing Yong's brilliance, this amalgamation made for a complicated and difficult to understand book, something Oliverio also stressed. "Hermeneutical Trialectic" is therefore useful for negotiating *Spirit–Word–Community*. Oliverio, "Interpretive Review Essay," 302, 310. See also, Oliverio, *Theological Hermeneutics*, 232–42.

392. Yong, *Spirit–Word–Community*, 9 (see 7–14 for further discussion; correspondingly, Yong, "Hermeneutical Trialectic," 26–28).

393. Yong, *Spirit–Word–Community*, 9 (see 7–14 for further discussion; correspondingly, Yong, "Hermeneutical Trialectic," 26–28).

sequential implications of the *filioque*,"[394] and his recognition of the Spirit as the bond of love between the Father and the Son, which led him to the Spirit as the natural interpretive starting point.[395] He presented the Spirit as the reconciler and mediator,[396] and overall "bringer-into-relationship," stating:

> Insofar as the Spirit is the bond of love between the Father and the Son and the one who reconciles each one of us to the other through Jesus, she is also the one who mediates between or brings into relationship the particularities of being. To that extent, then, our hermeneutical situation is always pneumatological and communal (and thereby Trinitarian).[397]

Yong further asserted that pneumatic interpretation can be Spirit-driven but not Spirit-centered for that position belongs simultaneously to the Spirit, the Father, and the Son. Reflecting on his approach he explained, "I was beginning to sense that a properly Pentecostal hermeneutic and theological method could and would indeed be pneumatically driven, but that such a pneumatological starting point should not lapse into a mere pneumatocentricism but ought to be both Christomorphic and patromorphic [*sic*] at the same time."[398] However, whilst, with this work, Yong recognized that an interpretive approach with a pneumatic starting point necessarily requires attention to both Spirit–Son and Spirit–Father relationships, he also did not overly attend to the Father's role. This is probably because, as is also the case here, he kept the focus pneumatic-trinitiarian, always discussing the Father with the Spirit and the Son. Nevertheless, if, as I have been suggesting, the Spirit–Father relationship has not been historically attended to in the same manner as the Spirit–Son relationship, then there is a clear case for seeking to rebalance this neglect within the pneumatic-trinitarian interpretive focus. For example, whilst agreeing with Yong that Western

394. Yong, *Spirit–Word–Community*, 17–18.

395. Yong, "Hermeneutical Trialectic," 27. Cf. Grenz discussing the Spirit as "the love between the Father and the Son" and "the Completer of [the triune] God's work in the world," and leading into consideration of pneumatic interpretation. Grenz, *Created for Community*, 161, 163 respectively (emphasis removed, 160–4 for discussion).

396. Cartledge's understanding of mediation is helpful here: "Mediation can be defined as the action whereby two distinct elements are brought together by an intermediary or third party. The term 'mediation' is often used when two estranged parties are brought back into a *reconciled relationship*. The person who facilitates such *reconciliation* is often called a 'mediator' or 'go-between.'" Cartledge, *Mediation of the Spirit*, 64 (emphasis added). See *Mediation of the Spirit*, 60–87 for discussion of pneumatic mediation engaging with renewal scholars and focusing on experience.

397. Yong, "Hermeneutical Trialectic," 27.

398. Yong, "Hermeneutical Trialectic," 27. Cf. Grenz, "Spirit and the Word," 365 (see 4.2.3). Noting that Yong's use of "Pentecostal" here is essentially "pneumatic."

theology has too often relegated the Spirit as an afterthought behind the Father and the Son, Western theology has also relegated *the Father* behind the Spirit and the Son. This patrological relegation has had, and does have clear hermeneutical implications for our understanding of pneumatic interpretation and interpretation of scripture more generally. My feeling is that these implications can at least partly be traced to the addition of the *filioque* clause to the Nicene Creed. With Moltmann, "the far-reaching decision in favour of the *filioque*," has led to an emphasis on the Spirit as the Spirit of the Son at the expense of attention to the Spirit as the Spirit of the Father, focusing on the redemptive aspects of the Spirit's work over the creational.[399] Space and remit limits the extent to which hermeneutical implications resulting from the *filioque* are explored here, but this is an area ripe for research. Theologians have considered—albeit not overly so—implications of the *filioque* on pneumatology in the renewal tradition,[400] including, notably, William Atkinson stressing neglect of the Father.[401] However, research for this work found no one who has recognized and begun to consider the implications of the *filioque* to understanding the Spirit's role in the interpretation of scripture.[402]

399. Moltmann, *Spirit of Life* (f.pub. 1991), 8. See 3.2.3.

400. See discussion in 3.2.3 in relation to Moltmann and Vanhoozer). Also Kärkkäinen and Ervin. Kärkkäinen stated, "If Pentecostals have paid little attention to the doctrine of the Trinity, the issue of *filioque* ('and the Son') has received even less attention. Nevertheless, many of the underlying issues at stake in the historic controversy over the *filioque* question have been of great interest to Pentecostals, even though most Pentecostals have yet to realize that fact." Kärkkäinen, "Trinity as Communion in the Spirit" (pub. 2002), 104 (104–8 for discussion). Ervin asserted that Pentecostals were largely ambivalent and inconsistent in their treatment of the *filioque* and recognition of its influence on pneumatology. Ervin, "Koinonia" (pub. 1987), 2–13. For more recent efforts addressing the implications of the *filioque* on pneumatology, see Atkinson, *Trinity After Pentecost* (pub. 2013), 127–30 and surrounding discussion (cf. fn. 401); Studebaker, *Pentecost to the Triune God* (pub. 2012), 118–20 and surrounding discussion; Vondey, *Beyond Pentecostalism* (pub. 2010) 87–88 and preceding discussion.

401. Atkinson explained, "The *filioque* clause is commonly regarded as problematic in that it relegates the Spirit in relation to the Son. . . . However, this is not its only problem. It also relegates the Father, so that the Father and the Son seem to be two equals in the procession of the Spirit, both equally primary as causes of the Spirit's existence and activity. This does not do justice to the biblical testimony, repeated often and in multiple ways, that the *Father alone* is the fount of all." Atkinson, *Trinity After Pentecost*, 127–28 (emphasis original). Also Smail, who critically engaged with the charismatic renewal (in 1980) as an active participant, and suggested that the movement "needs to know the Father." Smail, *Forgotten Father*, 13.

402. Moltmann has come closest. His thoughts on the *filioque* were also external to pneumatic interpretation, but I related them by engaging these insights with his "Trinitarian Hermeneutics of 'Holy Scripture.'" See 3.2.3.

Yong's pneumatic-trinitarian focus is helpful in drawing out on an important communal aspect vital to this developing understanding of pneumatic interpretation. Following Yong's perspective but relating it more directly to scripture; because pneumatic interpretation is always pneumatic-trinitarian, the Spirit, through scripture, works in ways that are also always communal. Effectively, the Spirit, through scripture, and as the bond of love between the Father and the Son, reconciles and mediates, working as a "bringer into relationship." Helpful to this communal understanding of pneumatic interpretation are Mark Cartledge's insights on pneumatic engagement with liturgy. Drawing on thoughts from Jeremy Fletcher and Christopher Cocksworth, Cartledge highlighted that the Spirit's language is one of love, involving relationship and words of love. Cartledge explained that this is evident within the triune relationship, in our relationship with the triune God, and in relationships with those around us. In all three interrelated situations, the Spirit leads in a language of love involving relationship and words.[403] Appropriating Cartledge's liturgical discussion to scripture further emphasizes that through scripture, the Spirit draws us into communal relationship with God as Father, Son, and Spirit, *and* each other. To pneumatically experience God *is* to experience relationship with God. Therefore, through the Spirit we have relationship with God as Father, Son, *and* Spirit, and this leads into our relationships with those around us.[404] Pneumatic interpretation therefore involves relationship with the triune God, *and* those in our community frameworks, *through* the written words of scripture.

These insights strengthen the perspective that seeking understanding of the Spirit's role in the interpretation of scripture requires attention on the Spirit's relationship with the Father as well as the Spirit's relationship with the Son. The Spirit–Father relationship deserves increased attention by renewal theologians. Pneumatic interpretation cannot help but be pneumatological, patrological and christological, and the Spirit–Father and Spirit–Son relationships contain particular, yet also mutual, theological implications (for example, creative and redemptive aspects, see 3.2 and 3.2.4). Additionally, the Spirit carries attributes particular to the Spirit, and yet also mutual with the Father and the Son,[405] reconciling and mediating, and bringing us into relationship with God as Father, Son, and Spirit, and with those around us.

403. Cartledge, "New *Via Media*" (pub. 2000), 277, citing Fletcher and Cocksworth, "Language of Love," 6. Cf. fn. 273 (Fletcher and Cocksworth); 1.6.1 (liturgical interpretation).

404. Cf. McDonnell, "Determinative Doctrine of the Holy Spirit," 150, stressing that when we experience God we experience first the Spirit, not the Father or the Son.

405. At this point in this analysis I acknowledge Richard Rohr (with Mike Morrell)'s

4.2.3 The Spirit creates (Stanley Grenz)

Like Moltmann (see 3.2.3), Stanley Grenz highlighted the creational nature of the Spirit's communication. Grenz suggested that as scripture is engaged with, "the Spirit addresses us" personally, and in this communication, "*the Spirit creates 'world.*'"[406] Grenz explained, "the world the Spirit creates is not simply the world surrounding the ancient text itself. . . . It is the eschatological world God intends for creation as disclosed in the text," continuing, "the Spirit's world-creating act does not arise out of nowhere, . . . it emerges directly out of the Spirit's own particular role within God's creative activity."[407] Following Grenz's perspective highlights that as the Spirit uses scripture as an instrument for personal communication, the Spirit creates eschatologically, according with God's creational purposes.[408] Grenz explicated further, suggesting that what the Spirit creates as scripture is engaged with, is new created life centered on Christ:

> The constructing of a world through the biblical text is ultimately the act of the Spirit. The world that the Spirit creates is nothing less than a new creation centered in Jesus Christ (2 Cor. 5:17). And this world consists of a new community comprised of renewed persons.[409]

Consequently, for Grenz, as the Spirit communicates scriptural truth personally, the Spirit creates and redeems in ways centered on Christ,[410] and

---

caution: "Sometimes, people try to over-define the Trinity. "*This* is the work of the Father," they say, confidently. "*This* is the role of the Son. And *this* is what the Spirit looks like." In attempting to parse out and diagram the persons of the Trinity, something is lost: the space between them. The inner life of the Godhead—this is a mystery that stretches language to its breaking point. The specific functions or roles of each person can be interesting to ponder, but frankly I don't think this is the important point. . . . The all-important thing is to get the *energy* and *quality* of the relationship between these Three—that's the essential mystery that transforms us. Finally, it's something you can experience only by resting inside of the relationships (prayer?), as when the disciples asked Jesus where he lived, and he offered this intimate invite: '*Come and see.*'" Rohr with Morrell, *Divine Dance*, 91 (emphasis original, referencing John 1:39).

406. Grenz, "Spirit and the Word," (pub. 2000), 362 (emphasis original). Also, *Grenz, Renewing the Center* (pub. 2000), 210; Grenz, *Created for Community*, 264; Becker, "Tenet," 47–48. *Created for Community* was published in 1999 (2nd ed., f.pub. 1996) but is included here to show Grenz's thought. Similarly, Moltmann, (chapter 3), Levison (chapter 5).

407. Grenz, "Spirit and the Word," 364.

408. Grenz, "Spirit and the Word," 365.

409. Grenz, "Spirit and the Word," 365.

410. Cf. Yong, "Hermeneutical Trialectic," 27, pneumatic interpretation is centered on the triune God. See 4.2.2 (Yong). Grenz's work suggests influence of Barth, *Holy*

this manifests as new communities comprised of redeemed and reconciled people. Furthermore, and complementing the pneumatic-trinitarian, communal emphasis drawn out in 4.2.2, this pneumatic interpretation will always be simultaneously personal and communal, creating, reconciling, and redeeming, and bringing eschatological new life and identity in accordance with God's purposes.[411]

Similarly to Macchia (see 4.2.1), although Grenz discussed the Father and the triune relationship surrounding his consideration of pneumatic interpretation,[412] he largely did not actively incorporate this *within* his discussions[413] where he concentrated on the Spirit–Son relationship. This is probably because Grenz placed the creational emphasis through John 1:

> Just as God created the world "in the beginning" through the act of speaking the Word, so also God creates "world" in the present by the Spirit speaking through Scripture. And what the

---

Spirit and the Christian Life, which has three chapters: the Holy Spirit as creator, reconciler, and redeemer respectively (cf. 1.6.1 (pneumatic ethics). Grenz used "renew," but continuing this work's emphasis, I use "redeem."

411. Grenz, "Spirit and the Word," 365–68. Critiquing Grenz's article, Vanhoozer was cautious of Grenz's claim that the Spirit creates life through engagement with scripture but admired Grenz's "overall vision that the Spirit leads people to reconceive their identities and world-view by means of the interpretive framework found *in* Scripture that recounts the eschatological event of Jesus Christ." Grenz used speech-act theory in his discussion and Vanhoozer disagreed with Grenz's application of locutions, illocutions, and perlocutions, suggesting that Grenz confused illocutions with perlocutions. Grenz, "Spirit and the Word," 361–64; Vanhoozer, "Speech Acts to Scripture Acts," 40–43 (42 [emphasis original]) (15–44 for speech-act theory and interpretation). For speech-act theory, see fn. 242.

412. E.g., consider this statement from Grenz, written outside the context of pneumatic interpretation: "The loving Father willingly created the world. And the Son willingly acted on behalf of the Father to make salvation available to fallen humans. But the divine work is not yet complete. *We* must be brought to share in the salvation the Father has planned and the Son has purchased. This is the task of the Spirit. Because he is the Spirit of the divine Father–Son relationship, the Spirit enters the world to complete the divine plan. The Spirit's goal is to bring us to share in the fellowship the Son enjoys with the Father." Grenz, *Created for Community*, 164 (emphasis original) within surrounding discussion 160–64 ("The Spirit and the Trinitarian Life").

413. E.g., consider this statement from Grenz, written the context of pneumatic interpretation: "As the Third Person of the Trinity sent into the world, the Spirit's mission is to complete the program of the Triune God. To this end, the Spirit is both the source of life and the power that renews life. . . . Central to the work of the Spirit in this enterprise is the Bible. By means of Scripture the Spirit bears witness to Jesus Christ, guides the lives of believers, and leads the people of God." Grenz, *Created for Community*, 164–65 within surrounding discussion 164–76 ("The Spirit and the Scriptures"). This is the only reference to the triune relationship within Grenz's consideration of pneumatic interpretation in *Created for Community*, *Renewing the Center*, or "Spirit and the Word."

> Spirit now constructs is a world centered in Jesus who is the one through whom all things find their connectedness (Col. 1:17). Through appropriating the Word written, therefore—that is, by means of the biblical text—the Spirit creates a world centered on Jesus Christ who is the Word disclosed.[414]

Showing his influence from reformed theology (see 4.2.1), and, arguably, his own hermeneutical leanings resulting from the *filioque*,[415] Grenz footnoted these ideas as a development of Barth's thought. However, by emphasizing the creational nature of pneumatic interpretation, and following his own thought, Grenz *did* point to the Spirit–Father relationship.[416]

4.2.4 The Spirit appropriates (Stanley Grenz, Clark Pinnock, Andrew Davies, and Scott Ellington, with Gordon Fee)

In chapter 2, scholars were all shown to acknowledge a relationship between the original content and surrounding framework presented in scripture and the Spirit's appropriation of scripture to contemporary situations. Some only recognized this *within* the historico-grammatical data presented in scripture whilst others began to explore how the Spirit might speak personally to situations *outside* those presented in scripture (see 2.1.2 and 2.5). Engaging with Hans Urs von Balthasar brought a perspective of pneumatic appropriation based around the nature of Christ, as he asserted that because all wisdom and knowledge is hidden in Christ, pneumatic truth—understood as the Spirit's (self)-interpretation of the triune God to us—is infinite and translatable through the ages (2.3.1 and 2.5).

These considerations led into discussions in chapter 3 such as the Spirit reaching through and beyond scripture, effecting and appropriating scriptural truth holistically in our lives (3.2.2), incorporating postmodernist methods of interpretation with historico-grammaticism (3.4.2 and 3.4.3), approaching interpretation by understanding Spirit, scripture, and community dynamically interrelating with each other (3.4.4), and questioning whether prophecy is an aspect of pneumatic interpretation and appropriation (3.4.5).

414. Grenz, "Spirit and the Word," 365. For creational emphasis external to pneumatic interpretation, considering each triune role, see Grenz, *Theology for the Community of God*, 375–78 (Father as the ultimate creator, Son as the intermediate agent of creation, and Spirit as the dynamic by whom God brings creation into existence [378]).

415. For the *filioque*, see Grenz, *Theology for the Community of God*, 62–65, 69–70, and 372 (voicing support).

416. Cf. fns. 412–3 (Grenz's trinitarian thought).

In this chapter, the caution was repeated (see 3.4.6, 3.4.1, and 4.1, 4.1.5), that overly focusing on frameworks for interpretation can, and has, inadvertently diverted attention away from the Spirit and into analysis of interpretive techniques and concepts. However, these explorations are also necessary to discerning the Spirit's relationship with scripture so this section considers contributions from Fee, Grenz, Pinnock, Davies, and Ellington to develop understanding of pneumatic appropriation.[417]

Arguing for a closer link between exegesis and Spirituality,[418] Gordon Fee detailed "an ongoing encounter with the living God—Father, Son, and Holy Spirit," throughout writing on his Philippians commentary. This encounter happened in two separate but interrelated ways. Firstly, Fee regularly became so affectively "overcome" as he exegeted the text "so as to articulate its meaning for the sake of others in the church" that he was "brought to tears, to joy, to prayer, or the praise." Secondly, he found that the Sunday sermons, liturgy, or sung worship at churches he visited during this time were always directly associated with the text he had been exegeting that week.[419] Fee stated, "It was as though the Lord was letting me hear the message played back in liturgical and homiletical settings that made

417. Other explorations included, Waddell, integrating intertextuality in the book of Revelation with the role of the Spirit and the role of the reader. Waddell, *Spirit of the Book of Revelation* (pub. 2006), chapters 2 and 3. Waddell sought "to delineate an interpretation of the role of the Spirit which integrates the text of Revelation, allusions within the text, and [his] own religious context of Pentecostalism" (4). He employed an intertextual approach because of its dual foci, being concerned with the effect of earlier texts upon later texts, explaining, "The interpreter must read in two directions. Not only does the old affect the new but the new affects the way in which one reads the old. In the intertextual approach, then, the reader also plays a significant part in the process of understanding" (3). Cf. fn. 350 (Waddell's pneumatic focus). Also, Allen, "'Forgotten Spirit,'" 51–66, analyzing the Spirit's eschatological readdressing of scripture, and the Spirit speaking directly in the book of Hebrews.

418. Fee, "Exegesis and Spirituality," 3–15. Fee referred to spirituality with a capital "S" based on his exegesis of the *pneuma* word group (5). Expounding this in "Some Reflections on Pauline Spirituality," 33–47—these two chapters are part of Fee, *Listening to the Spirit in the Text* (pub. 2000)—Fee explained that *pneumatikos* was "almost exclusively a Pauline word in the New Testament" (34, fn. 2), and translation should be an upper case Spirituality, reflecting Paul's primary use of *pneumatikos* as an adjective for the Spirit (34, cf. 37). He asserted that 1 Corinthians 2:6—3:1 was the central passage in the Pauline corpus to understand this, highlighting Paul's juxtaposing of the *pneumatikoi* ("Spirit people") with *psychikos* ("the person who is merely human, without the Spirit of God") (35, 36 respectively). Fee suggested that the adverb *pneumatikōs* (used in 1 Cor 2:14), instead of being translated "spiritually discerned," is better translated "discerned by means of the Spirit" (34, fn. 2). Essentially, Fee asserted that in 1 Corinthians 2:6—3:1, Paul talked *explicitly* of pneumatic discernment.

419. Fee, "Exegesis and Spirituality," 3.

me pause yet one more time and 'hear' it in new ways."[420] Fee considered what happened to him so significant that he recounted it in the preface to his commentary,[421] and wrote "Exegesis and Spirituality" through his experience.[422] Aligning with the emphasis here of the centrality of intimate relationship with God through pneumatic encounter to pneumatic interpretation, and no doubt writing from his own experience, Fee reasoned, "The first place that exegesis and Spirituality interface is the exegete's own soul—that the aim of exegesis is Spirituality, which must be what the exegete brings to the exegetical task, as well as being the ultimate aim of the task itself."[423]

Fee experienced pneumatic appropriation. He encountered the triune God through pneumatic encounter, receiving the message he was endeavoring to interpret and communicate in his personal, contemporary situations, in ways that helped him to interpret and communicate Philippians. His illustration *did not*, however, address the Spirit's communication to personal situations beyond those which are presented in scripture, This is perhaps unsurprising as Fee was producing an exegetical commentary, but he also did not address this in "Exegesis and Spirituality."[424] Grenz and Pinnock, however, *did* address this, similarly asserting that the Spirit appropriates scripture personally in ways reaching *beyond* but always cohering *with* the relevant scriptural passage in its original historical location. Grenz stated that this act of communication "parallels in certain respects that of the ancient community; nevertheless it is unique."[425] Pinnock, meanwhile, continued to describe this (see 3.2.2) as the Spirit fusing past and present horizons, opening scripture up with "'controlled liberty'" in ways honoring both the original meaning and the words needing to be opened up.[426]

420. Fee, "Exegesis and Spirituality," 4.

421. Fee, *Paul's Letter to the Philippians*, xiii–xiv, restated in Fee, "Exegesis and Spirituality," 4.

422. Fee, "Exegesis and Spirituality," 4.

423. Fee, "Exegesis and Spirituality," 7.

424. Elsewhere, Fee stated that the Spirit can use the language of scripture to speak personally in ways "out of their original context," but argued that "the help and power in this case comes from the Spirit speaking prophetically, not from the meaning of Scripture itself." Fee, "Why Pentecostals Read Their Bibles Poorly," 8, and fn. 1. Here, I differ, arguing that the Spirit speaks *through*, and *uses*, the words of scripture *and* their original surrounding historical framework. Cf. fn. 123 (charismatic exegesis and *sensus plenior*); 3.4.5 ("pneumatic" interpretation in early Judaism and the role of prophecy).

425. Grenz, "Spirit and the Word," 362.

426. Pinnock, "Work of the Spirit" (pub. 2009), 165. Also, Pinnock with Callen, *Scripture Principle*, 239.

Grenz and Pinnock both stressed that understanding the framework surrounding the scriptural text in its original historical location was an important aspect of discerning the Spirit's appropriation of scripture to personal and contemporary situations external to those presented in scripture,[427] and Grenz underlined that the Spirit always communicates within and through a surrounding historical and cultural framework.[428] A counter argument here is that not all who read scripture are academically trained and approaches that emphasize the historical context are therefore exclusive.[429] However, understanding that scripture was written, and is interpreted within surrounding contexts does not necessarily require academic training. Pneumatic appropriation is expounded here partly because of its translatability: although deepening in knowledge of the historical context can enrich understanding, the *essence* is also easily communicable to those less academically equipped. This is to say that we engage in intimate relationship with the triune God from our life contexts, and we also read scripture understanding that surrounding the stories, poetry, letters (and so forth) were particular situations, some easily identifiable and some requiring more effort to understand. Through these stories, poetry, and letters and their surrounding situations, the triune God, through the Spirit, speaks to us personally in and through our own life contexts. This enriches our understanding of scripture, of our situations, of ourselves, and, most importantly, deepens our relationship with God.

To help understand the Spirit's communication within and through a surrounding historical and cultural framework, Grenz suggested viewing scripture as "a paradigmatic event," a historical occurrence that captures our imagination and shapes ongoing life experience. He posited that as the Spirit interprets scripture to us, the memory of the relevant scriptural passage is preserved but reinterpreted (that is to say, *appropriated*) in light of our personal and contemporary situations.[430] Grenz further stated:

> This goal of the Spirit in appropriating the text is not reached with the mere recounting of the biblical story. Instead, as the narrative is retold (or reread), the Spirit transports the contemporary hearers (or readers) into the text. Or, stated in the opposite manner, the Spirit recreates the past as narrated by the

427. Pinnock, "Work of the Spirit," 165–67. Also, Grenz, "Spirit and the Word," 362, 366–67.

428. *Grenz, Renewing the Center,* 209–10.

429. E.g., Cheryl Bridges Johns, "Meeting God in the Margins," 20.

430. Grenz, "Spirit and the Word," 366. On paradigmatic events, see Coleman, *Issues of Theological Conflict*, 109–10.

text within the present life of the community, both individually and corporately.[431]

Davies also aligned, calling this aspect of pneumatic interpretation "*redeployable revelation*—in other words, the expectation that God the Spirit can and will use his Word to speak beyond its original significance into any location, context or heart of his choosing."[432] Rather than discussing the written words and their original historical location, Davies addressed "the entire testimony of the seamless robe of scripture."[433] He explained that scriptural interpretation involved not just discernment "of the surface of the text alone" but also "seek[ing] to allow the Spirit to speak to us from beneath the words."[434] Here Pinnock concurred, writing that scripture "can come to 'mean more' than was originally intended, achieving a 'fuller sense and a deeper meaning,' intended by God, but not clearly expressed by a human author."[435] Davies reasoned that beneath the written words lies a deeper sense with "a quintessential moral core," and interpretations claiming to be pneumatic will always cohere with this testimony.[436] In Davies's understanding therefore, the Spirit appropriates scripture *and* the testimony beneath the words to personal lives and situations, and this pneumatic interpretation has ethical import.

Discussing a Pentecostal approach to interpretation, Scott Ellington suggested that historico-critical[437] and postmodern approaches were both

431. Grenz, "Spirit and the Word," 367. Similarly, Pinnock, "Work of the Spirit," 166.

432. Davies, "Reading in the Spirit" (pub. 2009), 304 (emphasis added). This was within discussion of pneumatic interpretation and how approaches from Pentecostal scholars might help with interpreting and appropriating some of the more ethically challenging parts of the Old Testament. Davies noted Thomas's article in the same issue of *Journal of Beliefs & Values*, which gave a history of Pentecostal hermeneutics and highlighted contributions from Sheppard, Ervin, McLean, Spittler, Moore, McKay, Thomas, McQueen, Archer, Waddell, and Lee Roy Martin (all noted in this work). Thomas, "Where the Spirit Leads," 289–302.

433. Davies, "Reading in the Spirit," 308.

434. Davies, "Reading in the Spirit," 308.

435. Pinnock, "Work of the Spirit," 166. Pinnock was probably thinking of *sensus plenior* (see fn. 123). Grenz's thought, presented here, and in 4.2.3 suggests that he also would not have disagreed. Also Minto, discussing partnership between the Spirit and the interpreter, leading to an opening up of "living faith-knowledge of the very spiritual paschal realities of which the text speaks," namely "knowledge of the mystery of the Trinity [which] is a share in God's knowledge of himself and his plan." Minto, "Charismatic Renewal and the Spiritual Sense of Scripture," 262–63.

436. Davies, "Reading in the Spirit," 308.

437. Pentecostal scholars tend to refer to historical criticism over historical grammaticism, but there are differences, with historical grammaticism being less rigid. For further, see Keener, "Refining *Spirit Hermeneutics*" (pub. 2017), 214–19, discussing

valuable but insufficient,[438] and advocated an alternative approach that he entitled, "Testimony as a Model for Appropriating Biblical Truth."[439] Ellington suggested that contained within scripture are testimonies that speak of "who God is and how God characteristically acts."[440] In Ellington's view, these testimonies can be appropriated *by us* to our own lives in light of fresh contextual experiences. The concern here, however, is with *the Spirit's role* in this appropriation. It is *the Spirit*, working in, through, and with the interpreter, their context, and the passage of scripture and its context, bringing the insight. Ellington's attention to the Spirit was at best implicit, focusing more on our role as interpreters or on the role of scripture. This was probably because his focus was the Pentecostal community and he engaged with postmodernist considerations that tended to emphasize interaction between the "text" and the interpreter at the neglect of the Spirit (compare 1.5; 3.4.1; 3.4.2; and 4.1). Perhaps also, quite simply, the Spirit's role was just not his main concern. Nevertheless, Ellington's insights are valuable. In particular they help strengthen an idea that through scripture, the Spirit works with our imaginations evoking truths present in relevant scriptural passages that show us God's character and action.[441] This interpretation and appropriation, as has been continually emphasized (compare, for example, 3.2.3), is holistic, and triune.

Following Grenz, and Pinnock, and incorporating Fee's personal illustration, develops understanding that in seeking the Spirit's leading in interpretation, we can be pneumatically "transported" into the scriptural text and its surrounding historical framework, and through it into our own personal and contemporary situations (or vice-versa), which will always cohere in some way with those scriptural passage(s) and their surrounding frameworks. Davies's contribution emphasized that beneath the words is

---

historical criticism as supposed to historical context (214–15), paying attention to the literary context (215–17), and the importance of the historical background and cultural context (217–19).

438. Ellington, "History, Story, and Testimony" (pub. 2001) 261–62. Ellington also engaged with the 1993 and 1994 *Pneuma* essays and surrounding discussion (249–53) (see 3.4.2 and 3.4.3).

439. Ellington, "History, Story, and Testimony," 255–57 (255).

440. Ellington, "History, Story, and Testimony," 256, acknowledging Brueggemann, *Theology of the Old Testament*, 117–20.

441. Cf. Ellington, "History, Story, and Testimony," 258–59. Within his discussion Ellington highlighted that treating scripture as story was helpful to understanding appropriation (253–55). He later expanded on this, using the Psalms and discussing the biblical theme of remembrance continuing a story and viewing the past "as a living narrative that is constantly reaching forward and being integrated with new experiences." Ellington, "Reciprocal Reshaping of History and Experience" (pub. 2007), 18–31 (24).

an ethical dimension that the Spirit also, and perhaps most importantly, interprets to us, whilst engaging with Ellington strengthens understanding that through the written words, the Spirit works with our imaginations and our current contextual experiences, showing us "who God is and how God characteristically acts." In this pneumatic appropriation, understanding of God's character and action, of ourselves, our situations, and the scriptural passages informing this dynamically unfolds as we journey through our life and surrounding situations.[442] In this process, the Spirit works eschatologically, creating, reconciling, and redeeming simultaneously in our lives and in the lives of those around us (whilst also noting ongoing consideration of pneumatic hindrance, discussed further in 4.3), in accordance with the triune God's creational, reconciliational, and redemptive purposes.

4.2.5 Evaluation

The Spirit communicates through scripture in ways that lead into relational knowledge of God as Father, Son, and Spirit, but scholars such as Macchia and Grenz concentrated on the Spirit–Son relationship and did not address the Father or the triune nature of pneumatic interpretation. Engagement with those considering pneumatic interpretation should be approached with this awareness. The Western addition of the *filioque* clause to the Nicene Creed is a factor here and Yong followed Moltmann (see 3.2.2) in highlighting its influence. Yong used the *filioque* to stress that the Spirit's role in interpretation had traditionally, and especially in Western Christianity, been subordinated to approaches beginning with the Son. Whilst agreeing with Yong, this work continues to emphasize, aligning with Moltmann (and Atkinson, external to pneumatic interpretation), that the Father's role has also been neglected, and this patrological relegation can also be traced to the *filioque*.

As the Spirit–Father relationship has not been historically attended to in the same way as the Spirit–Son relationship, there is a clear case for seeking to rebalance this when considering pneumatic interpretation. With Yong, a pneumatic starting point for interpretation cannot centralize the Spirit and should naturally lead into consideration of the Spirit, the Father, and the Son, and their respectively particular, yet also mutual, roles.

Engaging with Yong has helped to identify the Spirit as the reconciler and mediator, and overall "bringer-into-relationship" (again noting that

442. Pinnock, "Work of the Spirit," 166–67, repeating Karl Rahner's analogy of falling in love, and again not discussing that Rahner's original discussion involved unfolding understanding of self as well as of dogma (see 3.3.3).

these attributes are, at the same time, particular to the Spirit, and yet also mutual with the Father and Son). Including Cartledge's liturgical discussion helped to highlight that through scripture, the Spirit reconciles and mediates, drawing us into relationship with God as Father, Son, and Spirit, *and* with those around us. Grenz's contribution added to this, presenting pneumatic interpretation as simultaneously personal and communal, creating, reconciling, and redeeming in our lives and in our relationships with those around us. This builds on chapter 3 where the personal aspect of pneumatic interpretation with the creational (Spirit–Father) and redemptive (Spirit–Son) aspects were emphasized (see 3.5).

Fee's personal illustration is a valuable account showing how some of this can practically manifest. His experience was simultaneously personal and communal as he was pneumatically drawn into a profound and ongoing affective, ethical, and cognitive relational encounter with the triune God that impacted him *personally*, and *simultaneously* helped him to interpret and communicate Philippians "*for the sake of others in the church*."[443] Using Grenz's description, the Spirit "transported" him into the Philippians' text and surrounding historical framework, and he heard the scriptures he was trying to communicate, pneumatically appropriated to him in the sermons, liturgy, or sung worship of churches he visited over the period he wrote his commentary, undoubtedly helping him identify what he felt needed communicating, but perhaps more importantly, transforming him personally.

4.3 INTIMATE RELATIONSHIP WITH GOD: AFFECTIVE, ETHICAL, AND COGNITIVE II

Considering the Spirit's appropriation to personal and contemporary situations beyond those presented in scripture, Davies cautioned that a problem is discerning whether our appropriations *are* pneumatic. He gave three guiding tools: 1) they will always cohere with the testimony of scripture (see 4.2.4);[444] 2) they will also always resonate with others in our community frameworks;[445] and 3) there will be an internal resonance of some kind

443. Fee, "Exegesis and Spirituality," 3 (emphasis added to stress the ethical component).

444. Davies, "Reading in the Spirit" (pub. 2009), 308. See 4.2.4.

445. "For my reading of the text to be more than just empty sophistry, it needs to find a home in hearts and minds beyond my own. The Spirit-inspired message needs to resonate in a Spirit-filled community." Davies, "Reading in the Spirit," 309. Cf. 3.4.4 (Thomas). Also, Lee Roy Martin, *Unheard Voice of God*, 53, 73.

regarding their personal significance.[446] Aligning with his first point, Davies noted that the Spirit interprets scripture to us in ways that always create opportunity for, but never compel ethical action.[447] These insights highlight that providing opportunity for ethical choice and action is a hallmark of the Spirit's interpretation of and through scripture. Furthermore, this leads back into appreciation that pneumatic interpretation is simultaneously personal and communal for ethical action always impacts those around us.

Tools such as those given by Davies[448] help guide in discerning whether our appropriations *might be* pneumatic, but can sensitivity to the Spirit be increased prior to this, thereby increasing possibility that our discernment and interpretation *will be* pneumatic? The solution offered here, lies with centralizing and prioritizing intimacy with the triune God through whom pneumatic discernment and interpretation comes. Interpreting and appropriating scripture pneumatically involves intimate relationship with God,[449] and affect, ethics, and cognition are three interrelating aspects of this relationship. In this section, thought from scholars, whose focus was varying aspects interrelating pneumatic interpretation with personal relationship with God, is recognized and developed. It therefore continues and builds on themes presented in 3.3. A further theme surfacing in this section is recognizing and incorporating the personal nature of the Spirit's communication within academic work. Consequently, this section also continues to discuss the Spirit's appropriation of scriptural truth to personal, and simultaneously communal, situations considered in 4.2.4.

4.3.1 Intimacy with God (Clark Pinnock, Rickie Moore, and Emerson Powery)

Pinnock suggested that considering Jesus's hermeneutical practices could help understand the Spirit's communication of scripture to personal and contemporary situations, and he highlighted that they were similar to those practiced in early Judaism and particularly at Qumran, where the community practiced divine appropriation of texts (discussed in connection with

446. "If it 'catches' in me and makes sense to me, then I can in some measure ascribe a sense of inspiration to my reading." Davies, "Reading in the Spirit," 309.

447. Davies, "Reading in the Spirit," 309.

448. Cf. Pink's four guiding tools in 2.1.1.

449. Discussion surrounding the Spirit communicating to and through non-Christians lies beyond the remits of this analysis, but I would argue that the Spirit's seeking to draw a person into relationship with the triune God is a hallmark of the Spirit's work regardless of how cognizant a person is of this.

David Aune in 3.4.5 and also in 5.3.3 with Archie Wright).[450] Emphasizing that Jesus wanted his followers to know scripture but *also* to be able to interpret the present time (Luke 12:54–57),[451] Pinnock argued that Jesus recognized a degree of historical relativity and employed a dynamic and pneumatic approach, understanding that scripture opens up and functions as the word of God in new, fresh ways.[452]

Using Jesus' interpretive practices as a contemporary model for pneumatic interpretation and appropriation raises two vital aspects. Firstly, Jesus's intimacy with the Father seems integral. As Pinnock wrote, "In the synoptic gospels, Jesus experienced the Spirit and was conscious of being the beloved Son of God. His intimate relationship with the Father was revealed in his 'Abba' prayers which were unlike anything in Judaism."[453] Pinnock highlighted that Jesus sometimes appeared to take liberties with scripture, or present scripture in a new light, but "he did it because he knew the will of God in this matter and at this time," emphasizing, "Jesus blended the original word of Scripture with its current significance for his hearers. It was his familiar practice."[454] Pinnock illustrated these aspects of Jesus's interpretive practices through Jesus's appropriation of Isaiah 61:1–2 in Luke 4:18–19, omitting Isaiah 61:2b—"the day of vengeance of our God"[455]—and through Jesus's opening up scripture to the two disciples on the road to Emmaus in Luke 24:13–32, enabling fresh recognition of Jesus and scriptural understanding. Whilst there is no reference to the Spirit in Luke 24, Pinnock argued generally that the wider context of Luke showed Jesus being pneumatically open and led.[456] The second vital aspect to recognize when using Jesus's interpretive practices as a contemporary model for pneumatic interpretation and appropriation is that Jesus was without sin (Heb 4:15), and in this respect his intimacy with the Father was unique.

450. Pinnock, "Work of the Spirit" (pub. 2009), 158–60.

451. Pinnock, "Work of the Spirit," 160–61.

452. Pinnock, "Work of the Spirit," 160–61. On Jesus's appropriation of scripture, see Keener, *Spirit Hermeneutics* (pub. 2016), 211–13.

453. Pinnock, "Work of the Spirit," 161.

454. Pinnock, "Work of the Spirit," 159–62 (159).

455. Pinnock, "Work of the Spirit," 159. For use of the Old Testament in the New Testament, see 1.6.1.

456. Pinnock, "Work of the Spirit," 162. Also on Luke 24:13–32, Richard Hays (without referencing the Spirit), presented the resurrected Jesus as the hermeneutical key through whom scripture is understood. "Reading Scripture in Light of the Resurrection," 229–38. Cf. Crinisor, "Paraclete and Prophecy," 276; and Pinnock with Callen, *Scripture Principle*, 195, each discussing the Spirit making known truths and insights previously hidden.

Similarly to Pinnock, Moore, using God's contrast between Job and his friends in Job 42:7, argued that Job's ability to speak the truth about God was related to his prayerfulness and time spent communing with God. Moore found this exploration of Job and his friends helpful to his own journey of learning to integrate his scholarship with his spirituality.[457]

Emerson Powery alluded to the relational nature of pneumatic interpretation when he argued that "according to the Gospel of Mark, one cannot know or understand the meaning (or narrative function) of the scriptural text without the proper engagement with or endowment by the Spirit."[458] Powery suggested that Mark 12:18–27, 35–37 firstly, presents the Spirit as the source of revelation and inspiration, and secondly, juxtaposes the Sadducees' failure to grasp the power of God and Jesus's ability to grasp it.[459] He reasoned that if *dynamis* (12:24) is viewed as a synonym for *pneuma*, the scriptural text interrelates Spirit and scripture and juxtaposes the Sadducees' interpretive practices with Jesus's.[460] Where the Sadducees failed, Jesus succeeded, providing correct pneumatic interpretation of scripture.

Pinnock's contribution most explicitly, together with Moore, and Powery's input, again emphasizes correlation between communion with God and truth brought by the Spirit through scripture. The contrasts between Job and Job's friends, and Jesus and the Sadducees, provide an important caution to pursue intimacy with God, through whom pneumatic interpretation comes (compare with 3.3.6, also 3.5).

4.3.2 Exegesis by the Spirit or the flesh (Francis Martin)

Following Pinnock, Moore, and Powery, engaging with thought from Francis Martin strengthens further the developing understanding of pneumatic hindrance brought through this analysis. Martin posited that there were two approaches to exegesis,[461] by the Spirit or by the flesh.[462] He explained flesh as "the innate drive of the human personality toward self-aggrandizement

457. Moore, "Raw Prayer and Refined Theology" (f.pub. 2000), 150.

458. Powery, "Spirit, the Scripture(s), and the Gospel of Mark" (pub. 2003), 186 (emphasis removed).

459. Powery, "Spirit, the Scripture(s), and the Gospel of Mark," 193, 197.

460. Powery, "Spirit, the Scripture(s), and the Gospel of Mark," 196–97.

461. Martin used "exegesis" to stress interpreting *and* communicating scriptural truth to others. Exegesis: critically interpreting and explaining a text, especially biblical. *Collins English Dictionary*, 687.

462. Francis Martin, "Spirit and Flesh" (pub. 2001), 6. As Martin noted, a draft of this paper was presented at the SPS conference in 1985 (3).

and self-preservation, . . . the direct result of human alienation from God and the consequent disorder in being."[463]

As Martin explained, exegesis by the Spirit or by the flesh are not mutually exclusive for "we are all tinged by the flesh in our thinking and activity even as we strive to live by the Spirit," but only *by* the Spirit can we "come into touch with the realities about which the text is speaking."[464] Martin considered how flesh—or, in this work's terms, immoral behavior—hinders pneumatic interpretation,[465] concentrating on four particular aspects: firstly, self-seeking (noting the Corinthian Christians as an example); secondly, sloth (not making an effort to understand scripture); and thirdly, personal sinfulness. Concerning this third aspect, Martin cautioned that those academically trained but ignoring immoral thoughts and behaviors will be hindered in accessing the true meaning of a text because ignorance of sin prevents understanding of the divine place. His insight is helpful, supporting Powery's contrast between the educated but ignorant Sadducees and Jesus,[466] and the beginning explorations of pneumatic hindrance in chapter 2 (see 2.1.1).[467]

Martin's fourth pneumatic hindrance was prejudice. Expounding this, he argued that this inherent characteristic, influenced by our surrounding community frameworks, causes us to pre-judge. Whilst not itself a negative feature, ignoring and not critically engaging with our own prejudices (that is to say, prejudgments) can hinder ability to pneumatically interpret.[468] Martin applied this to those using historico-critical methods but not incorporating the Spirit's personal appropriation of scripture,[469] which he attributed to the Enlightenment's rationalistic influence on Christian scholarship,[470] and

463. Martin, "Spirit and Flesh," 8.

464. Martin, "Spirit and Flesh," 6.

465. Also discussing the relationship between sin and pneumatic interpretation was Brown, *Holy Spirit and the Bible*, 167–68.

466. Noting that Powery did not mention the Sadducees' education. Comparably, Berkouwer used the Pharisees to illustrate pneumatic hindrance (see 2.1.1)

467. Martin, "Spirit and Flesh," 12–13.

468. Martin, "Spirit and Flesh," 14–16,

469. Martin, "Spirit and Flesh," 20–26. Cf. fn. 437 (historico-grammatical).

470. Martin, "Spirit and Flesh," 16–20 ("Philosophical Prejudice"). Cf. Ellington: "A predominantly rationalist worldview unnecessarily restricts both our approach to Scripture and the ways in which we make ourselves available to hear from God. By excluding the supernatural and focusing instead exclusively on the rational, much modern scholarship has become impoverished in the way it understands God to be present and has distanced itself from that which millions of Christians experience as an important part of their faith." Ellington, "Pentecostalism and the Authority of Scripture" (pub. 1996), 36. For Enlightenment influence on Christian theology and

described as "contextually limited exegesis" versus "complete exegesis."[471] He implied a fracturing of understanding amongst some contemporary scholars using historico-critical methods, involving tendency to appreciate content in and context surrounding scripture, but not always cognitively applying this to personal context and relationship with God. However, this suggestion is hard to defend because it is based around scholars *not* showing how their interpretive work affected personal life and relationship with God, or conversely, *not* showing how personal life and relationship with God impacted their interpretive work.[472] Fee, for example, detailed personal impact of his exegesis (see 4.2.4), but others may have had equally profound, but unshared, experiences. Craig Keener (discussed in chapter 5) is one such scholar. Keener has described how prophecies and dreams often drive him back to scripture with fresh perspective, but he does not always share these experiences in his writings, nor would it be always appropriate to do so.[473] In this instance, and against Martin, an argument from silence is a weak, and itself prejudiced, argument.

From Martin's contribution, three interrelating emphases strengthen and support developing themes. Firstly, for those in or identifying with the renewal tradition, and indeed all Christian scholars (see 1.2)[474] interpreting scripture and communicating scriptural truth in academic work is part of intimate relationship with the triune God through pneumatic encounter, within a surrounding community framework of committed and accountable Christian relationships.[475] The Spirit brings us into community and works in us to remove pneumatic hindrances but paradoxically, however, active ethical effort is also required to recognize and address, both critically

scriptural interpretation, cautioning against modernist *and* postmodernist influences, see N. T. Wright, "Challenge of the Enlightenment," 52–63.

471. Martin, "Spirit and Flesh," 25, acknowledging Ricoeur but noting that he developed the distinction independently. For Ricoeur on appropriation, see *Interpretation Theory*, 43–44, 91–94 (cf. fn. 65 [postmodern and philosophical approaches to interpretation]).

472. Cf. The emphasis of chapter 3 that pneumatic interpretation is dynamically interrelated to pneumatic interpretation of self. See, for example, 3.4.6.

473. Keener was responding to my discussion of *Spirit Hermeneutics* in *Pneuma* (2017), which probed this area. Keener, "Refining *Spirit Hermeneutics*," 204–5; Mather, "Welcoming *Spirit Hermeneutics*," 160–61. Remembering this work's resting position on prophecy as an aspect of pneumatic interpretation (see 3.4.5).

474. Cf. Martin, "Spirit and Flesh," 27; Minto, "Charismatic Renewal and the Spiritual Sense of Scripture," 262–63.

475. Martin, "Spirit and Flesh," 30. Also, Davies's guidance that if our discernment is pneumatic it will also resonate with others in our community frameworks. Davies, "Reading in the Spirit," 309.

and personally, influence of our ethical conduct on pneumatic discernment and interpretation.[476] Secondly, recognition of the Spirit's personal appropriation of scripture should be engaged with critically and personally when interpreting and communicating scripture academically.[477] Finally, for (believed) pneumatic interpretation to be evident to others, this personal appropriation requires conveying somehow in one's interpretive work. Fee's personal account, and Moore's, and McQueen's in chapter 3 (see 3.3.4 and 3.3.5), all illustrate this critical and personal engagement, conveying (believed) pneumatic interpretation of scripture and self.

4.3.3 Hearing scripture through relationship with God (Lee Roy Martin)

Engaging with three speeches from Yahweh to the Israelites in the book of Judges,[478] Lee Roy Martin developed an interpretive approach to scripture based around hearing scripture through engaging in relationship with God.[479] Integrating his Pentecostal faith expression with his academics formed Martin's approach (see 4.1.3). Because of his chosen texts, Martin considered pneumatic interpretation when explaining his interpretive approach but not when discussing the text. However, when considering interpretive method, direct attention to pneumatic interpretation was minor, giving way to interpretation as a Pentecostal (compare 3.1).

Martin argued that truly hearing scripture can only come through engaging in personal relationship with God via the Spirit,[480] and that through this interaction, God confronts and transforms the hearer, and community of hearers.[481] He discussed the relationship between hearing and

476. Cf. the affective-ethical paradox identified through the analysis that when we are the most affectively receptive to God we are also the most ethically willing to modify behavior, and in order to be in a state of open receptivity to God, and pneumatically discern and interpret, active effort is required. See, for example, 2.3.3; 2.5; 3.3; 3.3.1; 3.5.

477. Cf. fn. 475 (Martin and Davies).

478. Lee Roy Martin, *Unheard Voice of God* (pub. 2008). The three speeches were Judges 2:1–5; 6:7–10; 10:6–16, through an angel, prophet, and Yahweh directly. See chapters 5 to 7 for analysis and chapter 8 for summary. Martin employed literary criticism (14–16), and interacted with the reader throughout his analysis. E.g., 125, 133, 216. Also on the book of Judges, Lee Roy Martin, "Purity, Power, and the Passion of God," (pub. 2005), 274–300.

479. Martin, *Unheard Voice of God*, 58, 230. See chapters 1 and 3 for interpretive method.

480. Martin, *Unheard Voice of God*, 73–74.

481. Martin, *Unheard Voice of God*, 62–63. As Martin showed through chapters 5 to 7, the three Judges speeches were to the Israelite community, and he emphasized the

obeying, cautioning that failure to hear signifies spiritual stubbornness or rebellion,[482] and emphasized the loving, joyful obedience that comes from hearing God.[483]

Whilst Martin attended to disobedience and failure to hear God,[484] exploring (pneumatic) hindrance through immoral behavior such as spiritual stubbornness or rebellion did not overly feature in his interpretive approach. Following other Pentecostal scholars,[485] Martin emphasized that *cognitively* hearing God through engaging with scripture comes through personal relationship with God, transforming *affect* and facilitating *ethical* obedience,[486] centering on, and discussing affective transformation.[487] Within his interpretive approach, therefore, Martin considered the affective-ethical aspect of pneumatic interpretation over the ethical-affective.[488]

4.3.4 Personal incorporations (Moore and Richard Bauckham, via Lee Roy Martin and Robby Waddell)

In roundtable discussions of *The Unheard Voice of God*[489] and *The Spirit of the Book of Revelation*[490] in *JPT*, the issue of evidencing pneumatic

community's role in interpretation in his interpretive approach. E.g., "Faithful hearing of the word of God is best accomplished within the context of the believing community and under the guidance of the Holy Spirit. The community offers accountability and support that serves both as a guardian for proper interpretation and as a witness to the transformative effect of the Scripture." (78–79).

482. This was within discussion of hearing and obeying in the Old Testament and Judges. See text for further references. Martin, *Unheard Voice of God*, 68–69, 75–77.

483. Martin, *Unheard Voice of God*, 71.

484. The Israelites failure to hear God's voice was a theme through chapters 5 to 7 and Martin emphasized God's faithfulness to them.

485. Martin noted Land, *Pentecostal Spirituality* (see 3.1). Also, Baker, "Pentecostal Bible Reading" (pub. 1995), 34–48 (see fn. 247). Martin, *Unheard Voice of God*, 70–71.

486. Cf. 3.3.2 (Johns and Johns). Aside from "affect," Martin did not use these terms, although he referenced Land's use of orthopathy, orthopraxy, and orthodoxy in *Pentecostal Spirituality*.

487. Martin, *Unheard Voice of God*, 70–71, 73–74, 77–79.

488. Cf. my suggestion in chapter 3 (3.3.6, and 3.5) of a working understanding that affect and ethics dynamically interrelate

489. Lee Roy Martin, *Unheard Voice of God* (pub. 2008). Discussion included Brueggemann, "Lee Roy Martin, The Unheard Voice of God"; Moore, "Welcoming an Unheard Voice" 7–14; Pope, "Lee Roy Martin, *The Unheard Voice of God*, 20–29; Lee Roy Martin, "Hearing the Book of Judges," 30–50. All pub. 2009.

490. Waddell, *Spirit of the Book of Revelation* (pub. 2006). Discussion included Bauckham, "Review of Robby Waddell," 3–8; Herms, "Review of Robby Waddell," 9–18; Macchia, "Book of Revelation," 19–21; Waddell, "Spirit of Reviews and Response"

interpretation by incorporating discussion of personal impact through one's interpretive work surfaced via critiques from Rickie Moore and Richard Bauckham.

Moore critiqued that lacking in Martin's study were specifics about how Martin, and the Pentecostal community Martin had in view, had been confronted by the text of Judges.[491] Moore suggested that Martin's hearing thesis could have been illustrated by somehow showing personal and communal impact akin to Larry McQueen having concluded his study of Joel by incorporating his own (believed) pneumatic encounter of the text with his academic interpretation.[492] Martin responded briefly, describing the early stages of his research where he struggled to discover anything he felt "worthy of an entire thesis." This struggle persisted until, through a (believed) pneumatic experience, his thoughts were reoriented when he "suddenly and surprisingly" realized, "I had been *reading* Judges but not *hearing* Judges, and I determined that the terminology of 'hearing' captured concisely my hermeneutical goal as a Pentecostal."[493]

Similarly, Bauckham critiqued Waddell for explicating a Pentecostal approach to interpretation integrated with exegesis of Revelation 11[494] and not adequately illustrating *how* his interpretation was pneumatic. Bauckham stated:

22–31. All pub. 2008.

491. Moore, "Welcoming an Unheard Voice," 13.

492. Moore, "Welcoming an Unheard Voice," 13. Moore would have undoubtedly also been thinking of his own work. Cf. 3.3.4 (Moore), and 3.3.5 (McQueen). Martin did allude to personal encounter (see Martin, *Unheard Voice of God*, 232) but was not explicit or detailed in the way Moore suggested he could have been.

493. Lee Roy Martin, "Hearing the Book of Judges," 32 (emphasis original). On the sudden and surprising nature of pneumatic interpretation, compare Macchia's beautifully written *Pneuma* editorial, Macchia, "Resurrection: A Dance of Life" (pub. 2005), 223–24. Watching a show in Las Vegas with his family, Macchia began pondering over the symbolism of life and death in the artistry and performance imagery. As he watched, a part of the show caught Macchia unawares. It brought to him an instant and deep realization, which he also later digested. This flash of insight impacted Macchia profoundly. It led him into a deeper appreciation of his own faith and understanding of the triune God, reflecting particularly on "the dance of the Holy Trinity into which Christ transports us" (224). This moment of understanding, brought through a Las Vegas show, was for Macchia, "the hermeneutical key that interpreted everything else for me" (223). Whilst he did not mention the Spirit or scripture in his account, it is reasonable to assume that this flash of insight *did* lead him back to scripture given that he described its impact on his faith and theology. Macchia's recounted experience may well be another example of pneumatic interpretation and appropriation.

494. See Waddell, *Spirit of the Book of Revelation*, chapters 2 and 3 for interpretive method, chapter 4 for exegesis of Revelation 11. Cf. fns. 350, 417 (Waddell's interpretive method).

> It is by no means obvious how such features of a hermeneutic should actually be manifest in an exegesis such as Waddell's of Revelation 11. But surely they should be manifest in some way? I find no claim that his interpretation was given to him when he, like John, was in the Spirit. I find only exegetical procedures and arguments fully comparable with those used by myself and many others. Where is the Spirit's role in interpretation that Waddell has so emphatically required?[495]

Waddell responded by explaining that he was wary of claiming pneumatic interpretation and detailing personal experience, also extending this wariness to other Pentecostal scholars and postulating that this was "perhaps because confessional approaches are devalued by the majority of scholars in academia." Conceding slightly, Waddell stated:

> This is my testimony. I believe the Lord has called me to research and write on the Apocalypse, providing interpretations of the text that will inform and transform the way this biblical book is viewed by Pentecostals and others alike. This does not mean (of course) that my interpretations will always be correct, which is where the role of the community comes into play.[496]

Waddell's caution that his interpretations will not always be correct is important and this is not to suggest that incorporating personal (believed) pneumatic impact *from* the interpretive work *with* the interpretive work somehow conveys that the interpretation is perfect. As is consistently asserted throughout the analysis, central to pneumatic interpretation is intimate relationship with the triune God through pneumatic encounter, and the interrelation between affect, ethics, and cognition as aspects of that relationship. Additionally, because God as Father, Son, and Spirit, is invisible and yet, at the same time, incarnate, with the Spirit's act of interpreting coming to light in Christ, the incarnate one, the Spirit's communication will carry God's invisible, yet incarnate nature. Our interpretations, whether personal or textual (or indeed both) will therefore, to one extent or another, *always* be fragmentary in discerning pneumatic truth. However, because the Spirit always speaks through and beyond scripture, interpreting and appropriating scriptural truth personally and simultaneously communally, in ways that cohere with scripture, (believed) pneumatic interpretation *of* scripture *can only be shown* by incorporating personal (believed) pneumatic impact into the interpretive work. Because the Spirit, by nature, always speaks

495. Bauckham, "Review of Robby Waddell," 5–6.

496. Waddell, "Spirit of Reviews and Response," 31.

indirectly and never directly, communicating truth about the Spirit must be done through something else. These factors therefore require those of us in academia (or indeed anyone writing about pneumatic interpretation) to recognize, critically engage with, and articulate—if we wish to show it—what we consider to be the Spirit's personal interpretation and appropriation. Furthermore, this *inescapably* places intimate relationship with God as Father, Son, and Spirit, through the Spirit, together with the affective, ethical, and cognitive aspects of this relationship, centrally within scholars' academic efforts.

Finally, Bauckham's response to Waddell suggests that he was challenged by Waddell's perspective. Bauckham also emphasized that his own exegeses of Revelation 11 were close to Waddell's and he had no idea of Pentecostal hermeneutics or even much awareness of hermeneutics generally at the time of his research.[497] Bauckham's similar exegetical findings could be an example of pneumatic interpretation unknowingly employed (see 1.2). The emphasis of pneumatic interpretation, is, after all, on *the Spirit* working in, with, and through the interpreter and the passage of scripture. A person does not necessarily have to recognize the Spirit's work for the Spirit *to* work. Moreover, the Spirit's self-effacing nature indicates that the Spirit often chooses to work in ways hidden and unseen. Quite possibly, Bauckham's exegeses *were* pneumatic, but Bauckham's prejudice[498] did not allow him to see it.

4.3.5 Evaluation

Pinnock, with Moore, and Powery, and Francis Martin, and Lee Roy Martin all highlighted varying aspects relating ethical conduct with intimate relationship with the triune God through the Spirit, and influence on cognition. Consistent with Pentecostal scholars considered in chapter 3 such as Land and Johns and Johns, Lee Roy Martin (within his interpretive method) emphasized affective-ethical transformation and influence on cognition, whilst Francis Martin stressed hindrances on pneumatic interpretation from immoral behavior, effectively emphasizing the ethical-affective relationship and influence on cognition. Engaging with and developing thought from Francis Martin raised the importance of considering and critically engaging with prejudgments formed through surrounding community frameworks

497. Bauckham, "Review of Robby Waddell," 4, citing Bauckham, *The Theology of the Book of Revelation* (Cambridge: Cambridge University Press, 1993); Bauckham, *The Climax of Prophecy: Studies on the Book of Revelation* (Edinburgh: T. & T. Clark, 1993).

498. See 4.3.2, remembering that prejudice is not necessarily a negative feature.

that may hinder (or facilitate) ability to recognize truth brought by the Spirit through scripture. For those in or identifying with the renewal tradition, and indeed all Christian scholars, interpreting scripture and communicating scriptural truth in academic interpretive work should be undertaken as an overflow from one's personal relationship with God (namely, intimate relationship with the triune God through pneumatic encounter). *Ideally*, this academic work should be carried out within a surrounding community framework of committed and accountable Christian relationships, and *necessarily* with critical and personal awareness of potential pneumatic hindrances from personal sin and prejudgment.

Moore and Bauckham's critiques of Lee Roy Martin and Waddell's contributions, helped solidify what had been suggested when considering Francis Martin's contribution; that for (believed) pneumatic interpretation to be evident to others, personal (believed) pneumatic impact needs to be conveyed somehow in one's interpretive work. This requires scholars to recognize and critically engage with the Spirit's appropriation of scriptural truth to personal situations and surrounding community frameworks. Discussion of pneumatic appropriation in 4.2.4 together with Davies's guidance introducing 4.3, further establishes that if this appropriation is pneumatic, it will cohere contextually. All of this, once more places intimate relationship with God through pneumatic encounter, and the affective, ethical, and cognitive aspects of that relationship, centrally within our academic efforts. Aspects of this personal relationship with God need not be conveyed, nor, as with Fee (and Keener) is it always appropriate to do so, but this personal relationship is central to our academic efforts as well as to our personal life.

Finally, Bauckham's dialogue with Waddell brought an important caution to this work's developing understanding of pneumatic interpretation. Whilst pneumatic awareness is required for critical engagement with pneumatic interpretation, one does not necessarily need to be *aware* of the Spirit's work for the Spirit *to* work. The emphasis of pneumatic interpretation is upon *the Spirit* working in, with, and through the interpreter and the passage of scripture. Whilst pneumatic interpretation involves ethical responsibility on our part, a person can carry this out without awareness of the impact of their conduct to receptivity of pneumatic truth. Herewith is a vital ecumenical stress, stated in chapter 1 (see 1.2), that pneumatic interpretation, whilst characteristic of renewal thought, cannot be limited to the renewal tradition, for, to one extent another, the Spirit through scripture communicates knowingly or unknowingly (on our part) to, with, and through all Christians.

4.4 EVALUATION

By engaging with renewal conversationalists in the 2000s, chapter 4 has continued from 1990s conversationalists considered in chapter 3 by discussing the Spirit's personal appropriation of scriptural truth in more detail. The emphasis that the Spirit speaks *through* and *beyond* scripture personally within our contemporary situations in ways that cohere in some way with the original content presented in scripture and its surrounding historical framework has been developed. An overriding emphasis brought out of thought in this decade was that *the Spirit, through scripture, speaks personally, and simultaneously communally*, and therefore, personal impact from pneumatic interpretation cannot be separated from our surrounding community frameworks.

Through scholars attending to the Spirit's theological relationship with scripture, consideration of the creational (Spirit–Father) and redemptive (Spirit–Son) aspects of the Spirit's communication was continued from chapter 3. By drawing on and building upon thought from scholars including Macchia, Yong, Cartledge, and Grenz, the importance of considering *all three* triune roles from a pneumatic starting point was stressed. This furthered discussion that as we engage with scripture, the Spirit (self)-interprets the Father, Son, and Spirit to us. Here, it was highlighted that the Spirit–Father relationship deserves increased attention within considerations of pneumatic interpretation, redressing historical neglect of focus. At this point, caution was given that these creational, redemptive, and reconciling roles are both particular to the Father, Son, and Spirit, and yet also mutual within the triune relationship. Subsequently, I presented that the Spirit, through scripture, draws us into knowledge of God as Father, Son, and Spirit, creating, redeeming and reconciling personally, and simultaneously communally, in our lives. Following this, attending to the Spirit's personal appropriation of scriptural truth through engagement with Fee, Grenz, and Pinnock helped practically to illustrate some of this discussion and strengthened understanding that the Spirit always speaks through and within surrounding historical and cultural frameworks. Davies emphasized that beneath the written words is an ethical dimension that the Spirit also, and perhaps most importantly, interprets to us, whilst Ellington's insights helped highlight that through scripture the Spirit shows us God's character and action.

Considering intimate relationship with God as Father, Son, and Spirit through the Spirit brought further discussion of the affective, ethical, and cognitive aspects of this relationship, together with continued discussion of the Spirit's personal and contemporary appropriation of scriptural truth.

Similarly to 1990s conversationalists, scholars showed appreciation of ethical-affective *and* affective-ethical aspects of pneumatic interpretation and relationship with God, and influence on cognition, with insights from Francis Martin helping to stress and explicate pneumatic hindrance. Following 1990s Pentecostal conversationalists (for example, Land, Johns and Johns), Lee Roy Martin emphasized the affective-ethical, influencing cognition (within his interpretive method), but also recognized hindrance from immoral behavior. Insights from Francis Martin and critiques from Moore and Bauckham helped established that for (believed) pneumatic interpretation to be illustrated, scholars need to incorporate personal, and simultaneously communal, (believed) pneumatic impact from their interpretive work within their contributions. This requires critical engagement and personal reflection on these more intimate aspects of the Spirit's communication through scripture as part of academic work.

Finally, engaging with contributions from 2000s conversationalists has further cemented that those considering the Spirit's role in interpretation should prioritize the Spirit and give secondary attention to cognitive frameworks of interpretation, whether they are those surrounding the relevant scriptural passage in its original historical location or those surrounding us as we engage with scripture today. This was highlighted by Pentecostal scholars increasingly drawing away from detailed and explicit attention to the Spirit's role in interpretation and focusing on issues relating to Pentecostal hermeneutical identity. Whilst valuable to Pentecostal hermeneutics, these conversations were also not inclusive of scholars across and identifying with the renewal tradition who similarly prioritized intimate relationship with the triune God through pneumatic encounter, and who were also considering the Spirit's role in the interpretation of scripture. Paradoxically, therefore, the Pentecostal hermeneutics' conversation was helping, but increasingly hindering, understanding of pneumatic interpretation across the renewal tradition.

5

Hallmarks of Pneumatic Interpretation Amidst Scholarly Diversity

2010 to 2018

From 2010 onwards, conversations about the Spirit's role in the interpretation of scripture continued to strengthen and expand. Further full-length studies reflecting various perspectives emerged, notably from Chris Green, Jacqueline Grey, Craig Keener, and Jack Levison.[499] Branching further afield was Amos Yong, who brought pentecostal hermeneutics[500] into conversation with theological interpretation of scripture.[501] Contributing

499. Chris Green, *Sanctifying Interpretation*; Grey, *Three's a Crowd*; Keener, *Spirit Hermeneutics*; Levison, *Inspired*. Also, David Johnson, *Pneumatic Discernment in the Apocalypse* (cf. 1.6.1 [discernment]); Noel, *Pentecostal and Postmodern Hermeneutics*; Oliverio, *Theological Hermeneutics*; Philemon, "Pneumatic Hermeneutics"; Wyckoff, *Pneuma and Logos* (see fn. 343).

500. See 4.1 for Yong's use of "pentecostal." Also discussed in 1.2.

501. Yong, *Hermeneutical Spirit*. For TIS, see 1.6.1. Yong explained he was drawn into TIS discussions as he sought "to understand more clearly what it meant to do theology, and read Scripture as part of this process, in light of the Pentecost event." Yong, *Hermeneutical Spirit* 13. His thesis was pneumatology can reinforce trinitarian discussions amongst those discussing theological interpretation of scripture (1). He addressed this conceptually and thematically through essays covering cultural and transformation interpretation, theological anthropology, pneumatological soteriology, and theological-scriptural interpretation (see 1.6.1, fns. 68 [cultural interpretation], 70 [liberation hermeneutics and social justice], 71 [religious pluralism], 81 [theology and the biological and physical sciences]).

evangelicals[502] included Kevin Vanhoozer,[503] who suggested historical reformed scholars were under-resourced amongst renewal scholars addressing pneumatic interpretation (compare 4.2.1).[504]

During this era, collections and colloquies were produced, signaling the maturity the conversation was approaching. In *Pentecostal Hermeneutics: A Reader*, Lee Roy Martin charted a chronological and thematic history of Pentecostal hermeneutics by collating and arranging published *JPT* articles spanning twenty-five years.[505] This valuable collection was presented with simplicity, allowing the original voices and contributions to speak independently yet coherently. Martin started with Rickie Moore's brief, seminal contribution (see 2.4.1), ending with his own work on affectively

502. Billings, *Word of God*, especially 105–48; Habets, "Reading Scripture," 89–104; Meadowcroft, "Spirit, Interpretation and Scripture"; Webster, *Domain of the Word*, 32–49 ("Resurrection and Scripture"), 50–64 ("Illumination"); Wyckoff, *Pneuma and Logos*. With minimal attention and hermeneutically prioritizing Christ, Bartholomew and Thomas, "Manifesto," 4–7; Bartholomew and Emerson, "Theological Interpretation," 160. Additionally, Senapatiratne, "Pneumatological Addition," 44–59, with response by N. T. Wright, "Word and the Wind," 160–66 (141–78 wider response). Pentecostal scholar Timothy Senapatiratne suggested improving Wright's presentation of scripture as a five-act play (see 1.6.1 [narrative approaches]) with a pneumatic component. Wright was not convinced by this argument (which involved incorporating the Wesleyan Quadrilateral) but agreed that there was a need to investigate more thoroughly how the Spirit works with the church as it reads and seeks to interpret and live under the authority of scripture (165), expressing appreciation for scholars involved in this research area (166). Wright also offered his own experience with Pentecostalism and the charismatic movement (142–44).

503. Vanhoozer, "Ascending the Mountain," 781–803; "Reforming Pneumatic Hermeneutics," 18–24; "Spirit of Light," 149–67; Vanhoozer and Treier, *Theology and the Mirror of Scripture*, 59, 73–75, 137–40.

504. Vanhoozer used John Calvin and Jonathan Edwards to argue that "it is not the Bible that needs illumining, but readers." Vanhoozer, "Spirit of Light," 164. He discussed the value of Calvin and Edwards's theology to pneumatic interpretation in both "Spirit of Light," 158–67, and "Reforming Pneumatic Hermeneutics," 21–23, also identifying (in both articles) Owen, *Causes, Ways, and Means* (1678), as valuable for understanding how the Spirit renews the human mind and enables understanding. Also highlighting reformed scholars and their theology were Philemon, "Pneumatic Hermeneutics," 125–63 (John Calvin, John Owen); Vondey, *Beyond Pentecostalism*, 49–51 (Martin Luther), 66–68 (Karl Barth); Webster, *Domain of the Word*, 50–64 (the Reformation, Thomas Aquinas, and Barth); Wyckoff, *Pneuma and Logos*, see fn. 499. Also, Zwingli, *Clarity and Certainty* (1522). Briefly discussing Huldrych Zwingli was Webster, *Holy Scripture*, 101–4.

505. Lee Roy Martin, *Pentecostal Hermeneutics: A Reader* (f.pub. as a collection 2013). Included were contributions from Johns and Johns, McKay, Thomas, Baker, Archer, Ellington, Waddell, Pinnock, and Davies, all incorporated in this analysis. Further smaller reflections/literature analyses included, Melissa Archer, *"I Was in the Spirit,"* 45–55; Chris Green, *Pentecostal Theology of the Lord's Supper*, 182–94; David Johnson, *Pneumatic Discernment in the Apocalypse*, 16–49; Parker, *Led by The Spirit*, 16–43.

reading the Psalms (discussed in 5.4.4). Another collection, *Constructive Pneumatological Hermeneutics in Pentecostal Christianity*, from Kenneth Archer and William Oliverio, illustrated the breadth now present within Pentecostal hermeneutics' discussions as contributors deliberated issues relating to the community surrounding the interpreter covering four broad areas: philosophy, biblical theology, social and cultural factors, and the social and physical sciences.[506] As Oliverio stated, many of the contributors stood in continuity with classical Pentecostal hermeneutics but the collection intended to broaden out across the renewal tradition. However, Archer somewhat contradicted this, advocating viewing Pentecostalism as a distinct theological tradition before entering into dialogue with other traditions and further academic dialogue on interpretation.[507] With more concentrated attention to scripture and clearer focus across the renewal tradition, Kevin Spawn and Archie Wright's colloquy, *Spirit and Scripture: Exploring a Pneumatic Hermeneutic* brought together scholars in or identifying with the renewal tradition and focused on discussing the Spirit's role in scriptural interpretation. These were mainly biblical scholars offering historical biblical perspectives. Spawn and Wright started with a history of pneumatic interpretation across the renewal tradition (see 1.2; 1.5), before contributor essays, with others responding. Spawn and Wright's strength was in their clear focus across the renewal tradition, intention[508] to focus

506. Archer and Oliverio, *Constructive Pneumatological Hermeneutics* (pub. 2016). Contributions are discussed accordingly in this chapter. Concerning philosophy and pneumatic interpretation, Westphal, "Spirit and Prejudice," 17–32; Glen Menzies, "Echoing Hirsch,' 83–98. Additionally, Joel Green, "Pentecostal Hermeneutics: A Wesleyan Perspective," 159–73 (also advocating integration of TIS). For further contributions overlapping with this analysis, see 1.6.1, fns. 68 (cultural interpretation [Castelo, Yong]), 73 (liturgical interpretation [Shin]), 80 (practical theology and the social sciences [Cartledge, Kay]), 81 (theology and the biological and physical science [Mitchell, and Tenneson et al.]). External to *Constructive Pneumatological Hermeneutics*, discussing culture: Kenneth Archer, "Pentecostal Hermeneutics," 317–39; Estrada, "Contextualized Hermeneutic," 341–55 (cf. fn. 68 [cultural interpretation]); discussing liberation hermeneutics and social justice: Davies, "Spirit of Freedom," 53–64; Kenneth Archer and Waldrop, "Hermeneutics," 65–78 (see also fn. 70 [liberation hermeneutics and social justice]). Concerning Luke-Acts: Stronstad, "Aspects of Hermeneutics," 32–58; Stronstad, "Lukan Model," 12–17; and concerning N. T. Wright, Senapatiratne, "Pneumatological Addition," 44–59 (see fn. 502 [evangelical approaches]).

507. Oliverio, "Introduction," 4–5; Archer, "Afterword," 316, cf. 323.

508. Spawn and Wright, *Spirit and Scripture* (f.pub. 2011). Critiquing the *Spirit and Scripture* essays in his response essay, Walter Moberly commented that a recurring trap those concerned with "historically oriented biblical interpretation" fall into is that whilst "it is right and proper to give an account of what certain biblical writers and characters may have thought and done," scholars often insufficiently discuss relevance for contemporary interpretation. Moberly observed that the essayists had fallen into

chiefly on the Spirit and scripture, and conclusion that the Spirit works with "all biblical scholars" as they seek to interpret scripture, not just the "self-proclaimed Spirit-filled scholar."[509] Whilst agreeing with their conclusion (compare 1.2; 4.3.5), as the analysis has thus far been showing, pneumatic interpretation also involves responsibility on our part.

Underlining a central aim of *The Interpreting Spirit* to locate and focus on uniting features of scholarly thought amidst hermeneutical diversity (see 1.1; 1.5), this penultimate chapter draws on and develops—and in this process celebrates—thought from scholars in this most recent period. It addresses Yong's discussion of the human imagination in relationship with the Spirit, before focusing on contributions from two contrasting but complementary scholarly groupings, the "Regent school" and the "Cleveland school." Amidst different starting points, foci, terminology, and methods, hallmarks of pneumatic interpretation, explicated throughout this analysis are recognized, thereby building and strengthening understanding of these distinctive features.

5.1 THE PNEUMATIC IMAGINATION (AMOS YONG AND FRIENDS)

In *Spirit-Word-Community* (see 4.2.2), Yong considered the human (Christian) imagination in relationship with the Spirit, and in connection with interpretation and discernment. He called this "the pneumatological imagination."[510] To maintain terminological consistency, I also reference

---

this trap and had insufficiently addressed *how* the Spirit works through scripture *today*. Moberly, "Pneumatic Biblical Hermeneutics," 165. Moberly's critique was insightful but not entirely fair for, 1) Thomas (see fn. 666) and Cartledge's (fn. 549) contributions were not historical biblical and both concentrated on contemporary application, balancing somewhat the historical biblical contributions; 2) Moberly did not critique Cartledge, or Herms (see fn. 609). Moberly was also responding most directly to Boda, who disagreed (see Boda, "Walking with the Spirit in the Word," 169). Essays came from Boda, "Word and Spirit," 25–45; Spawn, "Principle of Analogy," 46–72; Archie Wright, "Second Temple Period Jewish Biblical Interpretation," 73–98; Herms, "Invoking the Spirit," 99–114; Thomas, "'What the Spirit is Saying to the Church,'" 115–29; Cartledge, "Text-Community-Spirit," 130–44. Responses came from Bartholomew, "Spirit and Scripture," 145–53; Dunn, "Role of the Spirit," 154–59 (Dunn's response is essentially another essay as he did not critique anyone), and Moberly, "Pneumatic Biblical Hermeneutics,' 160–65. For questions each essayist was asked to address, see Spawn and Wright, *Spirit and Scripture*, xvii. Contributions are discussed accordingly in this chapter.

509. Spawn and Wright, "Cultivating a Pneumatic Hermeneutic," 197.

510. Yong, "Pneumatological Imagination," 119–218, chapters 4 to 6. Yong provided historical background (123–32), summarized the pneumatic imagination (133–41),

this as "the pneumatic imagination."[511] Published in 2002, analysis of Yong's contribution is incorporated at this point because those engaging with his thought were writing post-2010 and this placement works well structurally.

William Atkinson helpfully summarized Yong's presentation of the pneumatological imagination, explaining that he made three important points. As Atkinson noted, Yong offered these points in the indicative ("the pneumatological imagination is . . ."), but Atkinson rephrased them in the imperative ("in order to be useful the pneumatological imagination *ought to be* . . .").[512] This rephrasing is significant, emphasizing a person's own ethical involvement. Atkinson stated:

> First, the pneumatological imagination ought to be powerfully charismatic in both a passive and active sense, recognizing that all human capacity for thought is a gift from a powerful God and then deliberately applying that thinking in an empowered way to the task in hand. Second, this form of imagination must be Christ-centered. The Spirit and the word must cohere. The imagination ought not to run wild but must be hemmed in to the concrete reality of the Christ-event. Thirdly, the pneumatological imagination must be value-driven. It will not suffice to take a value-free phenomena and especially to powers that are evidently at work in the world. There are good powers and there are evil powers. This imagination must be discerning; it must be critical.[513]

---

and connected it with interpretation (141–49). In chapter 5, he then used pragmatist, Charles Sanders Peirce's epistemology to provide "an alternative, albeit technical, account for how the imagination functions to engage the world." (151, 91–96 for Peirce). In chapter 6, Yong incorporated semiotics, discussing "ethical and aesthetic norms which shape our interpersonal relationships and our engagement with the world," and in this process, considered "how engaging others and the world . . . leads us to encounter the divine." (185). For definitions of semiotics and pragmatics, see fn. 75.

511. Wolfgang Vondey has also considered the role of the imagination. See Vondey, *Beyond Pentecostalism* (pub. 2010), 16–46 (with historical discussion [17–26], and incorporating Yong [38–40]). Also, Vondey, *Pentecostalism* (pub. 2013), 42–48 (incorporating Yong [87–88]). In *Beyond Pentecostalism*, 26–46, Vondey retained contemporary discussion of the imagination in relation to classical Pentecostalism, but in *Pentecostalism*, 9–27, used "Pentecostalism" as overarching terminology for the renewal tradition. This was also the case in Vondey, *Pentecostal Theology* (pub. 2017), 4. However, in *Pentecostalism* and *Pentecostal Theology*, Vondey's perspective was still oriented around classical Pentecostalism (cf. Jacqueline Grey, see 5.3.4, fn. 611).

512. Atkinson, *Trinity After Pentecost* (pub. 2013), 14, quoting and referencing Yong, "Pneumatological Imagination," 134.

513. Atkinson, *Trinity After Pentecost*, 14, referencing Yong, "Pneumatological Imagination," 134. For Atkinson, "word" here was scripture. For Yong, "Word" included scripture but was also wider. Cf. 4.2.1 (*Logos* incorporation), fn. 390 (Yong's use of

Also engaging with Yong's discussion was Oliverio, who suggested that "the function of what [Yong] calls the 'pneumatological imagination' is the place of human freedom in which the fallible and provisional work of discernment occurs."[514] Oliverio's suggestion, following Atkinson's summary, indicates that Yong's convoluted and sometimes abstract presentation of the pneumatic imagination bears similarities to this work's ongoing consideration of pneumatic interpretation and associated terminology, pneumatic discernment, pneumatic appropriation, and pneumatic hindrance. Following Atkinson's overview and Oliverio's descriptor, four observations of Yong's understanding of the human imagination in relationship with the Spirit can be made.

5.1.1 The heart and the imagination

Firstly, as stated in 1.3, this work understands the heart as the locus of discernment, and consequently interpretation, from which affect, ethics, and cognition stem (see 1.3). Yong's explication complements this for he recognized the imagination as ethically passive and active (compare 2.3.3), with affective, cognitive, and "spiritual" components.[515] He also connected the heart *with* the imagination. This was most explicit in his historical discussion where he reasoned that whereas contemporary Western Christianity had been influenced by philosophical thought subordinating the imagination to reason, the people of God in the Old Testament, and also in the New Testament,[516] are seen to have understood the imagination in ethical terms. As Yong explained, these ancient writers and early communities therefore connected the heart and imagination, understanding the heart as the focal point for good and evil, and recognizing a person's capacity to act accordingly.[517] Yong advocated returning to a way of thinking, rooted in Old

"Word").

514. Oliverio, *Theological Hermeneutics* (f.pub. 2012), 240.

515. E.g., Yong described the imagination as "a synthesis of passive and active components (being functionally relational)," and "a cognitive blend of the affective and spiritual aspects of a human being." Yong, "Pneumatological Imagination," 123 (see also, 123–29, 134, 136–37, 216). He also recognized an aesthetic element, and incorporated this when discussing ethics and semiotics (185–214) (Cf. fn. 510 [overview]). For Yong's understanding of "spirit," see fn. 529.

516. Yong referenced "Hebrews" but this was inaccurate. Cf. fn. 324 (Wenell, and Gorman).

517. Yong, "Pneumatological Imagination," 125, 129, 130–31 Also, Vondey, *Beyond Pentecostalism*, 19–20. Vondey drew on Brueggemann, "Imagination as a Mode of Fidelity," 13–36. Brueggemann tangentially linked the Spirit when discussing the imagination, the heart and scriptural interpretation in the Old Testament. Yong, and Vondey's

Testament thought, that understands the imagination dynamically interrelated with the heart as "an aspect of cognition that is holistically imbued with affectivity, and driven volitionally [ethically][518] toward the beautiful, the true and the good."[519] These aspects of Yong's discussion reinforce the understanding discussed at length in these pages in relation to pneumatic interpretation, and particularly in chapter 2, that the Spirit works in and with us *holistically*, involving affect, and ethical action, as well as cognition. When we recognize the heart as the locus of discernment, affect and ethics emerge as inescapable aspects of the interpretive (and imaginative) process alongside cognition.

5.1.2 Christ-shaped and trinitarian-shaped

Secondly, Yong emphasized the "christomorphic shape and trinitarian character" of the pneumatic imagination.[520] The life and mind of Christ is the model, and the Spirit works in us, "transmuting or transforming the shape of the human imagination into that of the mind of Jesus Christ's."[521] Discussions in 2.3.1, 3.2, and 4.2 focused on the relational nature of the triune God from the starting point of the Spirit, emphasizing neglect of attention to the Father. This established that the Son cannot be understood apart from the Spirit and the Father; therefore, the Spirit's holistic interpretation of the Son to us is *also* a holistic (self)-interpretation of the Father, and of the Spirit. Yong recognized this regarding the Father, explaining, "the truth which Jesus is simply reflects the truth of the Father, and our being conformed to the image of Jesus means the restoration of the image of the Father in us as well."[522] However, as this work has stressed (see, for example, 2.3.1), this is also a holistic interpretation of the Spirit because, as the Spirit interprets the Son, and the Father to us, the Spirit is also *self*-interpreted.[523] Yong did

reasoning for emphasizing Old Testament thought over New Testament thought was that the New Testament writers were also influenced by ancient Greek philosophy. Concerning philosophical influence: Yong, "Pneumatological Imagination," 123–32; Vondey, *Beyond Pentecostalism*, 16–25. Yong and Vondey both drew on Kearney, *Wake of Imagination*, 39–49 (37–79). See Vondey's discussion for further sources.

518. Yong used varying terms to describe behavioral aspects of the pneumatic imagination including ethics, moral codes, normative conduct, and volition.

519. Yong, "Pneumatological Imagination," 129.

520. Yong, "Pneumatological Imagination," 216.

521. Yong, "Pneumatological Imagination," 136.

522. Yong, "Pneumatological Imagination," 175 (similarly, 171). See also 4.2.3.

523. See, for example, 2.3.1. See also discussion of the kenotic personhood of the Spirit in Atkinson, *Trinity After Pentecost*, 58–62. Atkinson defined "kenosis" as

not address this pneumatic self-interpretation but he did emphasize communal aspects (similarly highlighted in 4.2.2). He stated, "Insofar as the Spirit consistently points beyond herself to the Father and the Son, so is the pneumatological imagination driven to engagement with the other that stand over and against the self."[524]

Consequently, in this work's terms, a person's imagination infused with the Spirit is affectively and ethically driven toward the nature of God as Father, Son, and Spirit, with Christ as the incarnate image. Moreover, the imagination infused with Spirit is also simultaneously personal and communal, also aligning with the triune nature of God.

5.1.3 Creational, relational, and fallible

Thirdly, Yong suggested that contained within scripture are root metaphors or images that "act as lures" and through the Spirit enact imaginative encounter as scripture is read.[525] He used a notion of root metaphors derived from Stephen Pepper, explaining them as

> formative cultural symbols or icons that enable large-scale coherent visions of the world and that thereby function normatively in the assessment of visions outside of that metaphoric framework because of their capacity to absorb and explain the other in its own terms.[526]

Yong centered on three root metaphors, also calling them "primordial experiences" (in other words, fundamental notions): "power," appreciating the Spirit's creational and life-giving nature and activity (compare 3.5, also

"*self- emptying*" (35, emphasis original), and "person" as "an entity with at least a potential sense of self and the capacity to relate to others" (58). Also, Studebaker, *Pentecost to the Triune God,* 146 (and preceding discussion), on the Spirit's identity.

524. Yong, "Pneumatological Imagination," 216.

525. Yong, "Pneumatological Imagination," 133.

526. Pepper's definition in Yong's words. Yong, "Pneumatological Imagination," 133, referencing Stephen Pepper, *World Hypotheses* (Berkley: University of California Press, 1942, n.p.). Noting Yong's caution about suggesting that the Spirit, through the imagination, functions normatively. For definition of metaphor, see fn. 76.

4.4);[527] the Spirit's relationality (see 5.1.2);[528] and "wind," recognizing the diversity of "spirits" operative in the world (discussed further in 5.1.4).[529]

Therefore, drawing from Yong's insights and phrasing in this work's terms, a way the Spirit communicates through scripture is by working on our hearts and imaginations (interrelated), bringing to mind images and symbols that *cohere with but reach creatively beyond* the scriptural narrative to our personal lives and surrounding situations. This pneumatic interpretation and appropriation is: 1) trinitarian, with Christ as the incarnate image; 2) affectively and ethically oriented and driven; and 3) simultaneously personal and communal.[530] However, as the analysis has been recognizing by discussing pneumatic hindrance, and as Yong also highlighted, we are people capable of error, prejudice, and immoral action, and so our pneumatic interpretation and discernment will always, to one extent or another, be partial and fallible.[531] Whilst this will always be the case, pneumatic hindrance can also be lessened by pursuing intimate relationship with God, through whom pneumatic interpretation is brought (for example, see 3.3.6; 4.3.5).[532]

527. Yong, "Pneumatological Imagination," 134–36. For later work exploring the Spirit's creational activity, see Yong, "Reading Scripture and Nature," 237–56. Cf. Davies, discussing the Spirit's creative work continuing after creation and sustaining life: "If the Father provides the creative impulse and the Word the structure and order of the universe, then it is the Spirit who breathes life into these dry bones of the cosmos—indeed, who *is* the life that animates them." Davies, "Spirit of Freedom," 58–68 (69 [emphasis original]).

528. Yong, "Pneumatological Imagination," 136–39.

529. Yong, "Pneumatological Imagination," 134, 139–41. Yong recognized various "spiritual" powers including divine, natural, human, and demonic. Oliverio explained, "[Yong] conceives of 'spirit' as a complex of tendencies which shape the behavior of *any* thing. This can represent things at various levels of aggregation, be they individuals, communities, institutions or things in the natural order. What seems to qualify something as 'spirit,' on his understanding, is that it has volition and that it is in motion, it is living." Oliverio, *Theological Hermeneutics*, 237 (emphasis original).

530. E.g., see Yong, "Pneumatological Imagination," 142–43 (receiving, imaginatively transforming, and "even add[ing] to what is passed on in a creative manner" [142]), 145–6 ("the imagination transcends the phenomena of the world by constituting it according to the values, affections, and intentions of the perceiver and experiencer" [145]), 160–62 (the Spirit transforms us into the image of Christ and engages us pragmatically, affectively, and "spiritually" [162 discussing the Spirit and scripture), 174–75 (Christ-shaped and trinitarian-shaped), 216 (summary). Yong combined discussion of metaphor, semiotics, and pragmatics through his discussion (see fn. 510 [overview], fn. 526 [metaphor]). For later application, see Yong's use of Stephen (Acts 6–7) to illustrate someone exhibiting a pneumatic imagination. Yong, "Reflecting and Confessing," 63–76.

531. Yong, "Pneumatological Imagination," 175–84, 210 (the partiality of knowledge), 139–41 (the diversity of "spirits"). Cf. 2.3.2 (invisible and incarnate).

532. Stephen Parker is a valuable dialogue partner here. *Led by The Spirit* was wider

5.1.4 Demonic influences

Fourthly, as Atkinson highlighted, Yong recognized that we live surrounded and influenced by various "spiritual" powers at work in the world, and within this Yong included the demonic.[533] Consequently, Yong's thought follows Vanhoozer's brief insight (see 3.3.1; 3.5) in highlighting an important and under-articulated issue, that in seeking the Spirit's guidance in scriptural interpretation, we should also be aware of, and critically engage with, the influence of evil spirits, howsoever understood, on our imagination and discernment, and therefore interpretation.

5.1.5 Evaluation

As Atkinson's summary and Oliverio's descriptor suggested, Yong's discussion of the human imagination in relationship with the Spirit (in those aspects as understood and presented here) complements and enhances this analysis of the Spirit's role in the interpretation of scripture, and dynamic interrelation of affect, ethics, and cognition as part of this process. The two offerings are both unique in approach and method, and there are different emphases. For example, this work is more concentrated on scripture, stresses the contextual coherence aspect of pneumatic appropriation by discussing frameworks surrounding the scriptural text and the interpreter,[534] and attends to intimate relationship with God. However, they unite in ad-

---

than pneumatic interpretation, "a 'practical theology' of Pentecostal discernment and decision making' (1), but his combined expertise in psychology, counseling, and theology provides a perspective unique amongst conversationalists. E.g., see his consideration of the psychological nature of pneumatic discernment and associated relationship with early childhood experiences. Parker, *Led by The Spirit* (2015 expanded), 131–62. Also, Regent University School of Psychology and Counseling, "Stephen Parker," n.p. Cf. my discussion in 2.2.3 concerning pneumatic interpretation and inner healing.

533. Yong, "Pneumatological Imagination," 134, 139–41. Cf. fn. 529 (Yong's understanding of "spirit"). For definition of evil spirit/demon, see fn. 258. Yong related this to the imagination, not scriptural interpretation.

534. Yong did consider context when engaging with Peirce's thought (see fn. 510), and also Daniel Patte's. See Yong, "Pneumatological Imagination," 161–63, discussing understanding scripture in its context and interpreting it to our context. Yong stressed, "a pneumatically nurtured imagination" (162) builds on this understanding by recognizing that with this comes personal transformation and communal engagement. See also Yong, "Pneumatological Imagination," 209–10 (analogy, and similarities and differences). Daniel Patte, "Critical Biblical Studies from a Semiotic Perspective," in Daniel Patte. "Critical Biblical Studies from a Semiotic Perspective." In *Thinking in Signs: Semiotics and Biblical Studies . . . Thirty Years After*, edited by Daniel Patte, 3–26. *Semeia* 81 (Atlanta: Society of Biblical Literature and Scholars, 2000).

dressing and highlighting similar aspects.[535] Yong's 'friends,' therefore, include Atkinson, Oliverio, (and Vondey[536]), and *all* scholars in or identifying with the renewal tradition discussed and celebrated thus far in this analysis whose thought collectively complements Yong's "pneumatological imagination" and who are also complemented *by* Yong's unique contribution.

5.2 TWO SCHOOLS OF THOUGHT

As noted at this chapter's start, within the 2010 to 2018 conversation were two broad and contrasting, yet complementary, scholarly groupings or schools of thought. "Regent school" thought is related to the Regent University School of Divinity in Virginia Beach, and "Cleveland school" thought is related to the Pentecostal Theological Seminary in Cleveland, Tennessee. Described by Yong as a "scholarly vanguard," Regent University School of Divinity has pioneered the emerging area of renewal studies since the early 2000s, identifying, researching and studying renewal movements throughout the history of the people of God.[537] Comparably, scholars associated with Pentecostal Theological Seminary have been at the forefront of Pentecostal hermeneutics' conversations since Moore's emphasis, in 1987, on pneumatically embodying the message of scripture (see 2.4.1).[538]

A significant number of scholars within the conversation have been associated with these two North American schools, but these schools of thought are not restricted to those currently or previously located at either school.[539] Rather, Regent University School of Divinity and Pentecostal

535. I read "Pneumatological Imagination" during my last few months of research. I note this to highlight that in this analysis I have been reaching complementary conclusions independently of Yong via a different approach and method. This has hallmarks of the qualitative research method, "triangulation," which Swinton and Mowat explain as "using multiple methods and multiple means of analysis, including using more than one person by the use of more than one method of data collection or one method of analysis" providing data "more rigour, breadth and complexity." Swinton and Mowat, *Practical Theology and Qualitative Research*, 215.

536. See fns. 511, 517 (Vondey).

537. See discussion in Coulter and Yong, *Spirit, The Affections, and the Christian Tradition*, ix–x; and Yong, "Conclusion: The Affective Spirit," 293–94 (294). Also, Regent University School of Divinity, "Center for Renewal Studies," n.p. Cf. discussion regarding charisms of groups and institutions in fn. 547.

538. Also Arrington (see fn. 195). Pentecostal Theological Seminary pursues theological learning through Church of God and Pentecostal roots, acknowledging Wesleyan-Pentecostal inheritance. Pentecostal Theological Seminary, "Story of PTSeminary," n.p.

539. As of January 2020, Dale Coulter, Kevin Spawn, and Archie Wright, were

Theological Seminary are here understood as hermeneutical thought hubs. They represent two broad and complementary research areas across the conversation where scholarly thought is generally identifiable with hermeneutical characteristics of that hub. Scholars identified as "Regent school" or "Cleveland school" have enough in common for it to be convenient to categorize them as such, whilst acknowledging that some would not identify themselves in this way and do not owe their views to those who work at Regent University School of Divinity or Pentecostal Theological Seminary. They have been categorized like this to emphasize a point, namely the *complementary* nature of thought related to pneumatic interpretation from those across or identifying with the renewal tradition.

5.2.1 The "Regent school"

"Regent school" scholars come from a range of ecclesial traditions including Pentecostalism. They mostly identify in, but some identify with (see 1.2) the renewal tradition. Scholars include Mark Boda, Jacqueline Grey, Craig Keener, Jack Levison, Kevin Spawn, and Archie Wright.[540]

The "Regent school" addresses pneumatic interpretation across, and surrounding,[541] a renewal spectrum.[542] These are mainly biblical scholars

current faculty at Regent University School of Divinity, with Mark Cartledge, Wolfgang Vondey and Amos Yong past faculty. French Arrington, Cheryl Bridges Johns, Jackie Johns, Steven Land, Lee Roy Martin, and John Christopher Thomas were current faculty at Pentecostal Theological Seminary, with Kenneth Archer, Chris Green, and Rickie Moore past faculty.

540. Also Ronald Herms (see fns. 574, 609). In keeping with his and this work's complementarity, Yong's thought crosses both "schools," as does Vondey's. Cf. fn. 511 regarding Vondey's thought orientation around classical Pentecostalism with stated renewal focus. As they were discussed in 5.1, Yong and Vondey's contributions are omitted from this discussion.

541. E.g., Keener addressed *Spirit Hermeneutics* to all committed to reading scripture experientially and seeking the Spirit's voice through scripture regardless of denomination or tradition, and Spawn and Wright emphasized that although the predominant contributors to the conversation about the Spirit's role in scriptural interpretation were renewal scholars, one did not *have* to be a renewal scholar to recognize or address the Spirit's role in interpretation. Keener, *Spirit Hermeneutics*, 3–4; Spawn and Wright, "Emergence of a Pneumatic Hermeneutic in the Renewal Tradition," 10–11, referencing Cartledge, and N. T. Wright's warnings against elitism. Cartledge "Empirical Theology" (pub. 1996), 119–21, and N. T. Wright, "How Can the Bible be Authoritative?" (pub. 1991), 16–17.

542. *Spirit and Scripture* arose from "Spirit and Scripture: A Symposium on Renewal Biblical Hermeneutics," held at Regent University School of Divinity in October 2008. Spawn, Wright, Graham Twelftree, and Yong were members of the organizing committee. Spawn and Wright, *Spirit and Scripture*, xiii.

and they focus on investigating ancient communities, their people, and their interpretive practices to inform contemporary understanding of the Spirit's interpretation of and through scripture. To varying extents, depending on their specialism, contemporary interpretation is addressed.[543] Two emerging and interrelated areas of enquiry are the influence of ethical conduct on pneumatic interpretation, and addressing aspects of pneumatic hindrance. Scholars tend to emphasize understanding the cognitive framework surrounding relevant scriptural passages in their original historical location.

This is a broad overview and individual contributions will be discussed. Whilst all "Regent school" contributions collectively and individually complement those from the "Cleveland school" (and vice-versa), some especially complement or align with the corresponding "school." This will be highlighted accordingly.[544]

5.2.2 The "Cleveland school"

The "Cleveland school" was named by James K. A. Smith after he identified a locus of thought coming from scholars at or associated with Pentecostal Theological Seminary.[545] "Cleveland school" scholars include Cheryl Bridges Johns, Chris Green, Lee Roy Martin, Rickie Moore, John Christopher Thomas, and Robert Wall.[546]

In their article, "The Pentecostals and Their Scriptures," Robby Waddell and Peter Althouse explained the core of the "Cleveland school's" ideology. Defending "Cleveland school" scholars' preference to focus on the final form of the text over the historical features, they stated, "The group [hold] a deep commitment to the spiritual experience of reading Scripture with an expectation of encountering God in and through the text. For them, the sacred text [is] no mere historical artifact; rather it [is] a place in which the Spirit would meet its readers and transform them into the image of Christ."[547]

543. Cf. Moberly's critique of the *Spirit and Scripture* essayists (fn. 508).

544. E.g., Grey's thought aligns with both "schools" but has a "Regent school" emphasis. Reflecting this, her contribution is considered at the end of 5.3. Similarly Robert Wall ("Cleveland school"), whose contribution is considered as 5.4 commences.

545. James Smith, *Thinking in Tongues*, 6, fn. 13.

546. Discussion concerns scholars and their thought post-2010 only.

547. Waddell and Althouse, "Pentecostals and Their Scriptures" (pub. 2016), 116. This article offers a useful short history of the conversation covering key developments including the "Cleveland school" and *Spirit and Scripture*. Waddell and Althouse offered these thoughts when discussing developments in 1993. They used the past tense ("the group also held . . .") but I adjusted their statement to use the present tense ("the group [hold]"). I would argue that this adjustment is valid because Smith also gave

The "Cleveland school's" strength lies with attention to this pneumatic experience. As Moore's precursor in 2.4.1 indicated, these scholars argue that we embody the scriptural message and understand that we do not just interpret scripture with the Spirit's help, but that the Spirit through scripture—or scripture, by the Spirit (see 5.4.2)—interprets us.[548] "Cleveland school" scholars emphasize affective and ethical aspects. Their primary cognitive framework of interpretation is the contemporary, and/or early, Pentecostal community. They therefore differ from, but more importantly, complement, "Regent school" scholars by focusing primarily on our experiences as we engage with scripture today.

5.2.3 Evaluation

This discussion has introduced two schools of thought within the conversation surrounding the Spirit's role in the interpretation of scripture from scholars in or identifying with the renewal tradition, and outlined hallmarks of "Regent school" and "Cleveland school" thought. Smith identified the "Cleveland school," but the "Regent school" is this work's classification. It is offered as a starting point for understanding alongside the "Cleveland school" to emphasize the contrasting yet complementary nature of thought from scholars across the conversation. In keeping with the work's stated overall purpose (see 1.1), the hope is that presenting these two broad research areas as schools of thought will strengthen understanding of hallmarks of pneumatic interpretation, and foster appreciation and understanding of different specialisms and contributions, working to build a stronger conversation overall.

---

his thoughts on the "Cleveland school" in the present tense. James Smith, *Thinking in Tongues* (pub. 2010), 6, fn. 13. Moreover, based on the understanding that a scholarly group or institution can have a God-given DNA or charism, *both* tenses are valid for that charism will have been present in both 1993 *and* 2010. Discussing institutions and their God-given charisms, see Gordon Smith, *Institutional Intelligence*, chapter 2. Of course charisms, as gifts of the Spirit, whether institutional or individual, also benefit from being nurtured: a charism can be present but not visible because it has not been nurtured, and it may recede from view because it has stopped being nurtured. Cf. fn. 529 (Oliverio on Yong's understanding of "spirit").

548. Ervin, Francis Martin, Pink, and Balthasar also provided (unknowingly) precursory contributions complementing Moore's insights, and which support the overall emphasis of this analysis that central to pneumatic interpretation is personal experience of intimate relationship with the triune God through pneumatic encounter, understanding affect, ethics, and cognition as dynamically interrelating aspects of this intimate relationship. See chapter 2.

5.3 THE "REGENT SCHOOL" APPROACH

This section considers contributions from scholars collectively termed as "Regent school," building an understanding of their individual and shared offering. Levison's emphasis on cultivating virtue and Keener's addressing of moral blindness is discussed, before highlighting Wright, Levison, and Boda's attention to ancient communities and their interpretive practices. The section closes by considering Grey's interrelation between Pentecostalism, scriptural interpretation, and the Old Testament.[549]

5.3.1 Cultivating virtue (Jack Levison)

In *Inspired: The Holy Spirit and the Mind of Faith*, Levison constructed a pneumatology from scripture across the Christian Bible, also incorporating surrounding early Jewish "scripture,"[550] to illustrate the connection between the Spirit and comprehension. Virtue (ethics) was an integral part of this connection.[551] Levison's pivotal exegesis was the same as his earlier, more comprehensive, *Filled with the Spirit*.[552] Before considering his

549. Miscellaneous contributions not discussed elsewhere in 5.3 included Cartledge discussing differences between Pentecostal and evangelical interpretive method. Cartledge, "Text-Community-Spirit," 130–42. Cartledge's terminology was confusing. My inference is that as a non-Pentecostal and like Pinnock, "Divine Relationality" (pub. 2000), 6, Cartledge championed classical Pentecostal scholars, emphasizing their approach to interpretive method with spirituality as integral, but concluded using renewal terminology and thereby stressing inclusivity across the renewal tradition. Also, McCall, "Baconian Common Sense Realism," 223–40; Sherman, "Mapping the Hermeneutical Waters," 21–39.

550. This work defines scripture within the Christian Bible (see fn. 2), but Levison, *Inspired* (pub. 2013), and also Wright, "Second Temple Period Jewish Biblical Interpretation" (see 5.3.3), used "scripture" more widely to include early Jewish literature surrounding scripture in the Christian Bible (e.g., Qumran). In *Filled with the Spirit* (see fn. 552), Levison used "literature." Discussing whether non-canonical texts are also scripture is beyond this work's remit. Briefly discussing complexities of terming "scripture," Levison, *Inspired*, 3, fn. 4.

551. Levison developed this across two areas: virtue and learning (chapter 1), and ecstasy and comprehension (chapter 2), before considering virtue and ecstasy within the inspired interpretation of scripture (chapter 3). He concluded with a proposal for pneumatology.

552. Levison, *Filled with the Spirit* (pub. 2009). This is a survey of the corpus of Israelite, Jewish, and early Christian thought, looking at pneumatology through the lens of what it means to be filled with the spirit (cf. fn. 554 [s/Spirit]). Levison emphasized his thought had developed since *Filled with the Spirit* and he credited critical reviews in *JPT* and *Pneuma* with helping develop this. Levison, *Inspired*, 8–9. This work therefore engages with *Inspired*, referencing *Filled with the Spirit* accordingly. For "pneumatic" interpretation in *Filled with the Spirit*, see 185–201, 347–61, 399–404.

understanding of the relationship between virtue and inspired (pneumatic) interpretation,[553] this grounding should be understood.

Levison argued that there is a clear strand of thought across this corpus that had been largely unnoticed and overshadowed by emphasis on subsequence and the gifts of the Spirit. This, he wrote, is the "long-held Israelite belief that the spirit[554] of God—not merely the soul or an essentially physical breath—was given at birth."[555] He argued that placing a starting point for pneumatology at the beginning of the biblical canon forces us to address this understanding.[556] Consequently, Levison recognized that we all "[have] the spirit-breath of God within us from birth,"[557] and throughout our lives, using Wright's explanation, "the individual either nurtures or ignores the divine spirit within."[558] However, as Wright stressed in his critique, Levison did not discuss the negative aspect in *Filled with the Spirit*, or address the influence of evil spirits on a person,[559] and this was also the case in *Inspired*.

553. Broadly, Levison used "inspired interpretation" where this work uses pneumatic interpretation, appropriation, and/or discernment.

554. Levison chose not to capitalize *spirit* and in deference to him, I do likewise when referencing his work. In doing this, he argued against dichotomy created by English translators having to choose whether to capitalize the word *spirit*. As Levison explained, "In Israel and the early church, however, this distinction simply did not come into play. One word, *ruach* or *pneuma*, could communicate *both* the spirit or breath of God within all human beings *and* the divine spirit or breath that God gives as a special endowment." Levison, *Inspired*, 19–20 (19) (emphasis original). For complementary perspective on *pneuma* translation, incorporating Chinese translation, with implications for personal communication with God, see Robert Menzies, *Language of the Spirit* (pub. 2010), 25–39.

555. Levison, *Filled with the Spirit*, 12.

556. Levison, "*Filled with the Spirit*: A Conversation with Pentecostal and Charismatic Scholars" (pub. 2011), 217–18. Responding, Macchia stated, "Levison wishes to highlight the uniqueness of the accent of Old Testament pneumatology on the Spirit of creation. In doing so, he shows us that there is in the Scriptures a deeper tension in relation to the issue of 'subsequence' that makes any difference between Paul and Luke seem like small potatoes. I speak of the tension between the pneumatologies of the two Testaments. The subsequence issue raised by Levison is not between faith and post-faith experiences but rather between the human vitality at birth and any further endowment of the Spirit!" Macchia later wrote, "*This* is indeed the subsequence issue on which we Pentecostals should be expending our scholarly energy." Macchia, "Spirit of Life," 70, 71 (emphasis original). Similarly, Waddell likened Levison's pneumatological argument to the debate between Dunn and Pentecostal scholars on Spirit baptism. Waddell, "Holy Spirit of Life," 210.

557. Levison, *Inspired*, 17.

558. Archie Wright, "Spirit in Early Jewish Biblical Interpretation," 45–46.

559. Wright, "Spirit in Early Jewish Biblical Interpretation," 45–46, and 36, fn. 4 concerning evil spirits.

Levison's pneumatology was controversial and *Filled with the Spirit* generated substantial response. *JPT* and *Pneuma*, for example, gave considerable space in their 2011 issues for critical reviews.[560] Some were less favorable,[561] but the majority were appreciative, albeit with cautionary elements.[562]

The main concern *for this work* was raised by Dale Coulter, who stated that Levison's work, and the responding reviews, highlighted two issues that those involved with developing renewal methodologies should heed. Coulter explained, "The first is the complex nature of the relationship between the human spirit and the Holy Spirit while the second concerns the 'mechanics' of such a relationship."[563] Whilst the analysis has not been assessing the human spirit,[564] it *has* been assessing the "mechanics" of relationship with God as Father, Son, and Spirit through pneumatic encounter, as we approach scripture seeking the Spirit's guidance. These "*mechanics*" concern: 1) the heart as the locus of discernment and interpretation; 2) the holistic, creational, redemptive, and reconciliational nature of truth brought by the Spirit through the interpretation of scripture; and 3) the dynamic interrelation between affect, ethics, and cognition, especially recognizing—in this context discussing Levison's contribution, and Keener's following—discussion of the paradox of affective receptivity and ethical willingness.[565]

560. *JPT* 20 (2011) 193–231, and *Pneuma* 33 (2011) 1–4, 25–93. Reviews included those from Macchia, Waddell, Wright, Charette, Stronstad, Turner, plus an editorial from Coulter, discussed in this section.

561. E.g., Charette, "'Something Completely Different,'" 59–62; Stronstad, "Review," 201–6. These reviews related to Levison's handling of Luke-Acts.

562. E.g., Max Turner: "For the ancient Israelite (according to Levison) the breath of God by which the human lives is the same as the holy spirit God has planted in him/her and by which YHWH orchestrates human activity to enhance creation and accomplishes his particular historical purposes with Israel. This is possibly the most original part of the book, and requires us to read nearly all references to 'holy spirit/spirit of God' without anachronistically reading them as 'the Holy Spirit', i.e. it is not the transcendent divine Spirit, occasionally on loan to humans; rather it is the immanent God-given anthropological spirit: the living heart, mind and soul, ever open to, and influenced by, the Lord himself. I found very many of his readings convincing, though with some caveats." Turner, "Levison's *Filled with the Spirit*," 195. See also, Macchia, "Spirit of Life," 69–78; Waddell, "Holy Spirit of Life," 207–12; Wright, "Spirit in Early Jewish Biblical Interpretation," 35–46.

563. Coulter, "Pentecostalism, Mysticism, and Renewal Methodologies," 1.

564. For perspective, see Welker, "Human Spirit," 134–42. Cf. fn. 529 (Yong's understanding of "spirit").

565. Also referred to as the affective-ethical paradox. See discussion in 2.3.3; 2.5; 3.3; 3.3.1; 3.5; 4.3.2. Cf. Coulter, stating that his and Yong's edited volume, *Spirit, The Affections, and the Christian Tradition*, "underscores the need for an ecumenical and cross-disciplinary exploration of affectivity in relationship to pneumatology and the

Levison argued that living virtuously cultivates cognitive[566] receptivity to the Spirit's communication. He cautioned, "God breathes the potential or capacity for virtue into everyone. God does not inbreathe actual virtue into everyone. The spirit of God within us must be taught, disciplined, cultivated."[567] He considered pre-Pentecost biblical figures alongside those in Acts or the epistles; characters like Daniel and Simeon, who illustrate lives spent in devotion and discipline, study and learning, and worship and prayer. Daniel's exceptional spiritual wisdom and insight is shown to arise out of his faithfulness and commitment to purity.[568] Simeon, a man "disciplined in devotion, hopeful, versed in scripture, and receptive to the holy spirit," pneumatically perceived the baby Jesus as the Messiah scripture had spoken of, his praises (Luke 2:28–32) "drenched in the language of Isaiah 40–55," illustrating the depth of his knowledge of scripture.[569]

Levison's understanding of virtue was dictated by the actions and attitudes exhibited by characters across the biblical canon and wider Jewish literature. He explained virtue as a malleable term encompassing a range of activities, not so much "a technical term for a particular way of life," but "a cipher for what is deemed to be holy, true and right" according to different authorial perspectives.[570] Virtue, for Levison, therefore included a range of

transformation of the human person." Coulter, "Introduction: Language of Affectivity," 6. For further, see 1.3.2.

566. This is my use of "cognition," applied in consideration of Levison's thought.

567. Levison, *Inspired*, 66, drawing on Philo. For Philo and virtue, see Levison, *Inspired*, 44–48, 66 (66) 139–43 (specific to interpretation). Also 135–38 discussing Ben Sira (see text for sources and discussion). For overview of Philo's life, works, and thought see Morris, "Jewish Philosopher Philo," 809–89; Sterling, "Philo Judaeus," 663–69. As Levison emphasized by such discussions, the idea that living virtuously helps with understanding scripture is not new. E.g., Athanasius (*circa* 295–373 CE) wrote, "In addition to the study and true knowledge of the Scriptures are needed a good life and pure soul and virtue in Christ, so that the mind, journeying in this path, may be able to obtain and apprehend what it desires, in so far as human nature is able to learn about God the Word. For without a pure mind and a life modeled on the saints, no one can apprehend the words of the saints." Athanasius, *Contra Gentes and De Incarnatione*, 275 (9.57).

568. Levison, *Inspired*, 32–38.

569. Levison, *Inspired*, 146–48 (146). Also Anna (Luke 2:36–38): "Anna, like Simeon, sees Jesus because she is well prepared: prayerful, devoted to fasting, and saturated by the vision of Isaiah" (183).

570. Levison, *Inspired*, 12. For further, see Sommers and Sommers, *Vice & Virtue*, 290–355, explaining roots of virtue philosophy in Greek thought and discussing different approaches and thinkers. Daniel Castelo, external to pneumatic interpretation and with Pentecostal-specific focus, considered the relationship between affect and virtue. Emphasizing their complementarity, Castelo stated, "when considered together, these two frameworks can provide a portrayal of the Christian life that begins with

ethical actions and conduct including courage, discipline, altruism, dietary simplicity, sexual purity, communal generosity, and sound reasoning.[571] An integral component in Levison's understanding was that although there may be points where we pneumatically receive intensification of insight, cognitive receptivity to the Spirit's communication emerges from a life spent cultivating virtue. On a situational basis, understanding often comes through a longer cognitive process[572] of "pondering and puzzling" upon scripture in light of specific, and sometimes unexpected, experiences or revelatory insights.[573] This unexpected aspect is important: the Spirit does not always act in the way we may anticipate, and truth brought by the Spirit can surprise. Subsequent dwelling on that experience or insight with scripture and in relationship with God and others in our community frameworks will facilitate understanding. Furthermore, the cultivation of virtue along with the process of pondering and puzzling following the initial experience or insight, brings, *pneumatically*, fresh understanding of scripture *and* personal transformation.

Levison's input concerning the ethical component of pneumatic interpretation is significant. In particular, his contribution strengthens the developing understanding of the correlation between ethical conduct and cognition, and relationship with pneumatic interpretation (see 4.3.5 for recent summary).[574] Moreover, Levison emphasized biblical (and early Jewish) figures shown to clearly prioritize intimate relationship with God. Therefore, although he did not specifically address this, he also implicitly recognized the affective component of pneumatic interpretation along with ethics and cognition.

God's prevenient activity and continues with the call to work out one's own salvation." Castelo, "Tarrying on the Lord," 31–56 (45). Cf. fns. 85 (affect), 84 (pneumatic ethics).

571. Levison, *Inspired*, 12.

572. Sometimes it is not practical to use affect, ethics, and cognition in one sentence. Although I recognize this process as cognitive, Levison was not, and neither am I, suggesting it was *solely* cognitive, but a cognitive process of reasoning interrelated with ethical action whilst in (affective) devotion to God.

573. Levison, *Inspired*, 101–5 (105, emphasis removed), using Peter's vision, and subsequent pondering and puzzling in Acts 10–11. On the unexpected nature of the Spirit's communication, see Yong, "Pneumatological Imagination," 160. Also compare Lee Roy Martin, Macchia, and Keener's sudden and surprising experiences (4.3.4, fn. 493, 5.3.2 respectively).

574. Complementary contributions included, Spawn, "Principle of Analogy," 67–70, discussing Job's growth of divine perspective through his growing knowledge of the heavenly court, establishing an interesting link between divine perspective and spiritual warfare; and Moberly, "Pneumatic Biblical Hermeneutics," 160–61, on the centrality of prayer (as part of relationship with God) to the faithful reading of scripture. Continuing Moberly's highlighting of prayer, Herms, "Response," 180–81.

5.3.2 Pneumatic hindrance (Craig Keener)

As Wright's critique helped address, Levison's focus was pneumatic cultivation and he did not consider how receptivity to, or discernment of, the Spirit's communication can be hindered. Aspects of Keener's thought, however, do provide insight into this important but neglected issue of pneumatic hindrance.

In *Spirit Hermeneutics*,[575] Keener developed a proposition for a Spirit-directed epistemology. He reasoned that this epistemology would provide "a necessary foundation for any Spirit hermeneutic, which grows from faithful relationship with God and trusting submission to what God says."[576] Within this discussion, Keener divulged his struggle to balance his academic work with his personal relationship with God. He shared this to emphasize the importance of integrating the academic side that pursues evidence, with a faith that recognizes that there must also be "a place for healthy trust."[577]

Keener suggested that "biblical faith" is a perspective that allows access to divine truth, "a spiritual sense, that allows us to see what is genuinely present yet is hidden from those who do not believe (2 Cor. 4:3–4)."[578] He emphasized that "biblical truth" is discerned through trust and dependence on God, who reveals truth in scripture. However, he also explained that unbelief is the opposing perspective to faith, hindering us from (cognitively) recognizing what is genuinely present in scripture.[579] Keener only indirectly discussed the Spirit in this discussion, but following his reasoning high-

575. Keener, *Spirit Hermeneutics* (pub. 2016). Identifying as "a charismatic, biblical scholar," Keener explained that his strongest contribution to the conversation was "by focusing on the biblical evidence itself." (1). He developed this in six parts: I) a first step toward considering how scripture speaks today; II) global readings of scripture and respecting and recognizing different cultural readings; III) the designed sense and the historical context (see fn. 43); IV) an Spirit-directed epistemology underpinning a Spirit hermeneutic; V) models for reading scripture evident within scripture itself; VI) uninformed or undisciplined populist readings of scripture. For further analysis, see discussion of *Spirit Hermeneutics* in *Pneuma* (2017), introduced by editors Waddell and Althouse, with peer essays and response from Keener. Waddell and Althouse, "An Editorial Note," 123–25; Oliverio, "Reading Craig Keener," 126–45; Spawn, "Interpretation of Scripture," 146–52; Mather, "Welcoming *Spirit Hermeneutics*," 153–61; Aker, "Craig S. Keener's *Spirit Hermeneutics*," 162–67; Grey, "Spirit *of* and Spirit *in*," 168–78; Kenneth Archer, "Spirited Conversation about Hermeneutics,"179–97; Keener, "Refining *Spirit Hermeneutics*," 198–240. Also, Keener, "Pentecostal Biblical Interpretation/ Spirit Hermeneutics," 270–83.

576. Keener, *Spirit Hermeneutics*, 287. See "Epistemology and the Spirit," 153–86.

577. Keener, *Spirit Hermeneutics*, 163–64, 29 (29).

578. Keener, *Spirit Hermeneutics*, 174–75 (175).

579. Keener, *Spirit Hermeneutics*, 175. Keener did not use the term cognition.

lights that truth the Spirit communicates through scripture can sometimes be concealed because our interpretive prejudgments do not allow us to recognize and receive it.[580] This reinforces the discussion in 4.3.2 and 4.3.4 in relation to Francis Martin and Richard Bauckham.

Elsewhere, Keener illustrated hindrance from prejudgment by sharing a personal experience of evil related to traditional African curses. In this experience, Keener and his family narrowly escaped being crushed by a large tree, which split and crashed in the spot they had been standing moments before. He explained, "The information that reached us from Congo soon after this event made clear that this was a direct and deliberate spiritual attack from which God had protected us."[581] This experience disrupted Keener's theology as he "did not understand biblically how a spirit could have power to do more than deceive and work in individuals." Not knowing how to resolve the tension between this personal experience of evil and his theological understanding of evil, "cognitive dissonance" persisted.[582]

Some years later, when reading Job 1, Keener "suddenly noticed" something afresh in the text: "Satan sent a strong wind, causing a house to collapse on Job's children" (Job 1:12, 19). In that moment, Keener identified what happened to him scripturally, connecting his experience with his theology.[583] Keener only implicitly linked the Spirit when recounting this story. Therefore, whilst he did not state as much, his interpretive prejudgment appears to have facilitated his *pneumatic* hindrance. Moreover, the moment of connection when he identified his own experience within the scripture he was reading appears to be an example of pneumatic appropriation (see 4.2.4).

Keener also emphasized that "Scripture is clear that human depravity affects our ability to perceive divine truth."[584] He called this "moral blindness," stressing that scripture also speaks of this "among God's own people."[585] This is important because it highlights that being a Christian

580. Keener, *Spirit Hermeneutics*, 175.

581. Keener, *Spirit Hermeneutics*, 116.

582. Keener, *Spirit Hermeneutics*, 116, 92 respectively.

583. Keener, *Spirit Hermeneutics*, 116. See 115–17 for pneumatic link. Cf. Lee Roy Martin's (believed) sudden and surprising pneumatic experience when searching for his thesis topic, which reoriented his perspective (4.3.4). Also, Macchia's revelation whilst watching a show in Las Vegas (fn. 493).

584. Keener continued, "Some depict this depravity as corruption of reason; others specify a fallenness of the will that resists divine truth. Still others, including myself, would doubt that reason and will are so easily disentangled." Keener, *Spirit Hermeneutics*, 177.

585. Keener, *Spirit Hermeneutics*, 171.

does not automatically guarantee pneumatic interpretation. Keener focused on the biblical evidence for moral blindness, considering sin's darkening of the mind, corporate blindness, temporary or partial blindness, and hostility toward truth.[586] He later followed this by stressing that disobedience hinders receptivity of truth, using Jesus's parable of the sower (Matt 13:11–15) to illustrate the importance of the manner in which a message is received, and contrasting Jesus's ethics with the Pharisees' ethics (compare 4.3.1).[587] Concluding, Keener emphasized that despite the reality of moral blindness, the Spirit is the ultimate inspirer and empowerer of our vision and receptivity.[588]

Within these aforementioned areas, Keener gave minimal attention to the Spirit's role. However, these aspects of his discussion are significant, for they highlight the lesser-explored area of pneumatic hindrance and impact on pneumatic interpretation.[589] His experience of evil in Africa and subsequent struggle to connect what had happened to him with his theology appears to be a useful example of pneumatic hindrance caused by prejudgment (as explained in 4.3.2, prejudgment itself is not necessarily a negative feature). When discussing moral blindness, Keener did not explore the relationship between immoral conduct and pneumatic interpretation any further than in his concluding summary, and further cross-disciplinary investigation concerning this area would be valuable. Although Keener recognized the value of majority world insights on spirits,[590] with his story showing direct experience, an aspect Keener surprisingly did not discuss was pneumatic hindrance caused by evil spirits.

586. Keener, *Spirit Hermeneutics*, 177–86. Darkening of the mind: Pharaoh's hardened heart in Exodus, and sin blinding the people's minds in Isaiah. Corporate blindness: the corporate sin depicted in Romans 1. Temporary or partial blindness: ignorance and sexual immorality causing blindness in Ephesians 4, and describing Jesus's disciples as half blind in Mark 8. Hostility toward truth: epistemic dualism in John's gospel, "those who embrace the truth and those who resist it" (182).

587. Keener, *Spirit Hermeneutics*, 207, 211–12, 214. See also Chris Green, "Provoked to Saving Jealousy," 180–92 regarding the hardening of Israel's hearts in Romans 9–11 and Paul's hermeneutical reworking of Hosea.

588. Keener, *Spirit Hermeneutics*, 186.

589. For smaller exploration, see Locker, "Seeing the Unseeable," 8–11. Also, Webster on "fallen intellect." Webster, *Domain of the Word*, 158.

590. Keener, *Spirit Hermeneutics*, 88–92.

5.3.3 Ancient communities and their interpretive practices (Archie Wright, Jack Levison, and Mark Boda)

Wright, Levison, and Boda considered ancient communities, their people, and their interpretive practices, giving some attention to contemporary application.[591]

Wright endeavored to show that "a 'Spirit-led' hermeneutic" was practiced in early Judaism before Christianity emerged and that these interpretive practices were taken up and used by Jesus and other New Testament figures.[592] Within this main focus Wright addressed contemporary application. He related discussions about pneumatic interpretation in the renewal tradition with interpretive methods practiced by the Qumran community.[593] For example, Wright compared the *pesharim* to contemporary "methods" of interpretation that this work has been explaining show the Spirit's appropriation of the scriptural text (see 3.4.5; 4.2.4) to the reader in their personal lives and surrounding circumstances.[594] He used Mark Stibbe's contemporary propagation of an objective (historico-grammatical principles) and subjective (the contemporary reader approaching scripture) hermeneutic to show their complementarity.[595] As Wright explained, "Both methods of biblical interpretation are marked with a key characteristic of a pneumatic hermeneutic—through the revelation of the holy spirit[596] the

591. See Moberly's critique that those concerned with "historically-oriented biblical interpretation" often fail to adequately address contemporary interpretation (fn. 508)

592. Archie Wright, "Second Temple Period Jewish Biblical Interpretation" (f.pub. 2011), 73–98 (74). Cf. 4.3.1 (Pinnock).

593. Wright, "Second Temple Period Jewish Biblical Interpretation," 74–75, 77–82, also drawing on Aune's discussion of charismatic exegesis (see 3.4.5).

594. Wright, "Second Temple Period Jewish Biblical Interpretation," 84, 72. Wright explained that "the *pesharim* of the Dead Sea Scrolls can be categorized as documents that represent a charismatic interpretation closely resembling that of the P/C [Pentecostal and charismatic] biblical interpretation of the twentieth and twenty-first centuries" (84). Cf. 3.4.5 (Aune regarding *pesharim*). Wright's explanation of aspects of interpretation at Qumran are useful for those unfamiliar with early Jewish interpretation. Levison also discussed interpretation at Qumran, without contemporary application in *Filled with the Spirit*, 185–88 (it was not his focus), and in *Inspired*, 138–39.

595. Wright, "Second Temple Period Jewish Biblical Interpretation," 84, fn. 56. For Stibbe, see 3.4.5.

596. Wright de-capitalized "Holy Spirit" when discussing interpretation at Qumran, explaining that "the role of the spirit in the Qumran documents is perhaps more covert than the spirit found in P/C communities." He continued, "The focus of the P/C community is on the 'Holy Spirit,' i.e. the Spirit of God, or the Spirit of the Trinity; whereas the QC [Qumran community] steers away from the capital 'H' and capital 'S' and focuses more on the 'holy spirit' of the individual." Wright, "Second Temple Period Jewish Biblical Interpretation," 80, also referencing Levison, *Filled with the Spirit* (see

interpretations are telling the story of what God is doing now through the eyes of the interpreter."[597]

Levison discussed pneumatic appropriation by the early Christians in the New Testament.[598] He offered that "the holy spirit brings out the *meaning* of ancient scriptures—texts known already to the speaker—for contemporary contexts," and argued that this happens through the speaker's sustained study and knowledge of scripture.[599] Simeon's song in Luke 2, discussed in 5.3.1, is an example of this.[600] Levison's consideration of Hebrews is also significant for this work's developing understanding of pneumatic appropriation. Here, he explained that Hebrews 3:7–8, 9:6–9, and 10:15–16 show the holy spirit doing three things: always communicating in the present; modifying or bending scripture to fit the needs of the recipients; and extending the original meaning into the recipient's world and giving it renewed meaning.[601]

Boda considered the Spirit's inscribing of the scriptural text on people's hearts in passages in Jeremiah and Ezekiel, and (interrelated) the hearing of

---

5.3.1).

597. Wright, "Second Temple Period Jewish Biblical Interpretation," 84. Recognizing that this work stresses *the Spirit's activity* over *our methodology*. Cf. fn. 26 (Spawn and Wright's pneumatic hermeneutic).

598. Levison, *Inspired* (pub. 2013), 145–84. Pneumatic appropriation is my term, not Levison's. Cf. fn. 566 (inspired interpretation). Noting their Jewish roots, Levison used the overarching term "early Christians," but of course some of these New Testament characters lived before and during Jesus's birth and upbringing. Cf. fn. 89 (people of God).

599. Levison, *Inspired*, 153 (emphasis original).

600. Levison, *Inspired*, 146–8. Levison also used the paraclete passages in John (particularly 14:26 and 16:12–14), arguing that the holy spirit sometimes guides by teaching in retrospect. This is important because it illustrates that pneumatic understanding may not come until after the event and reinforces limits on ability to pneumatically "know" in the present. Levison, *Inspired*, 148–51. Relatedly, discernment was raised in *Spirit and Scripture* as a key issue. Cf. Cartledge, "Pneumatic Hermeneutics," 187; Dunn, "Role of the Spirit," 155–56; Moberly, "Pneumatic Biblical Hermeneutics," 163–4; Thomas, "'What the Spirit Is Saying to the Church,'" 118; Thomas, "Discerning Dialogue," 184; Archie Wright, "We Are Not All Pentecostals," 179.

601. Levison, *Inspired*, 162 (154–62 for discussion of Hebrews). Cf. also fn. 417 (Allen). Dunn and Levison both discussed Paul's appropriation of Israel's past scriptures, concentrating on 2 Corinthians 3 and Exodus 34. Dunn warned that Paul's contrast between the letter and the Spirit "warns us" that if we are not careful, "we can build a system around Scripture, a system of dogma, or confessions of faith, or ecclesiastical system, or ritual traditions, that actually stifle what the Spirit may be seeking to say through Scripture." Dunn, "'The Letter Kills,'" 177. Levison, *Inspired*, 171–77. Also, Chris Green, "Provoked to Saving Jealousy," 190, on Paul hermeneutically bending Hosea 2:25 (in Rom 9:25–26) past breaking point; Vanhoozer, "Ascending the Mountain," 781–803 (transfigural interpretation).

ancient messages in new ways appropriate for the communities in 2 Kings 22–23 and Nehemiah 8–10.[602] Complementing "Cleveland school" thought, Boda summarized that 2 Kings 22–23 and Nehemiah 8–10 highlight the importance of the scriptural text and the community's reception of the message "in a way that engages their inner affections and outer [ethical] behaviour."[603] This therefore also implies a cognitive component since to receive the Spirit's interpretation requires cognition. Boda emphasized that whilst in 2 Kings and Nehemiah the messages are given through "scribal figures," in Jeremiah and Ezekiel, "the scribal and prophetic functions . . . are infused into the community as a whole."[604] Relating this to contemporary interpretation[605] (and complementing Levison's discussion using Simeon), Boda recognized that there are certain people and communities who "nurture the presence and experience of the Spirit in their lives and midst" and have an anointing to guide others in pneumatic interpretation.[606] He suggested that these people and communities are identifiable through observing "their spiritual, theological, ethical, and interpretive practice."[607] Aligning with this work's central stress, Boda's overriding emphasis was that "key to a pneumatological hermeneutic is a recovery of the role of Scripture as prompter to relationship with the triune God."[608]

Wright, Levison, and Boda's contributions all show the value of studying ancient communities, their people, and their interpretive practices when considering pneumatic interpretation. These biblical scholars, in keeping with their specialisms, started with and focused on the ancient communities and people shown in scripture and early Jewish texts (compare 3.4.4; 3.4.6). From these vantage points they addressed contemporary application. Each, with differing language, discussed the Spirit's appropriation of the scriptural text to the reader in their personal lives and circumstances. Their awareness of these ancient communities and how they interpreted with the "Spirit"—or how the Spirit interpreted them—is especially helpful in identifying patterns of pneumatic behavior, present both then *and* now. As Levison and Boda recognized, diligent study of scripture appears to nurture awareness of

602. Boda, "Word and Spirit," (f.pub. 2011), 25–45; "Walking with the Spirit in the Word" (f.pub. 2011), 169–72. For Jeremiah and Ezekiel references, see Boda, "Word and Spirit," 34–38.

603. Boda, "Word and Spirit," 40.

604. Boda, "Word and Spirit," 40, 39 respectively.

605. This was after reading Moberly's critique (fn. 508).

606. Boda, "Walking with the Spirit in the Word," 170. This was in relation to the scribal figures in 2 Kings 22–23 and Nehemiah 8–10.

607. Boda, "Walking with the Spirit in the Word," 170.

608. Boda, "Walking with the Spirit in the Word," 171.

the Spirit's interpretive activity—*if* approached as part of intimate relationship with God (a caution they would doubtless agree with). Boda's contribution shows evidence of the affective, ethical, (and cognitive) components of pneumatic interpretation that are so central to this analysis.[609]

5.3.4 Pentecostalism, scriptural interpretation, and the book of Isaiah (Jacqueline Grey)

Using the book of Isaiah, Grey proposed an interpretive approach to the Old Testament that interrelated the interpreter, and surrounding contemporary community framework, with the scriptural text, and surrounding historical community framework.[610] Her priority was providing an interpretive approach that helped Pentecostals[611] interpret scripture to personal life and surrounding community situations in ways consistent with their spirituality and assisting critical reflection of self and scripture (and surrounding cognitive frameworks).[612] She incorporated the Spirit's role when discussing a

609. Additionally, Ron Herms explored "pneumatic constructions in the communicative strategy of Revelation." Recognizing the author's spirituality, Herms argued that the book's communicative strategy is one renewal communities also experience. Herms sought "to take seriously the literary-narrative dimensions of the text while recognizing that the author presumed a certain understanding of, and participation in, the described spirituality and religious experience on the part of the hearers/readers." Herms therefore actively interrelated the interpreter and surrounding community framework with the ancient community shown in Revelation. Herms, "Invoking the Spirit," (f.pub. 2011), 99–114 (quotes, 99 and 100, fn. 2 respectively). See also, Herms, "Response," 180–82. Considering pneumatic discernment and interpretation through the book of Revelation is an emerging research area, particularly amongst Pentecostal scholars. See David Johnson, *Pneumatic Discernment in the Apocalypse*; and Thomas, "Mystery of the Great Whore," 111–36, discussing the discussing the unfolding nature of pneumatic discernment. Johnson's focus was also pneumatic discernment and therefore wider than pneumatic interpretation, and specific to Pentecostalism.

610. Grey, *Three's a Crowd* (pub. 2011). Grey's later, 'When the Spirit Trumps Tradition" (pub. 2016), 143–57, shows increased attention to the interpreter and surrounding contemporary framework, using Thomas's Acts 15 model (see 3.4.4).

611. Grey used "Pentecostal" terminology to refer to "common and inclusive spirituality" across the renewal tradition hallmarked by personal experience of the Spirit. Grey, *Three's a Crowd*, 35. However, she interacted mainly with classical Pentecostal scholars when discussing the renewal tradition (chapter 2) and renewal interpretive approaches. Accordingly, her terminology is retained.

612. Grey, *Three's a Crowd*, 187. Grey critically engaged with and actively incorporated postmodernist thought (127–33, also throughout), Pentecostal hermeneutics (chapter 3), Old Testament theology (chapter 4), and semiotics (chapter 5). She also incorporated qualitative research, engaging with sample groups of (mainly classical) Pentecostal readers, comparing their interpreting and reasoning processes (9–11, Appendix, and throughout).

Pentecostal approach to scripture and so pneumatic references were often implicit rather than explicit. Grey stated:

> It is crucial that to be consistent with the tradition of the Pentecostal community—the reader, their experience of God and spirituality are allowed to "speak" with the Old Testament text. It is likewise crucial for the theological consistency of the Pentecostal community that the Old Testament texts be allowed to "speak" to the reader their own message, one both relevant to their historical context and part of the redemptive story of the people of God.[613]

Grey advocated an interpretive approach that recognized and interrelated three components: "me," "them," and "us."[614] "Me" referred to the individual approaching Isaiah, anticipating and trusting that the Spirit will speak from the scriptural passages into their "unique situation and context."[615] Although Grey did not use these terms, she presented that this pneumatic interpretation and appropriation, whilst cognitive, also brings affective-ethical transformation.[616]

"Them" referred to the original community the author of Isaiah addressed within their historical and cultural situation.[617] Grey emphasized that "rather than subsume the culture and historical situation of the text into the situation of the reader (literalism) the context of the text and its meaning for 'them' must be voiced."[618] She explained that identifying "them" will be more specific according to a person's level of critical skills, knowledge, and resources, but within this is an over-arching principle that appreciation of the historico-cultural framework surrounding scripture in its

613. Grey, *Three's a Crowd*, 99.

614. Grey, *Three's a Crowd*, 155, 190.

615. Grey, *Three's a Crowd*, 163. Grey's incorporation of postmodernist thought meant she sometimes referred to "text" when she could have spoken more directly of the Spirit. E.g., "The text speaks to the Pentecostal reader with insight into the reader's own context and situation. This model proposes that the Pentecostal reader asks: what does the text mean to *me*? Through the process the text can speak to the Pentecostal reader." (163 [emphasis original]), noting her surrounding discussion concerned the Spirit's personal appropriation of scriptural truth. Cf. Ellington (4.2.4).

616. Grey, *Three's a Crowd*, 162–64, citing Johns and Johns (see 3.3.2).

617. Grey, *Three's a Crowd*, 164–70. Grey noted that "within the realm of biblical studies . . . the identification of the recipients of biblical texts is typically *unclear*" and a research area involving detailed critical analysis (164–65 [164], emphasis original).

618. Grey, *Three's a Crowd*, 164. Similarly, fn. 43 (Keener on original context and original meaning).

original historical location is achievable and important for *all* seeking to (pneumatically)[619] interpret and appropriate scriptural truth.[620]

"Us" concerned what the text means to "us" as a contemporary Christian and/or Pentecostal community, recognizing continuity and discontinuity between the contemporary and ancient community. She emphasized reading christologically alongside making effort to stand between the Old Testament and New Testament communities, interpreting with an overarching redemptive-history framework.[621] It is questionable how pneumatic her approach was at this point, for her starting point and emphasis was christological, not pneumatic (compare 4.2.2). However, pneumatic interpretation was not Grey's central focus.

Within her explication of "them," Grey also advocated approaching scripture as testimony, understanding that within the scriptural passages we read are truths or testimonies about God's character and actions.[622] As Grey explained, these truths were presented to the original community in the passages (or to whom the passages were originally addressed) within their specific historical cultural situations and yet are also presented to us as we read the passages in our contemporary historical cultural situations.[623] Because these truths show "principles of God's character and relationship with the world" they are both translatable *across*, yet also particular *to* specific historical cultural situations.[624]

619. Grey's pneumatic references were here implicit.

620. Grey, *Three's a Crowd*, 164–6. "A more simple reflection on the Old Testament Scripture should not obstruct academics, and more detailed 'scientific' study of context should not intimidate lay readers" (165). Cf. my similar reasoning in 4.2.4.

621. Grey, *Three's a Crowd*, 170–76 (170).

622. Grey, *Three's a Crowd*, 165–70. Discussion incorporated Ellington (see 4.2.4); Brueggemann, *Theology of the Old Testament*, 117–20; Childs, *Biblical Theology*, 358, 379; Ricoeur, *Essays*, 119–54. Ellington and Grey both drew on these same pages in Brueggemann, *Theology of the New Testament*. Ellington's influence on Grey is noted, as is Brueggemann's influence on them both.

623. Grey, *Three's a Crowd*, 165, 169.

624. Grey, *Three's a Crowd*, 168. Here Grey also highlighted contradictory, confusing aspects of the Old Testament to the contemporary reader, emphasizing the translatability, yet also, particularity. Cf. 4.2.4 (Davies regarding the moral core beneath the written words that the Spirit interprets to us). See also Grey's discussion of "Us." For complementary approach, cf. Spawn's discussions of analogy in conceptualizing the Spirit's role in interpretation and applying to interpretation in the renewal tradition. Spawn, "Intersection of Biblical Testimony and Experience," 3–7, using 1 Kings 17:17–24. Also, Spawn, "Principle of Analogy," 46–72; and Spawn, "Analogy and the Scholar's Shared Experience," 173–76, both using the story of Job as a case study. See also fn. 574 (Spawn). Also, Stovell, "Kingdom Pneumatic Hermeneutics," 8–11.

Whilst Grey's attention to the Spirit was mostly implicit through focusing on the Pentecostal interpreter, her contribution is valuable in providing practical interpretive principles for interpreting and appropriating scripture for Christians in or identifying with the renewal tradition who accentuate the Spirit's role in their hermeneutical considerations. "Implicit" is not intended disparagingly for Grey was partly able to present this practical study by focusing on the interpreter and interpretive method. This shows the value of contributions like Grey's, but they require balancing with those that *do* explicitly address the Spirit's role. This analysis has been working to do just this.

Finally, engagement with Grey's contribution underscores two interrelated and key principles presented through this analysis in varying forms. Firstly, the Spirit always communicates through and within cognitive frameworks of interpretation; the framework surrounding scripture in its original situation, and the contemporary community framework surrounding the interpreter. Both frameworks, using Grey's words, "must be voiced." Secondly, as we read scripture, the Spirit interprets the triune God to us.[625]

5.3.5 Evaluation

Contributions from these "Regent school" scholars strengthens understanding of distinctive features of pneumatic interpretation accordingly.

Levison's stance that living virtuously cultivates cognitive receptivity to the Spirit's communication emphasizes and furthers understanding concerning the ethical and cognitive components of pneumatic interpretation. Moreover, because Levison highlighted figures that prioritized intimate relationship with God, discussing attributes such as their devotion and prayerfulness, he also implicitly addressed affect. His contribution therefore addresses the ethical-affective aspect of the paradox of affective receptivity and ethical willingness, balancing affective-ethical contributions. Drawing from Levison's understanding and in this work's terms, daily cultivation of ethical conduct whilst in intimate, affective relationship with God, influences cognitive reception of truth brought by the Spirit through scripture. Levison's example of Simeon (Luke 2) related this directly to pneumatic interpretation and appropriation. Subsequent engagement with

625. For comparison between Grey, *Three's a Crowd*, and Chris Green, *Sanctifying Interpretation*, see Boone, "Pentecostal Worship and Hermeneutics," 119–22. Boone suggested that Grey and Green's propositions on scriptural interpretation showed two trajectories in Pentecostal approaches to scriptural interpretation: Grey's "revised Protestant hermeneutic," and Green's focus on transfiguration (119). For Green, see 5.4.3.

Boda concerning people who nurture the Spirit's presence also supports this understanding.

However, as Wright recognized, Levison did not discuss the negative aspect or consider the influence of evil spirits on a person. Only Vanhoozer, Yong, and Wright have so far briefly highlighted the issue of pneumatic hindrance caused by evil spirits (see 3.3.1; 3.5; 5.1.4; 5.3.1), and this area deserves attention. Scholars addressing pneumatic hindrance more widely have mainly been writing outside Pentecostal hermeneutics' conversations, and similar focus from Wright and Keener supports this understanding. Although Keener gave minimal attention to the Spirit's role (within these parts of *Spirit Hermeneutics*), engagement with his consideration of unbelief and moral blindness strengthens understanding concerning pneumatic hindrance. In particular, interaction with his discussion reinforces the discussion in 4.3.2 and 4.3.4, emphasizing further that although the Spirit is the ultimate inspirer and empowerer of our vision, cognitive receptivity to the Spirit's interpretation of and through scripture is not automatically guaranteed. Keener's personal account was a useful example of pneumatic hindrance (from prejudgment), and pneumatic appropriation.

Wright, Levison, and Boda's contributions all show the wealth of considering ancient communities, their people, and their interpretive practices. From these areas of expertise they then addressed contemporary pneumatic interpretation. Their focus is especially helpful with recognizing possible patterns of pneumatic interpretation, present both then and now. Each, with differing language, discussed the Spirit's appropriation of the scriptural text, and Boda's contribution showed the affective, ethical, and cognitive components of pneumatic interpretation. Grey gave more consideration to contemporary interpretation but was less focused on the Spirit. Her contribution is valuable, providing practical interpretive principles recognizing cognitive frameworks for interpretation: the historical cultural frameworks surrounding relevant scriptural passages in their original situation, and the contemporary frameworks surrounding the interpreter and the interpretive community.

5.4 THE "CLEVELAND SCHOOL" APPROACH

This section considers contributions from scholars collectively termed as "Cleveland school," building an understanding of their individual and shared offering. Following 5.2.2, additional introduction to "Cleveland school" thought is given through Moore, before considering further individual considerations from Robert Wall, Cheryl Bridges Johns, and Chris

Green. It finishes by integrating Lee Roy Martin's discussion of affectivity with pneumatic interpretation and appropriation.

5.4.1 Scripture as a sacramental, sacred place of transformation (Rickie Moore)

Moore used the term, "altar hermeneutics," coined by one of his seminary students, to emphasize the depth and profundity of scriptural interpretation when "brought within the place or sacred zone of encounter with God."[626] In this work's terms, Moore saw that vital to scriptural interpretation was prioritizing personal experience *of* and intimate relationship *with* God through pneumatic encounter.[627] Attributing contributions from Cheryl Bridges Johns, Daniel Castelo, Green, and Robert Wall,[628] Moore stressed "view[ing] Scripture sacramentally as a means of grace that facilitates divine-human encounter in a way that is beyond our control, our management, our capacity to manipulate or even fully to understand."[629] His emphasis was that "we need Scripture to interpret us more than Scripture needs us to interpret it,"[630] further stating:

> If we see Scripture as means to our epistemological ends, then we will continue to be trapped, as we have been, in a hermeneutical process that is constantly hinging on our capacity to explain or to explain away Scripture's many limitations, tensions, complexities, dissonances, incoherencies, contradictions, obscurities, ethical difficulties, and so forth—a hermeneutical process that will have us ever knowing but never coming to the knowledge of the truth.[631]

626. Moore, "Altar Hermeneutics" (pub. 2016), 149. For more on altar hermeneutics, see Vondey's consideration of the altar in Pentecostal theological method. Vondey, *Pentecostal Theology*, 37–59, 256–71 (and various other places in the text). Cf. 1.6.1 (liturgical interpretation).

627. Moore did not define his use of "Pentecostal" but it was mostly with small "p," also using "pneumatic." His pneumatic references were not always explicit but implication was present.

628. Cheryl Bridges Johns, "Grieving, Brooding, and Transforming" (pub. 2014), 141–53; Castelo, "Tarrying on the Lord" (pub. 2004, see fn. 570); Chris Green, *Sanctifying Interpretation* (pub. 2015, see 5.4.3); Wall, "Waiting on the Holy Spirit" (pub. 2013), 37–53. Moore also credited Francis Martin's influence (see 4.3.2).

629. Moore, "Altar Hermeneutics," 152–53.

630. Moore, "Altar Hermeneutics," 155.

631. Moore, "Altar Hermeneutics," 156.

Moore's point was that this group (or school)[632] were asking, what if God's goal in giving scripture is not so much about conveying knowledge but more about "transacting a salvation that surpasses knowledge," what then, do our interpretive interactions with scripture look like?[633] Perhaps this is optimistic but it does not seem so much a desire to discredit approaches that start with scripture and surrounding historico-grammatical framework as much as it is a yearning to suggest that the primary purpose of reading scripture is relational encounter with God that exposes and transforms, and from there, facilitates pneumatic interpretation of both scripture and self.

5.4.2 Waiting on the Spirit (Robert Wall), and meeting with God (Cheryl Bridges Johns)

Wall applied "the Pentecostal practice of 'waiting on the Holy Spirit'" to scriptural interpretation, using Acts 1:4 as support.[634] He emphasized approaching scripture in an attitude of worship and communion with God, meditating prayerfully upon scriptural passages over a period of time and waiting for the Spirit to "breath fresh meaning into its reading."[635] Drawing on uneducated Peter's pneumatic appropriation of Israel's scriptures in

632. Additional to fn. 628, Kenneth Archer, "Pentecostal Hermeneutics," 331–32; Melissa Archer, *"I Was in the Spirit,"* 45–54; Boone, "Pentecostal Worship and Hermeneutics," 111, 123–24; Cheryl Bridges Johns, "Transcripts of the Trinity," 155–64; Cole, "Taking Hermeneutics to Heart," 264–74. Also, Coombs, "Reading in Tongues," 264–66; Ellington, "Knowing God More and Less," 20–28; Ellington, "Locating Pentecostals at the Hermeneutical Round Table," 206–25; Chris Green, "Beautifying the Beautiful Word," 103–19; Green, "Provoked to Saving Jealousy," 191–92; Green, *Pentecostal Theology of the Lord's Supper*, 182–90; Green, "Then Their Eyes Were Opened," 196–201 (see fn. 73 [liturgical interpretation]); Green, "'I am Finished,'" 150–66 (however, Green accentuated Christ in his hermeneutical consideration and so, in this work's terms, was arguably no longer a renewal voice); Greves, "Daughter of Courage," 151–67; Bob Johnson and Moore, "Soul Care for One and All," 129–30; David Johnson, *Pneumatic Discernment in the Apocalypse*, 46–9; Lee Roy Martin (see 5.4.4); Glen Menzies, "Echoing Hirsch," 97, discussing reading as a spiritual experience; Redick, "'Let Me Hear Your Voice,'" 187–200; Thomas, "'What the Spirit is Saying to the Church,'" 117–22.

633. Moore, "Altar Hermeneutics," 156.

634. Wall, "Waiting on the Holy Spirit" (pub. 2013), 37, acknowledging Castelo, "Tarrying on the Lord," for helping his thought. Wall is Methodist but his language ("tarrying") and scholarly engagement were classically-Pentecostal oriented. Seattle Pacific University, "Robert Wall," n.p. Although unclear, he probably intended his use of "Pentecostal" on small "p" basis (see 1.2). Cf. fn. 544 (Grey and Wall).

635. Wall, "Waiting on the Holy Spirit," 53. Cf. Levison's discussion of pondering and puzzling (5.3.1).

Acts 4:8–13,[636] Wall emphasized that whilst academic rigor is important, ultimately "the authority of the faithful reader to retrieve spiritual meaning from a sacred text . . . is not based upon academic preparation but upon spiritual maturity."[637] Concluding, Wall emphasized that the Spirit, working within the reader's familiarity with scripture, empowers the reader to "reread the text with extraordinary intellectual [cognitive] acuity when adapting it for a new day."[638] Wall's thought was more clearly oriented to contemporary interpretation than Levison or Boda's (see 5.3), but alignment between all three contributions is noted.

Scripture, for Cheryl Bridges Johns, is a sacred space where, by the Spirit, we meet with God and "are known and read more than we know and read."[639] She offered "a view of the Bible as living subject whose existence is grounded in the economic life of God . . . serv[ing] as a sanctified, Spirit-filled vessel in service of restoring creation."[640] This work emphasizes that *through* scripture, the Spirit holistically (self)-interprets the triune God to us, but Johns emphasized that the Spirit *fills* the written words and in this process *scripture* "mediate[s] the presence of the triune God," particularly "the real presence of Jesus."[641] She posited that "*by* the Spirit," the words of scripture become pregnant, not just with meaning but "with the eternal

636. Wall, "Waiting on the Holy Spirit," 53. Wall earlier acknowledged Levison within his discussion (52). See Levison, *Filled with the Spirit*, 349–50, *Inspired* (2013), 153–54, discussing Peter's inspired interpretation of scripture in Acts 4. Cf. 5.3.1; 5.3.3. Pneumatic appropriation is my term, not Wall's.

637. Wall, "Waiting on the Holy Spirit," 53.

638. Wall, "Waiting on the Holy Spirit," 53. Complementing Wall, Vanhoozer and Treier, using 1 Corinthians 2–3 explained that God is Lord over history (1 Cor 2:9), and people have to wait for the Spirit to bring revelation (1 Cor 2:10–12). Until the Spirit brings this revelation it remains a mystery. The revelation is divine and self-revealing as the interpretation given by the Spirit reveals God. They emphasized, "Despite the spiritual nature of the speaking and hearing involved, true understanding remains human activity involving cognition." Vanhoozer and Treier, *Theology and the Mirror of Scripture* (pub. 2016), 138.

639. Cheryl Bridges Johns, "Grieving, Brooding, and Transforming" (pub. 2014), 145–49 (149). Similarly, Cheryl Bridges Johns, "Transcripts of the Trinity" (pub. 2014), 160–63.

640. Johns, "Grieving, Brooding, and Transforming," 145, drawing from Webster's understanding of sanctification as "a process in which, in the limitless freedom of God, the creaturely element is given its own genuine reality as it is commanded and moulded to enter into the divine service." Webster, *Holy Scripture* (pub. 2003), 27, as cited by Johns, "Grieving, Brooding, and Transforming," 148, noting that Webster preceded this, emphasizing that sanctification is *the Holy Spirit's work*. Contrary to Webster's and this work's position, Johns's position could be seen as inferring that *scripture* sanctifies.

641. Johns, "Grieving, Brooding, and Transforming," 147.

life of God," and "the Bible thus becomes an avenue for us to enter into the mysterious, wonder-filled life of God."[642]

Therefore, in Johns's understanding, but in this work's terms, as we read scripture, the Spirit draws us into intimate, transformative relationship with God, bringing reconciliation, sanctification, and restoration, simultaneously personally and communally.[643] Whilst she emphasized the triune nature of God, Johns focused on the Spirit–Son relationship, explicating that as we read scripture, Christ is made present by the Spirit.[644] Like Macchia (see 4.2.1), she did not actively discuss the Father when discussing the Spirit and scripture.

Johns's perspective was within her "Spirit–Word" discussion[645] where she used "Word" with a twofold sense, at the same time referring both to scripture and Christ as *Logos* (although she did not explicitly state this).[646] This "Spirit–Word" position can be traced to Land's analogy of the Spirit's forming of Christ in Mary and the Spirit using scripture to form Christ in us (see 3.2.1). It has been further influenced by Pentecostal scholars interacting with reformed theology, which Johns did, and which hermeneutically prioritizes the Son (see 4.2.1).[647] The issue is threefold. *Firstly*, this position forays into discussions about the nature of scripture; a much larger discussion area beyond this work's remits, and not all using the terminology may realize this. *Secondly*, the "Spirit–Word" position can lead to focusing more on scripture and less explicitly on the Spirit. *Thirdly*, the position *does not actively acknowledge the Father*. However, having made these observations, space and focus do not permit dwelling on them further and would also lead away from this work and Bridges Johns' shared emphasis on transformative communion with the triune God brought by the Spirit as we read scripture.

642. Johns, "Grieving, Brooding, and Transforming," 148 (emphasis added).

643. E.g., Johns, "Transcripts of the Trinity," 163–64. She emphasized communion with the people of God in scripture ("the first witnesses"), as well as with God and those around us. Also, "Grieving, Brooding, and Transforming," 145, 147, 149.

644. Johns, "Grieving, Brooding, and Transforming," 147.

645. Johns, "Grieving, Brooding, and Transforming," 47–48; "Transcripts of the Trinity," 163–64.

646. See Green, *Sanctifying Interpretation*, 121–22, considering Cheryl Bridges Johns's understanding of scripture.

647. See also Johnson and Moore, "Soul Care for One and All," 128–30, discussing the "Spirit–Word" position, crediting Land, and Barth's thought.

5.4.3 Sanctifying interpretation (Chris Green)

In *Sanctifying Interpretation*, Green aimed "to make a case for thinking differently about how and why we read Scripture, focusing on the ways the Holy Spirit uses our readings to work sanctification in and through us."[648] Understanding sanctification as "what it means to be holy, and how God works holiness in and through us,"[649] Green posited that traditional evangelical approaches to interpreting scripture had over-emphasized *how we know* when "the real work of interpretation" lies with *how* "God works in and through our readings of Scripture to form us into Christlikeness."[650] Although he did not use these terms, he effectively argued that scholars had overly focused on cognition, neglecting affective and ethical aspects and he sought to rebalance this. Wanting to correct "a habit of describing sanctification in terms of overcoming sin rather than in terms of being conformed to Christ,"[651] Green did not discuss ethical conduct influencing pneumatic interpretation. Instead, he emphasized the Spirit's (affective-ethical) work of sanctification enacted in and through us as we read scripture. This was contrariwise to Levison's ethical-affective stress (see 5.3.1), yet also complements it for both emphasized partnering with God in their discussions. One perspective could be that Green's emphasis was at the expense of highlighting personal responsibility to engage with the Spirit's work of sanctification and influence on cognitive receptivity. However, this disservices Green's offering for it was not his focus and for well-argued reasons of wanting to redress the holiness movement's emphasis on sanctification as overcoming sin.[652]

Green argued, "We are called to share in Christ's vocation, joining him in bringing to bear God's holiness for the good of all creation."[653] He explained that to share in Christ's vocation is also to share in Christ's identity. Therefore, aspects of Christ's life such as learning obedience through suffering and priestly mediation—"connecting God to the people and God's

648. Green, *Sanctifying Interpretation* (pub. 2015), 161. Green wrote from his classical Pentecostal perspective, addressing all across the renewal tradition (2). For critiques, see Boone, "Pentecostal Worship and Hermeneutics," 119–22 (see fn. 625 [Boone]); Mather, "Chris E. W Green," 562–64.

649. Green, *Sanctifying Interpretation*, 1.

650. Green, *Sanctifying Interpretation*, 113, also stating that "we need to shift away from *epistemological* accounts to *soteriological* ones" (113, emphasis original). Cognition, of course, is part of *both* approaches.

651. Green, *Sanctifying Interpretation*, 64 (emphasis original).

652. Also discussed in Mather, "Chris E. W. Green," 562–64.

653. Green, *Sanctifying Interpretation*, 109. This was the first part of his discussion (5–60).

people to one another"—are part of *our* vocation and identity.[654] Continuing, he considered how we are sanctified, what holiness looks like, and what it means to co-operate with the Spirit.[655]

Integrating vocation and holiness with scriptural interpretation, Green explicated that reading scripture pneumatically (affectively and ethically) draws us into holiness, "(trans)forming us for our vocation as Christ's co-sanctified co-sanctifiers."[656] Wanting to redress interpretive methods addressing how we know, Green emphasized that whilst believing God uses scripture to bring divine revelation—receptivity to which of course involves cognition—he held that "Scripture has the deeper purpose of making us *wise*." He stated:

> Only in wisdom are we able to fulfill our vocation and enter fully into the salvation made known to us in the Scripture's witness to Christ. In other words, Scripture read with and in the Spirit, actually works to conform us to Christ, materializing his character in us, incorporating us into his identity.[657]

Although wisdom also involves cognition,[658] Green's stress was that whilst cognitive vision is renewed, it is our sanctification and conformation that is most important, not what we can or cannot "see."[659]

Whilst noting this work's stress on the Spirit through scripture, (self)-interpreting the triune God to us, with Christ as the incarnate image,[660] Green's point, in this work's terms, was that as we read scripture, the Spirit

654. Green, *Sanctifying Interpretation*, 15–16, 30 (30).

655. Green, *Sanctifying Interpretation*, 63. This was the second part of his discussion (61–106).

656. Green, *Sanctifying Interpretation*, 109. This was the third part of his discussion (107–60).

657. Green, *Sanctifying Interpretation*, 110 (emphasis original).

658. Cf. Vanhoozer and Treier explaining that the Spirit connects us with God's wisdom but despite this, "true understanding remains human activity involving cognition, . . . discerning judgments involve both cognition and volition." In this statement, Vanhoozer and Treier recognized the roles of ethics and cognition in pneumatic interpretation but not affect. Vanhoozer and Treier, *Theology and the Mirror of Scripture* (pub. 2016), 137–38 (138) (part of their statement is also given in fn. 638).

659. Green, *Sanctifying Interpretation*, 111. Green advocated shifting from evangelical approaches to interpretation and using early Pentecostal hermeneutics as an alternative approach (109–23). Whilst appreciating his reasons for doing this, he also effectively replaced one cognitive framework with another.

660. Green did discuss trinitarian aspects (e.g., see 63–106), mainly external to scriptural interpretation. His main focus was relationship between the Spirit and the Son, and with scripture and the person reading scripture. Cf. 5.4.2 (Cheryl Bridges Johns).

works in us affectively, ethically, and cognitively, holistically interpreting Christ to us and transforming us into that interpretation. This pneumatic process facilitates ethical action on behalf of others and ourselves, enabling our vocational calling.

Green wove an abundance of thought provoking, interrelated themes through *Sanctifying Interpretation*, including recognizing the *limitations* of interpretation. This involved "remain[ing] always in apprenticeship to the Spirit . . . [when] learning to hear and speak faithfully," and recognizing that "our judgments and interpretations are trustworthy only if they remain tentative," for "no reading, except for God's reading at the Last Judgment can be a final reading."[661] Therefore, because "we are not yet at the End," we will always be "reaching beyond our interpretive grasp" when we approach scripture.[662] These final, highlighted emphases support the theme, commenced in 2.3.2, and seen most recently in 5.1.3, that truth the Spirit communicates through our engagement with scripture is *both interpretable and beyond interpretation, reachable, yet nevertheless also beyond grasp.*

In summary, Green's affective-ethical offering balances and complements Levison's ethical-affective contribution. Green's desire to redress over-attention to cognition amongst scholars discussing interpretation is commendable but it is also an unavoidable aspect of pneumatic interpretation, and interpretation more generally. Engagement with his important contribution has further emphasized the theme that there are limitations on our ability to grasp truth brought by the Spirit through engagement with scripture.

5.4.4 Affectivity, pneumatic interpretation, and pneumatic appropriation (Lee Roy Martin)

Lee Roy Martin focused on affect evoked in a believer through "hearing" (see 4.3.3) different psalms.[663] Explaining that "emotions are temporary responses to surrounding stimuli, but affections are lasting dispositions, our deepest desires,"[664] Martin therefore separated emotion from affect, under-

661. Green, *Sanctifying Interpretation*, 50, 81, 147 respectively.

662. Green, *Sanctifying Interpretation*, 147.

663. Lee Roy Martin, "Delighting in the Torah" (pub. 2010), 708–27 (Psalm 1); Martin, "Encountering God with the Psalmist" (pub. 2013) 131–47 (Psalm 63); Martin, "Longing for God" (pub. 2013), 54–76 (Psalm 63); Martin, "Presidential Address 2014," 355–78 (Psalm 107); Martin, "Psalm 130" (unpublished 2018); Martin, "Psalms in Early Pentecostalism" (pub. 2017), 725–46. Martin edited and brought these articles into a collection, published 2018. Martin, *Spirit of the Psalms*.

664. Martin, "Presidential Address 2014," 357.

standing affect slightly differently to here, where affect is viewed as an overarching descriptor of emotion and desire.[665] Martin largely did not explicitly discuss the Spirit, focusing instead on scripture, his Pentecostal context, and particular affections like joy, gratitude, lament, love, and compassion.[666] He explained, "The affective approach calls for the hearer to attend to the affective tones that are present in the text and to allow the affections of the hearer to be shaped by the text."[667]

For Martin, interpreting affectively involves four components: 1) recognizing and acknowledging the affective aspects within a particular passage of scripture; 2) critical awareness of our own desires as we engage with this passage. We may sometimes hope that our desires reflect the affective aspects of the passage at hand, but emotion and desire are powerful "pulls" and this will not always be the case. Critical awareness of our own emotions and desires is therefore vital; 3) corresponding with component two, keeping open to emotional impact as we engage with the passage; and finally, 4) allowing ourselves "to be transformed by the affective experiencing of the psalm."[668] Discussing Psalm 63, which he argued particularly resonated with Pentecostal spirituality, Martin explained, "Through the hearing of the Psalms the desires of the heart are transformed and redirected toward God so that the affections of gratitude, trust, and love (affections that foster worship) are generated and nourished."[669]

As this work has been emphasizing, it is by the Spirit through engagement with scripture that affect is transformed and redirected toward God as Father, Son, and Spirit. Relating affective interpretation more explicitly with the Spirit, Martin recounted a testimony from Daisy Wilkins given in an early Pentecostal periodical. Wilkins explained that throughout her

665. This influence stems from Land, *Pentecostal Spirituality*. See 3.1.

666. Thomas also considered affect within his context as a Pentecostal and New Testament scholar. He related affect to the five works of Christ held by Pentecostal holiness groups. Implicitly referencing the Spirit through the Pentecostal interpreter, Thomas posited that as the interpreter engages with their surrounding community and scripture, they undergo affective transformation. He further emphasized that this transformation also involved a journey of unfolding insight. Thomas used the fivefold gospel in his discussion (Jesus as savior, sanctifier, baptizer in the Spirit, healer, and soon-coming King). He therefore related affective transformation more with Christ than with the Spirit. Thomas, "'What the Spirit is Saying to the Church'" (f.pub. 2011), 116–17. Later, Thomas considered the Spirit more explicitly (128–29), discussing the Spirit's presence through the interpretive process, in personal formation within community and with scripture.

667. Martin, "Longing for God," 55. Also in Martin, *Spirit of the Psalms*, 23–46 (24).

668. Martin, "Longing for God," 59–60 (60).

669. Martin, "Longing for God," 60.

recent illness she had felt the Spirit's comforting and empowering presence and cited Psalm 23. Martin emphasized, "The Holy Spirit cheered and strengthened her so that she could say with David, 'thy rod and thy staff, they comfort me' (Ps. 23:4). The affections of joy and gratitude are evident in the testimony."[670]

Wilkins's account with Martin's analysis indicates that the Spirit *affectively* and *ethically* interpreted Wilkins, bringing *cognitive* insight of affective aspects in Psalm 23, which aligned (transformed and redirected) her human affections with God's affections. This affective alignment enabled her to persevere (ethical action) through difficulty and consequently Wilkins drew deeper in intimate relationship with God.[671] Furthermore, her account with Martin's analysis also suggests that the Spirit affectively, but also ethically and cognitively, *appropriated* aspects of Psalm 23 to Wilkins's personal life and surrounding framework (and vice-versa). Martin explained, "Her experience, therefore, *mirrors* that of David as expressed in Ps 23. She has chosen to live in the world of the psalm and to claim its confession of trust as her own."[672]

Martin's recounting of Wilkins's experience therefore emphasizes that the contextual coherence of pneumatic appropriation can be affective as well as cognitive (for example, compare 3.4.5). Furthermore, reconsidering Davies's thoughts on the ethical dimension beneath scripture's written words (see 4.2.4) in view of this discussion emphasizes that this contextual coherence can also be ethical.[673]

670. Martin, "Psalms in Early Pentecostalism," 738, citing *AF*, 1/12 (1908) 4. Also in Martin, *Spirit of the Psalms*, 185–209 (198–99). Wilkins testified, "I have been quite sick since I wrote you all last. . . . I am praising God for His keeping power that keeps me through health and sickness. Even through my darkest hours, the room was filled with angels singing sweet songs to cheer and strengthen me in faith. Many nights when everyone else would be asleep, the Holy Ghost would come in mighty power and fill my heart so that I could only say what good old David did in the 23rd Psalm. Praise the Lord!"

671. Cf. Johnson and Moore, writing external to pneumatic interpretation: "The Spirit transforms the distorted affections of the heart, the thinking of the mind, and behavioral propensities of the Fall. The thirst for holiness expressed through full surrender opens the life to transformation. The Holy Spirit purifies our hearts, renews our minds, and teaches us to act in ways consistent with the Kingdom." Johnson and Moore, "Soul Care for One and All," 133.

672. Martin, "Psalms in Early Pentecostalism," 738 (emphasis added) drawing on Goldingay, *Psalms I*, 345. John Goldingay. *Psalms Volume 1: Psalms 1–41*. Baker Commentary on the Old Testament Wisdom and Psalms. Edited by Tremper Longman III (Grand Rapids: Baker Academic, 2001).

673. I did not articulate this as explicitly in 4.2.4. Cf. Davies on the Spirit communicating through scripture in ways creating opportunity for, but not compelling, ethical action (4.3).

Martin's own earlier thought affirms this perspective. In *Biblical Hermeneutics* he considered pneumatic interpretation, also discussing what this work has been calling pneumatic appropriation.[674] Martin stated:

> The same Spirit that inspired the Scriptures now helps us to understand the Scriptures. The authority of Scripture is not in the church, not in the interpreter, not even in the text; the authority is in God the Holy Spirit. The Holy Spirit continues to give revelation, to give new, fresh expressions of God's Word from the living God. God takes the words which he spoke many years ago, and through the Spirit he gives a new application for us today.[675]

Whilst Martin did not discuss contextual coherence, he *did* emphasize truth communicated by the Spirit through our engagement with scripture to personal and contemporary contexts. He also recognized this as *the Spirit's* communicative activity rather than our interpretive methodology. This illustrates the contemporary perspective of pneumatic appropriation that Archie Wright mentioned when he compared this contemporary "practice" with "Spirit-led" interpretive methods practiced by the Qumran community (see 5.3.3).

Finally, Martin also alluded to affective and ethical aspects, referencing heart understanding and character formation.[676] This unintentional (on his part)[677] allusion to affect and ethics follows a consistent pattern across the "Regent school" and "Cleveland school" (and chapters 2 to 4 preceding), with scholars including Levison, Boda, and Green using various terminology but all essentially discussing affect, ethics, and cognition in relation with pneumatic interpretation.

5.4.5 Evaluation

This work emphasizes not that *scripture* interprets us but that *the Spirit through scripture* interprets us. In this understanding, as we approach scripture seeking to interpret its written truth, the Spirit reaches through and beyond scripture's written words, (self)-interpreting us affectively, ethically,

674. Martin, *Biblical Hermeneutics* (pub. 2011), 47–50.

675. Martin, *Biblical Hermeneutics*, 47.

676. Martin, *Biblical Hermeneutics*, 49. Martin also stressed that, through the Spirit, understanding of scripture is enabled and without the Spirit, scripture's meaning is hidden (49). Cf. Ervin (2.4.3).

677. This contribution from Martin preceded his work on affect. Probably, the affective emphasis of his later work was present, just not yet explicated.

and cognitively, and working in ways that create, redeem, and reconcile simultaneously personally and communally in our lives. This pneumatic interpretation is a holistic (self)-interpretation of God as Father, Son, and Spirit, with Christ as the incarnate image. Consequently, cognitive understanding of scripture, of self, and of God is brought, but through and with affective and ethical transformation. Cognition is not the primary focus, but it is also an integral, inescapable aspect. Furthermore, this process is also dynamic, understanding that the Spirit works in our lives in ways that lead us toward scripture and so the basis for interpretation does not always start with scripture (see 3.4.4). Much of this emphasis complements thought from "Cleveland school" scholars, but Moore, Cheryl Bridges Johns, and also Green, focused more on scripture itself than this work has, and potential reasons for this were clearest when interacting with Johns's "Spirit–Word" discussion.

Wall's focus on approaching scripture in an attitude of intimate relationship with God cements further the centrality of this relationship to pneumatic interpretation. His stress on meditating prayerfully on scriptural passages waiting for the Spirit to bring fresh insight together with focusing on spiritual maturity complements Levison's corresponding focus on spiritual maturity, relationship with God, and pondering and puzzling, and also Boda's thoughts on those who nurture the Spirit's presence (see 5.3).[678] Wall's recognition that the Spirit works with our familiarity of scripture highlights the practicality that spending time reading scripture as part of communion with God is important.

Johns and Green also focused on intimate, transformative relationship with God brought by the Spirit as we read scripture. Johns emphasized the triune nature of God but focused on the Spirit–Son relationship, explicating that as we read scripture Christ is made present by the Spirit. Like Macchia in 4.2.1, Johns did not actively discuss the Father when discussing the Spirit and scripture and her thought showed similar influence as Macchia's from engagement with reformed theology. Green also focused on the Spirit–Son relationship but his stress was not trinitarian. His emphasis on remaining in apprenticeship to the Spirit when learning to hear and speak faithfully complements perspectives from Levison and Keener in 5.3. Green's affective-ethical contribution contrasts yet complements Levison's ethical-affective offering as both scholars emphasized relationship with God. Furthermore, Green's corresponding stress on our interpretations always remaining tentative aligns with Yong's recognition of partiality (5.1.3). This reinforces the continuing emphasis within these chapters, based around the invisible and,

678. Cf. 3.3.3 (Rahner, through Pinnock).

in contrast, incarnate nature of God and God's communication, that truth the Spirit communicates through our engagement with scripture—because this truth (self)-interprets God as Father, Son, and Spirit to us—is both interpretable and beyond interpretation; reachable, yet nevertheless also beyond grasp (see 2.3.2; 4.2).

Despite limited attention to the Spirit, Martin's attention to affect evoked in a believer through hearing different psalms is valuable, especially his focus on particular affections like joy, gratitude, lament, love, and compassion. As this work emphasizes, it is *the Spirit* that transforms and redirects our affectivity as we engage with scripture as part of relationship with God. Daisy Wilkins's 1908 testimony with Martin's analysis highlighted affective, ethical, and cognitive aspects of the Spirit's interpretation of Wilkins and her engagement with Psalm 23. This complements especially with Boda's consideration using 2 Kings 22–23 and Nehemiah 8–10 (see 5.3.3). Wilkins's account with Martin's analysis also helped in recognizing that the contextual coherence of pneumatic appropriation can be affective and/or ethical (with cognition). Martin's own earlier thought affirmed this perspective and he discussed the contemporary perspective of pneumatic appropriation that Wright compared with "Spirit-led" interpretive methods practiced by the Qumran community (see 5.3.3). As Martin recognized, and as this work takes care to consistently stress, the concern is with the Spirit's communicative activity over our interpretive methodology. This emphasis can be hard to balance for pneumatic interpretation necessarily also includes involvement on our part.

5.5 EVALUATION

Although terminology and approach differed, thought from scholars identified as "Regent school," and "Cleveland school," preceded by analysis of Yong's consideration of the human imagination in relationship with the Spirit, all collectively identified affective, ethical, and cognitive components of the Spirit's communication through and beyond scripture (Yong, Levison, Keener, Boda, Grey, Moore, Wall, Johns, Green, Martin). Secondly, contributions from scholars in both "schools" also collectively highlighted intimate relationship with God as a central factor of pneumatic interpretation (Levison, Keener, Boda, Moore, Wall, Johns, Green, Martin). Thirdly, contributions across both "schools" helped to further address what this work has been terming as pneumatic appropriation (Keener, Wright, Levison, Boda, Grey, Martin). Finally, thought from Yong, Wright, and Keener helped address the lesser-focused area of pneumatic hindrance. Levison did not discuss pneumatic hindrance but he did address the ethical-affective aspect of the paradox of affective receptivity and ethical willingness, balancing affective-ethical contributions. This further highlighted the paradox that when we are the most affectively receptive to God we are also the most ethically willing to actively make room for the Spirit by modifying behavior, and to be in a state of passive reception, active behavior is also required. Whilst the Spirit is the ultimate inspirer and empowerer of our vision, receptivity to the Spirit's interpretation through and beyond scripture is also not automatically guaranteed.

These features build on similar foci by scholars across or identifying with the renewal tradition since 1970 highlighted and addressed in chapters 2 to 4. This affirms the emphasis on these aspects of pneumatic interpretation and associated terminology (pneumatic appropriation, pneumatic discernment, and pneumatic hindrance) within this analysis. *More importantly*, however, this indicates that these are hallmarks of the Spirit's communication through scripture and our receptivity to this interpretive activity. Although, like this work and Yong's, there are different emphases, starting points, and methods, these distinctive features *unite* scholars across both "schools" and the conversation overall. The aim throughout has been to focus on common, uniting features of scholarly thought over differences, and analysis in this chapter has underlined this focus. Whilst differences do also require noting (such as when interacting with Cheryl Bridges Johns's "Spirit–Word" discussion), overly focusing on them distracts from recognizing and attending to commonalities. It can be hard to focus on similarities over differences but it is worth the effort, for these *common, uniting themes* amidst the diversity of scholarly approach, focus, and opinion, reinforce our understanding of these distinctive and unifying features of pneumatic interpretation.

6

Reflections and Closing Analysis

6.1 CLOSING A HISTORICAL AND PNEUMATOLOGICAL ANALYSIS

THIS WORK HAS ASKED, what *is* the Spirit's role in the interpretation of scripture? This notoriously difficult question to address[679] has been approached by engaging with a conversation surrounding this topic that has been taking place amongst renewal scholars[680] since 1970. The approach was taken[681] recognizing that the Spirit never communicates directly but always through another object or movement, and that the Spirit communicates in ways that unify and which celebrate the other. Accordingly, chapters 2 to 5 have charted historical progress, but concentrated on identifying common, uniting features of scholarly thought amidst hermeneutical diversity. The work has therefore had a twofold and interrelated purpose: 1) to build understanding of pneumatic interpretation by drawing on and developing—and in this process celebrating—such scholarly thought; and 2) to offer something that might foster appreciation and understanding between scholars.

Within the analysis have been consistent references to "the conversation" and "conversationalists." This has been to emphasize that whilst scholars may not always have recognized this outside their related discussion

679. See discussion in 1.4 and 1.5.

680. For definition of a renewal scholar, conversationalist, or voice, see fn. 4. Also discussed in 1.2.

681. I am unsure whether I chose the approach or that the approach chose me. Perhaps, as I began exploring this area of research, the Spirit *through* the approach—and my affective, ethical, and cognitive engagement with it—chose me.

areas (that is to say, Pentecostal hermeneutics), they are part of a wider conversation about the Spirit's role in the interpretation of scripture from like-minded people who emphasize the Spirit and accentuate the Spirit's role in their hermeneutical considerations.

This final chapter reflects back over these pages, drawing together key themes and offering a closing perspective of pneumatic interpretation and associated terminology pneumatic discernment, pneumatic appropriation, and pneumatic hindrance. The diachronic arrangement of chapter 6, with chapters 2 to 5 preceding, emphasizes an aspect of the Spirit's communicative nature discussed in chapter 1, that the Spirit unfolds truth over time. This aspect of pneumatic interpretation was also addressed in chapter 3 (see 3.3.3), which highlighted that as we[682] engage with scripture, over a period of time the Spirit works to draw us deeper into relationship with God, unfold scriptural truth, and bring recognition and understanding of both scripture and self.

In a similar way, as I have journeyed through researching and writing *The Interpreting Spirit*, my understanding of pneumatic interpretation and associated terminology has also gradually unfolded. This is perhaps especially so regarding pneumatic appropriation and pneumatic hindrance. The analysis is ending but my understanding will continue to unfold beyond its close as the Spirit continues to reveal truth and I try to work in partnership with the Spirit to affectively, ethically, and cognitively understand and communicate that truth. There has also been an ongoing and unfolding personal journey throughout my research and writing, but I have chosen not to include many personal details. What happened *to* me and *in* me as I researched, wrote, and thought about ways the Spirit communicates through scripture, also involved others. Our stories are never solely our own, for they intertwine and interconnect with those around us. Pneumatic interpretation is always simultaneously personal and communal.

Consequently, taking the diachronic nature of the Spirit's communication into account, these reflections are deliberately open-ended, presented and offered as they have evolved, and at this point in their unfolding of understanding. My hope is that the Spirit in relationship with other scholars will take and develop the thoughts offered here as the conversation about the Spirit's role in the interpretation of scripture continues.

682. For use of "our," "we," and "us" in this work, see fn. 1.

6.2 REFLECTIONS

Chapter 1. Laying the foundations

This chapter introduced the work and provided a grounding understanding of the renewal tradition as global charismatic movements and scholars in these groups who emphasize the Spirit and accentuate the Spirit's role in hermeneutical considerations (1.2). It was also explained that the choice of renewal terminology was to stress inclusivity of scholars across or identifying with the renewal tradition (as understood in this work's terms), and to reduce confusion over Pentecostal and charismatic terminology. Following this, in 1.3, working pneumatic terminology was offered, and an understanding of affect, ethics, and cognition given, placing the heart as the locus of discernment, from which affect, ethics, and cognition stem. This foundational chapter closed with limitations and an introductory outline, but first, further grounding for the approach was given (1.4; 1.5). A note on interpretive method addressed the focus on *the Spirit's* interpretive activity over our interpretive methodology, alongside intention to identify common, uniting features of scholarly thought in line with the four identified aspects of the Spirit's interpretive nature discussed in 1.1. Subsequently, a brief hermeneutical theology of the Spirit was offered, focusing especially on the Spirit's self-effacing nature. This established that because we experience the Spirit indirectly *through* another object or movement,[683] our hermeneutical considerations can divert into focusing on whatever it is the Spirit is communicating through rather than attending to the Spirit. These objects or movements include the written words of scripture and their surrounding historico-grammatical framework; the contemporary community framework surrounding us as we approach scripture; affect, ethics, and cognition; and the Father and the Son. As explained, whilst these "diversions" are natural and necessary, *overly* concentrating on these object(s) or movement(s) that the Spirit communicates through actually steers attention *away* from the Spirit. Therefore, as illustrated by the work's twofold, historical and pneumatological approach, studies concerning the Spirit's communication require balanced attention to whatever it is the Spirit might be communicating through—and in that process celebrating—in order to consider the Spirit's role.

683. See fn. 10 for definitions of object and movement.

Chapter 2. Pneumatic interpretation is holistic: 1970 to 1989

The second chapter traced the beginnings of the conversation about the Spirit's role in the interpretation of scripture from 1970 to 1989 as the renewed emphasis on and experience of the Spirit brought by the charismatic movement started influencing hermeneutical conversations. Thought from evangelical, charismatic, Roman Catholic, and Pentecostal scholars was considered and it was established that the identified components of pneumatic interpretation—*affect, ethics, and cognition*—were themes from these conversational beginnings. As would be consistent throughout the analysis, these components were evident amongst scholars' written thought via a variety of different terms and explanations. This period saw the birth of Pentecostal hermeneutics and marked the beginnings of Pentecostal scholars' pursuit for a distinct theological and ecclesial identity within the academy. However, not every scholar using Pentecostal hermeneutics' terminology meant this in reference to Pentecostalism but as an approach to scripture incorporating pentecostal or charismatic experience. Hence, confusion over Pentecostal hermeneutics' terminology existed from these conversational beginnings.

A primary theme evident across evangelical, charismatic, Roman Catholic, and Pentecostal contributions was that the Spirit, through scripture, works *holistically* in our lives. Viewing the heart as the locus of discernment helped to appreciate this holistic understanding. Chapter 2 therefore commenced the emphasis that we do not just interpret scripture but that the Spirit, through scripture, *interprets us*. Scholars like Francis Martin and Howard Ervin emphasized that a major purpose of the Spirit's role in interpretation was to bring union with Christ. Martin described this as bringing all aspects of a person into union with Christ, and Ervin described this as joining ontologically with the mind of Christ. However, by engaging with aspects of Hans Urs von Balthasar's pneumatology, a central emphasis of this work began that this union was not just in relation to Christ, emphasizing the Father alongside the Son, with the Spirit. This commenced the suggestion that as we read scripture, the Spirit (self)-interprets God as Father, Son, and Spirit to us, recognizing Christ as the incarnate image. Balthasar emphasized that the illuminating Spirit takes complete possession of us as the Spirit interprets the Son who interprets the Father to us. Drawing from and developing his thoughts on the incarnate and, by contrast, invisible nature of God *and* God's communication, helped illuminate that the truth the Spirit communicates through scripture—because this truth (self)-interprets God as Father, Son, and Spirit to us—is both interpretable and beyond interpretation; reachable, yet nevertheless also beyond grasp.

Another integral component, *the paradox of affective receptivity and ethical willingness* (otherwise knows as the affective-ethical paradox), was first identified by engaging with Balthasar's pneumatology. In this understanding, as the Spirit works in us (interprets us), affect and consequently ethics are transformed and brought into alignment with God as Father, Son, and Spirit, yet at the same time, active ethical effort is also required. This interrelation between affect and ethics impacts cognition, facilitating pneumatic interpretation. The paradox, therefore, is that it is when we are the most affectively receptive to God that we are also the most ethically willing to modify behavior, yet in order to be in a state of open receptivity to God, and pneumatically discern and interpret, active effort is also required. Furthermore, whilst the Holy Spirit of God is all-powerful, the Spirit is at the same time vulnerable to obstruction through human rebellion because of God-given freedom of individual choice. Immoral behavior obstructs the Spirit, preventing this process and hindering pneumatic interpretation and discernment, but room is made for the Spirit by being affectively receptive to God and ethically willing to actively modify behavior.

Pneumatic hindrance[684] was also identified by those including evangelical, Arthur Pink, and Roman Catholic charismatic, Francis Martin. Like Balthasar, evangelical scholars, particularly Pink, recognized a relationship between affect, ethical conduct and pneumatic interpretation. They identified the heart as the locus of discernment and cautioned that when our hearts (and minds) were not in harmony with the Spirit, interpretation and discernment would be hindered. Pink's four relating qualifications facilitating pneumatic interpretation—impartiality, humility, prayerfulness, and seeking primarily not to acquire scriptural knowledge but to grow closer in personal relationship with God, and be transformed by God's teaching—were especially relevant. Illustrating the relationship between affect and ethics, Pink juxtaposed worldly affections with affections from the Spirit; he cautioned that partiality, pride, and not recognizing dependence on the Spirit to reveal truth, were particular hindrances. Drawing upon and developing Martin's thoughts on inner healing as a contemporary, charismatic interpretation of being set free from the body ruled by sin (Rom 6) presented an understanding that past experiences, which have caused emotional hurt, can hinder pneumatic interpretation and discernment. Inversely, inner healing—*healing of the heart* through the work of the Spirit—can help correct these pneumatic hindrances. This again illustrated the affective and ethical components of pneumatic interpretation. It also highlighted that

684. As with pneumatic interpretation and pneumatic appropriation, pneumatic hindrance was this work's term, applied as respective contributions fitted the description.

sometimes it is not our own ethical actions but the actions of others that cause emotional harm, damage the heart, and effect pneumatic hindrance. Distorted discernment and interpretation can, of course, lead to distorted conduct, increasing potential to cause emotional harm to others, and thus continuing the cycle.

As 1.3 outlined, *pneumatic appropriation* is an act of communication brought by the Spirit through our engagement with scripture to personal and contemporary contexts, which coheres with the original passage and its surrounding context in some way. Analysis of this aspect of pneumatic interpretation began by engaging with contributions from those discussing historico-grammatical methods. Charismatic and Pentecostal conversationalists were more cautious of incorporating these methods than evangelical scholars, but *all* acknowledged a relationship between the original content and context presented in scripture and the Spirit's appropriation of this to contemporary situations. Evangelical conversationalists only recognized pneumatic appropriation within the historico-grammatical data presented in scripture. However, they still perceived a relationship. Returning to Balthasar's pneumatology provided a perspective of pneumatic appropriation based around the nature of Christ, as he asserted that because all wisdom and knowledge is hidden in Christ, pneumatic truth, understood as the Spirit's (self)-interpretation of the triune God to us, is infinite and translatable across different contexts through the ages.

Chapter 3. Through and beyond scripture I: 1990 to 1999

Themes similar to affect, ethics, and cognition were also seen in Steven Land, *Pentecostal Spirituality*. To honor the influence of Land's work upon renewal scholarship and Pentecostal scholarship especially, elements of his discussion were used as a framework for this 1990s chapter. It gave theological consideration to the Spirit's relationship with scripture, discussed intimate relationship with God as affective, ethical, and cognitive, and considered frameworks (or contexts) for interpretation. Aligning with Land, cognition was identified as an aspect of intimate relationship with God *and* as a framework facilitating understanding.

The primary theme of chapter 2 had been that pneumatic interpretation was holistic. As analysis of the Spirit's role in the interpretation of scripture reached its second chronological era of consideration, it was becoming increasingly evident that pneumatic interpretation cannot be understood solely in relation to scripture. Concepts drawn and developed from these 1990s renewal conversationalists were showing that the Spirit always works *through* and *beyond* scripture's written words in ways that create, redeem, and effect and/or appropriate scriptural truth affectively, ethically, and cognitively in our lives. In other words, as we approach scripture seeking the Spirit's guidance in interpretation, the Spirit also reaches through scripture and interprets us.

Reflecting on the Spirit's relationship with scripture established this theme, with Land's thoughts helping to highlight that whilst scripture is the medium, the purpose is forming a life for God. Here, it was argued that those considering pneumatic interpretation should take seriously the Spirit's relationship with the Father as well as the Spirit's relationship with the Son. Jürgen Moltmann's theology, aligning with Balthasar's in chapter 2, was integral, drawing forth an understanding of the *creational* (Spirit–Father) aspect of pneumatic interpretation alongside the *redemptive* (Spirit–Son) aspect. The creational (Spirit–Father) aspect also helped appreciate why we can argue that the Spirit *does* communicate new things over against scripture's content as it is read. Furthermore, understanding (again aligning with Balthasar) that the Spirit (self)-interprets the Father, the Son, and the Spirit to us as scripture is engaged with strengthened understanding that the new things communicated will always remain in mutual relationship with scripture's written content. It was therefore suggested that Land's emphasis that the Spirit uses scripture to form Christ in us be adjusted to recognize that the Spirit's formation—or *(self)-interpretation*—is triune and not singularly related to Christ. In this theological understanding, scripture, therefore, does not go beyond the Spirit, because scripture reveals the triune God and this is a work of the Spirit *through*, in mutual relationship *with*, but also *beyond*, written scriptural content. The Spirit always reaches through and beyond scripture, effecting and/or appropriating scriptural truth holistically (creationally and redemptively) in our lives. In this way we interpret scripture but through this process the Spirit reaches through scripture and interprets us. As the Spirit (self)-interprets the Father, Son, and Spirit to us, we are pneumatically transformed into that (self)-interpretation.

Engaging with those who intentionally incorporated personal relationship with God within their hermeneutical considerations further strengthened this theme. Discussion here recognized intimate relationship with God as affective, ethical, and cognitive, with conversationalists showing collective recognition of the importance of pursuing intimate relationship with God, through whom pneumatic interpretation of scripture and self comes. The chief contributory insight gleaned from engaging with contributions from these conversationalists was of the dynamic interrelationship between affect and ethics, and the resulting influence on cognitive reception of truth brought by the Spirit through scripture.

Insights from Land, Paul Lee, and Vanhoozer helped strengthen the paradox that when we are most affectively receptive to God we are also the most ethically willing to modify behavior, and in order to be in a state of receptivity to God, active effort is required. Rickie Moore and Larry McQueen's personal accounts emphasized this further, conveying affective receptivity alongside active willingness to modify conduct, influencing their cognition. Whilst tending to emphasize the integration of their Pentecostal faith over explicitly discussing the Spirit's work, Moore and McQueen both described ongoing relational experiences with God through pneumatic encounter that brought affective, ethical, and cognitive transformation in their understanding of scripture and self. McQueen emphasized that his transformation of understanding directly related to his relationship with God, and his detailing of his affective pain as his cognitive understanding was adjusted suggested the removal of pneumatic hindrances. Moore described how his progressive encounter with Deuteronomy over a number of years impacted his ethics as he began to recognize and adjust the ways he had been thinking and behaving that he felt were hindering his ability to discern truth. Vanhoozer and Clark Pinnock were distinctive in emphasizing that immoral conduct, and evil spirits (Vanhoozer) can cause pneumatic hindrance.[685]

Cognition had been identified as an aspect of intimate relationship with God through whom pneumatic interpretation (of scripture and self) comes. Aligning with Land, who stressed the role of the Pentecostal community in shaping understanding, cognition was now also recognized as *a framework supporting knowledge*; in other words, a mental structure or process by which knowledge is acquired. As the conversation developed from the previous era's discussions over context and how the Spirit interprets scripture to us in our personal situations, scholars considered various cognitive frameworks and contexts for interpretation that incorporated the Spirit and allowed for personal faith expression. This led into discussions concerning application of postmodernist thought, use of historical grammaticism, involving understanding the framework surrounding the text in its original historical location, and community, involving understanding the framework surrounding ourselves as we approach scripture. It was through these discussions that emphasis, *for Pentecostals*, shifted from the Spirit's role in interpretation toward interpretation as a Pentecostal. Effectively, and illustrating the argument in 1.4 and 1.5, increasing focus on interpreting as a Pentecostal actually started to decrease attention on the Spirit. Those writing outside Pentecostal hermeneutics and less concerned about community

685. For definition of evil spirits and the demonic, see fn. 258.

identity (for example, Lee, Pinnock, Vanhoozer) tended to retain primary focus on the Spirit.

Lengthy, heated discussions occurred over use of postmodernism and historico-grammatical methods, typified by that between Timothy Cargal and Robert Menzies. Their articles illustrated evolving positions concerning the role of historico-grammatical approaches that would continue throughout the conversation. Generally, some Pentecostal scholars saw Menzies's position as an example of rational, evangelical principles of interpretation they were trying to rebalance or move away from as part of their quest for Pentecostal hermeneutical identity. However, whether they aligned with Cargal or Menzies, *all* considering historico-grammatical approaches within pneumatic interpretation and Pentecostal hermeneutics were seeking to address the relationship between the original meaning of the scriptural text and contemporary interpretation *in some way*, with differences lying in particular emphases and starting points. Therefore, all conversationalists recognized that the context or cognitive framework *mattered* and so in this respect they were not as different from each other as they perhaps thought they were.

John Christopher Thomas provided a healthy balance to interpretive approaches starting with scripture and the historico-grammatical data. His recommendation of an approach to interpretation incorporating the contemporary situation and surrounding cognitive framework, the Spirit, and scripture and surrounding cognitive framework, dynamically interrelating with each other was brave and pioneering. Thomas recognized that dependence on the Spirit's leading (as in Acts 15) was crucial, therefore prioritizing personal relationship with God. As emphasized, providing all three elements *were* held in balanced, dynamic relationship, Thomas's approach was preferable because it centralized intimate relationship with God, recognized the two frameworks (or contexts) and retained focus on the Spirit. Complementing Thomas's emphasis was David Aune (and James Dunn, see chapter 2), whose contribution showed that charismatic exegesis in early Jewish communities like Qumran was noticeably similar to contemporary renewal explorations of pneumatic interpretation and appropriation. Interaction with Aune's work highlighted the value of looking to ancient communities to inform contemporary understanding, and this was subsequently illustrated via the discussion of prophecy.

Thus, this second chronological era of consideration closed with an understanding that pneumatic interpretation of scripture is dynamically interrelated with pneumatic interpretation of self, and self-in-community; placing personal relationship with God centrally within consideration of the Spirit's role, and emphasizing the Father as well as the Son with the

Spirit. Analysis in this era also showed that interpretive frameworks that do not centralize the triune God will *hinder* developing understanding of how the Spirit works to communicate truth through scripture. This applies to those *over-using* both postmodernist and historico-grammatical frameworks. A framework for understanding pneumatic interpretation should draw us primarily toward intimate relationship with God, not into a medley of interpretive methods and concepts.

Chapter 4. Through and beyond scripture II: 2000 to 2009

Chapter 4 discussed the value and problem with Pentecostal hermeneutics before following a similar outline to chapter 3. It continued explicating the principle that the Spirit communicates *through* and *beyond* scripture's written words in ways that cohere in some way with the original passage and its surrounding historical framework. The overriding theme drawn and developed from renewal conversationalists in this era was that the Spirit through scripture, and working in our lives in ways that lead us toward scripture, communicates *personally and simultaneously communally*, and therefore, personal impact from pneumatic interpretation cannot be separated from our surrounding community frameworks. Building from chapter 3, this pneumatic interpretation was recognized as *reconciliational* as well as *creational* and *redemptive.*

The chapter further established that those considering pneumatic interpretation should prioritize the Spirit and give secondary attention to cognitive frameworks of interpretation, whether they are those surrounding relevant scriptural passages in their original historical location or those surrounding us as we engage with scripture today. This was highlighted by Pentecostal scholars increasingly drawing away from detailed and explicit attention to the Spirit and focusing on issues relating to Pentecostal hermeneutical identity. Whilst valuable to Pentecostal hermeneutics, these conversations were also not inclusive of scholars across and identifying with the renewal tradition who similarly prioritized relationship with the triune God through pneumatic encounter, and who were *also* part of the conversation. The conversation was reaching a stage where Pentecostal scholars writing in Pentecostal hermeneutics were the dominant voices, and those in or identifying with the charismatic movement were the minority voices struggling to be heard. Paradoxically, therefore, Pentecostal hermeneutics' discussions were helping, but increasingly hindering, understanding of pneumatic interpretation across the renewal tradition.

The analysis was highlighting that the Spirit through scripture (self)-interprets the Father to us as well as the Son and the Spirit. Conversationalists, however, largely continued to show inattention to the Spirit–Father relationship. Frank Macchia and Stanley Grenz discussed trinitarian aspects of pneumatology, but when considering the Spirit and scripture, they focused on the Spirit–Son partnership and did not address the Father or the triune relationship. This seems to have been at least partly influenced by their engagement with reformed theology. Amos Yong did focus on the triune relationship (his scope was wider than scripture), but he also did not overly focus on the Father. Potential reasons for this inattention are twofold; a tendency amongst some conversationalists to combine "Word" as scripture and Christ as *Logos*,[686] and hermeneutical implications resulting from the addition of the *filioque* clause to the Nicene Creed. Yong used the *filioque* to stress that the Spirit's role in interpretation had traditionally, and especially in Western Christianity, been subordinated to approaches beginning with the Son, but concurring with Moltmann (chapter 3), and William Atkinson, I stressed that the Father's role has *also* been relegated. With Moltmann, "the far-reaching decision in favour of the *filioque*"[687] has led to an emphasis on the Spirit as the Spirit of the Son at the expense of attention to the Spirit as the Spirit of the Father, focusing on the redemptive aspects of the Spirit's interpretive work over the creational. This patrological relegation, or inattention, has had and does have implications for understanding the Spirit's role in the interpretation of scripture, which, within space and remit constraints, I have been working to redress.

Accordingly, exploration of the creational (Spirit–Father) and redemptive (Spirit–Son) aspects of pneumatic interpretation identified in chapter 3 continued, aided particularly by engaging with aspects of Grenz's thought. His focus on the creational aspect of pneumatic interpretation addressed the Spirit–Father relationship despite Grenz himself largely not discussing the Father. Arguably this showed Grenz's own hermeneutical leanings resulting from the *filioque*. Interacting further with Grenz, and with ideas from Yong and Mark Cartledge brought a perspective of the Spirit as reconciler and overall "bringer-into-relationship." Their thought, largely wider than (Yong), or external to (Cartledge) the Spirit and scripture, helped highlight that as we engage with scripture, the Spirit reconciles, drawing us into

686. This will be discussed when reflecting on chapter 5.

687. Moltmann, *Spirit of Life*, 8. For Atkinson, and also Tom Smail, see fn. 401. Atkinson's focus was external to pneumatic interpretation but as with other Spirit-focused theologians discussed in this work (e.g., Balthasar, Moltmann, Yong), engaging with his thought helps provide insight into the Spirit's role in the interpretation of scripture. For further, see fn. 83.

relationship with God as Father, Son, and Spirit, *and* with those around us. Pneumatic interpretation was therefore presented as creational, redemptive, and reconciliational, *and* simultaneously personal and communal.[688] The Sprit *through* scripture, or working in our lives in ways that lead us *toward* scripture, (self)-interprets God as Father, Son, and Spirit to us, creating, redeeming, and reconciling personally *and* simultaneously communally, in *our* lives *and* in the lives of those around us.

Subsequent engagement with contributions from Gordon Fee, Grenz, Pinnock, and Scott Ellington helped practically to illustrate some of this discussion and strengthened understanding that the Spirit always speaks through and within surrounding historical and cultural frameworks. Andrew Davies's emphasis that beneath the written words is an ethical dimension that the Spirit also interprets to us began to expand understanding concerning the ethical aspect, which would resonate further in chapter 5. Particularly valuable was Fee's account of "an ongoing encounter with the living God—Father, Son, and Holy Spirit,"[689] throughout writing on his Philippians commentary. His experience was simultaneously personal and communal as he was pneumatically drawn into a profound and ongoing affective, ethical, and cognitive relational encounter with the triune God that impacted him *personally*, and *simultaneously* helped him to interpret and communicate Philippians "*for the sake of others in the church*."[690] Using Grenz's description, the Spirit "transported" him into the Philippians text and surrounding historical framework, and Fee heard the scriptures he was trying to communicate, pneumatically appropriated to him in the sermons, liturgy, or sung worship of churches he visited over the period he wrote his commentary, undoubtedly helping him identify what he felt needed communicating. Fee experienced pneumatic interpretation *and* pneumatic appropriation.

Considering intimate relationship with the triune God through pneumatic encounter brought further discussion of affect, ethics, and cognition, alongside continued discussion of pneumatic appropriation. Contributions from these renewal conversationalists showed the affective-ethical *and* ethical-affective aspects of pneumatic interpretation (and relationship with God), and influence on cognition. Aligning with 1990s Pentecostal scholars,

688. As stated, these creational, redemptive, and reconciliation roles are both *particular* to the Father, Son, and Spirit, yet also *mutual* within the triune relationship. Thus, whilst the differentiation is helpful, we must also be wary of overly defining the trinitarian roles. See fn. 405 (Richard Rohr with Mike Morrell).

689. Fee, "Exegesis and Spirituality," 3.

690. Fee, "Exegesis and Spirituality," 3 (emphasis added to stress the ethical component).

Lee Roy Martin, in his interaction with speeches from Yahweh to the Israelites in the book of Judges, emphasized the affective-ethical, influencing cognition, but also recognized hindrance from immoral behavior. Pinnock's comparison of Jesus's hermeneutical practices with those practiced in early Judaism and Qumran were valuable, emphasizing again the worth of looking to ancient communities to inform contemporary understanding. Also helpful was Pinnock's stress that Jesus wanted his followers to know scripture but *also* to be able to interpret the present time. Using Jesus's interpretive practices as a contemporary model for pneumatic interpretation and appropriation raised two important points. Firstly, Jesus's intimacy with the Father was integral. As Pinnock suggested, Jesus experienced the Spirit and was secure in his identity, knowing he was God's beloved Son. Connected with this, Jesus also appeared to take liberties with scripture or present it in a new light because he knew God's will in specific situations and contexts. Secondly, Jesus was without sin, and his intimacy with the Father was therefore unique. Offerings from Emerson Powery and Rickie Moore complemented these understandings. Collectively, these contributions correlated intimacy with God with pneumatic interpretation and appropriation. The contrasts given by Powery and Moore between the Sadducees and Jesus (Powery), and Job's friends and Job (Moore), provided an important caution to pursue intimacy with God through whom receptivity to the Spirit's interpretation of and through scripture comes.

Francis Martin's exploration of two mutually inclusive approaches to interpretation, by the Spirit or by the flesh, brought further insight to the area of pneumatic hindrance. His consideration of *prejudice* aligned with Pink's emphasis on partiality in chapter 2. As Martin emphasized, prejudice is an inherent characteristic influenced by our surrounding contexts, causing us to prejudge. It is not itself a negative feature but ignoring and not critically engaging with our own prejudgments can make it so. Martin's insight highlighted the importance of being critically aware of prejudgments resulting from our surrounding community frameworks that may hinder (or help) pneumatic interpretation. Consideration was then given as to how conversationalists, and indeed all Christian scholars, might facilitate pneumatic interpretation in academic work. This included: 1) approaching academic work as an overflow from personal relationship with God; 2) ideally undertaking the work within a surrounding community framework of committed and accountable Christian relationships; and 3) necessarily with critical and personal awareness of potential pneumatic hindrances from personal sin and prejudice. Following this reflection, engaging with Moore and Richard Bauckham's critiques of Lee Roy Martin and Robby Waddell's books helped solidify that if (believed) pneumatic interpretation is to be *evident* to others, personal (believed) impact should be conveyed somehow in one's academic work. This therefore requires awareness and engagement with the Spirit's appropriation of scriptural truth to one's personal situation(s) and surrounding community framework(s). As analysis in this era was cementing, if this appropriation is pneumatic, it will cohere contextually in some way. This once more placed intimate relationship with God through pneumatic encounter, and the affective, ethical, and cognitive aspects of this relationship, centrally within academic efforts. Of course, aspects of this personal relationship need not be conveyed, nor is it always appropriate to do so, but relationship with God should be central to our academic efforts as well as to our personal life.

Finally, Richard Bauckham's dialogue with Robby Waddell brought an important caution that whilst awareness of the Spirit's interpretive activity is a prerequisite for those critically engaging with pneumatic interpretation, one does not necessarily need to be *aware* of the Spirit's interpretive work for the Spirit *to* work. Pneumatic interpretation always involves ethical action on our part but this can be carried out without awareness of its relationship with affect and impact on cognition. Herewith came a vital ecumenical stress, also stated as this analysis commenced, that pneumatic interpretation, whilst characteristic of renewal thought, cannot be limited to the renewal tradition, for to one extent or another, the Spirit through scripture, and working in our lives in ways that lead us toward scripture, communicates knowingly or unknowingly (on our part) to, with, and through all Christians.

Closing this reflection of chapter 4, I realize afresh how intrinsically interconnected pneumatic appropriation is with pneumatic interpretation. This was becoming apparent in my thinking when writing chapters 4 and 5 especially, but now my appreciation is even more pronounced.[691] I continue to offer these unfolding insights as I move to reflect upon chapter 5 and bringing this analysis of the Spirit's role in the interpretation of scripture to a close.

Chapter 5. Hallmarks of pneumatic interpretation amidst scholarly diversity: 2010 to 2018

In this final era of consideration, the analysis drew on contributions from the most recent conversationalists. Chapter 5 underlined a core aim outlined in

691. This might be an example of the Spirit unfolding truth over time in my own understanding. It could also be an example of the Spirit guiding by teaching in retrospect. Cf. fn. 600 (Levison).

1.4, to focus on *uniting features* of scholarly thought amidst hermeneutical diversity, and in this process, draw together an understanding of pneumatic interpretation. It looked at Amos Yong's discussion of "the pneumatological imagination"[692] before addressing contributions from two broad, and contrasting yet complementary scholarly groupings, the "Regent school" and the "Cleveland school."[693] Whilst starting points, focus, terminology, and approach differed, uniting hallmarks of pneumatic interpretation, expounded throughout the analysis were discovered.

Yong's attention to the human (Christian) imagination in relationship with the Spirit complemented and enhanced this analysis. Both unique in approach, method, and terminology, and with different stresses (see 5.1.5), Yong's discussion within *Spirit–Word–Community* and this full-length work nevertheless united in addressing and highlighting similar aspects. This had hallmarks of the qualitative research method, triangulation, where different approaches, people, and methods are used to collect data on the same topic, ultimately reinforcing, deepening, and widening understanding of that subject-area.[694] Yong's "friends" therefore (the title given to this section) included not just those interacting with Yong's thought (William Atkinson, L. William Oliverio, and Wolfgang Vondey), but *all* renewal conversationalists celebrated in these pages whose thought, drawn and developed in this analysis, collectively complements Yong's "pneumatological imagination" and who are also complemented *by* Yong's unique contribution. Engagement especially helped appreciate that the Spirit can communicate with us through scripture by working on our hearts and imaginations, which are interconnected. In this interpretive action, the Spirit brings images and symbols to mind that *cohere with* but also *reach creatively beyond* the scriptural narrative to our personal lives and their surrounding situations. This pneumatic interpretation and appropriation is trinitarian with Christ as the incarnate image, affectively and ethically oriented and driven, and simultaneously personal and communal.

This work and Yong's also united in highlighting, albeit via different language and terminology, that as people we are fallible; capable of error,

692. As explained in 5.1, 'Pneumatological Imagination' was published in 2002 as part of *Spirit–Word–Community*. It was included at this point because those interacting with it were writing post-2010 and this placement worked well structurally.

693. This terminology alluded to two North American schools, influential within renewal scholarship, Regent University School of Divinity, a pioneer of the emerging area of renewal studies, and Cleveland Pentecostal Seminary, an established hub for Pentecostal hermeneutics' discussions. Grouping was not restricted to scholars previously or currently located at either school. See 5.2.

694. See fn. 535 (triangulation).

prejudice, and immoral action, and, Yong recognized, also live surrounded by various "spiritual" powers at work in the world, including the demonic.[695] Our pneumatic discernment (otherwise known as the pneumatological imagination), and consequently, pneumatic interpretation, will therefore always, to one extent or another, *also* be fallible and partial.[696] As this analysis has reasoned, whilst this will always be the case, pneumatic hindrance can be lessened by pursuing intimate relationship with God, through whom pneumatic interpretation and appropriation is brought.

Subsequently, the analysis addressed the "Regent school" and then the "Cleveland school." "Regent school" scholars came from a range of ecclesial traditions including Pentecostalism. Most identified *in*, but some identified *with*, the renewal tradition. They included Mark Boda, Jacqueline Grey, Craig Keener, Jack Levison, Kevin Spawn, and Archie Wright. Collectively, these conversationalists addressed pneumatic interpretation across, and surrounding, a renewal spectrum. Being mainly biblical scholars they focused on investigating ancient communities, their people, and their interpretive practices to inform contemporary understanding of the Spirit's interpretation of and through scripture. To varying extents depending on their specialism, they all addressed contemporary interpretation. Two emerging and interrelated areas of enquiry were the influence of ethical conduct on pneumatic interpretation, and addressing pneumatic hindrance. These scholars tended to emphasize understanding the cognitive framework (or context) surrounding relevant scriptural passages in their original historical location.

Levison's position that living virtuously (ethical action) cultivates receptivity to the Spirit's communication significantly aided the developing understanding of the ethical and cognitive components of pneumatic interpretation. As Levison emphasized people in scripture who prioritized intimate relationship with God, emphasizing their devotion and prayerfulness, he also implicitly addressed affect. His contribution therefore addressed the ethical-affective aspect of the affective-ethical paradox first identified in chapter 2, balancing affective-ethical contributions. Following Levison's understanding but in this work's terms, daily cultivation of ethical conduct whilst in intimate, affective relationship with God, influences cognitive receptivity of truth brought by the Spirit through scripture. Levison's example of Simeon (Luke 2) related this directly to pneumatic interpretation and appropriation.

695. See fn. 529 (Yong's understanding of spirit). Also fn. 258 (definition of evil spirit/demon).

696. See the complementary emphasis in chapter 2 of the interpretable and, at the same time, interpretable nature of truth brought by the Spirit through scripture.

As the critique from Wright helped address, Levison's focus was cultivation and he did not consider pneumatic hindrance. Within this area of pneumatic hindrance are questions concerning the influence evil spirits can have on us.[697] Throughout this analysis, only Vanhoozer, Yong, and Wright have been found to very briefly highlight issues of pneumatic hindrance caused by evil spirits, with Vanhoozer alone directly addressing this within scriptural interpretation.[698] It is perplexing that such minor attention has been given to this area and it deserves greater attention. Spiritual powers at work in the world surround us as we live out our personal and professional lives in their various situations and locations. These powers include evil spirits that would seek to distort understanding (Eph 6:12). By consequence therefore, this is always the wider, surrounding context whenever we engage with scripture, whether the situation is personal, academic, or a mixture of both. If the Spirit works in, with, and through our affectivity, ethical action, and cognition, it follows that evil spirits can attempt to do likewise, aiming to counterfeit and counteract the Spirit's interpretive activity. The Holy Spirit of God is all-powerful but the presence of evil spirits working to distort our understanding is also a clear and present reality. These are initial thoughts, and further consideration of this important research area lies beyond these pages.

Conversationalists addressing pneumatic hindrance more widely have also mainly been those writing outside Pentecostal hermeneutics' conversations,[699] and Keener's consideration of unbelief and moral blindness in *Spirit Hermeneutics* supported this theme. Within the aspects of his discussion included in chapter 5, Keener gave minimal attention to the Spirit's role. Nevertheless, engagement with these insights assisted understanding of this lesser explored area. In particular, it helped reinforce that although the Spirit is the ultimate inspirer and empowerer of our vision, cognitive receptivity to truth brought by the Spirit through scripture is also not automatically guaranteed. Keener's recounted personal experience of evil, struggle to connect what had happened to him and his family with his theology, and sudden realization of what had happened years later whilst reading a passage in Job, appears to be a valuable illustration of pneumatic

697. Remembering that this analysis is addressed to the Christian reader. See fn. 1, also fn. 25 (the Spirit's communication to non-Christians).

698. Also Atkinson without reference to the Spirit. See 3.3.1.

699. My hypothesis here is that those within Pentecostal hermeneutics' discussions have cautiously avoided what could be construed as works-based theology. Pink (2.1.1), Francis Martin (2.2.3, 4.3.2), Balthasar (2.3.3), Lee, Vanhoozer (3.3.1), Pinnock (3.3.3), Powery (4.3.1), Yong (5.1.4). Acknowledging Lee Roy Martin (4.3.3). Remembering that Yong's use of "Pentecostal" was mainly in the small "p" sense (see 1.2, 4.1).

hindrance from prejudgment, and pneumatic appropriation, reinforcing discussion of these aspects in chapter 4.

Contributions from Wright, Levison, and Boda highlighted the value of considering ancient communities, their people, and their interpretive practices when considering pneumatic interpretation. In keeping with their expertise, these biblical scholars started with and focused on the ancient communities and people shown in scripture and early Jewish texts. From this predominant focus they addressed contemporary application, and each discussed the Spirit's appropriation of the scriptural text to personal lives and situations. Wright followed Aune (chapter 3), and Pinnock (chapter 4) in highlighting interpretive practices at Qumran, underlining the worth of looking to this ancient community to inform contemporary understanding. Drawing on insights from Boda highlighted once more the affective, ethical, and cognitive aspects of pneumatic interpretation. Levison, and similarly Boda, recognized that diligent study of scripture appears to nurture one's awareness of the Spirit's interpretive activity—*if* approached as part of intimate relationship with God, a claim they would doubtless agree with.

Grey gave more consideration to contemporary interpretation but was less focused on the Spirit. However, her mostly implicit attention to the Spirit's role allowed provision of valuable and practical principles for interpreting and appropriating scripture. Engagement with Grey's contribution underscored two interrelated and core principles presented through this work in varying forms. Firstly, the Spirit always communicates through and within a cognitive framework of interpretation: the framework surrounding scripture in its original situation, and the contemporary community framework surrounding the interpreter. Both frameworks should be recognized and respected. Secondly, as we engage with scripture, the Spirit interprets the triune God to us.[700]

"Cleveland school" scholars included Cheryl Bridges Johns, Chris Green, Lee Roy Martin, Rickie Moore, John Christopher Thomas, and Robert Wall. Using Robby Waddell and Peter Althouse's explanation, these, mainly Pentecostal, scholars focused on "the spiritual experience of reading Scripture with an expectation of encountering God in and through the text," whereby the Spirit meets the reader, transforming them into the image of Christ.[701] "Cleveland school" scholars emphasized affect and ethics and their primary cognitive framework of interpretation was the contemporary

700. Grey did not discuss trinitarian aspects. Her contribution also aligned with both "schools" but had a "Regent school" emphasis. Reflecting this, it was considered as the "Regent school" discussion closed. Likewise Robert Wall, whose contribution was considered as discussion of the "Cleveland school" opened.

701. Waddell and Althouse, "Pentecostals and Their Scriptures," 116.

and/or early Pentecostal community. They therefore differed from, but more importantly, *complemented* "Regent school" scholars by focusing primarily on contemporary readers' experiences as they engage with scripture today.

Much of the emphasis from "Cleveland school" scholars complemented this analysis especially the emphasis on intimate, transformative relationship with God brought by the Spirit as we read scripture. However, Moore, Johns, and also Green, focused more on scripture itself than this work has. Whereas this work has stressed that the Spirit, *through* scripture, interprets us, their emphasis tended to be on scripture *by* the Spirit enacting transformation in our lives. Potential reasons for this emphasis were clearest when interacting with Cheryl Bridges Johns's "Spirit–Word" discussion. Johns used "Word" with a twofold sense, seemingly simultaneously referring to scripture *and* Christ as *Logos* (although she did not explicitly state this). This position, which other, mainly Pentecostal scholars also follow,[702] can be traced to Land's appealing comparison between the Spirit's forming of Christ in Mary with the Spirit using scripture to form Christ in us (chapter 3).[703] The position has been further influenced by Pentecostal scholars like Frank Macchia interacting with reformed theology (chapter 4), which Johns also did. The issue is threefold. Firstly, this position forays into discussions about the nature of scripture, a much larger discussion area, beyond this work's remit, and not all using the terminology may realize this. Secondly, partly because of the terminology, the "Spirit–Word" position can lead to focusing more on scripture and less explicitly on the Spirit. Thirdly, the position *does not actively acknowledge the Father* and therefore relegates the Father's role (and once again returning to hermeneutical implications resulting from the *filioque*). Space and focus did not permit dwelling on these issues further and to do so would have led away from mine and Johns's shared emphasis on transformative communion with the triune God brought by the Spirit as we read scripture.[704]

Aside from this, Green's attention to the Spirit's (affective-ethical) work of sanctification enacted in and through us as we read scripture contrasted Levison's affective-ethical stress, yet also complemented it for both emphasized partnership with God in their discussions. Furthermore, Green's emphasis on remaining in *apprenticeship* to the Spirit when learning to hear and speak faithfully corresponded with similar emphases from Levison and Keener, whilst his accompanying stress on our interpretations always

702. E.g., see fn. 380 (Macchia, Moore, Waddell).

703. Possibly even to Moore (chapter 2).

704. Cheryl Bridges Johns emphasized the triune nature of God but did not actively discuss the Father.

remaining *tentative* aligned with Yong's recognition of partiality. These last two emphases supported the continuing stress, based around the invisible and, by contrast, incarnate nature of God and God's communication, that truth the Spirit communicates through our engagement with scripture—because this truth (self)-interprets God as Father, Son, and Spirit to us—is *both interpretable and beyond interpretation; reachable, yet nevertheless also beyond grasp.*

Like other Pentecostal conversationalists, Martin mostly did not explicitly discuss the Spirit.[705] Instead, he focused on scripture and his Pentecostal context, and particular affections like joy, gratitude, lament, love, and compassion evoked in a Christian believer through hearing different psalms. As this work has emphasized, it is *by the Spirit* through engagement with scripture that affect is transformed and redirected toward God as Father, Son, and Spirit. Daisy Wilkins's 1908 testimony with Martin's analysis highlighted affective, ethical, and cognitive aspects of the Spirit's interpretation of Wilkins and her engagement with Psalm 23, which complemented Boda's consideration using 2 Kings 22–23 and Nehemiah 8–10. Wilkins's account with Martin's analysis suggested that the Spirit affectively and ethically *interpreted* Wilkins, bringing cognitive insight of affective aspects in Psalm 23, which aligned her human affections with God's affections. This affective alignment enabled her to persevere (ethical action) through difficulty, and consequently Wilkins drew deeper in intimate relationship with God. Furthermore, Wilkins's account with Martin's analysis *also* suggested that the Spirit affectively and ethically, as well as cognitively, *appropriated* aspects of Psalm 23 to Wilkins's personal life and surrounding framework (and vice-versa). Affect seems to have been evoked in Wilkins in ways that *cohered* with the part of the psalm that resonated most with her personal situation. This corresponded with an invigorated cognition, which subsequently steered her ethical action. This realization was helped by remembering Davies's stress of the ethical dimension beneath the written words (chapter 4), which first brought to light that the contextual coherence of pneumatic appropriation can be affective and ethical (with cognition). Martin's own slightly earlier thought affirmed this perspective as he had discussed the contemporary perspective of pneumatic appropriation that Wright compared with "Spirit-led" interpretive methods practiced by the Qumran community.

Writing chapter 5, I realized afresh that my aim throughout *The Interpreting Spirit* had been to focus on *common, uniting features* of scholars'

705. See 4.1 for a reminder of the reasoning behind this often-implicit attention. Also 1.4 and 1.5.

thought over differences. Whilst differences are important, overly focusing on them can distract from recognizing and attending to commonalities. It often requires more effort to locate and focus on these uniting hallmarks, but it is the stronger position, for, as Psalm 133 tells us, where there is unity there is blessing. Thus, the final era of consideration concluded by underlining that amidst different emphases, foci, terminology, and methods, contributions from scholars identified as "Regent school," and "Cleveland school," preceded by interaction with Yong's discussion of the imagination in relationship with the Spirit, collectively identified affective, ethical, and cognitive aspects of the Spirit's communication through and beyond scripture, and recognized intimate relationship with God as a central factor. Engagement also helped to further understanding of pneumatic appropriation and pneumatic hindrance. This affirmed the work's stress on these features, but *more importantly* indicated that these are *hallmarks* of the truth brought by the Spirit through and beyond scripture, and our receptivity to this interpretive activity.

6.3 CLOSING ANALYSIS

As this closing chapter commenced, I explained that my understanding of pneumatic interpretation and associated terminology had gradually unfolded throughout this analysis. The Spirit unfolds scriptural truth over time, and just as my particular understanding has evolved through undertaking this work, our understanding of how the Spirit brings truth through our engagement with scripture will also always continually unfold. Furthermore, in keeping with the invisible and, in contrast, incarnate nature of God and God's communication, the truth the Spirit communicates through scripture—because this truth (self)-interprets God as Father, Son, and Spirit to us—is *both interpretable and beyond interpretation; reachable, yet nevertheless also beyond grasp.* Our understanding of how the Spirit brings truth through scripture will always, to one extent or another, be fragmentary and incomplete; yet this recognition has not and should not stop the pursuit. I therefore offer this closing analysis at this resting point in the unfolding of my own understanding.

Pneumatic interpretation cannot be understood solely in relation to scripture because, as we read scripture, the Spirit works *through* and *beyond* the written words interpreting *and* appropriating—for I realize now at the end of this analysis that the two terms are intrinsically interrelated—scriptural truth holistically in our lives in ways that cohere in some way with the scriptural narrative and surrounding historical context or framework.

This pneumatic interpretation and appropriation is affective, ethical, and cognitive, also creational, redemptive, and reconciliational, and simultaneously personal and communal. *All* these aspects transform and draw us holistically into knowledge of, and relationship with, God as Father, Son, and Spirit, to whom the Spirit, through scripture, ultimately points. As we read scripture, therefore, the Spirit (self)-interprets and appropriates God as Father, Son, and Spirit to us, recognizing Christ as the incarnate image. This process is also dynamic, understanding that the Spirit works personally in our lives (and surrounding community frameworks) in ways that lead us toward scripture (and surrounding historical frameworks), and so the basis for pneumatic interpretation does not always start with scripture.

Central is intimate relationship with God as Father, Son, and Spirit, through whom pneumatic interpretation and appropriation of scripture and self comes. Whilst Christ is the incarnate image of this transformative communication, especially recognizing the affective, ethical, and cognitive components, the Spirit, through scripture, and working in our lives in ways that lead us toward scripture, also affectively, ethically, and cognitively, holistically interprets and appropriates to us *the Father*, whose love for us was so great that the Father gave us the Son—and thereby providing a supreme example of affective-ethical action. The Son cannot be understood apart from the Father, and so the Spirit's holistic interpretation and appropriation of the Son to us is *also* a holistic interpretation and appropriation of the Father. Jesus came from the Father to show us the Father; to see Jesus in the written words of scripture or in the affections or actions of our neighbor in ways that remind and lead us toward scripture *is* to see the Father, and as we are being transformed into the image of Jesus, the Spirit is also working in us the image of the Father. Furthermore, this pneumatic communication is *also* a holistic *self*-interpretation and appropriation, for, as the Spirit interprets the Son and the Father to us, *the Spirit* is also self-interpreted.

The Spirit, therefore, through our engagement with scripture, and working in our lives in ways that lead us toward scripture, works affectively and ethically, bringing cognitive understanding of both scripture and self, and drawing us deeper into holistic knowledge of, but more importantly, *intimate relationship with*, God as Father, Son, and Spirit, to whom the scriptural narrative, and therefore the Spirit through scripture, ultimately points. Cognition is an important and inescapable aspect of pneumatic interpretation and appropriation, but ultimately it is intimate, transformative relationship that is most important, not what we can or cannot "see."

However, this analysis has also shown that there is an ethical-affective aspect, influencing cognition. The paradox is that it is when we are most affectively receptive to God that we are also the most ethically willing to modify behavior, yet in order to be in a state of open receptivity to God, and pneumatically discern and interpret—and *be* pneumatically interpreted and appropriated—active effort is also required. Every relationship requires effort and our relationship with the triune God through pneumatic encounter is no different. As we cultivate this intimate relationship, cognitive receptivity to the Spirit's communication (through scripture, and in ways leading us toward scripture) grows. Jack Levison's illustration, using Luke 2:25–32, of Simeon's devotion to God, familiarity with scripture, and pneumatic comprehension of the baby Jesus as the Messiah scripture had spoken of, was a beautiful example of this. However, part of cultivating this intimate relationship also involves recognizing and addressing aspects that can hinder ability to perceive, discern, or receive truth brought by the Spirit through scripture and in ways steering us toward scripture, and this area has received the least attention. The analysis has highlighted a number of aspects related to pneumatic hindrance, including hindrances from evil spirits seeking to distort understanding, and as this work closes, I return to the subject of inner healing raised in chapter 2. Past experiences that have caused emotional hurt in some way can hinder ability to receive truth brought by the Spirit through scripture (or to receive truth in our lives in ways that steer us toward scripture), for it is in these areas where our heart is damaged and our discernment distorted. Inner healing, *healing of the heart through the work of the Spirit*, can help correct this, bringing freshness of vision and understanding of both scripture and self—in ways that are affective, ethical, and cognitive, creational, redemptive, and reconciliational, and simultaneously personal and communal—but this also necessarily involves an attitude of humility and willingness to be pneumatically transformed and reordered. Central once again is intimate relationship with *our* triune God through pneumatic encounter through whom pneumatic interpretation and appropriation of scripture and self comes, and to whom the Spirit through scripture, and working in our lives in ways that lead us toward scripture, ultimately points.

The value of personal accounts

Over the course of researching and writing this work, people have sometimes asked me what a pneumatic reading of scripture looks like. My answer is always the same: a pneumatic reading of scripture never stays just a reading, for the Spirit is concerned with so much more than just our minds. Truth brought by the Spirit through scripture, or, in our lives in ways leading us toward scripture, will manifest differently in each of us according to our different situations and contexts, but the hallmarks of pneumatic interpretation, as given here, remain the same. Robby Waddell was understandably cautious about discussing his personal (believed) pneumatic experience as he wrote *The Spirit of the Book of Revelation*. He felt that some scholars in academia can devalue such approaches. If this is the case, then perhaps it is because as academics we tend to prioritize cognition over affect and ethics. Personal accounts and insights, such as those from Rickie Moore, Gordon Fee, and Craig Keener,[706] have been integral to this analysis because they have helped to present an idea of ways that pneumatic interpretation can manifest in a person's life. My own story, briefly mentioned as this chapter commenced (see 6.1), has involved a journey of prayer for others. This journey—or perhaps the Spirit working through the journey—which has run alongside and intertwined with my research and writing, has been working in a number of ways. Amongst them, a deep and holistic appreciation has been instilled in me that *all* understanding, regardless of whether it is pneumatic, involves the interrelation of affect, ethics, and cognition. In chapter one of his letter to the Philippians, Paul spoke of longing for the Philippians "with the affection of Christ Jesus" (verse eight). It has sometimes felt, as I have prayed for those I believe the Lord has called me to care for in this way—and therein lies my affective-ethical action—*that similar affection present in Paul is also present in me.*[707] Most importantly perhaps, this personal journey, running alongside and intertwined with this work, has been one where, as I have been approaching scripture and my personal situations, seeking the Spirit's guidance, the Spirit also seems to have been reaching through scripture and those situations (in ways leading me towards scripture), and *interpreting me.*

6.4 CLOSING WORD

This work has been an analysis of the Spirit's role in the interpretation of scripture. It has been approached by engaging with a conversation surrounding this topic that has been taking place amongst scholars in or identifying with the renewal tradition since 1970. In choosing to consider pneumatic interpretation (and appropriation) via this approach, I have

706. Also Larry McQueen (chapter 3), Lee Roy Martin, Robby Waddell, and Richard Bauckham (chapter 4), and Daisy Wilkins (chapter 5). Without reference to the Spirit or scripture, Frank Macchia (fn. 493). For Waddell, see 4.3.4.

707. Of course, this affective-ethical action is dynamically interrelated and correlated with cognition. Affect propels me to prayer (ethical action), and as I continue to bring those I care for to the triune God (through pneumatic encounter) in this way, affect and cognition in me has grown. The affection of Jesus is also essentially the affection of the Father, and through the Father and the Son, the Spirit becomes known.

intended that it would also be seen as a celebration of continually unfolding renewal thought. Much like an orchestra comprised of different instruments and sections, each renewal voice, and family of renewal voices makes their own sound. All are individually valued, with their particular tones and melodies, but together there is also a collective richness, depth, complexity, and complementarity that only the whole orchestra can bring.

In an article published in 2000, Clark Pinnock, championing Pentecostals in academia, stated that their gift to the academy was an ability, as "biblical and practical people" to communicate "the personal nature of God's relationality."[708] He stressed that Pentecostals had not fully realized the uniqueness of their contribution and needed to, stating:

> It is time for Pentecostals to realize that they have a distinctive doctrine of God implicit in their faith and that they need to make it explicit—not just for purely academic purposes but for revival too, because Christianity is only as dynamic as its understanding of God.[709]

Whilst endorsing Pinnock's comments, this work has shown that they apply, not just to Pentecostals, but to *all* those across or identifying with the renewal tradition who prioritize personal experience *of* and intimate relationship *with* God as Father, Son, and Spirit through pneumatic encounter. This priority is central to discussions of pneumatic interpretation in the renewal tradition and has been the core theme around which this work has revolved. *It is now time*, therefore, for scholars to recognize that this distinctive characteristic is not just particular to those in the Pentecostal tradition.

This analysis has only focused on the renewal tradition inasmuch as it has drawn and developed—and in this process celebrated—thought from those who emphasize the Spirit and accentuate the Spirit's role in their hermeneutical considerations. Whilst other features also characterize renewal spirituality,[710] the focus on the Spirit is *the* overriding and defining feature uniting renewal Christians across their varied ecclesial traditions. Without this common focus there would be no renewal tradition, and when aspects particular to the tradition become the main focus, attention to the Spirit can actually lessen. The self-effacing nature of the Spirit is to always look beyond the Spirit toward the other, and so, as people characterized by a uniting emphasis on the Spirit, I humbly suggest that renewal scholars

708. Pinnock, "Divine Relationality," 6, 5 respectively.

709. Pinnock, "Divine Relationality," 6.

710. See 1.2 for discussion.

should correspondingly always seek to prioritize welcoming others into this conversation and others like it regardless of their ecclesial background.

Bibliography

Aker, Ben. "Craig S. Keener's *Spirit Hermeneutics: Reading Scripture in Light of Pentecost* and the Need for an Ecumenical Reading of Acts 2." *Pneuma* 39.1–2 (2017) 162–67.

Allen, David M. "'The Forgotten Spirit': A Pentecostal Reading of the Letter to the Hebrews?" *JPT* 18 (2009) 51–66.

Anderson, Allan Heaton. *An Introduction to Pentecostalism: Global Charismatic Christianity*. 2nd ed. Cambridge: Cambridge University Press, 2014.

———. "Pentecostalism." In *Global Dictionary of Theology*, edited by William A. Dyrness and Veli-Matti Kärkkäinen, 641–48. Nottingham, UK: IVP, 2008.

Anderson, Bernhard W. *The Living Word of the Bible*. London: SCM, 1979.

Anderson, Gordon L. "Pentecostal Hermeneutics Part 1." *Paraclete* 28.1 (1994) 1–11. Accessed May 8, 2018. http://enrichmentjournal.ag.org/top/holyspirit_articledisplay.cfm?targetBay=1b574def-b227-4617-bfc7-a02cdb926902&ModID=2&Process=DisplayArticle&RSS_RSSContentID=15177&RSS_OriginatingChannelID=1170&RSS_OriginatingRSSFeedID=4486&RSS_Source=.

———. "Pentecostal Hermeneutics Part 2." *Paraclete* 28.2 (1994) 13–22. Accessed May 8, 2018. http://enrichmentjournal.ag.org/top/holyspirit_articledisplay.cfm?targetBay=1b574def-b227-4617-bfc7-a02cdb926902&ModID=2&Process=DisplayArticle&RSS_RSSContentID=15178&RSS_OriginatingChannelID=1170&RSS_OriginatingRSSFeedID=4486&RSS_Source=.

Anglicans Online. "The Nicene Creed." Accessed March 20, 2020. http://anglicansonline.org/basics/nicene.html.

Apel, Willi, *Harvard Dictionary of Music*. 2nd ed. Cambridge: Harvard University Press, 2000.

Archer, Kenneth J. "Afterword: On the Future of Pentecostal Hermeneutics." In *Constructive Pneumatological Hermeneutics in Pentecostal Christianity*, edited by Kenneth J. Archer and L. William Oliverio Jr., 315–27. New York: Palgrave Macmillan, 2016.

———. "Biblical Imagery: The Metaphorical Symbols of the Holy Spirit." *The Pneuma Review* (2011). Accessed October 11, 2018. http://pneumareview.com/biblical-imagery-the-metaphorical-symbols-of-the-holy-spirit/.

———. "David K. Bernard, *Understanding God's Word: An Apostolic Approach to Interpreting the Bible*." *Pneuma* 29.1 (2007) 131–32.

———. "Early Pentecostal Biblical Interpretation." *JPT* 18 (2001) 32–70.

———. "Pentecostal Hermeneutics and the Society for Pentecostal Studies: Reading and Hearing in One Spirit and One Accord." *Pneuma* 37.3 (2015) 317–39.

———. "Pentecostal Hermeneutics: Retrospect and Prospect." *JPT* 8 (1996) 63–81.

———. *A Pentecostal Hermeneutic: Spirit, Scripture and Community*. 2005. Reprint with new Preface. Cleveland, OH: CPT, 2009.

———. "Pentecostal Story: The Hermeneutical Filter for the Making of Meaning." *Pneuma* 26.1 (2004) 36–59.

———. "Spirited Conversation about Hermeneutics: A Pentecostal Hermeneut's Response to Craig Keener's *Spirit Hermeneutics*." *Pneuma* 39.1–2 (2017) 179–97.

Archer, Kenneth J., and L. William Oliverio Jr., eds. *Constructive Pneumatological Hermeneutics in Pentecostal Christianity*. New York: Palgrave Macmillan, 2016.

Archer, Kenneth J., and Richard E. Waldrop. "Liberating Hermeneutics: Toward a Holistic Pentecostal Mission of Peace and Justice." *JEPTA* 31.1 (2011) 65–78.

Archer, Melissa L. *"I Was in the Spirit on the Lord's Day": A Pentecostal Engagement with Worship in the Apocalypse*. Cleveland, OH: CPT, 2015.

Arrington, French L. "Hermeneutics, Historical Perspectives on Pentecostal and Charismatic." In *Dictionary of Pentecostal and Charismatic Movements*, edited by Stanley M. Burgess and Gary B. McGee, 376–89. 1988. Reprint with corrections. Grand Rapids: Zondervan, 1993.

———. "The Use of the Bible by Pentecostals." *Pneuma* 16.1 (1994) 101–7.

Asia Pacific Theological Seminary. "Asian Journal of Pentecostal Studies Volumes." Accessed July 21, 2018. https://www.aptspress.org/asian-journal-of-pentecostal-studies/volumes-and-articles-of-ajps/.

Athanasius. *Contra Gentes and De Incarnatione*. Edited and translated by Robert W. Thomson. Originally written approximately 323 CE. Oxford: Clarendon, 1971.

Atkinson, William *Now Read This: How to Feed Your Spirit from the Pages of God's Word*. Eastbourne, UK: Kingsway. 1996.

Atkinson, William P. *Trinity After Pentecost*. Eugene, OR: Pickwick, 2013.

———. "Worth a Second Look? Pentecostal Hermeneutics." *Evangel* 21.2 (2003) 49–54.

Aune, David E. *Apocalypticism, Prophecy, and Magic in Early Christianity*. Tübingen: Mohr Siebeck, 2006.

———. "Charismatic Exegesis in Early Judaism and Early Christianity." In *The Pseudepigrapha and Early Biblical Interpretation: JSPSup.14*, edited by James H. Charlesworth and Craig A. Evans, 126–50. Sheffield, UK: Sheffield Academic Press, 1993.

———. "Christian Prophecy and Charismatic Exegesis." In *Prophecy in Early Christianity and the Ancient Mediterranean World*, 339–46. Grand Rapids: Eerdmans, 1991.

Autry, Arden. "Dimensions of Hermeneutics in Pentecostal Focus." *JPT* 3 (1993) 29–50.

Bader-Saye, Scott. "Listening: Authority and Obedience." In *The Blackwell Companion to Christian Ethics*, edited by Stanley Hauerwas and Samuel Wells, 156–68. 2004. Reprint, Oxford: Blackwell, 2006.

Baker, Robert O. "Pentecostal Bible Reading: Toward a Model of Reading for the Formation of Christian Affections." *JPT* 7 (1995) 34–48.

Balthasar, Hans Urs von. "The Interpreter." In *Theo-Logic III: The Spirit of Truth*, translated by Graham Harrison, 61–104. German original 1987. San Francisco: Ignatius, 2005.

———. "Preliminary Remarks on the Discernment of Spirits." In *Explorations in Theology IV: Spirit and Institution*, translated by Edward T. Oakes, 337–51. German original 1974. San Francisco: Ignatius, 1995.

———. *Theo-Logic III: The Spirit of Truth*. Translated by Graham Harrison. German original 1987. San Francisco: Ignatius, 2005.

———. "The Unknown Lying Beyond the Word." In *Explorations in Theology III: Creator Spirit*, translated by Brian McNeil, 105–16. German original 1967. San Francisco: Ignatius, 1993.

Barth, Karl. *Church Dogmatics, Volume I: The Doctrine of the Word of God, Part 2*. Edited by G. W. Bromiley and T. F. Torrance, and translated by G. T. Thomson and H. Knight. Edinburgh, T. & T. Clark, 1956.

———. *The Epistle to the Romans*. 1933. 6th ed. Translated by Edwyn C. Hoskyns. Oxford: Oxford University Press, 1968.

———. *The Holy Spirit and the Christian Life: The Theological Basis of Ethics*. 1938. Reprint, Translated by R. Birch Hoyle. Louisville: Westminster John Knox, 1993.

Bartholomew, Craig G. "Postmodernity and Biblical Interpretation." In *Dictionary for Theological Interpretation of the Bible*, edited by Kevin J. Vanhoozer et al., 600–607. London: SPCK, 2005.

———. "Spirit and Scripture: A Response." In *Spirit and Scripture: Exploring a Pneumatic Hermeneutic*, edited by Kevin L. Spawn and Archie T. Wright, 145–53. 2011. Reprint, London: Bloomsbury T. & T. Clark, 2013.

Bartholomew, Craig G., et al. *After Pentecost: Language & Biblical Interpretation*. The Scripture and Hermeneutics Series 2. Carlisle, UK: Paternoster, 2001.

———. *Out of Egypt: Biblical Theology and Biblical Interpretation*. The Scripture and Hermeneutics Series 5. Milton Keynes, UK: Paternoster, 2004.

———. *Renewing Biblical Interpretation*. The Scripture & Hermeneutics Series 1. Carlisle, UK: Paternoster, 2000.

Bartholomew, Craig G., and Heath A. Thomas. "A Manifesto for Theological Interpretation." In *A Manifesto for Theological Interpretation*, edited by Craig G. Bartholomew and Heath A. Thomas, 1–26. Grand Rapids: Baker, 2016.

———, eds. *A Manifesto for Theological Interpretation*. Grand Rapids: Baker, 2016.

Bartholomew, Craig G., and Matthew Y. Emerson. "Theological Interpretation for All of Life." In *A Manifesto for Theological Interpretation*, edited by Craig G. Bartholomew and Heath A. Thomas, 257–74. Grand Rapids: Baker, 2016.

Bauckham, Richard. Review of Robby Waddell, *The Spirit of the Book of Revelation*. *JPT* 17 (2008) 3–8.

Beale, G. K. *Handbook on the New Testament Use of the Old Testament: Exegesis and Interpretation*. Grand Rapids: Baker Academic, 2012.

Beck, James R. ed. *Two Views on Women in Ministry*. 2nd ed. Grand Rapids: Zondervan, 2005.

Becker, Matthias. "A Tenet Under Examination: Reflections on the Pentecostal Hermeneutical Approach." *JEPTA* 24.1 (2004) 30–48.

Berkouwer, G. C. *Holy Scripture*. Grand Rapids: Eerdmans, 1975.

Bernard, David K. *Understanding God's Word: An Apostolic Approach to Interpreting the Bible*. Hazelwood, UK: Word Aflame, 2005.

Berrin, Shanni L. "Pesharim." In *Encyclopedia of the Dead Sea Scrolls: Volume 2*, edited by Lawrence H. Schiffman and James C. VanderKam, 644–47. Oxford: Oxford University Press, 2000.

Billings, J. Todd. *The Word of God for the People of God: An Entryway to the Theological Interpretation of Scripture*. Grand Rapids: Eerdmans, 2010.

Bird, Thomas. "Experience over Scripture in Charismatic Exegesis." *CTQ* 45 (1983) 5–11.

Bloesch, Donald D. G. "A Christological Hermeneutic: Crisis and Conflict in Hermeneutics." In *The Use of the Bible in Theology: Evangelical Options*, edited by Robert K. Johnson, 78–102. Atlanta: John Knox, 1985.

———. *Holy Scripture: Revelation, Inspiration & Interpretation*. Carlisle, UK: Paternoster, 1994.

———. "The Sword of the Spirit: The Meaning of Inspiration." *Themelios* 5.3 (1980) 14–19.

Boda, Mark J., "Walking with the Spirit in the Word: A Response." In *Spirit and Scripture: Exploring a Pneumatic Hermeneutic*, edited by Kevin L. Spawn and Archie T. Wright, 169–72. 2011. Reprint, London: Bloomsbury T. & T. Clark, 2013.

———. "Word and Spirit: Scribe and Prophet in Old Testament Hermeneutics." In *Spirit and Scripture: Exploring a Pneumatic Hermeneutic*, edited by Kevin L. Spawn and Archie T. Wright, 25–45. 2011. Reprint, London: Bloomsbury T. & T. Clark, 2013.

Boone, R. Jerome. "Pentecostal Worship and Hermeneutics: Engagement with the Spirit." *JPT* 26 (2017) 110–24.

Boring, M. Eugene. "The Prophet as Interpreter of Scripture." In *Sayings of the Risen Jesus: Christian Prophecy in the Synoptic Tradition*, 95–103. Cambridge: Cambridge University Press, 1982.

BRILL. "Journal of Pentecostal Theology." accessed July 21, 2018. https://brill.com/view/journals/pent/pent-overview.xml.

Bromiley, Geoffrey W. "The Church Fathers and Holy Scripture." In *Scripture and Truth*, edited by D. A. Carson and John D. Woodbridge, 199–220. Leicester, UK: IVP, 1983.

Brown, Paul E. *The Holy Spirit and the Bible: The Spirit's Interpreting Role in Relation to Biblical Hermeneutics*. Fearn, UK: Christian Focus, 2002.

Brownlee, W. H. "Biblical Interpretation among the Sectaries of the Dead Sea Scrolls." *BA* 14 (1951) 54–76.

Bruce, F. F. *The Canon of Scripture*. Downers Grove, IL: IVP, 1988.

Brueggemann, Walter. "Imagination as a Mode of Fidelity." In *Understanding the Word: Essays in Honour of B. W. Anderson*, edited by James T. Butler et al., 13–36. JSOTSup.37. Sheffield, UK: JSOT, 1985.

———. *Interpretation and Obedience: From Faithful Reading to Faithful Living*. Minneapolis: Fortress, 1991.

———. "Lee Roy Martin, the Unheard Voice of God: A Pentecostal Hearing of the Book of Judges." *JPT* 18 (2009) 15–19.

———. *Theology of the Old Testament: Testimony, Dispute, Advocacy*. Minneapolis: Fortress, 1997.

Buchanan, Colin, et al., eds. *The Charismatic Movement in the Church of England*. London: CIO, 1981.

Bultmann, Rudolph. "γινώσκω, γνῶσις, ἐπιγινώσκω, ἐπίγνωσις, καταγινώσκω, ἀκατάγνωστος, προγινώσκω, πρόγνωσις, συγγνώμη, γνώμη, γνωρίζω, γνωστός (Bultmann)." In *Theological Dictionary of the New Testament I*, edited by Gerhard

Kittel and Geoffrey W. Bromiley, and translated by Geoffrey W. Bromiley, 689–719. 1964. Reprint, London: Eerdmans, 1995.

Burgess, Stanley M., and Eduard M. van der Maas, eds. *The New International Dictionary of Pentecostal and Charismatic Movements*. Grand Rapids: Zondervan, 2002.

Byrd, Joseph. "Paul Ricoeur's Hermeneutical Theory and Pentecostal Proclamation." *Pneuma* 15.2 (1993) 203–14.

Caponi, Francis J. "Aspects of the Pneumatologies of Karl Rahner and Hans Urs von Balthasar." *New Theology Review* 20.1 (2007) 7–17.

Cargal, Timothy B. "Beyond the Fundamentalist-Modernist Controversy: Pentecostals and Hermeneutics in a Postmodern Age." *Pneuma* 15.2 (1993) 163–87.

Carson, D. A. *Showing the Spirit: A Theological Exposition of 1 Corinthians 12–14*. Grand Rapids: Baker, 1987.

Cartledge, Mark J. "Affective Theological Praxis: Understanding the Direct Object of Practical Theology." *IJPT* 8.1 (2004) 34–52.

———. "Charismatic Movement." In *Encyclopedia of the Bible and Its Reception: Volume 5*, edited by Dale C. Allison Jr. et al., 9–11. Berlin: de Gruyter, 2012.

———. "Charismatic Spirituality." In *The Bloomsbury Guide to Christian Spirituality*, edited by Richard Woods and Peter Tyler, 214–25. London: Bloomsbury, 2012.

———. "Empirical Theology: Towards an Evangelical-Charismatic Hermeneutic." *JPT* 9 (1996) 115–26.

———. "Locating the Spirit in Meaningful Experience: Empirical Theology and Pentecostal Hermeneutics." In *Constructive Pneumatological Hermeneutics in Pentecostal Christianity*, edited by Kenneth J. Archer and L. William Oliverio Jr., 251–66. New York: Palgrave Macmillan, 2016.

———. *The Mediation of the Spirit: Interventions in Practical Theology*. Grand Rapids: Eerdmans, 2015.

———. "A New *Via Media*: Charismatics and the Church of England in the Twenty-First Century." *ANVIL* 17.4 (2000) 271–83.

———. "Pneumatic Hermeneutics: A Reply to Respondents." In *Spirit and Scripture: Exploring a Pneumatic Hermeneutic*, edited by Kevin L. Spawn and Archie T. Wright, 186–90. 2011. Reprint, London: Bloomsbury T. & T. Clark, 2013.

———. *Practical Theology: Charismatic and Empirical Perspectives*. Carlisle, UK: Paternoster, 2003.

———. "Text-Community-Spirit: The Challenges Posed by Pentecostal Theological Method to Evangelical Theology." In *Spirit and Scripture: Exploring a Pneumatic Hermeneutic*, edited by Kevin L. Spawn and Archie T. Wright, 130–44. 2011. Reprint, London: Bloomsbury T. & T. Clark, 2013.

Castelo, Daniel. "*Diakrisis* Always *En Conjunto*: First Theology Understood from a Latino/a Context." In *Constructive Pneumatological Hermeneutics in Pentecostal Christianity*, edited by Kenneth J. Archer and L. William Oliverio Jr., 197–209. New York: Palgrave Macmillan, 2016.

———. "Tarrying on the Lord: Affections, Virtues and Theological Ethics in Pentecostal Perspective." *JPT* 13.1 (2004) 31–56.

Catechism of the Catholic Church: The CTS Definitive & Complete Edition. 2nd ed. London: Catholic Truth Society, 2016.

Chandler, Daniel. *Semiotics: The Basics*. London: Routledge, 2002.

Charette, Blaine B. "'And Now for Something Completely Different': A 'Pythonic' Reading of Pentecost?" *Pneuma* 33.1 (2011) 59–62.

Childs, Brevard S. *Biblical Theology of the Old and New Testaments: Theological Reflections on the Christian Bible*. London: SCM, 1992.

Chilton, Bruce. "Rabbinic Literature and the New Testament." In *The World of the New Testament: Cultural, Social, and Historical Contexts*, edited by Joel B. Green and Lee Martin McDonald, 413–23. Grand Rapids: Baker Academic, 2013.

Christenson, Larry. "Biblical Interpretation in the Charismatic Renewal." In *Welcome Holy Spirit: A Study of Charismatic Renewal in the Church*, edited by Larry Christenson, 41–48. Minneapolis: Augsburg, 1987.

———. "Introduction: A View from Within." In *Welcome Holy Spirit: A Study of Charismatic Renewal in the Church*, 11–12. Minneapolis: Augsburg, 1987.

———, ed. *Welcome Holy Spirit: A Study of Charismatic Renewal in the Church*. Minneapolis: Augsburg, 1987.

Clark, Matthew Spencer. "An Investigation into the Nature of a Viable Pentecostal Hermeneutic." DTh diss., University of Pretoria, 1997.

Cole, Casey S. "Taking Hermeneutics to Heart: Proposing an Orthopathic Reading for Texts of Terror via the Rape of Tamar Narrative." *Pneuma* 39.3 (2017) 264–74.

Coleman, Richard J. *Issues of Theological Conflict: Evangelicals and Liberals*. Grand Rapids: Eerdmans, 1980.

Collins English Dictionary. 12th ed. Glasgow: Collins, 2014.

Congar, Yves. "The Renewal in the Spirit: Promises and Questions." In *I Believe in the Holy Spirit: Volume II: 'He is Lord and Giver of Life,'* 145–212. In *I Believe in the Holy Spirit: The Complete Three-Volume Work in One Volume*. Translated by David Smith. 1983. Reprint, French original 1979–80. New York: Crossroad, 2019.

Coombs, Clayton. "Reading in Tongues: The Case for a Pneumatological Hermeneutic in Conversation with James K. Smith." *Pneuma* 32.2 (2010) 261–68.

Coulter, Dale M. "Introduction: The Language of Affectivity and the Christian Life." In *The Spirit, the Affections, and the Christian Tradition*, edited by Dale M. Coulter and Amos Yong, 1–28. Notre Dame, IN: University of Notre Dame Press, 2016.

———. "Pentecostalism, Mysticism, and Renewal Methodologies." *Pneuma* 33.1 (2011) 1–4.

———. "The Whole Gospel for the Whole Person: Ontology, Affectivity, and Sacramentality." *Pneuma* 35.2 (2013) 157–61.

———. "What Meaneth This? Pentecostals and Theological Inquiry." *JPT* 10.1 (2001) 38–64.

Coulter, Dale M., and Amos Yong, eds. *The Spirit, the Affections, and the Christian Tradition*. Notre Dame, IN: University of Notre Dame Press, 2016.

Cox, Harvey. "Your Daughter's Shall Prophesy." In *Fire From Heaven: The Rise of Pentecostal Spirituality and the Reshaping of Religion in the Twenty-first Century*, 123–57. London: Cassell, 1996.

Crinisor, Stefan. "The Paraclete and Prophecy in the Johannine Community." *Pneuma* 27.2 (2005) 273–96.

Cross, Terry. "A Proposal to Break the Ice: What Can Pentecostal Theology Offer Evangelical Theology?" *JPT* 10.2 (2002) 44–73.

Cullmann, Oscar. "The Tradition." In *The Early Church*, 59–99. 1956. Reprint, London: SCM, 1966.

Dalton, William J. "The Composition, Inspiration and Interpretation of the Bible." In *The Roman Catholic/Pentecostal Dialogue 1977–1982: A Study in Developing Ecumenism, Volume II*, edited by Jerry L. Sandidge, 122–45. Frankfurt: Lang, 1987.

Davies, Andrew. "Reading in the Spirit: Some Brief Observations on Pentecostal Interpretation and the Ethical Difficulties of the Old Testament." *Journal of Beliefs and Values* 30.3 (2009) 303–31.

———. "The Spirit of Freedom: Pentecostals, The Bible and Social Justice." *JEPTA* 31.1 (2011) 53–64.

———. "What Does it Mean to Read the Bible as a Pentecostal?" *JPT* 18 (2009) 216–29.

Dempster, Murray W. "Paradigm Shifts and Hermeneutics: Confronting Issues Old and New." *Pneuma* 15.2 (1993) 129–35.

Dimat, Deborah. "Qumran: Written Material." In *Encyclopedia of the Dead Sea Scrolls: Volume* 2, edited by Lawrence H. Schiffman, James C. VanderKam, 739–46. Oxford: Oxford University Press, 2000.

Dorman, Ted M. "Holy Spirit, History, Hermeneutics and Theology: Toward an Evangelical/Catholic Consensus." *JETS* 41.3 (1998) 427–38.

Dostal, Robert J. *The Cambridge Companion to Gadamer*. Cambridge: Cambridge University Press, 2002.

Dulles, Avery. "The Bible in the Church: Some Debated Questions." In *Scripture and the Charismatic Renewal: Proceedings of the Milwaukee Symposium December 1–3, 1978*, edited by George Martin, 5–27. Ann Arbor, MI: Servant, 1979.

———. "Scripture: Some Recent Protestant and Catholic Views." *Theology Today* 37.1 (1980) 7–26.

Dunn, James D. G. *Jesus and the Spirit: A Study of the Religious and Charismatic Experience of Jesus and the First Christians as Reflected in the New Testament*. London: SCM, 1975.

———. "'The Letter Kills, But the Spirit Gives Life' (2 Cor. 3:6)." *Pneuma* 35.2 (2013) 163–79.

———. *The Living Word*. London: SCM, 1987.

———. "The Role of the Spirit in Biblical Hermeneutics." In *Spirit and Scripture: Exploring a Pneumatic Hermeneutic*, edited by Kevin L. Spawn and Archie T. Wright, 154–59. 2011. Reprint, London: Bloomsbury T. & T. Clark, 2013.

Dunnett, Walter M. *The Interpretation of Holy Scripture*. New York: Thomas Nelson, 1984.

Edwards, Jonathan. "A Careful and Strict Inquiry into the Prevailing Notions of the Freedom of Will." In *The Works of Jonathan Edwards I*, 3–93. 1834. Edited by Edward Hickman. Edinburgh: Banner of Truth Trust, 1979.

———. "A Dissertation on the Nature of True Virtue." In *The Works of Jonathan Edwards I*, 122–42. 1834. Edited by Edward Hickman. Edinburgh: Banner of Truth Trust, 1979.

———. *The Religious Affections*. 1746. Reprint with slight variations. Edinburgh: Banner of Truth Trust, 2014.

Elbert, Paul. "Contextual Analysis and Interpretation with Sensitivity to the Spirit as Interactive Person: Editor's Explanation and Welcome to JBPR." *JBPR* 1 (2009) 1–14.

———. "Spirit, Scripture and Theology Through a Lukan Lens: A Review Article." *JPT* 13 (1998) 55–75.

———. "Toward a Pentecostal Hermeneutic: Observations on Archer's Progressive Proposal." *AJPS* 9.2 (2006) 320–28.

Ellington, Scott A. "History, Story and Testimony: Locating Truth in a Pentecostal Hermeneutic." *Pneuma* 23.2 (2001) 245–63.

———. "Knowing God More and Less: Reading and Experiencing Exodus 33:11–23." *JPT* 23 (2014) 20–28.

———. "Locating Pentecostals at the Hermeneutical Round Table." *JPT* 22 (2013) 206–25.

———. "Pentecostalism and the Authority of Scripture." *JPT* 9 (1996) 16–38.

———. "The Reciprocal Reshaping of History and Experience in the Psalms: Interactions with Pentecostal Testimony." *JPT* 16.1 (2007) 18–31.

Ellis, E. Earle. *Prophecy and Hermeneutic in Early Christianity: New Testament Essays.* Tübingen: Mohr, 1978.

Erickson, Millard J. *Christian Theology.* 1984. 2nd ed. Grand Rapids: Baker, 1998.

Ervin, Howard M. "Hermeneutics: A Pentecostal Option." In *Essays on Apostolic Themes: Studies in Honor of Howard M. Ervin*, edited by Paul Elbert, 23–35. Peabody, MA: Hendrickson, 1985.

———. "Koinonia, Church and Sacraments, A Pentecostal Response." *Bibliography and Biography* 6 (1987) 1–32. Accessed August 15, 2018. http://digitalshowcase.oru.edu/ervin_bio/6/.

———. "The Ties That Divide." In *The Roman Catholic/Pentecostal Dialogue 1977–1982: A Study in Developing Ecumenism, Volume II*, edited by Jerry L. Sandidge, 238–60. Frankfurt: Lang, 1987.

EPTA. "History of EPTA." Accessed July 21, 2018. http://www.eptaonline.com/history-of-epta/.

———. "JEPTA." Accessed July 21, 2018. http://www.eptaonline.com/jepta/.

Estrada III, Rodolfo Galvan. "Is a Contextualized Hermeneutic the Future of Pentecostal Readings?" *Pneuma* 37.3 (2015) 341–55.

Evangelical Alliance. "Basis of Faith." Accessed July 13, 2018. http://www.eauk.org/connect/about-us/basis-of-faith.cfm.

———. "What Is an Evangelical?" Accessed July 13, 2018. http://www.eauk.org/connect/about-us/what-is-an-evangelical.cfm; accessed July 13, 2018.

Farah, Charles Jr., and Steve Durasoff. "Biographical and Bibliographical Sketch." In *Essays on Apostolic Themes: Studies in Honor of Howard M. Ervin*, edited by Paul Elbert, xi–xiv. Peabody, MA: Hendrickson, 1985.

Fee, Gordon D. "Exegesis and Spirituality: Completing the Circle." In *Listening to the Spirit in the Text*, 3–15. Grand Rapids: Eerdmans, 2000.

———. *Galatians: A Pentecostal Commentary.* Blandford Forum, UK: Deo, 2007.

———. "The Genre of New Testament Literature and Biblical Hermeneutics." In *Interpreting the Word of God: Festschrift in Honor of Steven Barabas*, edited by S. J. Schultz and M. A. Inch, 105–27. Chicago: Moody, 1976.

———. *Gospel and Spirit: Issues in New Testament Hermeneutics.* 1991. Reprint, Grand Rapids: Baker Academic, 2010.

———. "Hermeneutics and Historical Precedent—A Major Problem in Pentecostal Hermeneutics." In *Perspectives on the New Pentecostalism*, edited by Russell P. Spittler, 119–31. Grand Rapids: Baker, 1976.

———. "History as Context for Interpretation." In *The Act of Bible Reading: A Multidisciplinary Approach to Biblical Interpretation*, edited by Elmer Dyck, 10–32. Downers Grove, IL: IVP, 1996.

———. *Paul's Letter to the Philippians.* Grand Rapids: Eerdmans, 1995.

———. "Some Reflections on Pauline Spirituality." In *Listening to the Spirit in the Text*, 33–47. Grand Rapids: Eerdmans, 2000.

———. "The Spirit and Ethical Life." In *God's Empowering Presence: The Holy Spirit in the Letters of Paul*, 877–81. Peabody, MA: Hendrickson, 1994.

———. "Why Pentecostals Read Their Bibles Poorly—and Some Suggested Cures." *JEPTA* 24.1 (2004) 4–15.

Fiorenza, Elizabeth Schüssler, "Toward a Feminist Biblical Hermeneutics: Biblical Interpretation and Liberation Theology." In *A Guide to Contemporary Hermeneutics: Major Trends in Biblical Interpretation*, edited by Donald McKim, 358–81. Grand Rapids: Eerdmans, 1986.

"Final Report of the Dialogue between the Secretariat for Promoting Christian Unity of the Roman Catholic Church and Leaders of Some Pentecostal Churches and Participants in the Charismatic Movement within Protestant and Anglican Churches, 1972–1976." *Pneuma* 12.2 (1990) 85–95.

"Final Report of the Dialogue between the Secretariat for Promoting Christian Unity of the Roman Catholic Church and some Classical Pentecostals, 1977–1982." *Pneuma* 12.2 (1990) 97–115.

"The Final Report. Word and Spirit, Church and World: The Final Report of the International Dialogue between Representatives of the World Alliance of Reformed Churches and Some Classical Pentecostal Churches and Leaders, 1996–2000." *Pneuma* 23.1 (2001) 9–43.

Fish, Stanley. *Is There a Text in This Class? The Authority of Interpretive Communities.* Cambridge: Harvard University Press, 1980.

Fletcher, Jeremy, and Christopher Cocksworth. *The Spirit and Liturgy*. Grove Worship Series 146. Cambridge: Grove, 1998.

Fodor, Jim. "Reading the Scriptures: Rehearsing Identity, Practicing Character." In *The Blackwell Companion to Christian Ethics*, edited by Stanley Hauerwas and Samuel Wells, 142–55. 2004. Reprint, Oxford: Blackwell, 2006.

Forbes, Christopher. *Prophecy and Inspired Speech in Early Christianity and Its Hellenistic Environment*. Tübingen: Mohr, 1995.

Fowl, Stephen E. "How the Spirit Reads and How to Read Scripture." In *Engaging Scripture: A Model for Theological Interpretation*, 97–127. Oxford: Blackwell, 1998.

———, ed. *The Theological Interpretation of Scripture: Classic and Contemporary Readings*. Cambridge: Blackwell, 1997.

———. *Theological Interpretation of Scripture: A Short Introduction*. Cascade Companions. Eugene, OR: Cascade, 2009.

Frame, J. M. "The Spirit and the Scriptures." In *Hermeneutics, Authority and Canon*, edited by D. A. Carson and J. D. Woodbridge, 217–35. Leicester, UK: IVP, 1986.

Fuller, Daniel P. "The Holy Spirit's Role in Biblical Interpretation." In *Scripture, Tradition and Interpretation: Essays Presented to E. F. Harrison Ahead of His 75th Birthday*, edited by W. Ward Gasque and William Sandford LaSor, 189–98. Grand Rapids: Eerdmans, 1978.

Gadamer, Hans-Georg. *Truth and Method*. Translated by Garrett Barden and John Cumming. London: Sheer & Ward, 1975.

Goldingay, John. "Interpreting Scripture (Part 2)." *ANVIL* 1.3 (1984) 261–81.

———. *Models for Interpretation of Scripture*. Grand Rapids: Eerdmans, 1995.

———. "Scripture as Inspired Word: Interpreting Prophecy." In *Models for Interpretation of Scripture*, 141–99. Grand Rapids: Eerdmans, 1995.

Gorman, Michael J., ed. *Scripture and Its Interpretation: A Global, Ecumenical Introduction to the Bible*. Grand Rapids: Baker Academic, 2017.

Green, Chris E. W. "Beautifying the Beautiful Word: Scripture, the Triune God, and the Aesthetics of Interpretation." In *Constructive Pneumatological Hermeneutics in Pentecostal Christianity*, edited by Kenneth J. Archer and L. William Oliverio Jr., 103–19. New York: Palgrave Macmillan, 2016.

———. "'I am Finished": Christological Reading(s) and Pentecostal Performance(s) of Psalm 88." *Pneuma* 40.1 (2018) 150–66.

———. "Provoked to Saving Jealousy: Reading Romans 9–11 as Theological Performance." *Pneuma* 38.1–2 (2016) 180–92.

———. *Sanctifying Interpretation: Vocation, Holiness, and Scripture*. Cleveland, OH: CPT, 2015.

———. "'Then Their Eyes Were Opened': Pentecostal Reflections on the Church's Scripture and the Lord's Supper." *Pneuma* 35.2 (2013) 220–34.

———. *Toward a Pentecostal Theology of the Lord's Supper: Foretasting the Kingdom*, Cleveland, OH: CPT, 2012.

Green, Joel B. *Hearing the New Testament: Strategies for Interpretation*. Grand Rapids: Eerdmans, 1995.

———. "Pentecostal Hermeneutics: A Wesleyan Perspective." In *Constructive Pneumatological Hermeneutics in Pentecostal Christianity*, edited by Kenneth J. Archer and L. William Oliverio Jr., 159–73. New York: Palgrave Macmillan, 2016.

———. "The Practice of Reading the New Testament." In *Hearing the New Testament: Strategies for Interpretation*, edited by Joel B. Green, 411–27. Grand Rapids: Eerdmans, 1995.

Green, Joel B., and Lee Martin McDonald, eds. *The World of the New Testament: Cultural, Social, and Historical Contexts*. Grand Rapids: Baker Academic, 2013.

Grenz, Stanley J. *Created for Community: Connecting Christian Belief with Christian Living*. 1996. 2nd ed. Grand Rapids: Bridge Point, 1999.

———. *Renewing the Center: Evangelical Theology in a Post-Theological Era*. Grand Rapids: Baker Academic, 2000.

———. "The Spirit and the Word: The World-Creating Function of the Text." *Theology Today* 57 (2000) 357–74.

———. *Theology for the Community of God*. 1994. Reprint, Carlisle, UK: Paternoster, 2000.

Greves, Abigail. "Daughter of Courage: Reading Judges 11 with a Feminist Pentecostal Hermeneutic." *JPT* 25 (2016) 151–67.

Grey, Jacqueline. *Three's a Crowd: Pentecostalism, Hermeneutics, and the Old Testament*. Eugene, OR: Pickwick, 2011.

———. "The Spirit *of* and Spirit *in* Craig S. Keener's *Spirit Hermeneutics*." *Pneuma* 39.1–2 (2017) 168–78.

———. "Through the Looking Glass: Reflections on the Re-evangelization of Europe through a Post-colonial Reading of Isaiah 2:1–5." *JEPTA* 37.1 (2017) 28–39.

———. "When the Spirit Trumps Tradition: A Pentecostal Reading of Isaiah 56:1–8." In *Constructive Pneumatological Hermeneutics in Pentecostal Christianity*, edited by Kenneth J. Archer and L. William Oliverio Jr., 143–57. New York: Palgrave Macmillan, 2016.

Groome, Thomas H. *Christian Religious Education: Sharing Our Story and Vision*. London: Harper & Row, 1980.

Grudem, Wayne. *The Gift of Prophecy in the New Testament and Today*. 1988. Reprint, Eastbourne, UK: Kingsway, 1992.

Habets, Myk. "Reading Scripture and Doing Theology with the Holy Spirit." In *The Spirit of Truth: Reading Scripture and Constructing Theology with the Holy Spirit*, edited by Myk Habets, 89–104. Eugene, OR: Pickwick, 2010.

Hanson, Paul D. "Scripture, Community and Spirit: Biblical Theology's Contribution to a Contextualized Christian Theology." *JPT* 6 (1995) 3–12.

Harrington, Hannah K., and Rebecca Patten. "Pentecostal Hermeneutics and Postmodern Literary Theory." *Pneuma* 16.1 (1994) 109–14.

Harrison, Ted. "Raising the C of E's Spirit Level, 17 May 2013." Accessed August 13, 2018. https://www.churchtimes.co.uk/articles/2013/17-may/features/features/raising-the-c-of-e-s-spirit-level.

Hauerwas, Stanley. *Sanctify Them in the Truth: Holiness Exemplified*. Edinburgh: T. & T. Clark, 1998.

———. *Unleashing the Scripture: Freeing the Bible from Captivity in America*. Nashville: Abingdon, 1993.

Hauerwas, Stanley, and Samuel Wells. "Studying Ethics Through Worship." In *The Blackwell Companion to Christian Ethics*, edited by Stanley Hauerwas and Samuel Wells, 1–50. 2004. Reprint, Oxford: Blackwell, 2006.

———, eds. *The Blackwell Companion to Christian Ethics*. 2004. Reprint, Oxford: Blackwell, 2006.

Haughey, John C., SJ. *Theological Reflections on the Charismatic Renewal: Proceedings of the Chicago Conference October 1–2 1976*. Ann Arbor, MI: Servant, 1978.

Hays, Richard B. *Echoes of Scripture in the Letters of Paul*. New Haven: Yale University Press, 1989.

———. "Reading Scripture in Light of the Resurrection." In *The Art of Reading Scripture*, edited by Ellen F. Davis and Richard B. Hays, 216–38. Grand Rapids: Eerdmans, 2003.

Hays, Richard B., and Joel B. Green. "The Use of the Old Testament by New Testament Writers." In *Hearing the New Testament: Strategies for Interpretation*, edited by Joel B. Green, 222–38. Carlisle, UK: Paternoster, 1995.

Heidegger, Martin. *Being and Time*. Translated by John Macquarrie and Edward Robinson. London: SCM, 1962.

———. *Logic: The Question of Truth*. Translated by Thomas Sheehan. Bloomington, IN: Indiana University Press, 2010.

Heisler, Greg. "The Spirit and Our Preaching: Why We Are Desperate for the Spirit's Illumination." In *Holy Spirit: Unfinished Agenda*, edited by Johnson T. K. Lim, 197–202. Singapore: Genesis, 2014.

———. *Spirit-Led Preaching: The Holy Spirit's Role in Sermon Preparation and Delivery*. Nashville: B&H, 2007.

Hempel, Charlotte. "Qumran Community." In *Encyclopedia of the Dead Sea Scrolls: Volume 2*, edited by Lawrence H. Schiffman and James C. VanderKam, 746–51. Oxford: Oxford University Press, 2000.

Hengel, Martin. *The Zealots: Investigations into the Jewish Freedom Movement in the Period from Herod 1 until 70 AD*. Translated by David Smith. Edinburgh: T. & T. Clark, 1989.

Henry, Carl F. H. *God, Revelation and Authority: Volume IV: God Who Speaks and Shows*. Waco, TX: Word, 1979.

Herholdt, Marius D. "Pentecostal and Charismatic Hermeneutics." In *Initiation into Theology: The Rich Variety of Theology and Hermeneutics*, edited by S. Marmela and A. König, 417–31. Hatfield, South Africa: J. L. van Shaik, 1998.

Herms, Ronald. "Invoking the Spirit and Narrative Intent in John's Apocalypse." In *Spirit and Scripture: Exploring a Pneumatic Hermeneutic*, edited by Kevin L. Spawn and Archie T. Wright, 99–114. 2011. Reprint, London: Bloomsbury T. & T. Clark, 2013.

———. "Response to *Spirit and Scripture* Responders." In *Spirit and Scripture: Exploring a Pneumatic Hermeneutic*, edited by Kevin L. Spawn and Archie T. Wright, 180–82. 2011. Reprint, London: Bloomsbury T. & T. Clark, 2013.

———. "Review of Robby Waddell, *The Spirit of the Book of Revelation*." *JPT* 17 (2008) 9–18.

Hocken, Peter. "Charismatic Movement." *The New International Dictionary of Pentecostal and Charismatic Movements*, edited by Stanley M. Burgess and Eduard M. van der Maas, 477–519. Grand Rapids: Zondervan, 2002.

———. *Streams of Renewal: The Origins and Early Development of the Charismatic Movement in Great Britain*. Exeter, UK: Paternoster, 1986.

Hooker, Morna. "Beyond the Things that are Written? St. Paul's Use of Scripture." *NTS* 27 (1981) 295–309.

Horgan, Maura P. "The Bible Explained (Prophecies)." In *Early Judaism and its Modern Interpreters*, edited by Robert A. Kraft and George W. E. Nickelsburg, 247–53. Atlanta: Scholars, 1986.

Ingraffia, Brian D., and Todd E. Pickett. "Reviving the Power of Biblical Language: The Bible, Literature and Literary Language." In *After Pentecost: Language & Biblical Interpretation*, edited by Craig Bartholomew et al., 241–62. The Scripture and Hermeneutics Series 2. Carlisle, UK: Paternoster, 2001.

Isgrigg, Daniel D. *Pilgrimage into Pentecost: The Pneumatological Legacy of Howard M. Ervin*. Tulsa, OK: Word & Spirit, 2015.

Israel, Richard D., et al. "Pentecostals and Hermeneutics: Texts, Rituals and Community." *Pneuma* 15.2 (1993) 137–61.

Johns, Cheryl Bridges. "Grieving, Brooding and Transforming: The Spirit, the Bible, and Gender." *JPT* 23 (2014) 141–53.

———. "Meeting God in the Margins, Ministry among Modernity's Refugees." In *The Papers of the Henry Luce III Fellows in Theology: Volume 3*, edited by M. Zyniewicz, 7–31. Atlanta: Scholars, 1999.

———. *Pentecostal Formation: A Pedagogy among the Oppressed*. Sheffield, UK: Sheffield Academic Press, 1993.

———. "Transcripts of the Trinity: Reading the Bible in the Presence of God." *ExAud* 30 (2014) 155–64.

Johns, Jackie David. "Pentecostalism and the Postmodern Worldview." *JPT* 7 (1995) 73–96.

———. "Yielding to the Spirit: The Dynamics of a Pentecostal Model of Praxis." In *The Globalization of Pentecostalism: A Religion Made to Travel*, edited by Murray W. Dempster et al., 70–84. Carlisle, UK: Paternoster, 1999.

Johns, Jackie David, and Cheryl Bridges Johns. "Yielding to the Spirit: A Pentecostal Approach to Group Bible Study." *JPT* 1 (1992) 109–34.

Johnson, Bob L., Jr., and Rickie D. Moore. "Soul Care for One and All: Pentecostal Theology and the Search for a More Expansive View of Spiritual Formation." *JPT* 26 (2017) 125–52.

Johnson, David R. *Pneumatic Discernment in the Apocalypse: An Intertextual and Pentecostal Exploration*. Cleveland, OH: CPT, 2018.

Johnson, Luke Timothy. *Scripture and Discernment: Decision Making in the Church*. 1983. Expanded and revised. Nashville: Abingdon, 1996.

Johnston, Robert K. "Pentecostalism and Theological Hermeneutics: Evangelical Options." *Pneuma* 6.1 (1984) 51–66.

Jones, James W. *The Spirit and the World: A Creative Theology Based on the Action of the Holy Spirit in Church and Community in Today's World*. New York: Hawthorn, 1975.

Kärkkäinen, Veli-Matti. "Authority, Revelation, and Interpretation in the Roman Catholic-Pentecostal Dialogue." *Pneuma* 21.1 (1999) 89–114.

———. "Authority, Revelation and Interpretation." In *Toward a Pneumatological Theology: Pentecostal and Ecumenical Perspective on Ecclesiology, Soteriology, and Theology of Mission*, 23–38. Edited by Amos Yong. Oxford: University Press of America, 2002.

———. "Hermeneutics: From Fundamentalism to Postmodernism." In *Toward a Pneumatological Theology: Pentecostal and Ecumenical Perspective on Ecclesiology, Soteriology, and Theology of Mission*, edited by Amos Yong, 3–22. Oxford: University Press of America, 2002.

———. "Pentecostal Hermeneutics in the Making: On the Way From Fundamentalism to Postmodernism." *JEPTA* 18.1 (1998) 76–115.

———. "Pentecostal Identity." In *Pentecostals in the 21st Century: Identity, Beliefs, Praxis*, edited by Corneliu Constantineanu and Christopher J. Scobie, 14–31. Eugene, OR: Cascade, 2018.

———. *Spiritus ubi vult spirat: Pneumatology in Roman Catholic-Pentecostal Dialogue (1972–1989)*. Helsinki: Luther-Agricola-Society, 1998.

———. "Trinity as Communion in the Spirit." In *Toward a Pneumatological Theology: Pentecostal and Ecumenical Perspective on Ecclesiology, Soteriology, and Theology of Mission*, edited by Amos Yong, 97–108. Oxford: University Press of America, 2002.

———. *Trinity and Revelation: A Constructive Christian Theology for the Pluralistic World*. Grand Rapids: Eerdmans, 2014.

Kärkkäinen, Veli-Matti, with Amos Yong, ed. *Toward a Pneumatological Theology: Pentecostal and Ecumenical Perspective on Ecclesiology, Soteriology, and Theology of Mission*. Oxford: University Press of America, 2002.

Käsemann, Ernst. *Perspectives on Paul*. Philadelphia: Fortress, 1971.

Kay, William K. "Philosophy and Developmental Psychology: Relevance for Pentecostal Hermeneutics." In *Constructive Pneumatological Hermeneutics in Pentecostal Christianity*, edited by Kenneth J. Archer and L. William Oliverio Jr., 267–78. New York: Palgrave Macmillan, 2016.

———. "Spiritual Discernment." In *Holy Spirit: Unfinished Agenda*, edited by Johnson T. K. Lim, 130–33. Singapore: Genesis, 2014.

Kearney, Richard. *The Wake of Imagination: Toward a Postmodern Culture*. London: Routledge, 1994.

Keegan, Terence J. *Interpreting the Bible: A Popular Introduction to Biblical Hermeneutics*. Mahwah, NJ: Paulist, 1985.

Keener, Craig S. "Pentecostal Biblical Hermeneutics/Spirit Hermeneutics." In *Scripture and Its Interpretation: A Global, Ecumenical Introduction to the Bible*, edited by Michael J. Gorman, 270–83. Grand Rapids: Baker Academic, 2017.

———. "Refining *Spirit Hermeneutics*." *Pneuma* 39.1–2 (2017) 198–240.

———. *Spirit Hermeneutics: Reading Scripture in Light of Pentecost*. Grand Rapids: Eerdmans, 2016.

Klooster, Fred H. "The Role of the Holy Spirit in the Hermeneutic Process: The Relationship of the Spirit's Illumination to Biblical Interpretation." In *Hermeneutics, Inerrancy, and the Bible*, edited by Earl D. Radmacher and Robert D. Preus 451–72. Grand Rapids: Zondervan, 1984.

Lakoff, George, and Mark Johnson. *Metaphors We Live By*. Chicago: University of Chicago Press, 1980.

Land, Steven Jack. *Pentecostal Spirituality: A Passion for the Kingdom*. 1993. Reprint with new Preface. Cleveland, OH: CPT, 2010.

Landrus, Heather. "Hearing 3 John 2 in the Voices of History." *JPT* 11.1 (2002) 70–88.

LaSor, William Sandford. "Prophecy, Inspiration, and *Sensus Plenior*." *TynBul* 29 (1978) 49–60.

Lederle, Henry I. *Theology with Spirit: The Future of the Pentecostal & Charismatic Movements in the 21st Century*. Tulsa, OK: Word & Spirit, 2010.

Lee, David. "Taking Ourselves More Seriously." *ANVIL* 6.2 (1989) 149–59.

Lee, Paul D. *Pneumatological Ecclesiology in the Roman Catholic-Pentecostal Dialogue: A Catholic Reading of the Third Quinquennium (1985–1989)*. Rome: Apud Pontificiam Universitatem S. Thomae, 1994.

———. "Scripture and Koinonia in the Spirit." In *Pneumatological Ecclesiology in the Roman Catholic-Pentecostal Dialogue: A Catholic Reading of the Third Quinquennium (1985–1989)*, 51–96. Rome: Apud Pontificiam Universitatem S. Thomae, 1994.

Levison, Jack. *Inspired: The Holy Spirit and the Mind of Faith*. Grand Rapids: Eerdmans, 2013.

Levison, John R. (Jack). "*Filled with the Spirit*: A Conversation with Pentecostal and Charismatic Scholars." *JPT* 20 (2011) 213–31.

———. *Filled with the Spirit*. Grand Rapids: Eerdmans, 2009.

Levison, John R., and Priscilla Pope-Levison. "Global Perspectives on New Testament Interpretation." In *Hearing the New Testament: Strategies for Interpretation*, edited by Joel B. Green, 329–48. Grand Rapids: Eerdmans, 1995.

Lewis, Paul W. "Towards a Pentecostal Epistemology: The Role of Experience in Pentecostal Hermeneutics." *The Spirit & the Church* 2.1 (2000) 95–125.

Lim, Johnson T. K. "Pneumatic Preaching." In *Holy Spirit: Unfinished Agenda*, edited by Johnson T. K. Lim, 203–7. Singapore: Genesis, 2014.

Lim, Timothy. *Pesharim*. Sheffield, UK: Sheffield Academic Press. 2002.

Lincoln, Andrew. "Hebrews and Biblical Theology." In *Out of Egypt: Biblical Theology and Biblical Interpretation*, edited by Craig Bartholomew et al., 313–40. The Scripture and Hermeneutics Series 5. Milton Keynes, UK: Paternoster, 2004.

Locker, Markus. "Seeing the Unseeable—Speaking the Unspeakable: From a Kenosis of Exegesis toward a Spiritual Biblical Theology." *JBPR* 4 (2012) 3–20.

Ma, Wonsuk. "Biblical Studies in the Pentecostal Tradition: Yesterday, Today, and Tomorrow." In *The Globalization of Pentecostalism: A Religion Made to Travel*, edited by Murray W. Dempster et al., 52–69. Carlisle, UK: Paternoster, 1999.

Macchia, Frank D. "The Book of Revelation and the Hermeneutics of the Spirit: A Response to Robby Waddell." *JPT* 17 (2008) 19–21.

———. *Justified in the Spirit: Creation, Redemption, and the Triune God*. Grand Rapids: Eerdmans, 2010.

———. "Pentecostal Theology." In *The New International Dictionary of Pentecostal and Charismatic Movements*, edited by Stanley M. Burgess and Eduard M. van der Maas, 1120–41. Grand Rapids: Zondervan, 2002.

———. "A Reply to Rickie Moore." *JPT* 17 (2000) 15–19.

———. "Resurrection: A Dance of Life." *Pneuma* 27.2 (2005) 223–4.

———. "The Spirit of Life and the Spirit of Immortality: An Appreciative Review of Levison's *Filled with the Spirit*." *Pneuma* 33.1 (2011) 69–78.

———. "The Spirit and the Text: Recent Trends in Pentecostal Hermeneutics." *The Spirit and Church* 2.1 (2000) 53–65.

———. "Spirit, Word, and Kingdom: Theological Reflections on the Reformed/Pentecostal Dialogue." In *Between East and West: A Radical Heritage: Essays in Honor of Jan Milič Lochman*, edited by Frank D. Macchia and Paul S. Chung, 77–91. Eugene, OR: Wipf & Stock, 2002.

———. *The Trinity, Practically Speaking*. Downers Grove, IL: IVP, 2010.

Marshall, I. Howard. "The Holy Spirit and the Interpretation of Scripture." In *Rightly Divided: Readings in Biblical Hermeneutics*, edited by Roy B. Zuck, 66–74. Grand Rapids: Kregel, 1996. First published in *Theological Review* (February 1979) 2–8. Page references are to the 1996 reprint.

Martin, Francis. "The Charismatic Renewal and Biblical Hermeneutics." In *Theological Reflections on the Charismatic Renewal: Proceedings of the Chicago Conference October 1–2 1976*, edited by John C. Haughey, SJ, 1–37. Ann Arbor, MI: Servant, 1978.

———. "Revelation and Understanding Scripture: Reflections on the Teaching of Joseph Ratzinger, Pope Benedict XVI." *Nova et Vetera*, English Edition, 13.1 (2015) 253–72.

———. *Sacred Scripture: The Disclosure of the Word*. Naples: Sapentia, 2006.

———. "Spirit and Flesh in the Doing of Theology." *JPT* 18 (2001) 3–31.

Martin, George. "Introduction." In *Scripture and the Charismatic Renewal: Proceedings of the Milwaukee Symposium December 1–3, 1978*, edited by George Martin, 1–4. Ann Arbor, MI: Servant, 1979.

———, ed. *Scripture and the Charismatic Renewal: Proceedings of the Milwaukee Symposium December 1–3, 1978*. Ann Arbor, MI: Servant.

Martin, Lee Roy. *Biblical Hermeneutics: Essential Keys for Interpreting the Bible*. Miami: Gospel, 2011.

———. "Delighting in the Torah: The Affective Dimension of Psalm 1." *OTE* 23.3 (2010) 708–27.

———. "Encountering God with the Psalmist: An Affective Approach to Psalm 63." *Ekklesiastikos Pharos* 95.1 (2013) 131–47.

———. "Hearing the Book of Judges: A Dialogue with Reviewers." *JPT* 18 (2009) 30–50.

———. "Longing for God: Psalm 63 and Pentecostal Spirituality." *JPT* 22 (2013) 54–76.

———, ed. *Pentecostal Hermeneutics: A Reader*. Leiden: Brill, 2013.

———. "Presidential Address 2014: 'Oh Give Thanks to the Lord for He Is Good': Affective Hermeneutics, Psalm 107, and Pentecostal Spirituality." *Pneuma* 36.3 (2014) 355–78.

———. "Psalm 130: The Hopeful Cry of Lament." Paper given at the Sixteenth Annual Clarence J. Abbott Lecture in Biblical Studies, February 2018.

———. "Psalm 150 and Pentecostal Spirituality." Paper given at the Society for Biblical Literature annual meeting, November 2017.

———. "Purity, Power, and the Passion of God: A Pentecostal Hearing of the Book of Judges." *Ekklesiastikos Pharos* 87 (2005) 274–300.

———. *The Spirit of the Psalms: Rhetorical Analysis, Affectivity, and Pentecostal Spirituality*. Cleveland, OH: CPT, 2018.

———. *The Unheard Voice of God: A Pentecostal Hearing of the Book of Judges*. JPTSup. 32. Blandford Forum, UK: Deo, 2008.

———. "The Use and Interpretation of the Psalms in Early Pentecostalism as Reflected in *The Apostolic Faith* from 1906 through 1915." *OTE* 30.3 (2017) 725–46.

Mather, Hannah R. K. "Chris E. W. Green. *Sanctifying Interpretation: Vocation, Holiness, and Scripture*." *Pneuma* 39.4 (2017) 562–64.

———. "Welcoming *Spirit Hermeneutics*: A Response to Craig S. Keener." *Pneuma* 39.1–2 (2017) 153–61.

May, Robert J. "The Role of the Holy Spirit in Biblical Hermeneutics." MTh diss., University of Wales, 1999, accessed February 2, 2018. https://biblicalstudies.org.uk/th_spirit.html.

McCall, Bradford. "A Contemporary Reappropriation of Baconian Common Sense Realism in Renewal Hermeneutics." *Pneuma* 32.2 (2010) 223–40.

McCartney, Dan, and Charles Clayton. *Let the Reader Understand: A Guide to Interpreting and Applying the Bible*. Wheaton, IL: BridgePoint, 1994.

McDonnell, Kilian. "The Determinative Doctrine of the Holy Spirit." *Theology Today* 39.2 (1982) 142–61.

McFague, Sally. *Metaphorical Theology: Models of God in Religious Language*. London: SCM, 1983.

McKay, John. "When the Veil is Taken Away: The Impact of Prophetic Experience on Biblical Interpretation." *JPT* 5 (1994) 17–40.

McLean, Mark D. "Toward a Pentecostal Hermeneutic" *Pneuma* 6.1 (1984) 35–56.

McQueen, Larry. *Joel and the Spirit: The Cry of a Prophetic Hermeneutic*. 1995. Reprint with minor alterations. Cleveland, OH: CPT, 2009.

———. *Toward a Pentecostal Eschatology: Discerning the Way Forward*. JPTSup. 39. Blandford Forum, UK: Deo, 2012.

Meadowcroft, Tim. "Spirit, Interpretation and Scripture: Exegetical Thoughts on 2 Peter 1:19–21." In *The Spirit of Truth: Reading Scripture and Constructing Theology with the Holy Spirit*, edited by Myk Habets, 57–72. Eugene, OR: Pickwick, 2010.

Menzies, Glen W. "Echoing Hirsch: Do Readers Find or Construct Meaning?" In *Constructive Pneumatological Hermeneutics in Pentecostal Christianity*, edited by Kenneth J. Archer and L. William Oliverio Jr., 83–98. New York: Palgrave Macmillan, 2016.

Menzies, Robert P. "Coming to Terms with an Evangelical History—Part 1: Pentecostals and the Issue of Subsequence." *Paraclete* 28.3 (1994) 18–28. Accessed May 3, 2018. http://enrichmentjournal.ag.org/200501/200501_heritage_pt1.cfm.

———. "The Essence of Pentecostalism." *Paraclete* 26.3 (1992) 1–9. Accessed June 22, 2018. http://enrichmentjournal.ag.org/top/holy_spirit/200708.cfm.

———. "Jumping off the Postmodern Bandwagon." *Pneuma* 16.1 (1994) 115–20.

———. *The Language of the Spirit: Interpreting and Translating Charismatic Terms*. Cleveland, OH: CPT, 2010.

Menzies, William W. "The Methodology of Pentecostal Theology: An Essay on Hermeneutics." In *Essays on Apostolic Themes: Studies in Honor of Howard M. Ervin*, edited by Paul Elbert, 1–14. Peabody, MA: Hendrickson, 1985.

———. "Synoptic Theology: An Essay on Pentecostal Hermeneutics." *Paraclete* 13 (1979) 14–21. Accessed January 31, 2018. http://enrichmentjournal.ag.org/Tools_of_the_Trade/article_display.cfm?targetBay=d8fa2daa-0f05-4f8b-b3e8-f65bba19df5b&ModID=2&Process=DisplayArticle&RSS_RSSContentID=20146&RSS_OriginatingChannelID=1170&RSS_OriginatingRSSFeedID=3344&RSS_Source.

Mey, Jacob. *Pragmatics: An Introduction*. 2nd ed. Oxford: Blackwell, 2001.

Minto, Andrew L. "The Charismatic Renewal and the Spiritual Sense of Scripture." *Pneuma* 27.2 (2005) 256–72.

Mitchell, B. K. (Bev). "Let There Be Life! Toward a Hermeneutic of Biological and Theological Interpretation." In *Constructive Pneumatological Hermeneutics in Pentecostal Christianity*, edited by Kenneth J. Archer and L. William Oliverio Jr., 297–14. New York: Palgrave Macmillan, 2016.

Moberly, R. Walter L. "Pneumatic Biblical Hermeneutics: A Response." In *Spirit and Scripture: Exploring a Pneumatic Hermeneutic*, edited by Kevin L. Spawn and Archie T. Wright, 160–68. 2011. Reprint, London: Bloomsbury T. & T. Clark, 2013.

———. *Prophecy and Discernment*. Cambridge: Cambridge University Press, 2006.

Molnar, Paul. "The Role of the Holy Spirit in Knowing the Triune God." In *Trinitarian Theology after Barth*, edited by Myk Habets and Phillip Tolliday, 3–47. 2011. Reprint, Cambridge: James Clarke, 2012.

Moltmann, Jürgen. *The Spirit of Life: A Universal Affirmation*. Translated by Margaret Kohl. 1992. Reprint, German original 1991. London: SCM, 1991.

———. "The Theology of Mystical Experience." In *Experiences of God*, translated by Margaret Kohl, 55–83. German original 1979. London: SCM, 1980.

———. "Trinitarian Hermeneutics of 'Holy Scripture.'" In *Experiences in Theology: Ways and Forms of Christian Theology*, translated by Margaret Kohl, 134–50. German original 2000. London: SCM, 2000.

Moo, Douglas J. "The Problem of *Sensus Plenior*." In *Hermeneutics, Authority and Canon*, edited by D. A. Carson and J. D. Woodbridge, 179–211. Leicester, UK: IVP, 1986.

Moore, Rickie D. "Altar Hermeneutics: Reflections on Pentecostal Biblical Interpretation." *Pneuma* 38.1–2 (2016) 148–59.

———. "'And Also Much Cattle?!' Prophetic Passions and the End of Jonah." *JPT* 11 (1997) 35–48.

———. "Canon and Charisma in the Book of Deuteronomy." *JPT* 1 (1992) 75–92.

———. "Deuteronomy and the Fire of God: A Critical Charismatic Interpretation." *JPT* 7 (1995) 11–33.

———. "A Letter to Frank Macchia." *JPT* 17 (2000) 12–14.

———. "A Pentecostal Approach to Scripture." In *Pentecostal Hermeneutics: A Reader*, edited by Lee Roy Martin, 11–13. Leiden: Brill, 2013. First published in *Seminary Viewpoint* 8.1 (1987) 4–5, 11. Page references are to the 2013 reprint.

———. "The Prophetic Calling: An Old Testament Profile and Its Relevance for Today." *JEPTA* 24.1 (2004) 16–29.

———. "Raw Prayer and Refined Theology: 'You Have Not Spoken Straight to Me, as My Servant Job Has.'" In *The Spirit of the Old Testament*, 150–63. JPTSup. 35. Blandford Forum, UK: Deo, 2011. First published in *The Spirit and the Mind: Essays in Informed Pentecostalism*, edited by Terry L. Cross and Emerson B. Powery, 35–48. Lanham, MD: University Press of America, 2000. Page references are to the 2011 reprint.

———. *The Spirit of the Old Testament.* JPTSup. 35. Blandford Forum, UK: Deo, 2011.

———. "Welcoming an Unheard Voice: A Response to Lee Roy Martin's *The Unheard Voice of God.*" *JPT* 18 (2009) 7–14.

Morris, Jenny. "The Jewish Philosopher Philo." In *The History of the Jewish People in the Age of Jesus Christ (175 B.C.–A.D. 135): Volume III:2*, Emil Schürer, 809–89. Revised and edited by Geza Vermes and Fergus Millar. Edinburgh: T. & T. Clark, 1987.

Nash, Ronald. *The Word of God and the Mind of Man: The Crisis of Revealed Truth in Contemporary Theology.* Grand Rapids: Zondervan, 1982.

Neusner, Jacob. *Introduction to Rabbinic Literature.* New York: Doubleday, 1994.

Noel, Bradley Trueman. "Gordon Fee and the Challenge to Pentecostal Hermeneutics: Thirty Years Later." *Pneuma* 26.1 (2004) 60–80.

———. *Pentecostal and Postmodern Hermeneutics: Comparisons and Contemporary Impact*, Eugene, OR: Wipf & Stock, 2010.

O'Brien, James A. "Summary and Conclusion." In *Scripture and the Charismatic Renewal: Proceedings of the Milwaukee Symposium December 1–3, 1978*, edited by George Martin. 97–118. Ann Arbor, MI: Servant, 1979.

O'Connor, Robert. "Pragmatism." In *Dictionary for Theological Interpretation of the Bible*, edited by Kevin J. Vanhoozer et al., 614–6. Grand Rapids: Baker Academic, 2005.

O'Donovan, O. M. T. "Christian Moral Reasoning." In *New Dictionary of Christian Ethics and Pastoral Theology*, edited by David J. Atkinson and David H. Field, 122–27. Leicester, UK: IVP, 1995.

Olhausen, William. "A "Polite" Response to Anthony Thiselton." In *After Pentecost: Language & Biblical Interpretation: The Scripture and Hermeneutics Series* 2, edited by Craig Bartholomew et al., 121–30. Carlisle, UK: Paternoster, 2001.

Oliverio, L. William, Jr. "An Interpretive Review Essay on Amos Yong's *Spirit-Word-Community: Theological Hermeneutics in Trinitarian Perspective.*" *JPT* 18 (2009) 301–11.

———. "Introduction: Pentecostal Hermeneutics and the Pentecostal Tradition." In *Constructive Pneumatological Hermeneutics in Pentecostal Christianity*, edited by Kenneth J. Archer and L. William Oliverio Jr., 1–14. New York: Palgrave Macmillan, 2016.

———. "Reading Craig Keener: On *Spirit Hermeneutics: Reading Scripture in Light of Pentecost.*" *Pneuma* 39.1–2 (2017) 126–45.

———. *Theological Hermeneutics in the Classic Pentecostal Tradition: A Typological Account.* 2012. Reprint, Leiden: Brill, 2015.

Owen, John. *Causes, Ways and Means of Understanding the Mind of God as Revealed in his Word.* 1678. In *The Complete Works of John Owen: Volume 4: The Work of the*

Spirit, John Owen, 118–235. Edited by William H. Goold. Edinburgh: Banner of Truth, 1995.

Packer, J. I. "Infallible Scripture and the Role of Hermeneutics." In *Scripture and Truth*, edited by D. A. Carson and John D. Woodbridge, 325–56. Leicester, UK: IVP, 1983.

———. *Keep in Step with the Spirit*. Leicester, UK: IVP, 1984.

Parker, Stephen E. *Led by the Spirit: Toward a Practical Theology of Pentecostal Discernment and Decision Making*. 1996. Expanded ed. Cleveland, OH: CPT, 2015.

Parry, Robin A. "Reader Response Criticism." In *Dictionary for Theological Interpretation of the Bible*, edited by Kevin J. Vanhoozer, et al., 658–61. London: SPCK, 2005.

Pentecostal Theological Seminary. "Story of PTSeminary." Accessed October, 15, 2018. https://www.ptseminary.edu/story-of-ptseminary.php.

"Perspectives on Koinonia: The Report from the Third Quinquennium of the Dialogue between the Pontifical Council for Promoting Christian Unity of the Roman Catholic Church and some Classical Pentecostal Churches and Leaders 1989." *Pneuma* 12.2 (1990) 117–42.

Philemon Tesafaye, Leulseged. "Pneumatic Hermeneutics: The Role of the Holy Spirit in Theological Interpretation of Scripture." PhD diss., Fuller Theological Seminary, 2018.

Pink, Arthur W. *Interpretation of the Scriptures*. 1977. Reprint, Grand Rapids: Baker, 1996.

Pinnock, Clark H., "Biblical Texts: Past and Future Meanings." *JETS* 43.1 (2000) 71–81.

———. "Divine Relationality: A Pentecostal Contribution to the Doctrine of God." *JPT* 16 (2000) 3–26.

———. "From Augustine to Arminius: A Pilgrimage in Theology." In *The Grace of God and the Will of Man*, edited by Clark H. Pinnock, 15–30. 1989. Reprint, Minneapolis: Bethany House, 1995.

———. "How I Use the Bible in Doing Theology." In *The Use of the Bible in Theology: Evangelical Options*, edited by Robert K. Johnston, 18–34. Atlanta: John Knox, 1985.

———. "The Role of the Spirit in Interpretation." *JETS* 36 (1993) 491–97.

———. "The Work of the Holy Spirit in Hermeneutics." *JPT* 2 (1993) 3–23.

———. "The Work of the Spirit in the Interpretation of Holy Scripture from the Perspective of a Charismatic Biblical Theologian." *JPT* 18 (2009) 157–71.

Pinnock, Clark H., with Barry L. Callen. *The Scripture Principle: Reclaiming the Full Authority of the Bible*. 1984. 2nd ed. Grand Rapids: Baker Academic, 2006.

Plummer, Alfred. *A Critical and Exegetical Commentary on the Second Epistle of St. Paul to the Corinthians*. Edinburgh: T. & T. Clark, 1915.

Pluss, Jean-Daniel. "Azusa and Other Myths: The Long and Winding Road from Experience to Stated Belief and Back Again." *Pneuma* 15.2 (1993) 189–201.

The Pneuma Review. "Tribute to Professor Ervin: Interview with Daniel Isgrigg." Accessed July 14, 2018. http://pneumareview.com/tribute-to-professor-ervin-interview-with-daniel-isgrigg/.

Poirier, John C., and B. Scott Lewis. "Pentecostal and Postmodernist Hermeneutics: A Critique of Three Conceits." *JPT* 15.1 (2006) 3–21.

Pope, Robert. "Lee Roy Martin, *The Unheard Voice of God: A Pentecostal Hearing of the Book of Judges*: A Theological Review." *JPT* 18 (2009) 20–29.

Porter, Stanley E. ed. *Dictionary of Biblical Criticism and Interpretation*. Abingdon, UK: Routledge, 2007.

Porter, Wendy J. "Liturgical Interpretation." In *Dictionary of Biblical Criticism and Interpretation*, edited by Stanley E. Porter, 206–10. Abingdon, UK: Routledge, 2007.

Power, David N. "The Holy Spirit: Scripture, Tradition, and Interpretation." In *Keeping the Faith: Essays to Mark the Centenary of Lux Mundi*, edited by Geoffrey Wainwright, 152–78. London: SPCK, 1989.

Powers, Janet Everts. "'Your Daughters Shall Prophesy': Pentecostal Hermeneutics and the Empowerment of Women." In *The Globalization of Pentecostalism: A Religion Made to Travel*, edited by Murray W. Dempster et al., 313–37. Carlisle, UK: Paternoster, 1999.

Powery, Emerson B. "The Spirit, the Scripture(s) and the Gospel of Mark: Pneumatology and Hermeneutics in Narrative Perspective." *JPT* 11.2 (2003) 184–98.

———. "Ulrich Luz's *Matthew in History*: A Contribution to Pentecostal Hermeneutics?" *JPT* 14 (1999) 3–17.

Rabens, Volker. *The Holy Spirit and Ethics in Paul: Transformation and Empowering for Religious-Ethical Life*. 2nd ed. Minneapolis: Fortress, 2014.

Rahner, Karl. "The Development of Dogma." In *Theological Investigations I: God, Christ, Mary and Grace*, translated with an introduction by Cornelius Ernst, 39–77. 1961. Reprint, German original 1954. New York: Seabury, 1974.

———. "Experience of the Holy Spirit." In *Theological Investigations XVIII: God and Revelation*, translated by Edward Quinn, 189–211. 1983. Reprint, London: Darton Longman & Todd, 1984.

———. "Man as the Event of God's Free and Forgiving Self-Communication." In *Foundations of Christian Faith: An Introduction to the Idea of Christianity*, translated by William V. Dych, 116–37. German original 1976. London: Darton Longman & Todd, 1978.

Ramm, Bernard L. *Protestant Biblical Interpretation: A Textbook of Hermeneutics*. 1970. 3rd ed. Grand Rapids: Baker, 1984.

———. *The Witness of the Spirit: An Essay on the Contemporary Relevance of the Internal Witness of the Holy Spirit*. 1959. Reprint, Eugene, OR: Wipf & Stock, 2011.

Ranaghan, Kevin. "Preface." In *Theological Reflections on the Charismatic Renewal: Proceedings of the Chicago Conference October 1–2, 1976*, edited by in John C. Haughey, SJ, vii–viii. Ann Arbor, MI: Servant, 1978.

Redick, Caroline. "'Let Me Hear Your Voice': Re-hearing the *Song of Songs* through Pentecostal Hermeneutics." *JPT* 24 (2015) 187–200.

Regent University School of Divinity. "Center for Renewal Studies." Accessed October 15, 2018. https://www.regent.edu/acad/schdiv/renewalstudies/.

Regent University School of Psychology and Counseling, "Stephen Parker, Ph.D." Accessed May 4, 2018. https://www.regent.edu/school-of-psychology-and-counseling/faculty/ph-d-stephen-parker/.

Ricoeur, Paul. *The Conflict of Interpretations: Essays in Hermeneutics*. Translated by Northwestern University Press. Edited by Don Ihde. 1974. Reprint, London: Athlone, 2004.

———. *Essays on Biblical Interpretation*. Edited by Lewis S. Mudge. 1980. Reprint, London: SPCK, 1981.

———. *Interpretation Theory: Discourse and the Surplus of Meaning*. Fort Worth: Texas University Press, 1976.

———. "Metaphor and Symbol." Translated by David Pellauer. In *Interpretation Theory: Discourse and the Surplus of Meaning*, 45–69. Fort Worth, TX: Texas University Press, 1976.

Riddell, Peter G. "Semiotics." In *Dictionary for Theological Interpretation of the Bible*, edited by Kevin J. Vanhoozer et al., 734–37. Grand Rapids: Baker Academic, 2005.

Robeck, C. M. Jr. "Charismatic Movements." In *Global Dictionary of Theology*, edited by William A. Dyrness and Veli-Matti Kärkkäinen, 145–54. Nottingham, UK: IVP, 2008.

———. "Classical Pentecostalism." In *The New International Dictionary of Pentecostal and Charismatic Movements*, edited by Stanley M. Burgess and Eduard M. van der Maas, 553–55. Grand Rapids: Zondervan, 2002.

Robinson, James M., and John B. Cobb Jr. *The New Hermeneutic*. London: Harper & Row, 1964.

Rohr, Richard, with Mike Morrell. *The Divine Dance: The Trinity and Your Transformation*. London: SPCK, 2016.

Runyon, Theodore. *The New Creation: John Wesley's Theology Today*. Nashville: Abingdon, 1998.

Ryken, Leland. "Literary Criticism." In *Dictionary for Theological Interpretation of the Bible*, edited by Kevin J. Vanhoozer et al., 457–60. Grand Rapids: Baker Academic, 2005.

Schiffman, Lawrence H. *From Text to Tradition: A History of Second Temple and Rabbinic Judaism*. Hoboken, NJ: Ktav, 1991.

Schneiders, Sandra M. *The Revelatory Text: Interpreting the New Testament as Sacred Scripture*. San Francisco: HarperCollins, 1991.

Schürer, Emil. *The History of the Jewish People in the Age of Jesus Christ (175 B.C.–A.D. 135): Volume I*. 1885. Revised English ed. Revised and edited by Geza Vermes and Fergus Millar. Edinburgh: T. & T. Clark, 1973.

———. *The History of the Jewish People in the Age of Jesus Christ (175 B.C.—A.D. 135): Volume III:i*. 1885. Revised English ed. Revised and edited by Geza Vermes et al. Millar. Edinburgh: T. & T. Clark, 1986.

Selwyn, Edward Gordon. *The First Epistle of St. Peter: The Greek Text with Introduction, Notes, and Essays*. 1947. Reprint, 2nd ed. Grand Rapids: Baker, 1983.

Senapatiratne, Timothy. "A Pneumatological Addition to N. T. Wright's Hermeneutic Done in the Pentecostal Tradition." In *Pentecostal Theology and the Theological Vision of N. T. Wright: A Conversation*, edited by Janet Meyer Everts and Jeffrey S. Lamp, 44–59. Cleveland, OH: CPT, 2015.

Serenius, Vernon A. P. *That They May Be One*. Alexandria, MN: Serenius, 1973.

Sheppard, Gerald T. "Biblical Interpretation After Gadamer." *Pneuma* 16.1 (1994) 121–41.

———. "Canonization: Hearing the Voice of God Through Historically Dissimilar Traditions." *Interpretation* 36 (1982) 21–33.

———. "Pentecostals and the Hermeneutics of Dispensationalism: The Anatomy of an Uneasy Relationship." *Pneuma* 6.1 (1984) 5–33.

Sherman, Steven B. "Mapping the Hermeneutical Waters: The Holy Spirit and the Revitalization of Interpretation." In *The Holy Spirit and the Christian Life: Historical, Interdisciplinary, and Renewal Perspectives*, edited by Wolfgang Vondey, 21–39. New York: Palgrave Macmillan, 2014.

Shin, Yoon. "Radical Orthodoxy, Pentecostalism, and Embodiment in Exodus 20: Re-envisioning a Pentecostal Hermeneutic for a Formative Liturgy." In *Constructive Pneumatological Hermeneutics in Pentecostal Christianity*, edited by Kenneth J. Archer and L. William Oliverio Jr., 121–42. New York: Palgrave Macmillan, 2016.

Smail, Tom. *The Forgotten Father*. 1980. Reprint, London: Hodder and Stoughton, 1990.

Smail, Tom, et al. *Charismatic Renewal: The Search for a Theology*, London: SPCK, 1993.

Smith, Gordon T. *Institutional Intelligence: How to Build an Effective Organization*. Downers Grove, IL: IVP, 2017.

Smith, James K. A. "The Closing of the Book: Pentecostals, Evangelicals, and the Sacred Writings." *JPT* 11 (1997) 49–71.

———. "Thinking in Tongues." *First Things* 82 (2008) 27–31.

———. *Thinking in Tongues: Pentecostal Contributions to Christian Philosophy*, Grand Rapids: Eerdmans, 2010.

———. *You Are What You Love: The Spiritual Power of Habit*, Grand Rapids: Brazos, 2016.

Sommers, Christina, and Fred Sommers. *Vice & Virtue: Introductory Readings in Ethics*. 4th ed. London: Harcourt Brace College, 1997.

Sparks, Kenton L. *God's Word in Human Words: An Evangelical Appropriation of Critical Biblical Scholarship*. Grand Rapids: Baker Academic, 2008.

Spawn, Kevin L. "Analogy and the Scholar's Shared Experience with the Testimony of Scripture." In *Spirit and Scripture: Exploring a Pneumatic Hermeneutic*, edited by Kevin L. Spawn and Archie T. Wright, 173–6. 2011. Reprint, London: Bloomsbury T. & T. Clark, 2013.

———. "The Interpretation of Scripture: An Examination of Craig S. Keener's *Spirit Hermeneutics*." *Pneuma* 39.1–2 (2017) 146–52.

———. "The Intersection of Biblical Testimony and Experience: Toward the Conceptualization of the Role of the Holy Spirit in the Interpretation of 1 Kings 17:17–24." In *Holy Spirit: Unfinished Agenda*, edited by Johnson T. K. Lim, 3–7. Singapore: Genesis, 2014.

———. "The Principle of Analogy and Biblical Interpretation in the Renewal Tradition." In *Spirit and Scripture: Exploring a Pneumatic Hermeneutic*, edited by Kevin L. Spawn and Archie T. Wright, 46–72. 2011. Reprint, London: Bloomsbury T. & T. Clark, 2013.

Spawn, Kevin L., and Archie T. Wright. "Cultivating a Pneumatic Hermeneutic." In Kevin L. *Spirit and Scripture: Exploring a Pneumatic Hermeneutic*, edited by Kevin L. Spawn and Archie T. Wright, 191–98. 2011. Reprint, London: Bloomsbury T. & T. Clark, 2013.

———. "The Emergence of a Pneumatic Hermeneutic in the Renewal Tradition." In *Spirit and Scripture: Exploring a Pneumatic Hermeneutic*, edited by Kevin L. Spawn and Archie T. Wright, 3–24. 2011. Reprint, London: Bloomsbury T. & T. Clark, 2013.

———, eds. *Spirit and Scripture: Exploring a Pneumatic Hermeneutic*. 2011. Reprint, London: Bloomsbury T. & T. Clark, 2013.

Spittler, Russell P. "Scripture and the Theological Enterprise: View from a Big Canoe." In *The Use of the Bible in Theology: Evangelical Options*, edited by R. K. Johnston, 56–77. Atlanta: John Knox, 1985.

SPS. "About Pneuma." Accessed July 21, 2018. http://sps-usa.org/pneuma/about-pneuma.

———. "Who We Are." Accessed July 21, 2018. http://www.sps-usa.org/home/who-we-are.

Seattle Pacific University. "Robert Wall." Accessed November 1, 2018. http://spu.edu/academics/seattle-pacific-seminary/seminary-faculty/wall-robert.

Sterling, Gregory E. "Philo Judaeus." In *Encyclopedia of the Dead Sea Scrolls: Volume 2*, edited by Lawrence H. Schiffmann and James VanderKam, 663–69. Oxford: Oxford University Press, 2000.

Stevens, R. Paul. "Living Theologically: Toward a Theology of Christian Practice." *Themelios*, 20.3 (1995) 4–8. Accessed September 19, 2018. https://theologicalstudies.org.uk/article_living_stevens.html.

Stibbe, Mark. "This is That: Some Thoughts Concerning Charismatic Hermeneutics." *ANVIL* 15.3 (1998) 181–92.

Stovell, Beth. "A Kingdom Pneumatic Hermeneutics." In *Holy Spirit: Unfinished Agenda*, edited by Johnson T. K. Lim, 8–11. Singapore: Genesis, 2014.

Strack, H. L., and G. Stemberger. *Introduction to the Talmud and Midrash*. Translated by Markus Bockmuehl. Edinburgh: T. & T. Clark, 1991.

Stronstad, Roger. "A Lukan Model of Pneumatic Hermeneutics." In *Holy Spirit: Unfinished Agenda*, edited by Johnson T. K. Lim, 12–17. Singapore: Genesis, 2014.

———. "Pentecostal Experience and Hermeneutics." In *Spirit, Scripture, and Theology: A Pentecostal Perspective*, 53–78. Baguio City, Philippines: Asia Pacific Theological Seminary Press, 1995.

———. "Pentecostal Hermeneutics: A Review Essay of Gordon D. Fee, *Gospel and Spirit: Issues in New Testament Hermeneutics*." *Pneuma* 15.2 (1993) 215–22.

———. "Review of John R. Levison's, *Filled with the Spirit* Part III, Early Christian Literature Chapter 3, 'Filled with the Spirit and the book of Acts.'" *JPT* 20 (2011) 201–6.

———. "Some Aspects of Hermeneutics in the Pentecostal Tradition." In *Pentecostals in the 21st Century: Identity, Beliefs, Praxis*, edited by Corneliu Constantineanu and Christopher J. Scobie, 32–58. Eugene, OR: Cascade, 2018.

———. *Spirit, Scripture, and Theology: A Pentecostal Perspective*, 53–78. Baguio City, Philippines: Asia Pacific Theological Seminary Press, 1995.

———. "Trends in Pentecostal Hermeneutics." *Paraclete* 22.3 (1988) 1–12. Accessed February 2, 2018. http://enrichmentjournal.ag.org/top/month_holyspirit.cfm.

Studebaker, Steven M. *From Pentecost to the Triune God: A Pentecostal Trinitarian Theology*. Grand Rapids: Eerdmans, 2012.

Sugirtharajah, R. S. "Postcolonial Biblical Interpretation." In *The Modern Theologians: An Introduction to Christian Theology Since 1918*, edited by David F. Ford with Rachel Muers, 535–52. 3rd ed. Oxford: Blackwell, 2008.

Swinton, John, and Harriet Mowat. *Practical Theology and Qualitative Research*. London: SCM, 2006.

Synan, Vinson. *The Holiness-Pentecostal Movement in the United States*. Grand Rapids: Eerdmans, 1971.

———. *The Holiness-Pentecostal Tradition: Charismatic Movements in the Twentieth Century*. 2nd ed. Grand Rapids: Eerdmans. 1997.

Tennison, D. Allen. "Charismatic Biblical Interpretation." In *Dictionary for Theological Interpretation of the Bible*, edited by Kevin J. Vanhoozer et al., 106–9. Grand Rapids: Baker Academic, 2005.

Tenneson, Michael, et al. "Surprising Bedfellows: Theology and Science Interpretation and Integration." In *Constructive Pneumatological Hermeneutics in Pentecostal Christianity*, edited by Kenneth J. Archer and L. William Oliverio Jr., 279–96. New York: Palgrave Macmillan, 2016.

Thiselton, Anthony C. "'Behind' and 'in Front of' the Text: Language, Reference and Indeterminacy." In *After Pentecost: Language & Biblical Interpretation*, edited by Craig Bartholomew et al., 97–120. The Scripture and Hermeneutics Series 2. Carlisle, UK: Paternoster, 2001.

———. *New Horizons in Hermeneutics: The Theory and Practice of Transforming Bible Reading*. London: HarperCollins, 1992.

———. "The New Hermeneutic." In *A Guide to Contemporary Hermeneutics: Major Trends in Biblical Interpretation*, edited by Donald K. McKim, 78–107. Grand Rapids: Eerdmans, 1986.

———. *The Two Horizons: New Testament Hermeneutics and Philosophical Description with Special Reference to Heidegger, Bultmann, Gadamer, and Wittgenstein*. Exeter, UK: Paternoster, 1980.

Thomas, John Christopher. *1 John, 2 John, 3 John*. Pentecostal Commentary Series. 2004. Reprint, Blandford Forum, UK: Deo, 2017.

———. "Discerning Dialogue." In *Spirit and Scripture: Exploring a Pneumatic Hermeneutic*, edited by Kevin L. Spawn and Archie T. Wright, 183–85. 2011. Reprint, London: Bloomsbury T. & T. Clark, 2013.

———. "Holy Spirit and Interpretation." In *Dictionary of Biblical Criticism and Interpretation*, edited by Stanley E. Porter, 165–66. London: Routledge, 2009.

———. "The Mystery of the Great Whore: Pneumatic Discernment in Revelation 17." In *Perspectives in Pentecostal Eschatologies: World without End*, edited by Peter Althouse and Robby Waddell, 111–36. Eugene, OR: Pickwick, 2010.

———. "Pentecostal Theology in the Twenty-First Century." *Pneuma* 20.1 (1998) 3–19.

———. "Reading the Bible from within Our Traditions: A Pentecostal Hermeneutic as Test Case." In *Between Two Horizons: Spanning New Testament Studies and Systematic Theology*, edited by Joel B. Green and Max Turner, 108–22. Grand Rapids: Eerdmans, 2000.

———. *The Spirit of the New Testament*. 2005. Reprint, Blandford Forum, UK: Deo, 2011.

———. "'What the Spirit is Saying to the Church'—The Testimony of a Pentecostal in New Testament Studies." In *Spirit and Scripture: Exploring a Pneumatic Hermeneutic*, edited by Kevin L. Spawn and Archie T. Wright, 115–29. 2011. Reprint, London: Bloomsbury T. & T. Clark, 2013.

———. "'Where the Spirit Leads'—The Development of Pentecostal Hermeneutics." *Journal of Beliefs and Values* 30.3 (2009) 289–302.

———. "Women, Pentecostals and the Bible: An Experiment in Pentecostal Hermeneutics." *JPT* 5 (1994) 41–56.

Thomas, John Christopher, and Kimberly Ervin Alexander. "'And the Signs are Following': Mark 16:9–20—A Journey into Pentecostal Hermeneutics." *JPT* 11.2 (2003) 147–70.

Torrance, Thomas F. "The Epistemological Relevance of the Holy Spirit." In *God and Rationality*, 165–92. 1971. Reprint, Oxford: Oxford University Press, 2000.

Treier, Daniel J. *Introducing Theological Interpretation of Scripture: Recovering a Christian Practice*. Grand Rapids: Baker Academic, 2008.

Trueman, Carl R. "Illumination." In *Dictionary for Theological Interpretation of the Bible*, edited by Kevin J. Vanhoozer et al., 316–18. Grand Rapids: Baker Academic, 2005.

Turner, Max. "Does Prophecy Denote Charismatic Exegesis, Preaching, or Teaching?" In *The Holy Spirit and Spiritual Gifts: Then and Now*, 206–12. Carlisle, UK: Paternoster, 1996.

———. "Levison's *Filled with the Spirit*: A Brief Appreciation and Response." *JPT* 20 (2011) 193–200.

Twelftree, Graham H. "Spiritual Powers." In *New Dictionary of Biblical Theology*, edited by T. D. Alexander and Brian S. Rosner, 796–802. Leicester, UK: IVP, 2000.

Vanhoozer, Kevin J. "Ascending the Mountain, Singing the Rock: Biblical Interpretation Earthed, Typed, and Transfigured." *Modern Theology* 28.4 (2012) 781–803.

———. "Discourse on Matter: Hermeneutics and the 'Miracle' of Understanding." In *Hermeneutics at the Crossroads*, edited by in Kevin J. Vanhoozer et al., 3–31. Bloomington, IN: Indiana University Press, 2006.

———. "From Speech Acts to Scripture Acts: The Covenant of Discourse and the Discourse of Covenant." In *After Pentecost: Language & Biblical Interpretation* edited by Craig Bartholomew et al., 1–49. The Scripture and Hermeneutics Series 2. Carlisle, UK: Paternoster, 2001.

———. "Reforming Pneumatic Hermeneutics." In *Holy Spirit: Unfinished Agenda*, edited by Johnson T. K Lim, 18–24. Singapore: Genesis, 2014.

———. "The Reader in New Testament Interpretation." In *Hearing the New Testament: Strategies for Interpretation*, edited by Joel B. Green, 301–28. Carlisle, UK: Paternoster, 1995.

———. "The Spirit of Light After the Age of Enlightenment: Reforming/Renewing Pneumatic Hermeneutics via the Economy of Illumination." In *Spirit of God: Christian Renewal in the Community of Faith*, edited by Jeffrey W. Barbeau and Beth Felker Jones, 149–67. Downers Grove, IL: IVP Academic, 2015.

———. "The Spirit of Understanding: Discerning and Doing the Word." In *Is There a Meaning in this Text? The Bible, the Reader and the Morality of Literary Knowledge*, 407–31. Leicester, UK: Apollos, 1998.

———. "The Spirit of Understanding: Special Revelation and General Hermeneutics." In *Disciplining Hermeneutics: Interpretation in Christian Perspective*, edited by Roger Lundin, 131–65. Leicester, UK: Apollos, 1997.

———. "The Spirit of Understanding: Special Revelation & General Hermeneutics." In *First Theology: God, Scripture & Hermeneutics*, 207–35. Downers Grove, IL: IVP, 2002.

Vanhoozer, Kevin J., and Daniel J. Treier. *Theology and the Mirror of Scripture: A Mere Evangelical Account*. London: Apollos, 2016.

Vanhoozer, Kevin J., et al., eds. *Dictionary for Theological Interpretation of the Bible*, London: SPCK, 2005.

Vatican. "*Dei Verbum*." Accessed March 13, 2018. http://www.vatican.va/archive/hist_councils/ii_vatican_council/documents/vat-ii_const_19651118_dei-verbum_en.html.

Vermes, Geza, *An Introduction to the Complete Dead Sea Scrolls*. 3rd ed. London: SCM, 1999.

Villafañe, Eldin. *The Liberating Spirit: Toward an Hispanic American Social Ethic*. 1992. Reprint, Grand Rapids: Eerdmans, 1993.

Volf, Miroslav. *Exclusion and Embrace: A Theological Exploration of Identity, Otherness, and Reconciliation*. Nashville: Abingdon, 1996.

Vondey, Wolfgang. *Beyond Pentecostalism: The Crisis of Global Christianity and the Renewal of the Theological Agenda*. Grand Rapids: Eerdmans, 2010.

———. *Pentecostalism: A Guide for the Perplexed*. London: Bloomsbury T. & T. Clark, 2013.

———. *Pentecostal Theology: Living the Full Gospel*. London: Bloomsbury, T. & T. Clark, 2017.

Vondey, Wolfgang, and Chris W. Green. "Between This and That: Reality and Sacramentality in the Pentecostal Worldview." In *Pentecostal Ecclesiology: A Reader*, edited by Chris E. W. Green, 211–32. Leiden: Brill, 2016.

Waddell, Robby. "The Holy Spirit of Life, Work, and Inspired Speech: Responding to John (Jack) R. Levison, *Filled with the Spirit*." *JPT* 20 (2011) 207–12.

———. *The Spirit of the Book of Revelation*. JPTSup. 30. Blandford Forum, UK: Deo, 2006.

———. "The Spirit of Reviews and Response." *JPT* 17 (2008) 153–60.

Waddell, Robby, and Peter Althouse. "An Editorial Note on the Roundtable Dialogue of Craig S. Keener's *Spirit Hermeneutics: Reading Scripture in the Light of Pentecost*." *Pneuma* 39.1–2 (2017) 123–25.

———. "The Pentecostals and Their Scriptures." *Pneuma* 38.1–2 (2016) 115–21.

Wainwright, Geoffrey. "Towards an Ecumenical Hermeneutic: How Can All Christians Read the Scriptures Together?" *Gregorianum* 76.4 (1995) 639–62.

Wall, Robert W. "A Response to Thomas/Alexander, "And the Signs are Following" (Mark 16:9–20)." *JPT* 11.2 (2003) 171–83.

———. "Waiting on the Holy Spirit (Acts 1:4): Extending a Metaphor to Biblical Imagination." *JPT* 22 (2013) 37–53.

Waltke, Bruce K. "Exegesis and the Spiritual Life: Theology as Spiritual Formation." *Crux* 30.3 (1994) 28–35.

Ward, Timothy. *Words of Life: Scripture as the Living and Active Word of God*. Nottingham, UK: IVP, 2009.

Webster, John. "Biblical Theology and the Clarity of Scripture." In *Out of Egypt: Biblical Theology and Biblical Interpretation*, edited by Craig Bartholomew et al., 352–84. The Scripture and Hermeneutics Series 5. Milton Keynes, UK: Paternoster, 2004.

———. *The Domain of the Word: Scripture and Theological Reason*. London: Bloomsbury, 2012.

———. *Holy Scripture: A Dogmatic Sketch*. Cambridge: Cambridge University Press, 2003.

Welker, Michael. *God the Spirit*. Translated by John F. Hoffmeyer. Minneapolis: Fortress, 1994.

———. "The Human Spirit and the Spirit of God." In *The Spirit in Creation and New Creation: Science and Theology in Western and Orthodox Realms*, edited by Michael Welker, 134–42. Grand Rapids: Eerdmans, 2012.

Wenell, Karen. "The Setting: Biblical Geography, History, and Archaeology." In *Scripture and Its Interpretation: A Global, Ecumenical Introduction to the Bible*, edited by Michael J. Gorman, 23–44. Grand Rapids: Baker Academic, 2017.

Wenk, Matthais. *Community-Forming Power: The Socio-Ethical Role of the Spirit in Luke-Acts.* 2000. Reprint, London: T. & T. Clark, 2004.

Wesley, John. "Letter to Charles Wesley, London, January 27, 1767." In *The Letters of the Rev. John Wesley, Volume V: February 28, 1766 to December 9, 1772*, edited by John Telford, 38–39. 1931. Reprint, London: Epworth, 1960.

———. *A Plain Account of Christian Perfection.* First ed. 1738, final rev. 1787. Peterborough, UK: Epworth, 1952.

———. "Sermon 13: On Sin in Believers—2 Cor. 5:17 (Mar. 28, 1763)." In *The Bicentennial Edition of the Works of John Wesley, Volume 1, Sermons I: 1–33*, edited by Albert C. Outler and Frank Baker, 314–34. Nashville: Abingdon, 1984.

———. "Sermon 17: The Circumcision of the Heart—Rom. 2:29 (Jan 1, 1733)." In *The Bicentennial Edition of the Works of John Wesley, Volume 1, Sermons I: 1–33*, edited by Albert C. Outler and Frank Baker, 398–414. Nashville: Abingdon, 1984.

———. "Sermon 40: On Christian Perfection—Phil. 3:12 (1741)." In *The Bicentennial Edition of the Works of John Wesley, Volume 2, Sermons II: 34–70*, edited by Albert C. Outler and Frank Baker, 97–124. Nashville: Abingdom, 1985.

———. "Sermon 76: On Perfection—Heb. 6:1 (Dec. 6, 1784)." In *The Bicentennial Edition of the Works of John Wesley, Volume 3, Sermons III: 71–114*, edited by Albert C. Outler and Frank Baker, 70–87. Nashville: Abingdon, 1986.

———. "Sermon 127: On the Wedding Garment—Matt 22:12, (Mar. 26, 1790)." In *The Bicentennial Edition of the Works of John Wesley, Volume 4, Sermons IV: 115–51*, edited by Albert C. Outler and Frank Baker, 139–48. Nashville: Abingdon, 1987.

Westerholm, Stephen. "Letter and Spirit: The Foundation of Pauline Ethics." *NTS* 30 (1984) 229–48.

Westphal, Merold. "Spirit and Prejudice: The Dialectic of Interpretation." In *Constructive Pneumatological Hermeneutics in Pentecostal Christianity*, edited by Kenneth J. Archer and L. William Oliverio Jr., 17–32. New York: Palgrave Macmillan, 2016.

Willard, Douglas. "Hermeneutical Occasionalism." In *Disciplining Hermeneutics: Interpretation in Christian Perspective*, edited by Roger Lundin, 167–72. Leicester, UK: Apollos, 1997.

Williams, J. Rodman. *Renewal Theology: Salvation, the Holy Spirit, and Christian Living: Systematic Theology from a Charismatic Perspective.* Grand Rapids: Zondervan, 1990.

Willis, John T. "Prophetic Hermeneutics." *Restoration Quarterly* 32.4 (1990) 193–207.

Winn, Albert Curry. "The Holy Spirit and the Christian Life." *Interpretation* 33.1 (1979) 47–57.

Wolterstorff, Nicholas. *Divine Discourse: Philosophical Reflections on the Claim That God Speaks.* Cambridge: Cambridge University Press, 1995.

Wright, Archie T. "Second Temple Period Jewish Biblical Interpretation: An Early Pneumatic Hermeneutic." In *Spirit and Scripture: Exploring a Pneumatic Hermeneutic*, edited by Kevin L. Spawn and Archie T. Wright, 73–98. 2011. Reprint, London: Bloomsbury T. & T. Clark, 2013.

———. "The Spirit in Early Jewish Biblical Interpretation: Examining John R. Levison's *Filled with the Spirit*." *Pneuma* 33.1 (2011) 35–46.

———. "We Are Not All Pentecostals: A Response to Dunn, Moberly and Bartholomew." In *Spirit and Scripture: Exploring a Pneumatic Hermeneutic*, edited by Kevin L. Spawn and Archie T. Wright, 177–79. 2011. Reprint, London: Bloomsbury T. & T. Clark, 2013.

Wright, Tom. *Scripture and the Authority of God*. 2nd ed. London: SPCK, 2013.

Wright, N. T. "The Challenge of the Enlightenment." In *Scripture and the Authority of God*, 52–63. 2nd ed. London: SPCK, 2013.

———. "How Can the Bible be Authoritative?" *Vox Evangelica* 21 (1991) 7–32.

———. *The New Testament and the People of God*. London: SPCK, 1992.

———. "The Word and the Wind: A Response." In *Pentecostal Theology and the Theological Vision of N. T. Wright: A Conversation*, edited by Janet Meyer Everts and Jeffrey S. Lamp, 141–78. Cleveland, OH: CPT, 2015.

Wyckoff, John W. *Pneuma and Logos: The Role of the Spirit in Biblical Hermeneutics*. Eugene, OR: Wipf & Stock, 2010.

Yocum, John. "Clarity of Scripture." In *Dictionary for Theological Interpretation of the Bible*, edited by Kevin J. Vanhoozer et al., 727–30. Grand Rapids: Baker Academic, 2005.

Yong, Amos. "Conclusion: The Affective Spirit and Historiographical Revitalization in the Christian Theological Tradition." In *The Spirit, the Affections, and the Christian Tradition*, edited by Dale M. Coulter and Amos Yong, 293–302. Notre Dame, IN: University of Notre Dame Press, 2016.

———. "Conclusion—Theological Interpretation of Scripture after Pentecost: Trinitarian Hermeneutics for the 21st Century." In *The Hermeneutical Spirit: Theological Interpretation and Scriptural Imagination for the 21st Century*, 257–66. Eugene, OR: Cascade, 2017.

———. "Foreword." In Craig Keener, *Spirit Hermeneutics: Reading Scripture in Light of Pentecost*, xvii–xxi. Grand Rapids: Eerdmans, 2016.

———. *The Hermeneutical Spirit: Theological Interpretation and Scriptural Imagination for the 21st Century*. Eugene, OR: Cascade, 2017.

———. "The Hermeneutical Trialectic: Notes towards a Consensual Hermeneutic and Theological Method." *HeyJ* 45.1 (2004) 22–39.

———. "Jubilee, Pentecost, and Liberation: The Preferential Option of the Poor on the Apostolic Way." In *The Hermeneutical Spirit: Theological Interpretation and Scriptural Imagination for the 21st Century*, 162–78. Eugene, OR: Cascade, 2017.

———. "The Light Shines in the Darkness: Johannine Dualism and the Challenge of Christian Theology of Religions Today." In *The Hermeneutical Spirit: Theological Interpretation and Scriptural Imagination for the 21st Century*, 197–221. Eugene, OR: Cascade, 2017.

———. "The Pneumatological Imagination: Epistemology in Triadic Perspective." In *Spirit-Word-Community: Theological Hermeneutics in Trinitarian Perspective*, 119–218. Eugene, OR: Wipf & Stock, 2002.

———. "Reading Scripture and Nature: Pentecostal Hermeneutics and Their Implications for the Contemporary Evangelical Theology and Science Conversation." In *The Hermeneutical Spirit: Theological Interpretation and Scriptural Imagination for the 21st Century*, 237–56. Eugene, OR: Cascade, 2017.

———. "Reflecting and Confessing in the Spirit: Called to Transformational Theologizing." In *The Hermeneutical Spirit: Theological Interpretation and Scriptural Imagination for the 21st Century*, 63–76. Eugene, OR: Cascade, 2017.

———. *Spirit of Love: A Trinitarian Theology of Grace*. Waco, TX: Baylor University Press, 2012.

———. *Spirit-Word-Community: Theological Hermeneutics in Trinitarian Perspective*. Eugene, OR: Wipf & Stock, 2002.

———. "The Science, Sighs, and Signs of Interpretation: An Asian American Post-Pentecost-al Hermeneutics in a Multi-, Inter-, and Trans-cultural World." In *Constructive Pneumatological Hermeneutics in Pentecostal Christianity*, edited by Kenneth J. Archer and L. William Oliverio Jr., 177–95. New York: Palgrave Macmillan, 2016.

———. "The Science, Sighs, and Signs of Interpretation: An Asian American Post-Pentecost-al Hermeneutics in a Multi-, Inter-, and Trans-cultural World." In *The Hermeneutical Spirit: Theological Interpretation and Scriptural Imagination for the 21st Century*, 27–42. Eugene, OR: Cascade, 2017.

———. "The Social Psychology of Sin: A Pentecostal Perspective." In *The Hermeneutical Spirit: Theological Interpretation and Scriptural Imagination for the 21st Century*, 141–61. Eugene, OR: Cascade, 2017.

———. "Theological Anthropology and the Spirit: The Lukan Imagination I." In *The Hermeneutical Spirit: Theological Interpretation and Scriptural Imagination for the 21st Century*, 79–138. Eugene, OR: Cascade, 2017.

———. "Understanding and Living the Apostolic Way: Orality and Scriptural Faithfulness in Conversation with African Pentecostalism." In *The Hermeneutical Spirit: Theological Interpretation and Scriptural Imagination for the 21st Century*, 43–62. Eugene, OR: Cascade, 2017.

———. "The Word and the Spirit or The Spirit and the Word: Exploring the Boundaries of Evangelicalism in Relation to Modern Pentecostalism." *TRINJ* 23.2 (2002) 235–52.

Zuck, Roy B. "The Role of the Holy Spirit in Hermeneutics." *BSac* 141 (1984) 120–29, accessed March 3, 2018. https://biblicalstudies.org.uk/article_spirit_zuck.html.

Zwingli, Huldrych. *Of the Clarity and Certainty or Power of the Word of God*. 1522. In *Zwingli and Bullinger: The Library of Christian Classics*, edited and translated by G. W. Bromiley, 59–95. Louisville, KY: Westminster John Knox, 2006.

Index of Ancient and Biblical Characters and Groups

Index of Names

Index of Subjects

www.ingramcontent.com/pod-product-compliance
Lightning Source LLC
LaVergne TN
LVHW050617100826
845148LV00011B/1628

* 9 7 8 1 7 2 5 2 7 3 1 8 4 *